ENTRANCES AND EXITS

MICHAEL RICHARDS

PERMUTED
PRESS

A PERMUTED PRESS BOOK

Entrances and Exits
© 2024 by Michael Richards
All Rights Reserved

ISBN: 978-1-63758-913-7
ISBN (eBook): 978-1-63758-914-4

Cover design by Cody Corcoran
Cover photo by Tony Duran
Art direction, design, and interior composition by Greg Johnson,
Textbook Perfect

PERMUTED PRESS

Permuted Press, LLC
New York ✦ Nashville
permutedpress.com

Published in the United States of America
1 2 3 4 5 6 7 8 9 10

To my family

Contents

PART 4 *Giddyup!*

PART 5 *You Gotta Listen to the Little Man*

Foreword

By Jerry Seinfeld

There were many things that bonded Michael Richards and me together. Cereal, interesting automobiles, Tony Curtis, but mainly it was prioritizing our personal life in a very distant second place to our comedy life.

Some funny people do comedy because of the fun or attention it brings if they can do it well. I think for Michael and me, it much more took the form of a "sacred mission." A deadly serious undertaking in which no effort can or will be spared. "Kill" and "die" are words comedians toss around very freely. Mostly it's because comedians love to exaggerate and overstate everything in hopes of getting a reaction. But for some comedy performers those words are not an exaggeration at all. They are literal.

We must "kill."

The audience "died laughing."

That line is a "killer."

I "died" out there tonight.

Within the comedy community there are only a small few that approach it like this and it's not by choice, it's by birth. It's what you are and how you're made. There's no thought, choice, or decision about it. You think nothing but, "I must make this funny moment work." The rest of your human life is but an annoying inconvenience.

I first became aware of Michael on *Fridays* because I was doing *Benson* across the hall at ABC Prospect Studios in the early '80s. I only did three episodes and was fired but I got to see Michael work, which of course changed both our lives forever. I have never just "liked" a comedian in my life. They're either just okay or if they can actually make me laugh, I fall madly, insanely in love with them.

It was definitely when I saw Michael do Dick Williams, a Hollywood fitness guru, on *The Tonight Show with Jay Leno* that I fell hopelessly, forever in love with him. The furrowed "trying to seem handsome" brow, the tension through the neck, arms, and shoulders to appear muscular, the black shoes and socks, the smooth playboy style of walking, it was over for me.

Poor Michael, he never had any idea that the second I heard he was available for the part of Kramer on *The Seinfeld Chronicles* the part was his and no one else had any chance. I went through the multi-layered network audition process so that Larry, Castle Rock, and NBC could imagine I would even consider another actor. Not for an instant. It was all a charade as far as I was concerned.

Michael, of course, was amazing in the audition and after the last one I'll never forget an NBC executive turning to me and commenting, "Well, if you want funny..." That's when I first understood TV networks are not actually in the entertainment field. I looked at this guy like, "What world do you live in?" Whatever it was, it wasn't the kill and die world that Michael and I lived in.

I never thought that the show would be very popular but I was determined that it was going to be funny. I have to say looking back on it all now, one of my very favorite things that I absolutely miss the most was just looking into Michael's eyes. It's the most beautiful view in the world of comedy. If you could only see the way they dance and jump up close when he's in the curl of the wave.

It was fun when we rehearsed but when the audience was in, the lights were up, and the cameras were on, and we knew that huge laugh we just got is going out to millions and millions of people, that was comedy big wave surfing. We were riding monsters and we knew it. And of course, it was wonderful when the show caught on and people got into it.

But the show I saw, Michael Richards six inches in front of my nose, was something else entirely. It was one of the greatest gifts for me personally having Michael's face right up to mine. It was that place that Michael and I always dreamed of being. A golden comedy heaven.

I guess there were other events in my life and in the world that took place between 1989 and 1998 but it's all faded and dim in my mind. It was Larry, Jason, Julia, and Michael. We hung on tight as we could for as long as we could. And honestly, the most vivid reality for me of creating it day after day, year after year, was that Michael/ Kramer and I really did live together. He envisioned it so strongly in his mind and I did too.

Most weeks were seven days long for me and I didn't have to pretend very hard, which I guess is called "acting," that our little apartment set was where we really lived. I also didn't have to act at all that I would love having such a fun live-in and/or adjacent to a friend that I was always excited to see—that was Michael.

We decided early on that no real-life rules would ever apply to Kramer. His apartment would be a Silly Putty fantasy that we would form into whatever comedic device we needed it to be. And of course, the character itself would also be infinitely re-inventible per each story like Harpo Marx, Stan Laurel, or Bugs Bunny. Whatever's funny, that's what Kramer would be. Some of it we thought of but a lot was inspired by what we saw in this wonder of Michael himself. And that was the one-of-a-kind comedy genius that Michael had. Only he could soar, dip, and dive so easily with this freedom.

I know Michael tortured himself to make this happen 180 times in a row over a decade, but I know it was why he was born. I would tease him about it and laugh at the twists and contortions that he would put himself through mentally and physically to do it, but it was really just part of the fun and pain of doing comedy. It was when we locked eyes in that apartment set that I knew I was in the best cult ever. Two insane lunatics spinning in an out-of-control comedy universe.

And it was when I felt the spin rate start to slow ever so slightly that I knew we had to get out. This was all way, way too much magic to turn into a transaction for profit enterprise. Not going to end it on that note. I wanted to keep flying on the wings of the comedy gods that had smiled on us for so long. Obviously, all the ingredients were fabulous, but for me, Michael will always be the bubbles that made the drink so tickly and tingly.

I'm sure you could see how often I was hanging on for dear life to keep from laughing when I was in a scene with him. Nothing ever felt as pure as just looking into Michael's eyes when we sat at the script read-throughs, when we "laid down some tracks" for the scene, and of course, when the red light came on and we played it for keeps.

That's the show I was watching.

That's my most indelible memory of doing it.

That's why I feel Michael and I will always be at the end of the hall, living right next to each other forever.

The Hair

We're on a break, and Jerry comes over to me during rehearsal early in the third season of *Seinfeld*. During these brief lulls, we usually lounge around in his apartment set. We make ourselves at home. In a way, we are home. For all the time we spend in this soundstage—five days, forty-five hours a week—the set has become our home.

Jerry is shaking his head slightly.

"Michael," he says, with a slightly bemused grin that makes him appear as if he's listening to a joke in his head before he tells it. "Michael. Michael."

I can't tell if there is trouble or if he is laughing to himself. Jerry has a way of reducing problems to nothing, often to silliness. It's the not-so-secret ingredient of the show. It's also Jerry in real life. The two are often indistinguishable.

Jerry can stay cool in any type of situation, to stand still and calmly assess circumstances as if it's a puzzle to figure out or some kind of word game that will eventually produce a punch line. It's an enviable quality, and I have attributed it to his having had good parenting, which he has acknowledged to me to be true.

As a result, Jerry doesn't flap easily. He genuinely plays it cool. Not me. I'm a flapper. I was raised around high-strung Italians, and they were not so buttoned up. They always let the goo out. So I say what I feel, no holding back. This is a vital side to Kramer too. He inadvertently shoots his mouth off, which the show's writers and I are realizing usually gets the ball rolling.

As comedians, Jerry and I are both ball rollers. He is more graceful, more methodical, and to the point. For his stand-up he carefully crafts his jokes word by word, rarely deviating from the genius he has put on the page, a true Apollonian. I am and have always been far more unpredictable onstage, riskier, off book, Dionysian.

I look at Jerry, who is looking at me, paused, as if we're both at a red light waiting for it to turn green.

I rev my engine. "So, what's up?"

He grins and says, "They're talking about your hair."

I think he is referring to the show's fans, wanting me to know that they're getting into Kramer's look. But no, he tells me it's the network. The network is concerned about the way my hair looks. Starting in the middle of our previous season, I let my hair grow and pulled it up, using a touch of hair gunk to keep it looking, well, *weirdly alive.*

"I'm Kramer," I say, running my fingers through my hair. "The man wants his hair this way."

Jerry nods. "They don't think the audience will like Kramer if he looks too crazy."

"Really?" I say. "Well, tell 'em I'm putting a scorpion tattoo on my neck."

Green light! I floor it. Kramer kicks in like a blower! There is no separating the two of us, especially when I'm around Jerry. (To this day, at seventy-four, around Jerry, I'm Kramer. I'm psychically bound to this character, and Jerry is also "Jerry" around me.)

"Jerry, look how these network people wear their hair! They're running the front office. They have to look normal! I'm not normal! I don't work in the office. The K-Man is eccentric! Every wild, weird, and goofy thing going on in New York City is running through this guy's blood. You know…Giddyup! Come on, let's go! Game on! We've got things to do! That's New York City! That's Kramer, Jerry! And it's all in the man's hairdo!"

Jerry is amused.

Then in an abrupt U-turn, I go from Kramer well over the speed limit into a slow cruising speed. "So, what'd you tell 'em?"

"I said, 'We're making a comedy.'"

Bingo! I come to a stop. Jerry gets it. He has always gotten me. "Done!" I say. "Let's have a bowl of cereal."

We sit down in the kitchen area of the set and pour ourselves two bowls of high-fiber, no-sugar cereal and move on to whatever. It is the last time the network or anybody on staff will ever question Kramer's look. But you know, I couldn't have changed even if they had mandated it. By this time, early in season three, only seventeen shows in, Kramer and I are irrevocably entwined, braided together from head to toe.

The hair, so essential, symbolizes the irrational that was and is and always will be the underlying feature not only of Kramer but of comedy itself.

This seemingly senseless spirit has been coursing through me since childhood. I've been under its almighty influence since the day I came into this world. I was raised by it, nourished by circumstances that shaped my love for the far out. I became a devotee of the best, most outrageous comedians on early television, and then in theater school at Valley College, then CalArts, but mostly at Valley College, I was drawn to the freakish and oddly humorous playwrights Ionesco, Pinter, Cummings, and Beckett…everything avant-garde—experimental, radical, the unacceptable or unorthodox in art and society. I felt it all within myself, especially the physical comedy, the body movements, so freakish and undignified, where I bumped into things, knocked stuff down, messed up situations, and often ended up on my ass.

This book is a hymn to the irrational, the senseless spirit that breaks the whole into pieces, a reflection of the seemingly absurdist difficulties that intrude upon me. It can be Harpo Marx turning me about, shaking up my plans, throwing me for a loop.

Upset and turmoil is with me all the time. It's at the basis of comedy. It's the pratfall that we all take. It's the unavoidable mistake that I didn't expect. It's everywhere I go. It's in the way that I am, both light and dark, good and not so good. It's my life.

PART 1

Got Any Meat?

CHAPTER 1

····························

If You Want Funny

If I'm not interested, I'm usually not at my best. And if I hadn't been able to perform, if I hadn't followed my interest in theater, I would've been a tramp wandering the earth, which is what I was interested in doing many years later. Actually, I've always been interested in tramping, but one step at a time.

Milton Berle once told me that saying a joke and playing a character are two different things, but if you can bring the two together, saying funny and doing funny, then you're making gold. This explains why I am sitting in Jay Leno's kitchen in March of 1989. He's been a fan of mine going back to *Fridays*, the late-night sketch comedy show that ran for three seasons on ABC starting in 1980, and even further back to when both of us were doing stand-up at the Improv comedy club. He is sitting in for Johnny Carson this week, and he wants me on the next night's show. He senses we can do something funny together.

He doesn't know what that is, and neither do I, not yet. But we're *interested*.

Jay suggests I reprise a character I created on *Fridays*, an absurd hipster and ladies' man named Dick. He was one of the show's memorable characters.

"Doing that character, whaddya think will be funny?" he says.

That's the golden question, isn't it?

"I could come in as a weight lifter," I say. "Dick as one of Hollywood's top personal trainers, a weight lifter to the stars."

Jay mulls the wafer-thin premise.

"All right," he says. "Can you sketch it out?"

"Yeah, let me work on it. I'll call you later."

A routine is already starting to take shape in my head.

* * *

A COUPLE OF HOURS LATER, I phone Jay from my house and tell him that I've figured it out. Jay comes up with the idea of plugging a new book from Dick. Aside from this and my brief premise, we agree to fly without a safety net; we'll improvise the whole thing. To Jay's credit, this doesn't seem like too big a deal working without a script. He trusts me and obviously himself. I'll *do* funny and he'll *say* funny. Together, we're going for the gold, Uncle Milty!

* * *

THE NEXT AFTERNOON I ARRIVE at *The Tonight Show* set on the NBC lot in Burbank with a barbell setup, a bucket of white chalk, a towel, and a rowing machine. I have some bits in mind that are similar to some funny moves I put on Dick back on *Fridays*—one sketch in particular that was called "Dick Goes to the Gym." I can open it up more with Jay, but as I get into costume—a woman's one-piece stars-and-stripes swimsuit, large blue shorts, and an oversized weight-lifting belt—I'm not quite sure how I'm going to do that. But I got one thing going through my head: if ya can't make it funny, make it interesting.

I'll just be Dick. I'll commit to the character and trust in this. Jay will be Jay, and he's very much at home with himself. Okay, Mikey, got it? Just be Dick. That should take us most of the way home. Everything else, the physical comedy, well, it can't be rehearsed anyway. It needs to be in the moment, natural. So, Giddyup!

* * *

When it's time for the sketch, Jay gets up from his desk and walks to the middle of the stage where my workout equipment is set up. He introduces me as his "distinguished guest, Hollywood's top fitness trainer to the stars," who is promoting his new book, *Health, Wow!* "Please welcome Dick Williams."

I step out from behind the curtains wearing my workout suit with a lit cigarette dangling from my mouth, plus Dick's trademark black socks and dress shoes. The studio audience roars. I flex, and they laugh harder. I snap a towel at Jay's rear end, and we're off. I get wacky on the rowing machine. I topple over my equipment. Jay sets me up perfectly. The whole thing works. Hail to the irrational!

An estimated five million people watch that episode of *The Tonight Show*, as they do most nights, and among them is New York–based comedian Jerry Seinfeld, who laughs as he watches the show in his apartment.

The next day Jerry calls his friend Larry David, another stand-up comedian with whom he has spent months creating and writing a half-hour TV pilot for NBC. He says to Larry, "I saw Michael Richards last night with Leno on *The Tonight Show*. Michael was hilarious. He could play Kessler."

Like me, Larry was a writer–cast member on *Fridays*, so he knows me, but I imagine him inhaling deeply, clenching his teeth, wincing a little as he does when annoyed or irritated, and finally, with a nay-saying groan to Jerry, "Ehhh, Kenny's got a ponytail. I'd like that for the character."

"Great," Jerry says. "Let's bring Michael in for a read."

* * *

FOUR MONTHS EARLIER, Jerry and Larry were working on a sitcom pilot. Both of them had done sets at Catch a Rising Star comedy club this one particular night and were hanging out together at the bar. Jerry mentioned that NBC was interested in doing a show with him, and he asked Larry if he wanted to work on it with him. Did Jerry have an idea? No, he had nothing—except himself, which was enough for a network to want to invest in him. He and Larry wandered into a nearby Korean grocery store, where lightning struck as they joked about things on the shelves. The show would be about two guys talking about stuff—stuff on the shelves, goofy stuff they did during the day, and the stuff going on in their lives.

They would stay close to themselves, write from there. There was no premise better than that! They knew themselves well enough. Certainly, they knew what made them laugh. Which was essential since neither of them had written a pilot script. But that didn't matter! They were the pilot. The whole thing would be about them.

I can hear their eureka moment… What we're doing right now, this is it! Two guys, us! Talking about whatever! That's the show!

It was something Jerry and Larry had done together for years: talked about their lives, other people's lives, everything. Jerry would star as himself, and his friend George would be modeled on Larry. *Cheers* had a bar; they'd have a coffee shop. They would talk about the minutiae and annoyances of living in New York and the relationships in their daily lives, the stuff they always talked about when they got together.

Depending on your point of view, it would be about everything, or it would be about nothing. Either way, they were onto something.

Jerry was managed by George Shapiro and Howard West. George was the nephew of comedy legend Carl Reiner. His show business connections ran deep, and he adored Jerry. More than that, he believed in him and believed Jerry was primed for success, which he was. After years of working in clubs, nonstop touring, and numerous *Tonight Show* appearances, he had climbed the ladder in the comedy firmament to a place where George and Howard were able to secure a deal for him to make his own comedy pilot for NBC.

Jerry and Larry finished writing the pilot in February. A few weeks later, Jerry sees me on *The Tonight Show*. Soon after, I get a call from my agent.

"They want you to audition for a pilot Jerry Seinfeld is doing for NBC," he says.

"NBC? But they canceled my show last year," I say, referring to the series *Marblehead Manor*, which ran on the Peacock network before getting the ax. "Did they ask for me?"

"It's coming from NBC. Jerry's writing the pilot with Larry David."

"Oh, those guys must've asked for me. Okay, yeah, I know Larry. We were on *Fridays* together."

"How about Jerry?" my agent asks. "Do you know him?"

No, I say. I knew of Jerry, though. At thirty-five years old, he is a bona fide stand-up comedian. Like Jay, Jerry is established, a pro, a headliner who's selling tickets. I am not surprised he has a TV deal.

Larry is in another category. Seven years older than Jerry, he has worked the stand-up scene since the early '70s. He, too, is a gifted writer, something he does with more assurance than telling jokes to an audience, which he did with an air of disdain that still came off as rather funny. It was a unique feature of his comedy act that worked. He was perpetually bothered and disgruntled, and though it didn't make him loveable, he was very much liked. It got him on *Fridays* and more recently on *Saturday Night Live*'s 1984–85 season that included Billy Crystal, Martin Short, Julia Louis-Dreyfus, and Christopher Guest.

Naturally, I tell my agent to send me the script for the audition. I am curious to see what the boys have come up with.

"What's it called?" I ask.

"*The Seinfeld Chronicles*."

* * *

NBC MIGHT NOT HAVE TOLD Jerry and Larry yet, but I am probably at the bottom of their network list or out altogether in the discard pile. I can hear the NBC execs say, "We had Michael on a show that didn't work. Sorry. What about Tony Shalhoub? Have you thought about him? How about Larry Hankin? There are a lot of funny guys out there."

Hollywood is tough. But for a guy on the cusp of forty, standing six feet three inches tall, with the physique of a spaghetti noodle, my life is pretty good. I own my own home. I work regularly in television and films. My résumé also includes a few plays at the Mark Taper Forum.

Stand-up comedy, which is live and a form of theater, is, for me, usually improvisational and raw, a place where I let it all out, like a dog off leash, though lately I'm losing interest in the whole stand-up scene. After my recent co-starring role with "Weird Al" Yankovic in his movie *UHF*, it's clear to me I am more of a character actor than a stand-up comic.

I've always felt this anyway, but now I am leaning into it. I'm going to audition for the Actors Studio and look into the Stella Adler Conservatory West.

* * *

I AM AT HOME PREPARING for my audition for the Actors Studio—memorizing the Jerry-and-the-dog monologue from Edward Albee's *The Zoo Story*—when a messenger delivers the pages for my NBC-*Seinfeld* audition. *The Seinfeld Chronicles* script is still a work in progress, but it's enough to give me a taste of the show, including a scantily written character named Kessler, the role for which Jerry envisions me.

The pages are not like any TV sitcom script I have read before in that it's just conversation, a lot of banter with very few stage directions.

It's interesting, kind of like *My Dinner with Andre*, but without the insight into the human condition. It's just the condition, which I think is better.

It is mainly two guys talking in a coffee shop, where they are occasionally interrupted by a snarky waitress who they know from being regulars. Then there is Kessler, a guy who lives in the apartment across the hall from Jerry. He barely has any lines. He walks into Jerry's apartment and says, "Got any meat?" In the next scene, he turns to George and asks how real estate is going.

I assume George works in real estate. I imagine Kessler must be a weirdo. There is no explanation or background for any of these people. There are no typical sitcom setups or jokes. It's just talk.

I'm intrigued. It's clear that this show is going to be about people and their ability or inability to navigate their lives in New York City. Since Kessler has few lines and really no story to go on in the pilot, I figure I'll go into the audition as a character, be in character. It won't be about saying funny. It will be about doing funny.

* * *

I AUDITION THREE TIMES. The first takes place in a conference room at NBC in Burbank, the same place I was a few weeks ago when I appeared on *The Tonight Show*. I walk in thinking NBC doesn't really want me. No one has said it directly, but the way the network's executives greet me with chilly, perfunctory hellos makes it seem like they are doing Jerry a favor by bringing me in. It doesn't matter to Jerry, though. He says he is a fan of mine and thanks me for coming in.

"Oh, well yeah, I wasn't going to stay at home," I say, affecting a look of seriousness that lands on Jerry and doesn't move until he starts to laugh.

Right. I'll make some faces. I just want to make Jerry laugh. I'm not thinking about the network...they don't want me anyway. But I'll perform well. I do want the room to laugh.

We sit down and subtly, like Jacques Tati, I study my chair and try to get comfortable. After a few moments, I stand and get another chair, a desk chair on wheels, which lets me glide awkwardly around the room toward Jerry. This gets laughs. Then I start with the first line. When Jerry says his line, I don't respond. I turn my head slowly and stare at him, like I have never seen him before, like I don't know what to say, and he cracks up.

The others in the room do the same. This is not just an audition; it's a performance. I'm giving them a character.

In the clubs, I used to open my act "in character" by standing onstage, acutely natural for five to six minutes while attempting to speak without saying anything. I pretended to have gone blank, to have forgotten my joke. I stood there all blanked out like Buster Keaton with the world falling apart around me. I covertly searched my pockets, trying to find the paper with my joke written on it. I find it. I glance furtively at my joke. Got it.

Slowly, I started my delivery, stuttering, then pausing, having forgotten the joke again. I look for the paper once more. Got it. Then apprehensively, I deliver, "A guy walks into an antique store and

10

says, 'What's new?'" It was the only joke I ever told in a club, and it worked. So here with Jerry, I'm doing my opener but without the joke. I'm in character, just staring at him, very subtly signaling to him to "do something because we're being watched."

Jerry isn't an all-out actor. He's a comic who knows comedy. He's watching me, and at this audition, in this moment, this man is my audience, and the best one I could hope for. He won't stop himself from laughing—and he is laughing.

I pick up on this immediately. And so I play to Jerry—something I will do for the nine seasons to come. But first things first. I have to get the job.

* * *

A FEW DAYS LATER, I return for a second audition. Same place, but with more people in the room. Some are from NBC. Others are from Castle Rock, the production company that Rob Reiner—Jerry's manager George Shapiro's second cousin—founded a couple years earlier. Castle Rock is making the pilot (the network will finance it and put it on the air). I look around the crowded room. Where's Larry?

I didn't see Larry David at my first audition, and he is AWOL from this one too. Strange. We'd worked together in the past…he's the producer and writer here…I let it go. Jerry warmly welcomes me back, appearing eager to play.

As we get rolling, I start fooling around with our dialogue, changing lines, and improvising new ones. Our chemistry this time is even better. Jerry doesn't know what I am going to do, but he gamely plays along, clearly enjoying himself and keen to see how it will all turn out. Me too. I am flying without a net. I stand up and move around the room. The physicality feels good to me. Talking to Jerry from over my shoulder, I walk toward the conference room door, open it up, and to my surprise, there is Larry, standing straight and tall, listening to the scene through the door.

He is clearly caught off guard when the door opens. I feign shock. "What the hell are you doing out here, you Peeping Tom!" I exclaim without breaking character. "I'm going to get the landlord. I'm sick and tired of you creeping around this building, you pervert. I'm calling the cops."

Then I slam the door shut, sit back down, and give Jerry the next line as if nothing out of the ordinary has happened. (Later, I find out that Larry worried his presence in the room might throw me off, so he listened from outside.) People in the room are dying. Near the end of the scene, I get up and open the door again. Larry is still there.

"You're a sick man, and you need help! A great deal of help!" I slam the door shut.

I leave. End of audition.

* * *

I AM USED TO GETTING HIRED right after the first audition. I have gone in twice now and killed. My chemistry with Jerry is obvious. Everyone laughed. I can come up with only two reasons why they haven't given me the job already: they don't know what they're doing, or my initial hunch about *Marblehead Manor* is correct—the network considers me used goods.

Later, Jerry will confide that I was right, NBC didn't want me from the get-go because of the canceling of *Marblehead Manor*, but he pushes for me, and that's the reason I am called back for a third audition. This one is in a plush suite at the swanky Century Plaza Hotel, which must be, I think, something they arranged as a convenience to NBC president Brandon Tartikoff, who is joined by NBC's head of comedy, Warren Littlefield, and their head of late night and specials, Rick Ludwin. It is clearly the final round. The pilot is scheduled to shoot soon. Decisions have to be made.

Arriving early, I wait in the lounge with a bunch of other actors, the cream of the crop who've made it this far. One guy comes in character, wearing pajamas and slippers. Sure, why not? I am wearing pants (thank God for that) and a button-down shirt. They send us up one by one on the elevator. I'm using it: mentally, I'm in the elevator of our building in NYC, going up to Jerry's apartment. But now, I walk into the hotel suite pretending it's my room. After only a few steps inside I stop abruptly, pretending to be shocked by the sight of everyone there.

"What are you people doing in my room?" Some laughs.

I slip into the bathroom, wait a moment, and then loud enough for them to hear me, I plead, "Oh, come on!" I flush the toilet. Returning to the room, drying my hands, I look at Jerry seductively.

"Darling, do you want me to get room service?"

I'm getting laughs.

"No, thank you," Jerry says. "I'm good."

"All righty. Shall we do our scene?"

Jerry cracks up.

"Yes, we should do something," he says.

I deliver the first line: "Got any meat?"

I don't want to repeat the business from the previous auditions. Without deviating from the dialogue, I climb up on the nearby table and go straight into a headstand, as if this is ordinary behavior, nothing unusual while we're having a conversation. Jerry plays it the same way. Nose up in the air. Eyes slightly pinched. Wearing a look that is somewhere between amused and befuddled. Classic Jerry.

Then I deliberately lose my balance, crash backwards, roll off the table, and fall awkwardly into an empty chair. Everyone in the room is stunned, waiting to see if I am injured. Me too. I sit up and say my last line as if nothing out of the ordinary has happened.

I get up from the chair, point to Larry and bark, "Pervert!" and walk out the door and back to the elevator.

Afterward, there is nothing for those left in the room to debate. *Marblehead Manor* is ancient history. Much later, George Shapiro told me that after I'd exited the room, Brandon Tartikoff said, "Well, if you want funny, go with that guy."

CHAPTER 2

Kessler

The date is April 28, 1989, and nothing about the pilot we are shooting feels right to me. Maybe it's just nerves before camera. I am always nervy before I shoot. I usually stay apart from everyone to gather myself.

When I auditioned for Larry and Jerry, I was playing silly and gave myself up to them. I was weirdly funny and off the wall, all out on a limb and having careless fun for their amusement. I didn't give a hoot whether NBC or Castle Rock liked me. I wanted to make my comrades in comedy laugh, so I played it up, and doing so, I went home foreseeing that they were going to cast me. I was right.

Now I'm on the set, but it all feels rather empty. I sense my character Kessler isn't going to come through well. Having recently finished the film *UHF*, I still have a hangover from the character I played, Stanley Spadowski. I think some of him is still on me, and there is only one day to shoot the pilot, one chance to get Kessler right.

This is going to be a long day. I'm inside Kessler, but unknowingly, far from the character into whom I will evolve, Cosmo Kramer.

He has not yet arrived. For the pilot, it's just Kessler and "he's looking for meat," a suitable metaphor for finding Kramer.

I wonder whether I will have time to get another pilot before the end of the year. What? I want to get out of here and escape to another show? I can't have this mindset and perform. I buck myself up. Come on, Michael, you signed on the dotted line. We all signed on the dotted line. Let's get the job done!

I've worked with all kinds of material before. Once, when I was assigned to act in a weak sketch on *Fridays*, Jack Burns, our ensemble director, noticed my uncertainty. He took me aside and said, "With your talent, if you fully commit to the material, if you give it all you've got, you are seventy percent there. That's enough for the audience to go on. The other thirty percent lands where it will."

It was excellent advice, and I can get by on Jack's encouraging words. I have read enough sitcom scripts to know the pages Jerry and Larry have written are smart, quirky, funny, and different. Is it too different to become mainstream? What does it matter! Our job is to make it funny, and funny is about as mainstream as you can get.

Jerry and Larry have never written a TV series. They are first timers who don't entirely know the rules, and they have inadvertently broken and continue to break many of them by simply doing their own thing. Thank God for that! This is their time—*our* time—to be funny, and NBC has given us the nod to make it funny or bust.

As for me, I'm waiting and waiting to get in front of the camera and work. I'm somewhat relaxed but also bugged by this feeling of coming up short for Kessler. Maybe I need something to eat. Yeah, eat a hardy lunch and get funny. Let's get the job done!

* * *

AFTER I WAS PICKED TO PLAY KESSLER, the focus was on casting Jerry's best friend, George Costanza, the character based on Larry.

Unlike Jerry, Larry had no interest in playing himself. But finding someone who fit his vision of himself was one of the hardest parts of putting together the show. Their search was exhaustive and included Danny DeVito, Larry Miller, Nathan Lane, and Steve Buscemi, to name a notable few.

For Larry, someone who wasn't exactly comfortable in his own skin and not particularly fond of anyone else's skin, it was next to impossible to find an actor who could assume his level of discomfort and irritability with warmth, intelligence, and humor.

Then he watched a videotape that Jason Alexander had sent from New York. A veteran of stage and TV, Jason had recently won a Tony Award for his work in the musical *Jerome Robbins' Broadway*. His talent, timing, and versatility were evident on the tape, so much so that Larry called off the search after watching it. "That's the guy," he said.

Jason, standing five feet five inches tall and with the physique of a fluffy pillow, bears no resemblance to Larry. It doesn't matter. He's a gifted actor, and brilliant, and that's what's needed to counter Jerry, who doesn't even pretend to be an actor. But there's more. For Larry, choosing Jason is personal in a way that is obvious to me. If you're going to hire someone to portray you, find someone who can do it better than you. And that's Jason.

As for me, I was told that Larry had reservations about me because I didn't look like the guy who inspired Kessler, Larry's real-life New York neighbor, struggling comic Kenny Kramer. Except I did. Kenny was tall and thin and had long features, like me. The difference was, he had a ponytail, which, on the day we shoot the pilot, Larry suggests I wear.

"A hairpiece?" I say.

He shrugs as if to say, "Why not?"

"My luck it'll fall off during a take, but that could be funny. Kessler wears a fake ponytail. Let me think about it."

"Maybe if we do more episodes," Larry suggests. I respond by imitating him, clenching my teeth and slowly inhaling and exhaling with a pondering "no."

Larry laughs. It's up to me to find Kessler on my own, just as it is up to Larry to write a show as he sees fit. We're both masters of our domain.

* * *

WE ARE ON A SOUNDSTAGE over at Hollywood's historic Desilu-Cahuenga Studios, where it is still possible to wander into some of the soundstages, as I do, and commune with the ghosts of *The Abbott and Costello Show*, *I Love Lucy*, *The Dick Van Dyke Show*, *Make Room for Daddy*, *The Andy Griffith Show*, and other comedy classics shot there during television's Golden Age.

The cast looks ready to me, but I'm not feeling ready right down to the way I'm dressed. Kessler's wardrobe is flat and has little character to it. (Kramer's distinctive look is vital to my development and understanding of the character, and it will take some time to grow out of Kessler and into Kramer. For now, Kessler is unformed and not so nattily dressed.) What's his story? There isn't much to go on, not enough backstory in the script, not any storylines to ramp up his life. Kessler is more of a device for getting laughs.

I fret about the naturalness of Kessler. Just how human is he? It gets to me, and to compensate, I fear playing him too broad, falling into caricature and unbelievability. Who is Kessler? This is the puzzle I've been given to figure out. If Jerry is playing himself, a working stand-up comedian, Kessler would need a job of some kind too. Obviously an eccentric man, to say the least, he will have to be amusing if Jerry is going to let him come in and out of his apartment. Jerry has to like this guy.

Wait a minute, this sounds like me, like Michael Richards being admitted into Jerry's show! Oh, I see, I'm playing myself too.

Why, yes! I'm naturally touched by a quirky spirit, an irrational ha-ha soul. Yes, Kessler-Richards is right up my alley. This explains why they wanted me to come in and read for a funny, irrational next-door neighbor. I am that neighbor. I am not and have never been consistently normal. How could anything about me be normal given my own backstory?

*　*　*

It begins in 1948, when my mother, Philomena Nardozza, a twenty-six-year-old Catholic girl living with her Italian parents, Antonio and Theodosa, in south central Los Angeles and working as a receptionist in a doctor's office, gets pregnant. Keeping this from her own parents and not knowing where to turn, she meets an older woman who is also pregnant but going to Mexico to get an abortion.

She and my mother form a plan. After this woman has her abortion, she will return to LA and take my mom to Mexico for the same procedure. However, my mother never hears from this woman again. After some weeks go by, she finds out the woman died in Mexico during the abortion.

Scared and desperate, she goes to the Catholic Archdiocese of Los Angeles. She feels unable to attend to a baby on her own. At home, unbeknownst, she is already witnessing in her mother the

18

early onset of schizophrenia. Her aging father also has health problems. He is a part-time barber but his take-home is meager. My mother, who works as a secretary-receptionist in a doctor's office, takes care of everyone, but she is overwhelmed, and now she must take care of...me!

The archdiocese encourages my mother to carry me to term and then give me up for adoption. As she begins to show, she confesses everything to my grandfather. He feels that a baby might help my grandmother "stick around." She is beginning to retreat, talking to herself in front of them, engaged in a conversation that has nothing to do with them. "Ma!" Both he and my mother interrupt my grandmother to bring her back to our world. "Ma!" So far, this works.

I am born at St. Anne's Maternity Hospital, July 24, 1949, at 4:43 a.m. This is a matter of fact according to my birth certificate, one of the few facts about my origin that I can uncover with certainty until I am in my fifties. It also says that my father is William Richards. That will be a source of inquiry for many years. Who was this man? Did he love my mother? Where is he now?

My mother changes her last name to Richards from Nardozza, and her first name Philomena to Phyllis. She is now Phyllis Richards. Why has she done this?

Whatever her reasons, it's all made up.

I am left at the maternity ward and tagged "Adopted." St. Anne's has a large maternity ward that is also set up as an adoption center. My availability and adoption is arranged early. A Catholic couple set on adopting a baby boy arrive the next day and take me home. I am now officially theirs, but only for a few weeks. This couple is in contact with my mother, who now yearns to see me. They kindly arrange for her to come to their house for a visit. When they put me in her arms and she holds me, she cries and wants me back in her life. She pleads with them to understand, and they do.

To everyone's relief, the details are quickly worked out, and my mother is able to take me home...home to my grandmother..."Ma" as we all call her.

* * *

My mother takes on a second job to make additional money. She has the one as a secretary-receptionist in a doctor's office and the other as a medical records librarian in a health clinic. She works from early morning until early evening. With my grandpa at the barbershop, I am usually in the arms of my grandma—"Ma." She holds me like a doll all the time and never puts me down. She rocks me and wraps me in a quilted blanket she had made years ago in Potenza, Italy, her hometown.

The times when she talks to herself don't interfere with her ability to care for me. Not yet. She keeps me clean and bottle fed.

For now, she can manage herself and me at the same time. She can be in two worlds—one with us and the other in some mysterious realm that comes and goes. Most of her conversations in the "realm" are in Italian. On bad days, and they aren't too frequent, she gets into heated arguments with someone "in there," and my mom or my grandfather call her back to us. As I get older, I learn to do the same. This doesn't upset me.

As crazy as things were and will get, my family loves me, and I have TV and *The Lone Ranger*, *Amos 'n Andy*, *The Adventures of Wild Bill Hickok*, and my pillows to wrestle.

By the time I am four, what's going on with Ma is normal to me. I have nothing else for comparison. Ma loves me. She is maternal to the core. My grandfather was right. My presence has kept Ma with us.

* * *

I can't remember much about my grandfather. He comes home in the afternoon tired from work but always with something for me hidden in his hand. I rush up to him and pry open his big hand to get my treat. My favorite is a roll of Life Savers candy.

20

One day my grandfather doesn't come home from the barbershop to lie down, as he does each day, being tired all the time. He collapses on Adams Boulevard suffering a fatal stroke. He is sixty-eight years old. I am turning six at the time. My mother cries that night in her bedroom, and I stand by her bed while my grandmother loudly insists that my mother do as she has done: "Live for the boy! Live for the boy!" Taking me in her arms, my mother hugs me, and I hold on to her.

It's around this time that my grandmother starts slipping deeper into her schizophrenia, requiring more and louder shouts of "Ma!" to bring her back. Sometimes, in the evening, she locks herself in the bathroom, where I can hear her through the door, arguing in Italian with the voices in her head.

Within a year, those voices begin to lead her out of the house. She has been living for me until her illness literally pulls her away. She wanders through the front door and down the driveway in her bathrobe and slippers, heading down Adams Boulevard, with all that busy traffic and noise, and maybe the spirit of her husband, my grandpa, somewhere on the pavement. I play a game where I follow her, thinking she can't see me. We get as far as half a mile from home before she senses my presence, stops, turns, and tells me in broken English to "go home."

She knows it's dangerous for me to be trailing her into the void.

"Go home, Mike!" she implores. "Go home."

"Where are you going, Grandma?" I ask.

"Go home, Mike! Go home."

She knows that I can safely find my way home and that I will be fine without her. And I am. I know my way back home, and I run there as fast as I can, imagining that I am taking my grandma home with me, carrying her on my back, because I know, unlike me, she can't make it back on her own.

I run as fast as I can.

* * *

My mother returns from work.

"Is Ma here?"

"No, Mom. She went away again."

"Have you eaten?"

"I had some peanut butter."

She broils a hot dog for me, with a slice of American cheese wrapped around it.

"Let's go," she says.

We get in her blue '52 Chevy Bel Air and drive to the police station. They have Ma. She's dirty and half-dressed with a police blanket around her. She sits silently in the back seat of the car, in the dark that hides her from herself. As we drive her home, I eye the Baldwin Hills in the distance, telling myself that I'm going to walk up there someday, and to Ballona Creek, where there are snakes and frogs and this weirdly colored water—discharge from the nearby Styrofoam plant.

Is this too far for me to walk? No one ever asks or wonders. I certainly don't. On my own, I already venture for miles on the railroad track along West Jefferson Boulevard, picking up small granite rocks that glitter in the sun. I pocket them like jewels and bury them under a large red-berried toyon bush—the ones that look like holly scattered throughout the foothills here. Hollywood, that's what it's sometimes called. The blue-bellied lizards here will guard my magic stones.

No matter how far I go, I can always find my way back home. But Ma can't. Next year, she will enter Norwalk Sanitarium, the Metropolitan State Hospital for the mentally ill. This will be her home for the rest of her life.

* * *

Who is this Kessler character who is out to get meat? He's lost and only at home in Jerry's apartment. If he can't make it there, he's stuck in the building, unable to get out? Who is this guy? I am looking at my script. "Got any meat?" Kessler could be hungry for the whole of life. The character stands unjustified, loosely written, undefinable. I have to make it all up, have to imagine a backstory to put flesh on Kessler's bones.

Where is Larry in all of this?

For the time being, I want to leave Larry alone while he's into shooting the other scenes for the pilot. He's up to his neck, working to get George and Jerry right. Larry knows funny. We've been in the trenches before, digging deep for laughs late at night in the clubs and during those grueling days on *Fridays*, scrambling each week to throw a show together. Larry knows the heat.

Jerry is equally focused but remarkably cool, like his alter ego, Superman, standing unfazed with hands on his hips as bullets bounce off him.

We're making comedy out of the mix, this cuckoo world that's always pushing us around, all round and round we go. I watch Larry go for laughs. Jerry's laughing it up too. Lee Garlington, as the waitress, plays along. She's very present, a very good actress, and literally serving Larry/George and Jerry through her role as the waitress. She plays smarter than they are. The boys need this. It's compensatory. They don't have to be smart all the time. It's too exhausting, too one-sided, and reeks of hubris if they do.

The day drags on. Finally, there's a break in the action and I get my moment with Larry. I am now standing with the source for Kessler. Larry is the one who wrote him into the show, and I want to know how he sees Kessler, who this guy is, and what his relationship with Jerry is all about besides the fact that he lives across the hall.

"How do you see Kessler?"

"I had this neighbor, Kenny Kramer. He was always thinking of ways to get by."

"He likes money?"

Larry snickers. "Yeah, he likes money."

"Kessler's got his own apartment. How does this knucklehead pay for it?"

"Kenny gets by. He figures out something."

"He's a moocher?"

Laughing. "Yeah, yeah, Kessler's always mooching."

"How about if he got the apartment ten years ago? It's a tiny studio, just an eight-by-eight room. Hardly any rent."

"Yeah, that could be."

I should leave Larry alone. Stop talking about Kessler. Just make it funny and leave it at that, but I'm curious to see what more Larry could say.

"What does Kessler do in the city?"

"Oh, he never leaves the building. He figures it all out from inside the building."

"He's always inside the building?"

"Yeah, he's got agoraphobia."

"So, he can only get as far as Jerry's apartment?"

This is hilarious to Larry. "Yeah, he's terrified to go anywhere else!"

"So Jerry's place is his whole world?" I ask.

"Right! For Kessler, going out on the town is going to Jerry's apartment."

Larry's done and so am I. It's like we're on *Fridays* again, rushing to build a sketch. There's never enough time. It's not perfect, but it's good enough. Larry was probably screwing around, but this background story intrigues me. Kessler is acutely introverted, stuck in his building. I'm an introvert and can feel stuck in myself. I had a grandmother who was "severely introverted" and stuck in herself. How does Kessler try to get out of himself to meet the world? It's all in Jerry's apartment. For me, everything happens there.

* * *

WE TAPE THE PILOT EPISODE without a studio audience. This is like Kessler unto himself without the world. We make up the studio audience's response to what we think is funny. Naturally, they're laughing at everything we do! Without the actual audience, without the real world responding, we are deeply introverted unto ourselves, which makes the soundstage seem vaster than it already is, an ocean of darkness with a small island of light in the distance—the coffee shop, where the action is for most of the day.

It's called Pete's Luncheonette, not Monk's Cafe, as it will come to be known. I spend much of the day and into the evening waiting to work, lying in the corner on the empty audience bleachers of the soundstage and listening to Jerry and Jason in the distance as they work and shoot their scenes. I'm Kessler all alone in the corner of his building, waiting for his turn in life, waiting to enter Jerry's apartment.

Jerry, who greeted me earlier with enthusiasm, is now fully engaged in his scenes with Jason, who not only impresses but intimidates me with his photographic memory and ability to change direction and add nuance instantly upon request. I quickly see the dynamic between the two of them, and with Larry hovering, watching, adding lines, totally involved in perfecting the material, I get that this will be the all-consuming thrust of the show.

Onto myself and running my lines, I write notes on the front and back of my script, including one that says, "Alone with the Alone." I run my lines, and though each time I do them in a way that feels good, I worry that I won't be able to get to that place again.

A satisfying delivery becomes more elusive as the hours pass. I get to the point where I am not sure if I can even remember the lines. It's because the character isn't on me yet and won't be for the shoot. I envy the apparent comfort the others display across the soundstage. Though Jason will say he channeled Woody Allen in the pilot, he is playing it through himself, as Jason Alexander. He is securely natural in his own skin.

At one point, Jerry looks at the cameras, the set, and grins. "So, this is how it's done. We'll keep it funny, and that should be that." Remarkable. It's that easy for him. He, too, is natural in his own skin.

What happened to the confidence I had in the audition? There I was relaxed. I improvised. I played around as a funny-bone actor.

Here I am playing someone outside myself, which Kessler is, obviously. The problem is that I am trying to play the character rather than be the character. This is different from playing myself, being natural in my own skin.

Kessler is just the beginning of something that I am not keyed into yet. It will come. I get up to take a walk. Larry sees me.

"Ponytail?" he says.

"I'm thinking of shaving my head and just leaving the sideburns," I say.

"Really?" Larry looks concerned.

He knows that I could possibly do this. I'm a freak, very tuned into the irrational. I reassure him with a smile that says, "Don't worry. I won't let you down." I wouldn't be in this show if he really thought otherwise. I know this, and it provides me with the fuel to deliver. I want him to feel right for casting me.

Buck up! Play it for laughs. I'm stuck inside a Kessler, who is stuck inside his apartment building. We're all stuck inside of something. The only way out for me is comedy. Play it for laughs. "Live for the boy" becomes live for the laughs!

* * *

I finish the day with the annoying sense of not having done enough with the part. Just two short scenes, little interaction with the others, and no strong connection to my character. If the pilot is picked up, how the heck will I fit into it?

My agent sends over a script for a movie with John Ritter. It's a comedy called *Problem Child*. Good; if the pilot doesn't go, maybe I'll be on the set with John Ritter. I don't know whether Jason, or even Larry and Jerry were also mulling other commitments or hatching backup plans, but I am quite sure that none of us had any idea of the extraordinary ways this pilot would begin to change our lives.

PART 2

Oh Mama!

CHAPTER 3

The Backstory

S tarting at a very young age, my imagination is the key to my survival. My mom works all day, my grandmother is slipping into her madness, and my grandfather is dead. One day in nursery school, I see a comic book with Prince Valiant on the cover. He's wearing armor and holding a big, shiny sword illuminated by the sun.

That image of the young hero is all I care about at school, Prince Valiant *and* the grape juice we get at snack time. My mother buys me a Prince Valiant sword and scabbard at the toy store. I wear it everywhere. Imagining myself as the warrior-knight, I ask my mother about my father for the first time. She tells me that he was killed in the war. I believe this and live with it for many years.

My father was killed in the war.

I like to fight the enemy, my pillow. It tries to kill me but I won't let it, and I see people fight on television, guns going off and people dropping to the ground. I think about my father in the war and getting killed. I fight my pillow as hard as I can.

At five, my mom gets me a bicycle. From then on, I am riding for miles. Despite my young age, I know the streets, and from Hauser and La Brea, I ride all the way to Culver City! I zip past the Helms Bakery trucks parked along Washington Boulevard and as far as the MGM studios. What's in there? I discover where I can crawl under a metal fence and walk around the studio's back lots. I hang out for hours on the sets of an old western town and a palace in ancient Egypt! Sometimes, I bring other kids to marvel at all this make-believe.

One morning, I'm watching Laurel and Hardy's short film *Hog Wild* on TV. They're trying to install a radio antenna on Hardy's roof, and in the background I see the Baldwin Hills. "Hey, I know those hills!" Then, the two are driving down Hauser Boulevard. "I know that street! I ride my bike on it all the time." At the end of the movie, they're driving out of control right through Culver City!

After that, whenever I'm outside riding my bike, I keep an eye out for Laurel and Hardy! They're around here somewhere. It's like I'm on TV with them.

Here I am at six, walking along the railroad track, my pockets full of magic stones, but I feel that ultimate power comes from the Baldwin Hills rising in the distance, too far away for now, but I will climb to the top someday, maybe when I'm seven, which is just in a few months. This huge amount of earth swelling up to the sky feels alive and a part of me as I scan the ridges as high as they can go. I think I am more at home in the Hills than in my house with Ma.

My mother worries. She knows she can't take care of me, not with all the hours she works, and my grandma is becoming less reliable, sometimes wandering away from the house and getting lost. My presence isn't enough to keep Ma at home anymore. I also feel my own urge to ride away on my bike and do what I want. Unlike my grandma, I get power from my stones, and no matter how far I roam, I can always find my way back home.

My mom's brother, Mike (I never see much of him), tells her to send me to a boarding school for first grade—Page Military

Academy here in Los Angeles, billed as "a big school for little boys."

At first, I imagine a connection between wearing a uniform and being close to my father, but I quickly grow to hate this place. I get the measles and I am sent to the infirmary. I pass the time with my *Prince Valiant* classics until the nurse takes them from my bedside and throws them away. "You're here to get well," she scolds me, "not read comics!"

One weekend when I am home, I make my way up to the top of the Baldwin Hills, and there I discover an army post! Amazed, I see uniformed soldiers with rifles slung over their shoulders patrolling the perimeter. I tell them that I go to Page Military Academy and wear a uniform too and that my father was a soldier who died in the war. They give me Juicy Fruit gum, and when I see them again, they greet me with a salute.

Back at Page, the older cadets order me to tear pages out of a textbook. They know I will get into trouble, and I do. The headmaster yells at me and calls my mother at work. I cry and plead with her to not send me back to Page. I don't want to go back to that school. Figuring out that I was duped by the older cadets, she places me in a day care center close to home until I am able to start second grade at the Catholic school where we go to church.

I don't like day care either. I sneak out and walk home to be with Ma and watch TV. The phone rings a lot, but Ma never answers it. Neither do I. Ma doesn't know anything about the day care center. She's content inside of herself and not in need of much. I have seen her sit on a sofa for hours, looking at nothing and appearing to be fine with that.

* * *

I CAN'T REMEMBER LEARNING how to read, but at this Catholic school where I go for second grade, we read out loud in class. I read with great emotion, punching up the words as I feel them. I don't know it, but I am performing and getting good reviews. My classmates compliment me during recess. They think I'm funny—and a good reader!

But my teacher dislikes how animated my reading gets, especially when it makes the class laugh! She stops calling on me to read, and as a result, I lose my interest in school.

It's not until I hear Sister talk about "God our Father," that we have a "loving Father" watching over us, that I am intrigued again. Sister tells us that if we all behave, we're going to the church tomorrow to see "our Father." Why hasn't my mom told me that I have another father? When I ask her about this, she tells me that I do have this Father, and that Sister will teach me more about him.

When Sister speaks of the Father, he sounds a long way off, in a distant place called Heaven. She once said that Moses was at the top of a mountain and saw the Father up there. I got to the top of my mountain and saw army men. They were sort of like my father. But Sister tells me that the Father in Heaven is my real father.

My real father?

Yes!

I can't wait to see him!

The day arrives. We are going to see God, our Father. Sister says this with a solemn reverence that heightens my anticipation. I keep my hands folded on my desk all morning. I pay attention and don't fidget or talk out of turn. Finally, Sister leads us single file into the church, crossing ourselves with the holy water, and walking down the red-carpeted aisle. Genuflecting, we shuffle into a row, where I end up kneeling next to Sister before the golden altar.

After a few minutes of waiting, I get anxious.

"Where's God?" I ask.

Sister points to the altar.

"But I don't see him."

The nun puts her finger to her lips for silence.

"Is he here now?" I ask.

"Shhhh." She's getting annoyed.

"How about now?"

She nods, intimating that yes, our Father is with us. He's at the altar. But I don't see him.

"In the box?" I ask.

She nods yes and puts her finger to her lips.

"Doesn't he want to come out?"

"Michael! Shush!"

She startles me. I won't ask any more questions.

I slump and lean back on the edge of my pew. This angers Sister, and she snaps at me to get up from the pew and kneel!

After school, instead of getting on the bus that takes me home, I return to the church to see my Father on my own. The church is empty. I head straight for the golden box on the altar and carefully open the little doors. Inside I find a white cloth napkin, just a napkin.

Walking home that afternoon, I start thinking that Sister and all the people going to the church and kneeling before the box with no god inside, it's all make-believe. They're pretending that God is in there, and now they want me to pretend too? They're kind of like my grandmother and her kind of make-believe, except they can find their way around without needing the police to pick them up to bring them back home.

Of course, I am too young and unaware to understand that the people in the TV shows I watch are also pretending. The Greek word for actor is *thespian*, which translated means "of the gods." One day I will find myself to be an actor on TV—a "god" in the box.

* * *

GRANDMA IS NOT HOME. I go up into the Baldwin Hills. There's a lot of rough brush, lizards, and jackrabbits, a king snake or two. Once a rattlesnake. There are some dirt roads, one that the soldiers in their trucks use. There are some oil-pumping rigs. Some of them are not working. They sit like prehistoric monsters petrified by time. The soil around them is stained with oil, and the air is still tainted by the muck. The army post up here can guard the "monsters." That's how it's done.

Looking at the city basin sprawling far and wide beneath me: The Baldwin Hills Dam and downtown LA is to the east. Across the city basin to the north, pitched on the hills opposite mine, is the Hollywood sign. To the west is the Pacific Ocean. I can see my house below on Blackwelder Street. The Hills uplift me. I feel larger than the city. I see all the hills surrounding Los Angeles. The mountains of Santa Monica loom higher than the sea, the clouds higher than the mountains, and the sun...what makes it so bright?

It's so round and higher than any mountain or building or church. The only thing that boxes it up is the night. I also love the moon. When I am outside at night, waiting for my mom to come home and feeling alone, I look up at the moon, and through my tears I see streaks of rainbow colors that comfort me. The moonlight soothes me, keeps me company, and makes me feel that I'm not really alone.

* * *

EACH SUNDAY FOR THE NEXT FIVE YEARS, my mother and I drive out to Norwalk to visit Grandma at the sanitarium. She's been committed to a lockdown ward, but they let her go outside into the visitor's garden, where we all sit together on a bench and eat ice cream cones from a vendor on the grounds. Ma doesn't speak much, and so it's just sitting together for a little while and then we leave. That's the usual visit.

My mother sells our house and moves to the San Fernando Valley. She buys a small two-bedroom tract house situated in a walnut grove (once a sprawling farm) in Van Nuys. I now attend St. Brigette Catholic School on Sherman Way. I'm in the fourth grade.

A math problem is presented on the blackboard, and Sister calls on me to work it out.

I don't understand this stuff and consequently, she gives me a page of these problems to do at home. "And don't come back to school without them," she adds.

I can't do the problems, so I don't go back to school. When my mother drops me off in the morning, I pretend to walk through the school gate, but then I turn around and head home. There I study the *TV Guide*, circling the programs and movies I want to watch all day, especially the comedies: *I Married Joan, I Love Lucy, The Phil Silvers Show,* and *My Little Margie,* whose star, Gale Storm, buttons her scenes by clucking her tongue, producing a funny sound like some of Kramer's funny utterances.

This goes on for two weeks before the school finally gets ahold of my mom and asks why I haven't been at school. Well, I have been; it's just another kind of school, one where I watch the finest character actors on TV. My mom is not happy. Through tears and breathless sobs, I explain that Sister told me not to return to school without completing the math problems, and, well, I couldn't do them and she wasn't around to help, so I took Sister at her word and didn't go to school.

I show the problems to my mother. She doesn't understand them either. She's furious—not with me to my surprise, but more with the school for letting me and her down.

"Get in the car!" she says.

We drive to the convent, find Sister, and my mom lets her have it. That's the end of Catholic school for me.

* * *

I'D RATHER GO TO THE PUBLIC SCHOOL where all the kids in my neighborhood go. I promise my mom I'll do better in school if I can go there. Though I flunk out of fourth grade, I'm still passed into the fifth, where I find myself at the top of the class and becoming best friends with Dave, the toughest kid and best athlete in the school.

I tell him and another tough kid from our class about an empty farmhouse in a nearby field and suggest the three of us should go there and explore it. The old farmhouse is dirty, dark, and spooky. "It might be haunted," I say. As we enter, I make a few scary sounds and convincingly fib about a dead person upstairs in the closet. Both Dave and the other kid bolt out of there. With the power of my imagination and my sense of fun, suddenly I'm the leader, the toughest one around. It's all make-believe, what you imagine yourself to be. Unknowingly, I'm thinking like an actor.

Dave has two older brothers, who call Dave and me "sticks" because we're so skinny. From this, I entertain them by hiking up my pants and playing a nerd à la Don Knotts, and they laugh. I like making them laugh. It comes easily for me. They have a friend named Lloyd, and I make everyone laugh by doing a funny impression of him.

One day, I do this impression in front of Lloyd. He gets mad and chases me around Dave's yard. I hop on top of a brick wall and scramble up to the roof of their garage. Lloyd tries to keep up, but from the roof, I wildly leap into a large sycamore tree, and, like Johnny Weissmuller's Tarzan, I swing from limb to limb until I'm back on the ground. This chase is like a few I'd seen in old film comedies with Keaton, Chaplin, or Laurel and Hardy. Everyone is laughing hard, even Lloyd. My antics busted them up.

From this day on, I am into slapstick comedy—big, broad, crazy antics, like riding my bike into trash cans, bumping into walls, or suddenly falling or tripping in grocery stores, movie theaters, or the middle of the street. Anything for a laugh, I'm on all the time. It's really the only reason for going to school—to make my friends laugh.

But I get to seventh grade at Mulholland Junior High, and I don't know where my friends are. We are put in different classes, different periods, all controlled by a bell that begins and ends everything. I can't help but think of Victor Hugo's Quasimodo, the freaky

36

Hunchback of Notre Dame, who said, "The bells made me deaf." In fact, I can't hear much of anything at school, until one day, some kids from the school's drama class come into my English class to perform a few scenes from a play.

I sit up and take notice. I'm interested! I'd like to try that! I find out that this drama class is an elective that I can take next semester. I can hardly wait!

* * *

On my first day in this class, the drama teacher hands out a mimeographed scene to each student. We're assigned parts and begin to read the scene. I take to it very easily and read well enough to keep my part as other students are replaced to give somebody else their turn to read. I am never replaced, and during the course of this first exercise, something happens to me: I regain the feeling I'd had when I read with expression in the first grade.

It's like reconnecting with a friend. Oh, there you are! Reading out loud is so natural to me. It's all I want to do.

Then the bell goes off and class is over. This is the first time I've ever disliked the bell ending a class. But Mr. Boardman, the drama teacher, asks me to stay so he can have a word with me. As the others file out, he introduces me to someone new—William Shakespeare. He has a few students working on a scene from *The Tempest*, and he would like me to play Caliban.

I agree, but I'm not sure what a Caliban is or what I'm getting into. I really liked the play reading, though, and knew that I was good at it. Now a teacher is telling me that I read very well and appear to have a knack for it, and he wants me to be in an acting scene. But the scene isn't for another English class, he says. It's for an open competition at UCLA in which junior high schools from all over Los Angeles will perform scenes from Shakespeare.

It's a big deal.

I respond with the diligence of a boy who craves this type of affirmation and opportunity to stand out. The language of Shakespeare doesn't hang me up. Caliban is a kind of monster, and I like that. I slip into character without any struggle. Mr. Boardman goes through the part with me word for word. I lower my voice and limp around the room. I've got it or it's got me, and by the time of the competition, I have morphed into Caliban, so childlike, crying for the lost island that his mother once gave him but Prospero took away. "Curse be that ye did so!"

I feel Caliban's lost island; I miss my Baldwin Hills!

I am Caliban! I slump to the ground.

"Which first was mine own king! And here you sty me in this hard rock whiles you do keep from me the rest o' the island!" Mr. Boardman is awed by my performance.

We advance to the finals. By this time, we have been at this competition all day, and I am exhausted, spent. We begin the scene, and I am deeply engaged in Caliban's anger toward Prospero, and then, suddenly, I go blank. I don't know my line. I stand onstage stuck in the mire of Caliban. "You taught me language!" But here I have no language to speak, only the feeling of being lost in empty space. I use it. I'm slowly moving convulsively through my space, and then I blurt out the line. It's all rather effective. We place third in this competition.

From this day on, I always work hard to know my lines, obsessively running them until they become second nature, which lets me soar through a character.

* * *

IMPRESSED BY MY WORK with Caliban, Mr. Boardman wants me for the lead in a school play he has written about an unruly "Spirit" character who causes kids to mess up the lunch area until he learns the folly of his careless ways. I throw myself into this role. My character wears a cape, and I drag my left leg as if it doesn't work. I grease my hair straight back and speak in a deep, gravelly voice. I have a facial twitch. I get laughs.

At the end of the play, redemption: the lunch tables are cleaned. The play is a hit with the whole school. When kids see me in the hallway, they ask me to play the "Spirit" for them. Even the teachers congratulate me. I am a star.

CHAPTER 4

Love

The summer before I start high school, my mother takes a better-paying job as the medical record librarian at the Conejo Hospital in Thousand Oaks. She buys a brand-new home, and I'm enrolled in Thousand Oaks High School. Changing schools yet again could be hard for me, but I'm all for it if there is a good drama teacher and class plays.

Mrs. Rose is the school drama teacher, and she is good. She directs the plays and also readies students for the National Forensic League. Competitive debating is at the core of the League, but they also offer two other competitive categories: Dramatic Interpretation and Humorous Interpretation. Mrs. Rose wants me to choose one of the categories and find a five-minute piece to present.

I'm not well read enough to know what to choose, but my English class comes through for me again. It turns out that sections from the play *Dino* by Reginald Rose are in my English book. I take the book home, one of the few schoolbooks that ever makes it that far. I put a pencil to the scenes, editing my piece down to five minutes.

With a clock on the table, I rehearse the piece repeatedly, timing myself to make sure I am on the dot, exactly five minutes.

Also, in the competition, you must hold your pages while you present your piece, so my mother types out the material for me. She can type 120 words a minute. It takes her no time at all. I meticulously place the pages into a clear plastic cover; they're easy to read, will stay clean, and free from getting wrinkled. I like the process of learning the material and becoming a character. Even holding the typed pages in the folder. It all feels good and comfortable and right.

For my performance, every detail is attended to, well rehearsed, and to the point until my lines are second nature. I'm ready to lift off.

I present *Dino* to Mrs. Rose and the drama class. Mrs. Rose loves it, and I'm registered to compete. I want to make her proud, and it turns out I have what it takes not only to compete in Dramatic Interpretation but also to win in the National Forensic League. For the rest of the school year, I am bused to different high schools throughout Ventura County for tournaments. I place first in each one, amassing an impressive collection of gold medals and reveling in the growing confidence I have in myself as a performer.

The next year I switch to Humorous Interpretation and go in search of a great piece. In the school library, I look through a book of old vaudeville material and come across a funny short story about a Captain Bligh who cheerfully invites people to come on board for a sail "to enjoy the cool breezes" but then demoralizes them with all his complicated commands for working the boats rigging. The piece has a few funny characters, and I have voices for them all.

I edit the piece, time it out, type it up on my mother's IBM Selectric, and perform it for class. I get the laughs I expected. Mrs. Rose is all for it, and so apparently are the judges who watch me in competitions and acknowledge I have a talent that lets me stand out at these events. I collect more gold medals and a reputation as the only kid in the county who's taken first place in both categories, Humorous and Dramatic Interpretation.

* * *

By my junior year, I have starred in school productions of *Arsenic and Old Lace*, *Outward Bound*, and *The Wizard of Oz*. But I am just getting started.

My friend William, a senior, is a skilled and prolific artist who paints as a symbolist and surrealist in the mode of Max Ernst and Salvador Dalí. He's turned his parents' house into a studio and has a painting going on in nearly every room. In a few years, he will be represented by one of the most prestigious galleries in LA. We regard each other as fellow artists and discuss the ideas that guide us with respect and certitude that we are onto something.

In addition to his own work, he designs and paints most of the backdrops for the Conejo Valley Players, a thriving community theater that movie and TV producer-director Dwight Hauser started almost a decade earlier in an old barn. Industry actors who know Dwight drop in to work there. William urges me to try out for their next play, a production of *Kiss and Tell*, which is a 1940s Broadway hit about teenage dating that was also turned into a popular movie starring Shirley Temple.

The timing is perfect. They're just starting to cast it. I audition with several other teenagers from around the county. The director likes me. She calls Mrs. Rose at school to get a bead on me. "Yes, I know Michael," she says. "Cast him." It's done. I become one of the leads in their production. My name is on posters across Ventura County, and my picture is in the local newspaper.

* * *

That summer I work the graveyard shift as an orderly at the hospital. I also begin my first serious relationship. Marilyn is a classmate of mine. She lives a block from the hospital. I leave funny notes in her mailbox, sometimes a few dorky hospital supplies, swabs, or an examination glove. It's easy to be with her. We fool around listening to Johnny Mathis. It's love.

I buy a '56 Chevy Nomad modified with a 427 hp engine and a Hurst four-speed shift on the floor. It's already the fastest car in Conejo Valley. I got it from a gas station owner who built the car for his son who'd just gotten drafted. I enjoy street racing. With a few friends, I sometimes head for the Valley and cruise through Bob's Big Boy on Van Nuys Boulevard picking up a race or two and extending my reputation as one of the fastest cars in San Fernando. What a car!

* * *

IT'S MY SENIOR YEAR of high school. For the League, I return to Dramatic Interpretation and create a piece of my own. I improvise the whole thing and take four gold medals.

But not everything is as bright and shiny as the American mags on my car. I fight with my mother all the time. On some school nights, it gets so heated that I drive to Marilyn's house or sleep in my car.

When I tell my mom I'm competing in Camarillo or Ventura, she asks, "Are they paying you for that?"

"Mom, I'm winning gold medals."

"Are they real gold?"

She doesn't get it. To her, I'm just working for free.

The situation worsens anytime I bring up my father, which I do because now that I'm older, what my mother has told me over the years doesn't add up.

"And my father didn't die in World War II! If I was conceived in 1948, my father couldn't have been killed in a war that ended in 1945!"

"Well, it was after the war."

"How could that be, Mom?"

"At the end of everything."

"The end of what, Mom?" I ask.

"When he died."

"When he died? How did he die, Mom?"

"I told you."

Finally, I explode. "Just tell me the truth! Stop lying to me!"

She's shaking "I didn't want to tell you before because you were so young, but he was killed in an automobile accident."

"Oh, so now that I'm older, I can hear that he died in a car accident?"

"It's hard for me to talk about it, Mike."

"So, he died in a car crash?"

"Yes."

"This is crazy, Mom. So he didn't die in the war! Where did he die?"

"I think in Arizona. I can't remember."

"In Arizona? What was he doing there?"

"He was working."

"Doing what?"

"He was an engineer in construction. He was driving back from there."

"And the accident happened?"

"Yes."

"He had a job in Arizona?"

"Yes."

"Was my dad born in California?"

"I think he was from Arizona."

"He was born in Arizona?"

"I think so. I don't want to talk about this anymore. It's too upsetting!"

She heads for the bathroom and closes the door like Ma, her mother, closing herself off in the bathroom. She looks crazy to me.

It bothers me that she cuts me off like this, but I can see it affects her too. It's clear she's covering up something that she just can't talk about. This makes me angry. Why is it so hard for her to talk about my father? Why can't she tell me the truth? All these years thinking he had died in the war, all the fantasies I had of him taking the bullet were bullshit. Okay, he died in a car crash. In Arizona.

* * *

I GET AN F IN ENGLISH, of all subjects, which prevents me from graduating with my class. Yet I stand on the dais at the honors ceremony with thirteen of the smartest kids in the school receiving their academic awards. Mine is from the National Forensic League. I'm not graduating from high school, but I receive the highest honor. So be it.

I end up getting my diploma after taking a few summer school courses—speed-reading and metal shop—while also juggling two jobs: my old orderly position at the hospital and an ambulance attendant on weekends. I'm a good attendant, but the work on the ambulance is intense. I see terrible things, especially on the freeways. These scenes take a toll, causing me to picture my father dying in a car wreck, and I don't want to think about him that way. I stop asking my mother about him. I also stop street racing.

Summer ends. I graduate from school…and this part of my life.

I just want to commit to being an actor.

CHAPTER 5

The Summer of '69

Without a plan, I follow my girlfriend to Ventura Junior College, where I take two classes: Greek Theater and Rehearsal and Performance 1. I star in two productions, a modern version of *Antigone* and Elmer Rice's *Street Scene*. After a performance of *Street Scene*, Jerry Mathers from *Leave It to Beaver* comes backstage. I'm meeting my past. How many days did I watch "the Beave" when I stayed home from school!

My mother takes a new job as a medical record librarian at the hospital in Panorama City. She moves back to our old house in Van Nuys, which she still owns and was leasing out.

Near the end of my semester at Ventura, I drive to the Valley to see my old friend Dave, who is enrolled at Pierce College. I check out their drama department, but it doesn't do much for me. Someone mentions Los Angeles Valley College, that their drama department is the best. Really? I drive over there, and it is impressive. They have three stages!

Overall, you can't beat any of these local junior colleges for twenty-eight bucks a semester! I can do several plays a year on beautiful stages, outfitted with lights and sound, a costume department, and a director and staff, all for less than a hundred dollars a year. Stick around for a few years and you've got seven plays under your belt.

I like the setup at Valley College and want to go there for my second semester. Marilyn wants to stay in Ventura County. She's starting to see another guy and wants to move on from me. She breaks my heart. The pain of splitting with my first love wrecks me. It really blows my mind. I feel like taking my life. After a week or so, I come to my senses and throw myself into my acting work. For the time being, I stay at my mom's house in the Valley until I can get situated on my own.

I sign up for a full semester of classes but realize this is way too ambitious and withdraw from everything except Acting 1 and Rehearsal and Performance 2. I'm at this school for acting, not to take a bunch of classes for my edification. I get edified through acting! I must get into a play! The head of the theater arts department, Patrick Riley, teaches the Acting 1 class. In the first week, we are practicing improvs and I slip in some of my League material. He's impressed. It helps me land the lead in the main stage production he's directing of Tennessee Williams's *Summer and Smoke*.

The play challenges me. Playing John Buchannan Jr. makes me realize my lack of life experience. I'm certainly no Laurence Harvey. I just haven't lived enough. Though I'm about to turn twenty, my mojo for seduction is undeveloped. But this changes as work on the play begins and I get close to the girl playing Alma, a gorgeous, talented girl who lights my fire. About this time, I blow the transmission to my car and I don't have the bucks to get it fixed. My mother will not give me the money. She insists I get a job. I see her point, but I'm in a play now, and that's all that matters.

But it works out. "Alma" drives me home each night, and we start it up. On and offstage, we are John Buchanan Jr. and Alma Winemiller sizzling with sex for each other.

* * *

MY MOTHER DOESN'T UNDERSTAND this obsession of mine for acting. She can't see the worth of acting as an art form, the whole range of theater, its history, and the incredible craft of television and film. Between this and the time I spend with "Alma," my mother wants to know what the hell I'm doing with my life. Why I'm not earning money.

"Acting *is* a job, Mom. I just don't get paid for it."

She wants my car fixed and a job to pay for it. It's rather practical and good thinking, but I don't need my car. I've got "Alma."

And there are numerous kindred spirits on the Valley College campus in Riley's acting class. A few become good friends, like Frank, whose James Dean obsession includes carrying a pack of cigarettes in his T-shirt sleeve and a switchblade in his pocket; Paul, who's serious and thoughtful; and Brad, my closest friend, a writer and deep thinker from a family of intellectuals. The editor of the college paper, Brad writes a glowing review of my performance in *Summer and Smoke* and adds another when I star in the next play, *Waiting for Godot*.

At this point, I am sleeping in a spare bedroom rent-free at his place, with my broken car parked out back, and working part time in the school cafeteria. It's enough to keep me fed.

The theater opens me up to everything. I am fascinated with madness, humor, and the absurd. Beckett is sublime. With *Godot*, I am clearly in a waiting pattern myself, not sure what is up next. Brad introduces me to the Beat poets. I read all the Beat literature and feel the depth of my age, the questioning of the counterculture, the musing of rock and rollers, the disturbing suffering of the Vietnam War. What are we fighting for? I read Ginsberg's *Howl*; his "holy, holy" cantos are my introduction to a spiritual life. I get into Kandinsky and Miró. Their abstractions inspire me. I feel secure and well informed with them around.

With Brad, I create Clique, an acting club that quickly becomes a driving force in our little theater department. We read Megan Terry and her take on improvisational theater. I direct and star in her one-act play *Keep Tightly Closed in a Cool Dry Place*. Brad writes a winning review. It's a Clique production, and it's a big, buzzy deal on campus.

* * *

ONE DAY CLIQUE IS MEETING in the Horseshoe Theater at Valley College. We're discussing another Clique production, a one-act that I've written. A film student walks into the theater and straight out asks if he can join the group. His name is Ed Begley Jr. I like him immediately, but Clique is a tight group. Can this guy act? He played a small part in *Summer and Smoke*, the Salesman, and I liked what he brought to his gum-chewing character. He's fearless and outgoing, and I can tell he's funny. This interests me more than anything.

Frank Doubleday stands up and challenges Ed. He wants to see how tough he is. Ed is amused and plays along. It's all acting, all improv—except for the switchblade Frank clicks open. That's real.

"You think you can just walk in here and get your way?" Frank says with a threatening sneer.

Ed, stepping straight into character, puts up his hands. "Maybe we can strike a deal."

"You got any money? Or do you want to die right here?"

Ed goes for his wallet and throws it to the floor. "I need to live. It's all I got."

Frank picks it up and pulls out the bills. "You got more than you need." He pockets the money. "You got a problem with that?"

Ed steps back. "Take what you want."

I jump into the fray. "No use wasting a life that could be useful around here. What's your name, boy?"

Frank interrupts. "I say we kill him!"

Paul steps forward. "He may have more money hidden in his shoes."

Brad is up now. "You were in that play *Summer and Smoke!*"

Ed denies the allegation. "You must be thinking of somebody else."

"I was in that play *Summer and Smoke!*" I say, not acknowledging that Ed was in the play too.

Brad walks over to me. "I tell you it's him. He was in that play!"

I move in on Ed. "Now don't lie to us, boy."

Frank gets louder. "I say we kill him!"

Ed breaks down. "Okay! Okay! I was in the play! I didn't mean to do it! Please don't kill me!"

He slumps to his knees and cries. It's so over the top that we all bust out laughing. Ed is right on. He's one of us. He's in.

* * *

AT THE TIME, Ed is not in any of the acting classes. Why should he be? I didn't know this, but he already has a talent agent, has guest-starred on *My Three Sons* and some other episodic TV, appeared in commercials, and has his SAG card! Also, his dad is the Academy Award–winning actor Ed Begley. Apart from all the showbiz stuff, I naturally gravitate toward Ed the way I will with Jerry Seinfeld years later. We are sympatico, on the same wavelength, and most importantly, into comedy.

But this new friendship is put on hold.

The school year ends, and I want to fly back east to polish the play I wrote with a friend, Richard. I had met the guy the summer before through my old girlfriend Marilyn. He was visiting Los Angeles. This is Richard, an English major at Princeton who was enamored by my ability to improvise characters.

One day, he tape-recorded me, transcribed and formatted my stream-of-consciousness dialogue into a one-act play, and submitted it to the director of the Princeton Players. They responded positively and want it for a fall production. So now I'm all hyped up to work on the play with Richard. He's home for the summer, so I can stay there with him and his parents in King of Prussia, Pennsylvania. I've got just enough money for a one-way ticket. I'm going for it. I'll find some kind of work to earn my flight back.

After just a week with Richard, the play is ready! What am I doing out here? I was way too impulsive flying to Pennsylvania, but I was so excited about working with Richard and getting the play in shape! Now that it's in shape, I'm ready to go home. There's one problem: I need money for a plane ticket! His dad has pull in the community and gets me a job in the shoe department at Wanamaker's. Perfect! In three weeks, I'll have my fare.

About a week into my job, I'm working the register and it's very busy with customers waiting in line. A hurried customer who doesn't want to wait shoves five bucks into my hand for a three-dollar pair of socks and walks away. For some stupid unconscious reason, I pocket this without putting it into the register. No good. That afternoon I am fired. Busted!

Too embarrassed to go back to Richard's house and face his father, I walk to the highway and stick out my thumb for New York City. I'll try for another job—to get into a play on or off-Broadway. Yeah, this is what I'm supposed to do! I am picked up right away by a dead ringer for actor Don Johnson, who I'd seen months earlier in the play *Fortune and Men's Eyes*.

The guy who picks me up, a smooth, friendly talker, tells me that he's a photographer who lives in a commune of artists on Long Island. With my height, he says that I have what it takes to be a fashion model and make some money until my acting career takes off. I can stay with the commune. It sounds good to me. It's nighttime when we get to his place, which is actually a room in someone's attic, not a commune full of artists. Once we're there and the door is shut, he says that he wants to "measure me" for the modeling job.

Duh!

I finally see what's up.

I'm caught in a situation that's something between seduction and rape just as it was in the play *Fortune and Men's Eyes*. It explains why I saw this guy as the Don Johnson actor in the play. But I was too unconscious to see that this projection was foretelling actual seduction. I suppose this "informing" from the gut happens a lot if only I were sharp enough to read the signs. But I'm not accustomed to thinking like this. When he brings out his measuring tape, well, it's clear that I'm being called upon to measure up the situation, to figure out fast what to do now!

Using my acting skills, I lead him to believe that I'm a young, confused man aching for love and understanding, and really into him, but instead use that ruse as an opportunity to grab my things and get the hell out of there.

I spend several hours curled up on a bench before catching a bus into the city, where I pass a couple of harrowing days trying to find an audition, a room in a flophouse, and ultimately survive the hard, unwelcoming streets of Manhattan. Without an agent, not belonging to Equity, I'm out in the wind. How ironic—I'm down to five bucks and that's it. Enough of New York. I locate an on-ramp to the highway and stick out my thumb for Los Angeles.

Within minutes, a good-natured guy in a semitruck stops and takes me on a long ride, dropping me off close to Oklahoma, right in the middle of nowhere. As I wait for another ride, I lean against a wooden signpost and notice skulls etched into it. Other hitchhikers have scrawled, "You're dead here," "I've been here for centuries," "Lose all hope." People talk about reading signposts—this one isn't hopeful, only portentous. I'm being "informed" again. I hope I don't die out here!

I'm there for nine hours before a car stops in the middle of the night with a man and a woman in the front seat. He tells me to get in and sit up front and punches her in the head when she first refuses to go into the back seat. Climbing over the seat, she's wearing a short muumuu and doesn't have any underwear. What a sight. Once we're all settled, I see that I am riding with a third-rate Bonnie and Clyde.

He's a career criminal and certified whack job with the complexion of a rope and covered with tattoos. "Lose all hope."

Drunk and dangerous, they get me involved in a petty theft of a car tire after one of ours gets a flat, and we all end up in a small-town jail in Cordell, Oklahoma, where I am charged with grand larceny. I am petrified and traumatized and might have rotted for a year or more if not for a sympathetic public defender and understanding sheriff who recognize me for what I am: an ignorant junior college student and unwitting participant who just wants to go home. "Clyde" is wanted for murder in another state, and the little fish that I am is set free.

Well, I'm certainly out in the world now. Being in the Cordell jail for a week and a half was edifying. It was a bedroom in a house with a few twin beds, steel bars on the only window, and a thick perforated metal door to the hallway. I cried most of the time I was in there. I missed "Alma." The jailer's wife felt so sorry for me, she brought me a can of peaches every day and some *Field and Stream* magazines.

* * *

As soon as I'm out of jail, I call my mother and plead with her to wire some money for a bus ticket. She reluctantly does so, but sends only enough to get me as far as Phoenix. She's big on doing things on your own: Get a job. Earn your keep. She will only help part of the way.

When I get off the bus in Phoenix, it's 114 degrees! In a swoon, I'm back to hitchhiking and eventually reach LA. Of course, the time will come when I do pay my mom back by buying her a house and depositing a big sum of money into her savings account. I will set her up for life.

I've lost fifteen pounds, and I'm wearing the same clothes I had on the day I started hitchhiking three and a half weeks ago! I'm a mess and wiped out from the whole experience. Food and a haircut help restore my appearance. Should I chalk this summer up to smoke? Certainly, this is some "life experience" that tells me to stay honest and be more prepared the next time I go to New York. Hitchhiking cross-country was a rough way to get back home. I was tramping, a touch of Ma in my soul. I was in the lower world, irrational, exposed to danger. Stealing five bucks led to this pratfall. Dishonesty led me astray.

I'm twenty years old edifying, breaking myself in. Getting rough about it. Learning the hard way. Going down in order to come back up.

I head to "Alma's" house. I miss her. Brad has already shared some of my stories with her. Romantically, she sees me as a "bad boy," some cool, misunderstood rebel, which makes her as eager to see me as I am to see her. At first sight, she wraps her arms tightly around me. But following our passionate reunion, it's clear this time together is going to be bye-bye. "How would you feel if I told you that I was seeing someone else?" she says.

I have heard this before, but this time, to my surprise, it doesn't hit me hard. After everything that I've just been through, I really don't give a damn.

I head over to the theater arts department at Valley College, where I sit outside and eat an ice cream cone. This college is my sanitarium. I have to get out of here. It feels small, not the bigger world that I just stumbled through. I walk over to Ed's apartment not far from the school. He thinks my romp back east on the road, the way I tell it, is funny.

This kicks off our interest in developing a comedy act. Out of the dark comes the light, a clown rising from the ashes.

CHAPTER 6

....

Next

The two of us start fooling around with comedy, and right away
we have an act—well, we call it an act—and, despite only a few
weeks of preparation, none in front of an audience, but in a burst
of inspiration and fearlessness, we audition for Doug Weston, the
owner of the Troubadour nightclub in West Hollywood. It's the
hottest club in town.

We arrive unannounced, wearing tattered tuxedos from the
production of *Waiting for Godot* that I was in at Valley, along with
World War II–era gas masks that we picked up at an army surplus
store in Hollywood. The character opposite me in the play was a lot
shorter than Ed, so his tuxedo is way too small, the hems of his pant
legs only reaching halfway below his knees. It's perfect lunacy. My
tux is unusually dirty. I always made a point of rolling around in the
dirt outside the club before going onstage. I've got plenty of dirt on
me for Doug.

A hippie wild man standing six feet six inches tall with straight brown hair to his shoulders, Doug peers at us through tiny wire-rimmed glasses.

"We're comedians," Ed says.

"Yeah, we're here to make people laugh," I add, making a funny face.

Doug is amused and puts us onstage on a trial basis that very night. The Troubadour is a dream come true for us. Lenny Bruce was arrested there in the early '60s. Buffalo Springfield played their first gig there. Bob Dylan, the Byrds, Richard Pryor, Nina Simone, Joni Mitchell, and James Taylor are also among those who helped make that stage a legendary space. We go on between the bands like Dada-inspired clowns.

In one bit, I'm a model plane and Ed starts me off, winding up the propeller, making sound effects, and flying me around the stage until the imaginary string tethering me to him snaps. Uh-oh! I'm unleashed and out of control. I finally crash hard onto a table and fall to the floor. The rowdy audience loves it. Doug gives us twenty-five bucks a night and has us come in three nights a week.

One afternoon we come around to pick up our check. We go upstairs to Doug's office. After some friendly chitchat, Doug asks me to lie on the floor so he can "stretch out" my limbs. I have no idea why, but whatever, I don't want to rock this money-making boat, and I comply. Doug rubs my legs and breathes deeply. Ah, so that's why. He's feeling me up. He opens my legs and moves his hands up toward my inner thighs. I'm not shocked or upset, probably because this is not as close to my experience on Long Island or my ride-along with the dangerous "Clyde" and his abused gal pal. I don't think Doug is going to go much further, but just in case, I interrupt his massage.

"Hey, Doug, maybe you could shine our shoes too," I joke.

He stops. I've snapped him out of this little fantasy of his. I get out from underneath him and stand up next to Ed. "We'll bring the shoes by later."

"We gotta get our check, Doug," Ed adds.

* * *

ONE MORNING CASS ELLIOT of the Mamas & the Papas drives her beautiful convertible Cadillac over to Ed's apartment, where I have crashed on the floor following a late night at the Troubadour. She leaves him the car in exchange for taking her to the airport. Ed's ability to know everyone, to have a Who's Who roster of friends, it's a thing with him. He dips himself into some scene, like a magnetic bar into sand, and comes out with celebrities all over him.

Now we have this Cadillac for the week. So be it. Ed and I zoom along the Sunset Strip with the convertible top down, putting up with the yellowish-brown smog throughout our fair city, donning our gas masks to make a statement, getting a thumbs-up from the hippies on the street. An older man pulls up alongside us at a red light, glares at us with disdain and growls, "You gotta be kidding."

"No, we aren't kidding," I say, pulling my mask off. "The world is ending in fourteen days. Get food and water, weapons, and a girl or guy, and dig in somewhere! Only a few of us will survive!"

He roars off either to get away from us or to do what I just said. Who knows? Who cares?

* * *

"YOU GUYS ARE WHACKED!" says Avery Schreiber, one half of the popular Burns and Schreiber comedy team, after seeing us one night at the Troubadour. It's a compliment, and he urges us to stay outlandish. The advice is appreciated, but the truth is, we don't "stay" like a well-trained dog. We have a few bits, but most of the time we're really wild and all over the place.

One night, Ed and I get a spot at the Ice House in Pasadena, and Ed, feeling like we're on top of the world, invites his dad, the great Ed Begley, to our show. But that night we're really off, not up to our best in a quiet room with only thirty people. We're used to a large rowdy crowd at the Troubadour. Onstage, we start fooling around with a twelve-foot ladder we came across backstage. It feels even taller and proves unwieldy.

I try to set this thing up à la Oliver Hardy and it falls into the audience almost landing on a couple at their table. Ed and I lift the ladder up and start whirling around in circles yelling for "help!" and getting all entangled as we fall off the stage into more tables. The audience sitting here backs off for safety. Ed and I are on the floor in this mess. I take hold of the top of one of the broken tables and turn it like a gigantic steering wheel of a car. "Get in! Let's get out of here!"

We're back onstage. Now we're getting the club's red light blinking furiously to stop the act and get offstage and we do just that. But I quickly return and ask for a round of applause for the "other members of our act who put so much time into staging our show," gesturing to the bewildered audience standing by their knocked-over tables. There's no laughs and just a smattering of applause. I'm sure the audience thinks we're maniacs who got into the building by mistake. A few people actually backed away from the stage when I came out again. They were frightened. The emcee comes out and tries to regain the room as Ed and I finally head backstage.

"We didn't get one laugh!" I say.

"No, we got some laughs," Ed protests.

"No, we got nothing," I insist.

Ed heads for the back of the room where his dad is sitting alone at a table. I sheepishly follow. We bombed. Ed is upbeat, as if we killed.

"Hi, Dad, how'd you like it?"

I'm way too embarrassed to ask. Mr. Begley just looks at us perplexed.

"I don't know what you're doing up there," he says.

"Neither do we," I say, kiddingly.

He doesn't think that's funny. He tries to study me as if I put his son up to this.

"Are you alright?" he asks. I think he's referring to our mental state.

"Yeah, we improvise a lot, Dad."

Mr. Begley gets up slowly.

"I'm tired, son," he says.

Ed gives him a hand and begins to walk him out of the club.

"Goodbye," he says to me.

I can't thank him for coming. I'm just feeling bad that we "perplexed" him.

I follow along and Ed sees his dad off.

Weeks later, Mr. Begley dies.

I don't think our act that night helped him any. Many years later, I kiddingly told Ed that we killed his father with that show.

* * *

SHORTLY AFTER THIS OUTRAGEOUS SHOW, I'm drafted into the army. Brad immediately pleads with me to flee to Canada. I know all about the war in Vietnam, and I understand his concern and the reasons he wants me to head north, but I'm up for going into the army and checking it out. I suppose those friendly soldiers who saluted me at the top of Baldwin Hills way back when have something to do with this sanguine acceptance of my fate. It's also another on-the-road adventure, a going away from home and finding my way back. I know I'll make it home even though people around me who hate the war think differently.

"You'll get killed in Vietnam."

"I don't feel that to be so," I say.

"It's a bullshit war. Why put yourself through it?"

"I'm going because *I know* I'm not dying in Nam."

"How can you be so sure?"

"Look at me." I make a goofy face. "Do you think the army is stupid enough to send me to Nam?"

CHAPTER 7

Drafted

I know it's cliché, but without a father in my life, the military does appeal to me—the maleness of it, the order, the discipline, the archetype of the warrior.

As confident as I am in not going to Nam, I still imagine that I could let a heavy military vehicle run over my foot if I need to get out of the war. It's a solid plan B. But I know I won't have to go through that kind of agony. I know that my place is not in a firefight killing people. It's just not in my cards.

Brad drives me to the induction center, the portal for entering the army. In order to enter, I have to empty out. Like a death to be born again, I return to nothing. "Listen, Brad. Sell all my stuff, sell my Nomad. The transmission is thrashed. Get what you can. A father sold me his son's car; the lad is going into the army. I'm in the service now, so sell the car. The papers are in the glove compartment. You've got the key. Catch ya in another lifetime."

I salute him. "Carry on, General."

Then I execute a sharp about-face and head for the building. Brad just stands there with his mouth open. He thinks I've lost my mind. I'm only out to gain it.

* * *

IN FRONT OF ME at the induction center, there are three different colored lines on the hallway floor to follow. According to my order to report, I'm blue, so I follow that line to my future. I start thinking about possible noncombatant roles I could take on. I could be in the medical corp. I could work in a dispensary like these army orderlies ahead. I have the background. Or better yet, I'll look into special services. Maybe I can make army films or something along those lines.

I strip and stand naked, blood is drawn, and questions are asked about drug use. If I keep my eyes crossed, I can say I'm into a lot of acid. "Over four hundred trips, man." Except they will check my blood, and I'm clean. I'm not a doper. They will know I'm faking it. Still, I can easily play lunacy. Don't speak. Never say a word. Don't answer any questions. Maybe just flap my arms, run down the hall, and throw myself out a window. That should do it.

I ask an army orderly how he got his job. "Applied for it," he says. I tell him that I use to be a hospital orderly and an ambulance attendant. "Put that down on your profile sheet."

"Thanks, man, I will."

* * *

MY FIRST TWENTY-FOUR HOURS are all about the food. It's delicious: scrambled eggs, hash browns, and toast for breakfast; the next day another big breakfast and a bag lunch of beef stew, an apple, and Jell-O as we ship out to our next destination. I'm transported to Fort Lewis in Washington State. We grab bunks, sleep, and wake up the next morning to reveille. Breakfast is wonderful. Waffles and

OJ. "Any more of that orange Jell-O?" A mess hall cook grimaces and shakes his head no. "Okay, just asking."

Our heads are shaved. Old clothes are exchanged for fatigues. Duffel bags are packed. At lunch, there's cherry Jell-O. I love the army!

Then we board trucks that take us off to basic training camp. The jostling of the ride puts me to sleep the way Ma rocked me as a child—until I am jolted awake by her arguing with someone in her head—blending into an angry man screaming, "Every piece of shit grunt in this fucking truck, get the fuck out NOW! MOVE! MOVE!" It's the drill sergeant.

I'm anchored by my eighty-pound duffel bag, looking more like a teenage Jerry Lewis than a trim William Westmoreland as I try to get out of the truck. It's still not fast enough for Sarge. "Get the fuck outta the truck!" he screams. What is wrong with this man? Is he in a lot of pain?

I don't know why the urgency, but what a voice! He'd make a great Zeus. Sarge can project, but his diction isn't that good. As close and loud as he is, I can't understand much of what he's saying. The force of his anger garbles some of his words. I am also distracted by his big red face and bulging veins, which look close to bursting.

Finally, I get off the truck and pull my bag along. It's so heavy that it throws me off balance.

"Where do I go?"

"You're going straight to hell, you son of a bitch! Get the fuck in line!"

"The bag is heavy."

"What the fuck did you say?"

For the first few weeks of basic training, I do little that is right or good enough for Zeus. I drop off the monkey bars at the slightest amount of pain, not to be defiant but because it hurts. "I don't like that burning sensation," I tell the sergeant. He does a beautiful double take, so incredulous at my admission that he can't find the words to yell at me. I trip on the obstacle course. Well, it's meant to obstruct, right? And I naturally gravitate to the pratfall. The Fool in me throws in a few extra for laughs. I hear my squad laughing. They're entertained. I'm back at the Troubadour.

When we march, I do it well—right foot, left foot—except, as my troop marches forward, I cannot resist marching in reverse, backwards. I knew this antic was coming. I'm really trying my best to be a soldier, but this antic is irresistible. I go for a laugh without getting caught for it. I'm very good at not being caught; that's part of the Fool's routine. Sarge doesn't catch me marching backwards or hiding in the bushes during combat training.

I'm one step behind…I mean, ahead.

However, there are times when I get nailed for not pushing myself hard enough, not going for the burn, not enduring the pain. "Richards!" Sarge yells. "Get in the fucking cockroach position! And die, cockroach, die!"

The cockroach position is when you lie on your back, the upper portion slightly raised with your head, and extend your arms straight up and your legs at forty-five degrees off the ground. You hold this position until you "die."

For whatever freaky physiological reason, I'm able to stay in this position for an unusually long time. The drill sergeant is yelling at me to "die, cockroach, die!" But I won't die. He orders me to get to my feet, but I continue to hold the position. I'm quivering, but I won't die. I will not cave in.

He decides he has no time to deal with this nut, the cockroach who refuses to die, and walks off yelling at someone else to get their shit together. I continue to hold the position. Finally, "Get the fuck up, Richards! Now!" I get up and stand at attention. He gets in my face. "So, you see, Richards! You can buck up, fuckhead! At ease!" he commands.

My unit now at ease looks at me in awe. Wow, that was weirdly challenging. But I understood something here. I can get through the burn and the suffering without giving into it. That's what the drill sergeant just pointed out to me, to "buck up!" Throughout the training ahead, if I was lagging, Sarge would yell out, "Buck up, fuck-head!" It always got me over the hump.

It reminds me of the scene in *Cool Hand Luke*, when Luke won't stop fighting Dragline. He holds the position no matter how much of a beating he's taking, and he wins that way. Luke was an ex-Marine. He knew how to "buck up!"

* * *

DURING BASIC TRAINING, I filled out the profile sheet listing my work experience. My job as a hospital orderly and an ambulance attendant serves me well. With basic training coming to an end, I'm ordered to report to medical school at Fort Sam Houston, Texas.

"Lucky you, Richards," a fellow draftee in my unit says. "Medics are the first guys killed in Nam."

Oh, what a nice thing to say!

"Where are you heading?" I ask.

"AIT." Advanced infantry training.

"Oh, lucky you. You'll be the first to lounge around the base and shop at the PX all day."

* * *

MEDICAL SCHOOL IS INTENSE. As part of the curriculum, I watch training films depicting every gruesome wound and all the traumatic death that occurs in battle. We see in graphic and gory detail what happens when human beings shoot at each other, blow each other up. The footage is real, straight from the battlefield! Not only do we see everything imaginable, but we are also instructed what to do in those situations—patching up guys screaming, collecting their guts, bagging it. Enough!

The things I saw as an ambulance attendant gave me some background to face this medical school, and despite some clowning around in basic training, I'm not a screwup. I can focus, and I do focus. But what I see in those films is horrible. What frightens me that day is the realization that war is in the cards for mankind. It may not be transcended but is part of the human condition. That plain truth is truly horrible.

It wakes me up to my humanity. I'm becoming a man, so warlike, knowing that this is what I am, what I am capable of, what is part of all of us, and there's nothing that we can do about this life and death that we are. War is part of the scenery. "Oh, the horror, the horror!" The wrath of man, like the wrath of God, is death-dealing war! So be it.

"Buck up!" I tell myself and become a healer, a medic, a man who can alleviate some of the inevitable suffering that befalls us.

Graduation from medical school goes by quickly. Still, it was a four-month course. I am now a medic with the rank of Spec 5, or "buck sergeant." I also qualify to carry a .45 pistol. I'm a warrior-medic, a man of war and peace. I am attached to a tank division, Old Ironsides at the army base known as the Rock in Baumholder, Germany, assigned to its medical corps. Before I leave the country, I'm given a two-week furlough.

* * *

ON LEAVE FOR TWO WEEKS.

I'm met at LAX by Brad, who's wearing bell-bottom jeans and a paisley-patterned shirt. His hair is longer, past his shoulders, and seeing me for the first time in months, he wears the same incredulous expression on his face that he did when he dropped me off at the induction center six months ago—his mouth hangs open as I walk toward him in my army uniform.

My hair is short. I've put on some healthy weight—I'm clearly well fed. And I'm beaming to be back. My shoes are shined. I'm sporting a few ribbons, medical insignia on my collars, and my Spec 5 rank on the arms of my jacket. Seeing Brad's reaction, buck the fuck up! I'm honed and to the point. I'm definitely in the army!

"Well, here's my new lifetime," I say.

Brad embraces me. "My dear brother, you've returned from the dead."

No matter how radical and antiestablishment Brad has become, my appearance is acceptable. He respects me. I look too elegant to be anything else for him. I'm feeling decent. I'm a medic. This is cool.

When I get into Brad's car, I notice the clutter in the back seat: papers and food wrappers, a sandy blanket, wrinkled towels, a bent-up cardboard box. It's a mess. Even the city looks messy and out of order. I've changed. In the army, I'm used to being in a tightly run situation, where everything is organized and in its place.

Brad offers me a cigarette and I take one. He lights his and passes the lighter.

"So, are you going to Nam?"

"I'll be stationed in Germany."

"That's great! So you're out of the fray. That's really great! You knew you weren't going!"

"No, I saw the fray in training as a medic."

"Pretty heavy?"

Definitely.

Brad cranks up a Credence Clearwater Revival song on the radio. "Remember this?"

"I do."

"I sold the Nomad and got what you paid for it," Brad says.

"Hold on to the money. I can't use it. If you see anything truly worthwhile, buy it for me," I say.

"Okay."

"My brother [Stan] bought a house in Santa Monica. Gale [his wife] is making pretty good money now," Brad says.

"How are they doing?" I ask.

"Stan is finishing up his dissertation at UCLA, and Gale is still working at the museum," he says. "Neil is working there now."

Neil is a friend of theirs.

Brad continues, "They had a Warhol installation and after the show, the museum just threw out most of the installation. Gale didn't know anything about it."

"Paintings?"

"No, Brillo boxes. To the museum it was just a bunch of junk. Neil took it all out of the trash and set this stuff up in his living room!"

Neil is like good ol' Kramer discovering the old Merv Griffin set in a dumpster and taking it home. Years later, this so-called junk fetches half a million dollars.

* * *

DURING THE DAY, Brad is busy at CalArts in their critical studies program. I buy some jeans and a few work shirts and hang out with Brad's brother, Stan. At his house, I sit around reading Ferlinghetti and listening to the Rolling Stones.

One night the craziest guy comes over to Stan and Gale's. This is Carlos Castaneda. He's involved in the anthropology department at UCLA and has become a rather famous author and mystic since the publication of his book *The Teachings of Don Juan: A Yaqui Way of Knowledge*. Carlos is into peyote and vision questing, whereas I am in the army feeling rather comfortable with my feet on the ground. But I am intrigued from the moment I overhear him talking to someone as they enter the room. "People are afraid of death," he says. "They should spend at least one night a week in a cemetery, just alone with all that death around you—to hear what the dead have to say. It's a way to get over fear."

"Carlos, this is Michael," somebody says. "He's in the army."

I'm now being introduced as someone who's "in the army." Maybe one of the dead? It doesn't bother me.

Carlos's eyebrows go up. "How are you doing with all of that?"

"I'm adjusted. I'm a well-adjusted man." I make a funny face.

He laughs. "When they tell you what to do, do you always do it?" he asks.

"I do the best that I can do."

Carlos suggests that we all go to a graveyard and spend the night. "To be alone with the dead, your dreams can become more intelligible," he says. "Dreams are from the realm of the dead. They are the language of the night. Most people avoid leaning into their dreams. They fear the dead."

"I'm up for it," I say. "Let's go!"

Carlos turns to Stan. "We should go to the veteran's cemetery in Westwood! We separate there, and each of us is alone for the night. Lay on a grave. Don't move. Just listen."

But nothing comes out of it. He's now talking about his work at UCLA.

Why go to a cemetery? What about the living dead? What about people who are unable to live life, too poor to afford life, or too unhealthy to enjoy it? Why not listen to them? See what they have to say about life and death and fear and dreams. You don't have to go to a cemetery for that. Listen to a few homeless people. That should do it. Carlos, you should meet my grandma. She has visions and talks to the dead. You don't need a cemetery for that.

After that night, I never see Carlos again. Years later, his work is revealed to be a fraud, the teachings he got from Don Juan were all a sham. Carlos, an imposter? I read his book, and whether it's true or false, I do admire his imagination.

My leave ends.

* * *

In Baumholder, with three other medics, we run the dispensary, which puts us in a prominent position. The men working in our division come in to see us for various injuries and ailments. If they're sick or hurting, we're the men they come to. We have the authority to write a prescription to excuse a man from work or send him to the doctor. When we're out in the field, I drive one of the two ambulances, or cracker boxes as they're called, in support of our tanks and numerous infantrymen.

My cracker box is a two-and-a-half-ton vehicle that turns into a mobile field hospital. During maneuvers I drive with Jamar, my attendant, sitting next to me. Our main task is to follow two tank squads—about twenty-four M60 tanks—wherever they go. This is about the most fun I have had in this army so far. I've got a floor-shifting six speed, all-traction four-wheel vehicle that can take nearly any kind of terrain short of entering deep water, which is the point. Tanks can go places. It's a pleasure to keep up.

We go out for a war game with other units acting as the enemy. The terrain is rugged. At night, the infantry guys camp out in their pup tents on the freezing cold ground, and in the even colder night air, while Jamar and I sit comfy in the Crackerbox. Sleep is minimal. We're off to an early start around 3:00 a.m. It's still dark, and night driving limits our lights to nearly nothing. Slit shields over our lights give us minimal light to follow. It's tricky driving and very slow going, but we roll along until we come to a stop.

Then: nothing. We don't move. After half an hour, I get out of our truck and walk over to command, where a few infantrymen are setting up a large field tent. It's looks like we're going to be here for a while. I salute a lieutenant.

"How's the war going, sir?" I ask

"We were killed an hour ago," he says.

"How did that happen?"

"Aircraft. Hit by a bomb." He's serious.

"But we were on the move a half hour ago."

"We didn't know we were dead."

"Oh, you just found out?"

"Yeah, we were hit an hour ago."

Wow. We're all driving around dead. I wonder what Castaneda would have thought about this, dead people talking to each other.

"Thank you, sir." I salute and head back to the Crackerbox to tell Jamar that we're dead. He takes his death well.

"Fine with me," he says. "Let's crank the heater and sit back till they tell us we're not dead anymore."

* * *

MY FRIEND BRAD HAS SENT ME some plays. I have works by Harold Pinter and five plays by Ed Bullins. I'm currently reading *Dutchman* by LeRoi Jones, later known as Amiri Baraka. One afternoon sitting around in the dispensary, I ask Jamar to read some of the pages from *Dutchman* out loud to me. Jamar is moved by the grit and the language of the play. "This is great stuff," he says. "We ought to get some of the brothers to read this."

A few days later, Jamar gets everybody in a room and they start reading pages from an Ed Bullins play. No one has read the play before or has any kind of theatrical background, but the material lights up the room. I step back. This is bigger than I am, as it should be.

I see the powerful effect this play—and this playwright—has on these men. Jamar beams with satisfaction of having invited the brothers and hearing them say, "We gotta read all these plays." It's clear that they could form a reader's theater.

There's a theater on base that's always empty. After checking it out, I approach the base's CO about using the theater for a show. He's open to it! There's no budget, of course, but so what? There can be a reader's theater, I can mount shows, assemble a cast!

As I'm mulling all this, a well-equipped theater company known as the V-Corps Training Road Show comes to the base for a day to present a play about race relations in the army. They set up their play in the very theater I have just received permission to use. It's called *The Weak Link*, and it's about a soldier who comes to terms with his own racial biases. As he goes through this transformation, the segregated reality of life in the army is highlighted, but it concludes with an inspiring we're-all-in-this-together message.

After the show, I go backstage and ask who's in charge of the production. I'm directed to Sgt. Randy Larsen. I recognize him as the actor who also starred as a colonel in the show. He turns out to be a Northwestern drama graduate who's been part of the road show since its inception. He plans to get his MFA in theater after his hitch is up. I forget to ask how "short" he is, how much time he has left before he's discharged. Right now, I'm hyperfocused on his play. I share my thoughts about the production, various ways to make it better, and then a bit of my background in theater.

"Would you like to be part of the road show?" he asks.

"Very much," I say, without realizing what this might mean.

"I'll look into things," he says. "We'll be in touch."

CHAPTER 8

The Road Show

Three days later, I'm transferred to Frankfurt to be a part of the army's V-Corps Training Road Show. Just like that!

The base in Frankfurt is part of the city, not off by itself as a military installation like in Baumholder. I report to a three-story apartment building about a block long within a German residential area. A regular clean-cut neighborhood. The road show is comprised of about twenty-five guys who all reside in one section of this apartment complex. All are on "civilian status." They don't wear uniforms. It's a big outfit that Randy oversees, a half-million-dollar operation including a white diesel semi with a large butterfly painted on both sides of the trailer and the name of the outfit painted underneath: V-CORPS TRAINING ROAD SHOW.

The trailer contains sets, lights, sound, and costumes and comes with a designated driver. There's also a standard green army bus with its driver for the cast and crew who travel to bases across Germany.

I am in my dress uniform, tie and all, carrying a duffel bag with just my kit and some additional clothing. I travel light. No more eighty-pound duffel bags for me. I step into the apartment foyer, where I'm greeted by Davis, who's wearing jeans, a button-down shirt, and polished black Florsheim dress shoes. He starred in the V-Corp production *The Weak Link* and was clearly the best actor in the show. He has talent.

"Hola! I'm Davis."

This man is upbeat. I like him immediately.

"How you doing?" I shake his hand.

"We're doing it, brother. Welcome to the road show!"

"It's an apartment building," I say.

"Right on. With a touch of Bauhaus. Look at this staircase. Pretty cool, huh?"

I don't know what Bauhaus is, but I like the staircase.

"Yeah."

"You got any civies? We don't wear uniforms around here."

"This is all I have."

"I can give you a shirt. You gotta get out of that shit."

When we reach the third floor, I see Randy walking toward us in the long hallway. He's dressed in loose tan pants and a white shirt and red Swedish clogs.

"Hello, Michael," Randy says in a relaxed tone that is distinctly nonmilitary.

"Hi, Randy. Should I salute you?" I say this half-jokingly. I want to kid with this man. I want to get off to a good start. I'm grateful to be in Frankfurt. I'm in a city. A neighborhood! I feel at home.

"Oh, no," he says. "We're at ease around here."

We enter his apartment, which he shares with his assistant, Ken, who handles the day-to-day operations. It takes me only a few seconds to pick up on their relationship. The two of them are a couple and don't make any attempt to hide it from me.

"You know, I'm taking a chance with you," Randy says. "I'm not sure what you really know about building a show. Your notes were outstanding, so I'm going on that alone." Ken pours me a glass of lemonade.

Randy proudly tells me about creating the road show and his responsibilities in meeting each week with the brass in the IG Farben Building, a massive structure that was once the military headquarters for a Nazi chemical plant but now serves as headquarters for all US military brass in Europe and is known as "the Pentagon of Europe." This is a bit overwhelming. I see the operation, and I'm intimidated by the administrative know-how that Randy and his "associate" possess. But the lemonade calms me down.

"I don't know how good of an actor you are, but I'd like to read you for the colonel," Randy says. "We'll do this tomorrow after lunch. I take it that you can get acquainted with the part by then. It's just a read, no need to memorize."

He hands me the script to the show. It's his whole world.

"Who's handling wardrobe?" I ask.

* * *

THE ENTIRE COMPANY IS ASSEMBLED in a large meeting room in our building for the read. Everyone is in their civies. I stick out in my uniform, but I don't give a shit. Randy introduces me to the company. Davis shouts out, "We gotta get Richards out of that uniform!" There's some laughter and chatter about how unhip a uniform is until Randy cuts them off. "I'm glad Richards is still in uniform to remind you that we're still in the army. In this road show, we have the privilege, the liberty to wear a uniform or not. Let's be cool about it." Randy is a good man and an obvious leader: sensitive, understanding, and trusting, but still tough enough to get the job done.

We read the play and I'm the colonel. I've already memorized most of the part. I set the pace and my acting is good. Randy is impressed. His hunch about me was correct. He's got his colonel.

Over the next few days, I am brought into the world of the road show. A number of people smoke opiated hash. I am invited into somebody's room for a hit, but I say no thanks and head for the door. I'm thinking about the look of my colonel, especially his dress shoes.

Standing in his shoes, I'm heading for character. I'm taking my new role seriously.

Randy takes me to meet the one-star general in charge of the V-Corps Training Road Show. This general is definitely taking his role seriously. His office is in the Farben Building. Our steps echo in the wide halls of this ominous World War II–era structure. It's clear you better have your shit together when you're in this place.

"General Stanton," Randy says, "Richards is quite capable of playing the colonel in *The Weak Link*. I highly recommend him for the part."

"Very well." The general nods before adjusting the aim of his steely eyes onto me. "If you need anything let me know directly."

I am scheduled to play the colonel a week and a half later in Mannheim and a few other bases along the way. We rehearse every day. Several people notice that I wear the colonel's shoes a lot. I explain it's a quirk of mine for getting into character. Randy is direct-ing, but he's open to me implementing changes. We switch some of the supporting parts around, putting the better actors in the best scenes. I alter some of the blocking.

We also work to straighten out the dialogue in the play so every-one feels more natural in their parts. "I know what it says in the script, but how would *you* say that line?" I ask. The subtle changes make all the actors stronger.

By the conclusion of the Mannheim tour, Randy knows that bringing me on board was the right decision. I can do no wrong in his eyes—even when I tell him that I'd like to wear my colonel's uni-form everywhere I go, especially when we enter the bases, "so I can *be* a colonel. Return all the salutes while I'm visiting the fort, inspecting my men."

Randy thinks it's a great idea, a way to promote the show, to have characters from the play outside the theater meeting the troops.

But I don't want to formally meet the troops as an actor from the show. I want to *be a colonel wherever I go*, certainly to feel how the bases respond to my rank. It will enhance my performance.

Not sure what to make out of a "full commitment to character," Randy suggests I "put in a request" to the general.

"It's essential," I say.

* * *

"THIS WILL ENHANCE MY PRESENCE onstage, sir. It will give me greater authenticity, not in playing a colonel, but by *being* a colonel. It's called 'Method acting,' sir."

I produce a copy of Konstantin Stanislavski's *Building a Character and Creating a Role*.

"He's Russian?" the general asks.

"Yes, sir."

"How Russian?" He chuckles.

"Sir, the Method is used by the finest actors in our country. The Actors Studio in New York is one of our best acting schools, and the teachers there utilize Stanislavski's technique."

The general looks through the book page by page rather quickly. He's speed-reading. I learned some of this in a speed-reading class one summer. He's good at it. The book is 230-plus pages. He goes through the text in ten minutes. He's remarkable. I see why he's a general. Finally, he hands the book back to me.

"Well, I can't put you in a war room, Richards, but I can give you officer's clearance. I expect that you can handle this responsibility and attend to our code of honor. I've seen footage of your performance, and I approve. You're representing our finest. Keep it that way. I expect nothing but excellence from you."

"Yes, sir," I say.

"Permission granted. Dismissed."

* * *

I TAKE THIS "PERMISSION" SERIOUSLY. From now on, I'm the colonel. Short of a little gray in my hair, which I use onstage, I dress as a colonel wherever I go, starting with breakfast in the officers' mess hall. I have three colonel uniforms in my locker. I travel as a colonel to all the bases. I am greeted as a colonel. I return saluting. I look sharp. I am the colonel. The company goes along with my "character work" and duly responds to me as "the colonel." They're amused. But I am the colonel, "To remind you all that we are still in the army!" I quote Randy. They love it.

I do not engage too much with actual officers. Only one time does an officer question my character. An MP is curious about my campaign ribbons and asks more about my time in action. I show him my MID (Military Intelligence Division) identification. He makes a call, and I'm cleared to be the colonel that I am.

* * *

ONE DAY, AS THE COMPANY SETS UP a show at a base, I am backstage running my lines, focused on my performance but also keeping an eye on all the activity involved in getting the show up. Through a large window in this backstage area, I see two soldiers out by a tree lighting up a bowl of hash. I step up to the window and tap on it to get their attention. They turn to see a full-bird colonel pointing to them to stay right where they are. I step out of the theater and go over to them. They slowly salute and I return it. I notice one of them surreptitiously drop their small pipe to the ground. They are terrified.

"What's going on, gentlemen?" I ask.

"Nothing, sir," one says.

"Don't lie to me, son. Pick up that bowl."

The silent one picks up the pipe. I look them over, letting the tension build. Finally, "I am here to remind you that we are still in the army," I say. "Carry on, gentlemen. Enjoy your day." I do my snappy about-face and I'm out of there.

At twenty-one, it's incredible the way this has all worked out for me—from draftee to medic to "the colonel." I don't know if anyone in the army is playing the part of a solider as smoothly as I am until I encounter one of the most extraordinary men I have ever met.

CHAPTER 9

The Burgermeister

I'm talking to Randy about the road show. I suggest scouring bases for writers, actors, directors, finding talent. He's all for it and adds, "V-Corps wants a new show addressing the army's drug problem."

"Good idea." If half the road show is opiated, I assume that half the army must be sky high too, including guys who are in the line of fire.

Randy has more news for me. In a few weeks, his time in the army is over. He's going home, and I am going to be his replacement. Ah, now I get it. I see the reason for my speedy transfer. It's not just playing the colonel in *The Weak Link*. I'm going to be responsible for the whole road show—acting, directing, production, twenty-five guys, trucks—plus putting together a new play on drugs.

Despite the immediate anxiety I feel from the weight of responsibility, I see the big picture here, the opportunity to create, and from that point on, I am all in. I am all about being an actor and director who will not only keep this show going but also put my stamp on it, going for first-class productions.

To develop the drug show right, I promote my understudy to colonel in *The Weak Link*, which frees me up from going on the road so I can concentrate on this new project. I continue to dress as a full bird "to remind you [me] that we are still in the army [still in *The Weak Link*]." I envision a workshop with a few actors improvising scenes that we can stitch together into a compelling story, the way I built the play years before that was going to be produced at Princeton.

The casting call for actors we'd sent to bases in and around Frankfurt brings fewer people than I expected, a mere four hopefuls: two dancers, a guy who claimed he was in a movie that was never seen, and Howard Ransom. But Howard is more than enough.

A young Black guy with a New Orleans drawl, he saunters into the green room straight up radiating self-assurance. His bravado is immediate. His presence fills the room. His charisma is incredible. This man can take over a crowd in seconds. He's probably already wondering how he can take over my gig. He'll be powerful onstage!

"What are we doing here?" he asks. "You guys acting?" (I am paraphrasing here to the best of my recollection. Howard's style of elocution is beyond my ability to replicate.)

"Yeah, we're in a play. We're here now to create a new show," I say.

"That's right. We're all in plays, doing lots of shows," he says.

"Are you an actor?" I ask.

"Oh, my man! That's all that's going on. It's all acting," he says, leaning into us. "Who's real around here is the question."

I get what he's saying. We're all playing parts. And I can tell Howard is always looking them over. He's a natural.

"What's your MOS?" I ask.

"I'm a cargo specialist. Loading and unloading freight," Howard says.

"What kind of freight?"

"Army goodies, food stuff, the chow that keeps our boys going." He laughs. "I'm in the grocery business."

"PX stuff?"

"We crate it and freight it."

Howard beams. He's a man who gets things done.

He is a streetwise Shakespeare, full of rapid-fire, off-the-cuff rhyming jive and a delivery that is mesmerizing. He is lightning in a bottle. I can't tell if he has come in character or really is this character, though soon enough I will have my answer. This is Howard. The man is real, utterly authentic.

I tell Howard the goal here is to create a play that addresses the drug problem in the army. He agrees it is a problem that needs a solution.

"Ah, yes," he says. "Salvation through the hope house. That's the name of your play. *The Hope House*. I'll enter as the Burgermeister and straighten everybody out."

In German, the Burgermeister is the master of the people, the master of the town, and Howard is indeed masterful. He just gave me the name of the show and his part within in. My mind is ablaze with a vision of the way this project could evolve: it will be about establishing Hope Houses on the bases—a clinic to get off drugs, to get counseling, developing a reassuring plan for a better life in the army, like my dispensary in Baumholder, a place to get well.

* * *

FOR THE AUDITION I HAND HOWARD *The Joyous Cosmology* by Alan Watts. "Howard, would you read a few lines from this book? Choose anything. Put it into your own words or read it as it is."

"I like that. A man should have choices in life," he says,

He randomly stops on a page and with great care reads: "All boundaries and divisions are held in common by their opposite sides and areas, so that when a boundary changes its shape, both sides move together."

He stops reading, looks up, and stares straight into me. "Yeah, moving together. I'm looking forward to it."

82

We hold this moment looking at each other. I can tell that Howard can take direction, that he and I can "move together," take all "sides and areas" for staging a play. He's genuinely present and clearly intelligent. This man is an artist.

It's up to me now.

As Randy said to me in Baumholder, "I'll look into things. We'll be in touch," I say.

I try to hide my enthusiasm but I know this is our star.

I want to build an entire show around this man. A request for Howard's transfer is submitted and Howard arrives as quickly as I did from Baumholder.

* * *

ON THE MORNING HOWARD IS DUE TO ARRIVE, the colonel is in the officers' mess having "my" usual breakfast: scrambled eggs and a German crusty roll with an assortment of jams. Occasionally I will indulge and have Griessbrei pudding and Eierkuchen, a German pancake nicely browned and slathered with applesauce. The head chef, a man named Luka, is a German contractor. He comes over to my table to greet me, as he frequently does.

"Good morning, Colonel."

"Good morning, Luka."

"Colonel, I have Eierkuchen this morning or Leipziger Lerche."

"I'm fine with the usual," I say. "Thank you."

I'm thinking of Howard and getting him situated. What room should he be in? Who will he get along with? Should I quarter him with two other Black guys in the road show, Will and Warren? They share a room. Another bunk and locker could be added without it feeling crowded. I'm segregating and this isn't cool, but I want Howard to feel comfortable here. Would he prefer being with the other Black guys? Will and Warren prefer it. Yet being heads, they like to smoke with Davis and the rest of the white road show smokers. The bowl unites them all. It's a peace pipe.

Is Howard a head?

I'm walking back to our quarters. Soldiers on furlough, dressed in their civies, check me out with great respect. Soldiers in uniform salute me. I'm one of the finest. It's all character work. Germans notice me. How can such a young man be so high in rank? He must be a brilliant soldier, a young Alexander coming into power. A kaiser in the making. Stanislavski, I salute you.

A jeep is parked in front of our building. And there he is: Howard. Standing by the jeep and looking up at the building, he's already out of uniform. His colorful sequined shirt sparkles in the sun—so does his gold watch, jeweled rings, and black-and-white vinyl shoes. He's wearing baby blue slacks and holds an ebony cane with a gold horsehead handle. He's got the driver, a muscular Black man in fatigues, carrying his tan leather suitcase with gleaming brass hardware. On Howard, I see no army issue at all. Incredible.

I approach him as the colonel. The uniform surprises him.

"That's mighty fine," he says. "You're a man of rank, sir."

Both he and the driver salute me. I return their salute.

"I'm in character," I say.

"Yes, indeed. You're the colonel. I know about the show. You're a man of conviction. I like that."

"You've seen *The Weak Link?*"

"I've seen pictures of you in the *Stars and Stripes.* I dig your gig."

"Cool."

"This is Thomas." He nods and carries Howard's suitcase into the building.

"Where's your issue?" I ask.

"Thomas already has it in my room."

Howard has already arranged for Will and Warren to move upstairs in a room occupied by two other heads.

"How did you make that happen?" I ask.

"They got a view of the world up there," he says. "Bigger room, balcony and all. I will provide them with some deck furniture." He looks up at the balcony. "There they are. You motherfuckers look nice up there! Don't be jumpin' now."

Will and Warren wave to us and salute. I return their salutation. Howard laughs.

"I'm keeping all the smokies upstairs. I can't be smellin' that shit. It fucks up my temperament."

Okay, so Howard's not a head.

He continues: "Besides, they should mingle. Those two motherfuckers were hiding out." I stare at him, mesmerized. Before I've even had a chance to welcome him, Howard has managed to get his own room and has the driver carrying in his luggage like a personal valet. Is he coming to be in my play? Or am I in his play?

"Yes, you've got a fine deal right here," he says. "You can be the colonel wherever you go?"

"That's right."

"You got the army backing you all up with this shit?"

I show Howard my MID identification.

"God damn! You are the smoothest cat I've ever met!"

* * *

A young Black civvy comes around with hash. He always shows up with his high-strung whippet on a leash. He deals small time, and probably provides most of the hash for the road show. I can't order the guy out of the building or restrict the company from hanging out with him. We're on civilian status, and civilians do come through. There's always a big game of Risk going on, and a few German university students usually come by to play. They don't smoke, but I'm not sure what they're up to. One evening I see one of these students go down into the basement of our building and look around. I follow him down there and want to know what he's doing. He plays like he's confused and got lost in the building. I know he's not lost. I tell him to beat it. I think it's a heads-up to keep the basement doors locked. We all have bikes, sports gear, furniture, road show supplies, army gear, and other personal effects down there. I realize we don't have much security. The doors are often unlocked. Anybody can come through the place, and it seems they do.

At a meeting that day, I introduce Howard and explain that he is going to help develop our new drug show. Then I state my concern for security. "Keep your room locked," I say. "Keep the front door and the basement door locked. Carry your key with you at all times."

Before anyone has time to ask a question, Howard, who was introduced only moments earlier, stands up.

"I just walked into this building and nobody said a thing. I could fill up a truck with all your shit and be outta here in no time, that's how lax you are. You go out, you lock your door. Any weird-lookin' motherfucker comes into this building should sign in downstairs. There's not a goddamn person in this room who knows who's been coming through here all morning. I saw some weird-looking strut come in here with a skinny-ass dog, walking down the halls like he owns the place."

"That's Terry," someone says.

"Well, Terry can kiss my ass!"

"Terry's okay, he comes around a lot," someone else says. "We know who he is."

"You don't know shit. He's scoping you. Selling you smoke. I know the man's game."

The room is silent. Howard sits down.

My turn.

"Okay, so we'll keep the front door locked. Use your key. I like the idea of signing in. Let's get a table and a logbook set up downstairs."

"Yeah, maybe put a few candies in a bowl to welcome our guests," Howard chuckles.

* * *

HOWARD AND I SET OURSELVES UP in the basement of the building. It's a large, open space that also houses stacks of duffel bags full of our army gear, thousands of pounds of this stuff.

"When you turn it in, where does it all go?"

"Army surplus," says Howard. "Sold right here in Europe or the States. It's all worldwide military surplus. Nothing goes to waste."

A year from now, I'll see John Lennon wearing army surplus on *The Dick Cavett Show*. Is that my jacket? Did it belong to someone I knew? Someone who didn't make it?

"The yippy-hippy look," Howard said. "Civilian cool. Sew some head shit on there, be pretty."

I think Howard's right. I think he's onto everything. I have a TEAC reel-to-reel tape recorder on a table. One of the road show crew is there to push record.

"Get that thing on," I tell him. "I want to record everything Howard says."

"That's right. In the basement, the lower world. I'm so low I've got no place to go but up," says Howard.

He stands and begins to improvise the opening of the show.

"I enter the auditorium," he says, staring off into the distance. "I strut down the aisle, and I've got my stick. Each time my point touches the ground there's a rumbling in the earth. You'll provide the sound, make what I'm doing sound real. Then we hear the sweet sound of a brush on cymbal, a nice mellow beat to it. A very steady cool…"

He enters alright, and eloquently speaks of the pitfalls of addiction, losing one's cool on drugs, how the dope made a fool out of him once upon a time.

We set the play in a clinic on base called the Hope House, and Howard plays the narrator, a guide and counseling spirit to those who come to the Hope House to get off the dope.

The Hope House is Howard's romp, a way to review himself. I just marvel at his knowledge of addiction. Howard is more like a man coming home from the war. He saw it all. I'm just hearing about it for the first time.

Though Howard is twenty-one, just like me, he's already lived several lifetimes. He's a former heroin addict. He was a pimp ("I had eleven darlings working my turf," he says). And a survivor. He lifts his shirt and shows me the scars from his wounds. He's been shot twice. "This is all going into the play," he says.

"I'm clean," he adds. "The Lord keeps it that way for me. Got drafted, decided I'd check it out. Now I'm here for the Hope House."

We improvise different situations playing soldiers struggling with addiction; different addicts tell their stories, their abuses, the lying and cheating, surviving violence, busting the law.

As much as Howard impresses me, he also frightens me. He's huge. He's strong. He's an old soul. This man is from the dead, from the underworld. He's a kingpin there. He rules from the depths. He's an artist, a con man, a charmer, an Orpheus. He's been shot twice and lived. He's been dead twice and lived. He's resurrected. I love him.

* * *

OUR SHARED SENSE OF PURPOSE brings out our best as we put the finishing touches on our draft. The show flows out of us, especially Howard, who bares his soul so that others can know the route he took to come back from the dead, to discover himself in a new light. His language is obscure, poetic, told in rhymes and riddles. Hard street stories and gunplay. I served a few weeks in a jail for stealing a tire. Small time. His stories come from the New Orleans underworld. Bigger crimes, far more danger.

"Welcome to Hope House," Howard says.

In just six days the script will be nearly finished. Howard embellishes every part, four characters in search of themselves, all of them addicts trying to regain consciousness. All the characters are different parts of Howard confronting his addiction: shooting up, hitting bottom, withdrawing from the smoke, the pills, "the monkey." For one of the characters, he turns to Jesus.

I am in awe as this show flows out of him.

Finally, our work—transcribed and put into script form—is given to the general for approval. Though a speed-reader, I hope he takes his time. Don't race through this, General. It's good and important, even profound—a poetic romp from inferno to redemption. Word comes back that the general likes the draft and wants me to prioritize the writing and development of *Hope House*.

* * *

A REAL DRUG SHOW IS GOING ON all around me. This army is getting dizzy from it all, and the general knows this. Years later, a report will come out that nearly 50 percent of all enlisted men serving in Vietnam have used opium or heroin, and 20 percent of them will have succumbed to addiction. To me, the numbers seem way short of the mark. During my time in the army, opiated hash is everywhere—and it isn't confined to the enlisted men and NCOs. Even the officers were into it. The hash pipes light up like so many stars in the universe, and there's also a lot of acid and heroin available for those who want it.

I don't see the harder stuff within the road show, but American civies hanging out in Germany are bringing in stuff, mostly hash from Afghanistan.

* * *

HOWARD AND I BECOME CLOSE. One night he takes me to the King's Club. It's a popular hangout for Blacks off base. Howard refers to it as "the headquarters." Heading out, I go to his room to get him. He comes out in an exceptional two-toned suit and matching hat with his beloved walking stick. He's magnificent.

"This is what I'll be wearing in the play," he says. "I am the Burgermeister."

* * *

We're cruising along in our company jeep. Howard is directing me to the King's Club. I have no idea where we are as we course
through the city. Howard seems to know every street, as should be
expected. He's the Burgermeister. This is his town. These are his
people. When we stop at a light, Howard tips his hat to the woman
he sees at the corner. He greets women as if they're all his ladies.

We arrive at the club. "Yes, I'm gonna show you a place that
jumps," he says.

When we go inside, I feel like I am the first white person entering this club, which does indeed seem like a headquarters for Blacks
in or out of the army. I sense most of them are civilians. Some wear
black berets and dark sunglasses. All are dressed well. I see a few
Black women close to their men.

I can feel the stares, the apparent trespass, but Howard's there
and his presence makes everything okay. I'm his guest, and he's the
Burgermeister.

A few guys come to Howard, and there's the usual dap and hugs.
Howard is clearly respected, the center of attention. Several people
sitting at a booth get up and greet Howard. Daps abound. I'm introduced as "the playwright." Howard slides into the booth.

"Loosen up, brothers," he says. "This man is a colonel in the army.
He's also the playwright."

"A colonel? What are you writing?"

"We're working on a show about drugs in the army," I say. "I'm
putting it together with Howard."

"What are you drinking?" Howard asks me.

"I'll have a glass of milk." Howard busts up. "With an ice cube," I
say. "No, forget the glass, I'll just drink it out of the carton."

"No, get a straw, motherfucker!" Howard laughs.

It's not a long evening. We simply have a beer and then we're up
on our feet. We're on the move and as we head for the door, Howard
has a low-key chat with a few guys I hadn't seen before and then
we're out into the night and back into the jeep.

Driving by the club, Howard, like a pope, raises his hand and gives those in front a salutation like a benediction. I'm the pope's driver. He's being chauffeured in his jeep. Yes, the pope is doing well in the army. Actually, we both are. I'm in charge of the road show, and Howard is making the scene.

* * *

ONE NIGHT WE TAKE A DRIVE into the city. Howard is in his fabulous suit, and I'm dressed as the colonel. We're zipping along when we're stopped by the German police. This isn't good. I don't want to implicate my character with another call to MID questioning my identity, and this time by the German police. Howard looks back at the police car. His expression changes.

"Oh, those two motherfuckers again," he says. "I've got no time for this shit."

"What? You know these guys?" I ask.

"Just wait here. I'll straighten this shit out."

Howard gets out of our vehicle and walks back to talk to the German police. Why are they stopping us? Is he speaking German? Nothing should surprise me when it comes to Howard. He returns a few moments later and simply says, "We're cool. Let's go."

"What was that all about?" I ask.

"Dumb uninformed police shit."

"Do you speak German?"

"I don't have time for language. All these Germans speak better English than we do. It's mandatory in their schools."

"What were you talking to the cops about?"

"Their nasty habits, that's for sure."

"Howard, I don't know what you're saying."

"That's what I said to those two motherfuckers."

* * *

Work on the play continues. The company will be away on the road for the next four days. Howard and I are expected to complete a second draft.

We work for a few hours that morning, and I'm confident with how things are going. I'm walking around upstairs going over things, when I suddenly hear a ruckus in Howard's room downstairs—first a bottle shattering against the wall, then a woman screaming, "Get your big ugly asses out of here!"

That doesn't sound good—and it isn't. Glancing out the window, I see an MP's jeep. Are they going through the road show building looking for contraband? The company isn't supposed to be holding while traveling, so their rooms are probably stacked, floor to ceiling, with hash. But all the doors to their rooms should be locked. How'd the MPs get in? Who left the front door open? Then I hear the girl scream again.

Howard usually has a woman in his room, but they don't usually get raided. This is serious. On my way to his room, I hear one of the MPs ordering Howard to salute and get at attention. Howard balks. "That's it," he says. "I can't work. You're fucking with me. Disturbing my process!"

When I finally get there, I see that a couple of MPs, both of whom are captains and wear silver helmets, have entered Howard's room. They see me and want to know who I am and why I'm out of uniform and why Howard has been drinking and entertaining a woman in his room.

"We don't wear uniforms around here," I say, as calmly as possible. "We're special operations."

"Doesn't anybody salute around here," one of the MPs snaps. Addressing me, he asks, "What's your rank?"

I tell them, "I could be a colonel, then what?"

I whip out my ID, knowing it says special operations MID. They give it a hard look and then leave without any explanation. Howard and I trade what-the-fuck looks.

Walking back to my room, I am impressed with the power I seem to have. But still, I wonder what that was all about. Within an hour, a messenger comes to the building and hands me an envelope. Inside are orders: I'm to report to the general's office right away.

I put on my plain suit and think about how I'm going to justify our "operation" for today. Should I tell the general and whoever else is in his office that Howard was getting into character and needs a woman in his room? The liquor bottle was a prop? I don't think so. I'll tell them the truth: we're on civilian status, and Howard was on a break. Period.

* * *

INSIDE THE GENERAL'S OFFICE, I am met by several officers and a few men in suits, none of whom I have ever seen before. They waste no time getting to the point. They tell me there is a black-market trade in weapons and other military stuff, and I have crossed paths with some of the people involved.

What? This is news to me, I tell them.

They ask me about the King's Club. One of the men wearing a suit opens a folder containing photographs showing people outside the club.

"What's going on in this picture?" he asks.

"I don't know any of these people. I just go there with Howard."

He shows me another photo. "Recognize anybody?"

"No, sir."

I notice a few pictures of me in the jeep as the colonel with Howard. There's another shot of Howard talking to the two German police officers who stopped us that night.

"Did you see those two officers at any other time with Corporal Ransom?" the interrogator continues.

"No, sir."

He shows more photos, one with the German university students standing around with some other people at the park in Frankfurt.

93

"Recognize any of these people?"

"Yeah, these two guys come around to play the board game Risk."

The interrogator circles the two I picked with a red marker.

I continue, "There was another guy with them once, and he went down into the road show basement and was looking around. I told him to leave."

"A lot of army issue down in that basement?" he asks.

"Yes, sir. Everything we got."

"The times you were at the King's Club, did you hear any discussions about guns? Things disappearing?"

This line of questioning, the people in the room, the way they're looking at me, the photos—it scares me. This is not about Howard drinking in his room with a woman. This is bigger, much bigger. I hope they can see that I'm not lying. That they know I'm not running drugs or guns or dealing army surplus on the black market. I think they've already come to that conclusion. I hope so.

And then they drop it on me: *They want me to continue to do what I am doing but make reports on people—who's doing what, be an informer.* This is big. This is not a role I can or want to play.

I explain as best as I can that I'm merely an actor in a show. I'm not a spy, not a snitch.

I am immediately dismissed. I walk back to our building wondering, Where do I go from here?

* * *

THE COMPANY WILL RETURN at the end of the week. How do I juggle all this, knowing that there's this investigation and knowing people in the road show could be involved? Who was playing Risk with those university students? Who else is under investigation? Who are the people in those pictures? Who's "taking" those pictures?

I'm scared. I know too much. It's like I've eaten the apple in Eden.

Soon there's a ring at the door of our building. When I get there, another messenger hands me a manila envelope. I open it on the spot, and inside are my discharge papers! What? I'm honorably discharged, four months early, with full pay and all benefits. End of road show, so long *Hope House*, adios colonel, goodbye US Army.

And Howard?

He is equally surprised. Not so much about the photos and the investigation but that I leave tomorrow!

All of it affects him deeply. I didn't know how much until the early morning hours when I'm startled awake by the sound of smashing glass in the hallway. I go out there and see Howard, shitfaced, swatting at the ceiling lights with his cane, creating mini explosions as he busts them one by one, shattering glass across the floor.

Howard is coming undone. I suppose if the road show comes to an end, everybody has to go. But I know the road show is here to stay. It's a very good thing the army has going.

I yell, "Stop this shit, you stupid fuck!"

That stops Howard. But then, he whirls around in anger and comes for me, lifting his cane to smash my head open. It stops inches from my face.

"Who the fuck are you talking to me like this? I will kill your ass!"

"This is the road show, man! I'm not running things anymore, but you are. All the work, the transcribing, it's your story, your *Hope House*, Howard!"

"What do you know about me?" he asks.

"That you can look into a wrong and make it right," I say. "You're the only fucker who can put together the *Hope House*. You're an artist, man!"

Howard stares straight into me again.

"You're the star, Howard."

PART 3

I'm Out There!

CHAPTER 10

Higher Intelligence

Four days later, I'm back in California, wearing my army trench coat with $3,700 (this is my savings from the army, equivalent to $27,172.94 today) stuffed in the pocket, driving a beat-up '54 Chevy with a rebuilt engine that I quickly bought in Venice for just fifty bucks. There's no way to get around LA without a car.

It's dark out, and I take the wrong turn down a one-way street. Luckily, there's no traffic, and so rather than make a U-turn, I speed ahead toward a cross street. Ah, shit! A car turns onto this street and is heading straight for me. Suddenly, there's a flashing red light on top of the oncoming car.

I stop my car and get out. The officer emerges, cautiously using his car door as a shield. I'm sure he thinks I'm a nut on the loose.

"I got confused. I didn't see a one-way sign," I gripe.

He slowly approaches me. "Can I see your driver's license and registration?"

"I don't have 'em. I just bought the car this morning. I have a transfer of title but not the actual registration. I just got out of the service." I hand him my military ID.

He looks it over.

"This all you have?"

I take out of my wallet my MID card and hand it to him. He studies it.

"What was your MOS?" he asks.

"V-Corps Training Road Show. I played a colonel."

He studies me for a moment. "Look, you can't drive without a driver's license."

"Yes, sir. I needed some wheels to get around..."

"I understand that. I'm a veteran too." He hands my IDs back. "Get your license."

"Right."

"I'm going to get back into my vehicle, and I'm not looking at you. You get in your car and do what you're going to do to get out of here safely, okay?"

"I really appreciate that."

"And welcome home...Colonel."

* * *

DRIVING THE WRONG WAY, figuring out which way to go, is indicative of where I am right now. A lot of restlessness around me. The antiwar movement is still on. The young so distrustful of the government, some giving the finger to the system, a lot of them smoking weed and taking acid to "break on through to the other side." So many people are dropping out and tuning in to some other side, but what am I tuning into? What am I here for in LA? For now, I'm off to the DMV to get my driver's license.

* * *

I LOOK INTO WHAT ED IS UP TO and he's into getting our act going again. Around this time, Rudy De Luca and Sammy Shore opened the Comedy Store on the Sunset Strip. It's an intimate theater in what was once a celebrity nightclub in the '40s and '50s and more recently a rock-and-roll hotspot for the likes of Jimi Hendrix and the Byrds.

Ed and I think it would be a hoot if we just crash this joint, streak it, roller-skate through the place butt-naked with eyeballs painted on our chests.

"We'll get arrested," I say with devilish glee. "It'll be good publicity."

And it would be. But we really don't want to deal with cops, and I don't ever want to be in jail again after that Cordell, Oklahoma incident. So we end up going to Western Costume, where Ed knows someone, naturally, and we settle on wearing traditional Yugoslavian carnival costumes, skirts and all. That night we roller-skate through the Comedy Store and right onto the stage, taking over somebody's act, speaking in gibberish, and falling down everywhere. We get huge laughs. Then we head for the door.

More people are outside, waiting to get in. They bust up laughing as we skate out of the place and right onto Sunset Boulevard weaving in and out of traffic!

Some years later, Rudy De Luca is casting and directing a film and instantly recognizes me as I enter his office for a part. "You!" he screams, jumping up from his chair. "It's you! You are the funniest, craziest motherfucker in the world!" He goes on about that night Ed and I skated into the Comedy Store. "Where the hell did you go after that?" he says. "You never came in again. Where did you go?"

"I was taken up by a flying saucer."

He laughs. He thinks I'm joking. I wasn't.

Soon I'll have my contact experience. But first one more gig with Ed.

I call the Shriners for their Fourth of July event in Griffith Park. Because I'm a vet, they listen to me. Oliver Hardy was a Shriner, a part of their Jester division, which was featured so well in Laurel and Hardy's hilarious film, *Sons of the Desert*. I come up with a preposterous routine. Ed and I will be in military tanks that we make out of refrigerator boxes with long cardboard cylinders sticking out like gun barrels. We intend to blow white pastry flour through them as if they're being fired.

Ed and I play two whacked-out tank drivers yelling at each other. He's the American, I'm the enemy. With our legs sticking out of the bottom of the boxes, we walk around ramming each other and firing our guns. The flour gets everywhere and during the crazy battle, Ed inadvertently drops the American flag on the ground. This is no "Honolulu Baby." The Shriners watching this nutty show immediately step in and shut us down. One of them picks up the flag and tells us to go.

Still in our boxes, covered in flour, we walk into the sunset. Kids run by with sparklers in their hands.

"We didn't get any laughs," I say.

"No, we got some laughs," Ed protests.

"No, we got nothing."

* * *

REALLY, AT THIS POINT, I want to be in plays, go back to school, use my GI Bill and study theater. My old friend Brad, using some of the money from selling the Nomad, went ahead and bought an old colorful circus wagon with spoked wooden wheels in Sun Valley for just twenty-five bucks. "Michael would love this thing!" he said.

He and a few folks around Tujunga got the wagon up to a level spot behind his cabin. As a welcome home gift, Brad gives me the wagon and the rest of the money from selling my stuff. I accept his gift, and this is what I'm living in now, my "Circus Wagon."

I place an old Persian-like carpet in there with my new Posturepedic twin bed (a big treat having slept on thin, spartan mattresses in the army), a table, a bookshelf, and some worn-out framed pictures of Yosemite Valley that I bought from a thrift store nearby. I put up some bamboo shades and run an extension cord for a few lamps inside. Outside, I surround the wagon with Hawaiian torches, and at night under the moon, this horseless wagon looks like a forlorn carny show on the prairie.

And I look like some sort of clown with a lime green bandana tied around my head, orange paisley patterned slacks, a blue denim work shirt, and yellowish leather chukka boots. When I go into the city at night, I slip on my army trench coat. Brad's new girlfriend, Norah, is pretty good at stitching, and she sews a few purple irises above the pockets of my denim shirt. These are the ribbons to my new uniform.

That summer in Tujunga it's over a hundred degrees every day, and without an air conditioner, the wagon is a sweatbox. During the day, I spend most of my time in Brad's cabin sitting near a window cooler, one of those goofy evaporator units with a water tray that must be kept filled, a big metal box droning away to defeat nature's heat while I'm reading Strindberg's *Inferno*.

* * *

IT'S 1971, AND MY CIRCUS WAGON LIFESTYLE is not that expensive. Thanks to the army, I have enough money to get by. Again, the harder proposition in this post-army chapter of my life is figuring out the right direction to go.

Resuming the act with Eddie is not in the picture. Although the two of us had made some headway with the act before I was drafted, he's really on his own with it now, and I'm not up for the club scene. I want to act in great plays.

Brad is the only person I know who understands this about me. He just graduated from CalArts, shaving off his remaining two years for an undergraduate degree by writing a two-hundred-page thesis incorporating the whole curriculum. Apparently it's brilliant, and the head of the film school, Gene Youngblood, graduates Brad early. Now he's heading off to Stanford with a full scholarship to pursue a graduate degree in English and their Creative Writing

Program. Inspired by this, CalArts and its acting program is on my mind.

I'm not into knocking on doors trying to get an agent, an 8 x 10 headshot, a SAG card, or an Equity membership. I'm young and feel more secure in school, a preeminent acting school like CalArts. Randy Larsen, who started the V-Corps Training Road Show, was going back to school for his MFA in theater. CalArts won't hurt me, I tell myself; it can only help. Of course, this school is a lot more than twenty-eight bucks a semester. It's more like $2,500 a semester.

As a veteran, Uncle Sam will pay my tuition, plus room and board, but only for about a year and a half at CalArts. I decide to shop around.

* * *

I SAW AN INCREDIBLE PICTURE of Mount Shasta somewhere and found out there is a community college with a theater arts department not far from this mountain in the historic gold rush area of Northern California. Yeah, the tuition here is a heck of a lot cheaper.

Shasta Community College is about six hundred miles from Brad's place, where I'm staying now. That gives me plenty of driving time in my old Chevy to think about things.

The scenery along the way is spectacular. The deserts, the great Sierras, forests, even the long stretch of Highway 5 looks good to me. It's nice to be back in the States. But during the six-hour drive, I realize that I'm too far from home. I need the vitality of the city. I feel like I'm driving away from myself.

But, having come this far north of Sacramento, I'm not turning around yet. Let's see Shasta College! It's beautiful up here. My old Chevy is running well. We're not all the way up here for nothing. Buck up!

Finally, I'm there and pull into the parking lot right in front of the theater arts building. Mine is the only car. Is there any life around here? It feels so desolate. The door to the theater is wide open. I walk in and look at the stage. It's small. The auditorium has low ceilings. All of it—the seating, the whole setup—is less than half of the main stage at Valley College. The theater seems sad to me, very alone and empty, the way I feel being there.

A man walks toward me from near the stage and says hello. He's the head of the drama school. He tells me about some of the shows they're going to be doing, a musical and some other play I've never heard of, but I'm not listening. I just want to get back in my car. I still have the whole afternoon to drive home and stop at CalArts on the way. How far is the campus in Valencia? It doesn't matter. As Edward Albee wrote in *The Zoo Story*, "It's one of those things a person has to do; sometimes a person has to go a very long distance out of his way to come back a short distance correctly."

* * *

HOURS LATER I TURN INTO the parking lot of CalArts. The sky is on the verge of getting dark, and yet the school doors are open. This is more like it. The place is huge. I know right away that I belong at this school. I bound up the steps to the administration office, which is closed, but a student who works there provides me with admission forms to the theater school. I notice an audition is involved and decide then and there that I'll present a scene from Megan Terry's *Keep Tightly Closed in a Cool Dry Place*, the play I did at Valley College. This time, I'll play all three characters.

Before leaving, I check out the main stage. It's a huge modular theater system that can be set up in multiple configurations: horseshoe, in the round, proscenium, or combinations of the three. It's only limited by imagination. The school's tech department must be first-rate. There are also four large rehearsal halls with lights and sound where shows can be produced. That's five theaters! This is definitely where I need to be. Done.

Not bad for a day's drive. I get back in my car confident that I'm going in the right direction.

* * *

MY AUDITION IS HELD in one of the four large rehearsal rooms. I am there with around forty other students also applying to get in. Each person gets up and does their piece in front of everyone, as well as the faculty, including the dean of the theater arts department, Michael Addison. I am ready. Playing three distinct characters, it's quite a showcase. Brad is there to lend his support. It couldn't have gone any better. On my way offstage, Michael Addison gives me a little nod. I know I'm in this school.

A few days after the audition, I get a call from the theater arts school that I've been accepted. What ensemble level I will be placed in will be posted on the first day of school. Whatever level, I'm ready for it all.

* * *

I ACQUIRE A DORM ROOM. I pack my meager belongings—a few books, clothes, and my Posturepedic mattress tied to the top of my Chevy—and move in. All situated that evening, I'm lying on my heavenly bed, resting and looking forward to my orientation seminar the next day, when there is a knock at my door.

"Who is it?"

"Uh, this used to be my room. I need something that I left in there. I need to get it back."

"What is it that you're looking for?" I ask without getting up from my comfortable bed.

"My soul is in there," the person says, "I need it back."

"No, your soul is not in here," I say.

"Well, I have to have it before I go."

He's giving me an ultimatum?

I repeat that his soul is not in my room anymore, but if I find it, I'll leave it with Stephanie Ross, our dorm mother. I hear him walk away. Is he coming back? Will he suddenly break through the door?

A half an hour later, Stephanie, who will go on to become the line producer for *The Tonight Show with Jay Leno*, tells me the guy at my door is "a burnout who fried his brain on acid" and is no longer a CalArts student. I'm to let her know if he comes around again. She'll call security and I'm wondering, What does a soul look like?

The soulless man doesn't come around again, though I'm always looking over my shoulder when I'm in the dorm, heading to my room. I imagine the guy approaching me or waiting for me with a gun or a knife, insisting that I give him back his soul or he'll do me in. Just in case, I put a little sign on my door: "If you lost your soul, check with lost and found in the housing office. It's not in this room anymore."

* * *

THERE'S A STUDENT BULLETIN BOARD in the hallway just outside the offices for the theater arts department. And thar she blows! I've been assigned to the MFA ensemble. What? I think that there has been a mistake. I go into the offices, and right to Michael Addison's, and there he is sitting behind his desk. I express my concern. He smiles and says, "You're in the advanced ensemble. Congratulations."

Shortly, I am assigned the role of Talthybius, the conscientious bringer of bad news, in *The Trojan Women*. This first year is like a slingshot into another realm of thought and searching. I take two classes in critical studies—one is a writing course with Deena Metzger. She's a poet, novelist, activist, and mystic who encourages just about everything that goes through my mind. I tell her that I'm not a very good writer and don't know grammar, but rather than get hung up on not knowing the rules of my language and therefore not writing at all, Deena says she is more interested in the person behind words, like the face behind a mask.

"People usually hide behind words or use language to fake people out. Get to the person. Write from there."

What?

Start with you, she advises. A mood, a feeling, find words for it. Pictures, illustrations, anything. It doesn't have to be just words; get to the "person" behind words. There is also a discussion that words are secondary to the natural world. Deena clarifies: it's the idea that the natural world speaks to us through images, not words. I am given an assignment to collect images that seem to *naturally* resonate with me and to then speak through these images. Find words that can go along with the images.

Fascinated and inspired, this intel-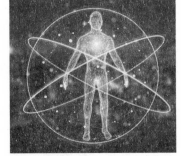lectual scavenger hunt is right up my alley. "In the beginning was the word," the Bible said. "In the beginning was the deed," Goethe said. The "deed" comes out of the "person." So, "in the beginning" is the "person," as "in the beginning" language was invented by man. Man comes before words. Deena is asking me to get back to "the first man" that I am. Whew! This is all rather new to me.

My second class is on Bertolt Brecht led by the eminent John Willett, considered the greatest living authority on Brecht. We read Brecht's plays out loud and discuss their political intent. *Galileo* has a big impact on me. Reading it leads to my interest in religion, not science, but to Galileo's opponent, the church, which had the power to shut down science. I become interested in how ideologies, censorship, and propaganda promote or obstruct innovative thinking.

I audition for a class in cabaret comedy, even though I'm not interested in a comedy workshop. What am I up to? I just want to act in plays, but here is a chance to meet the director, Sabin Epstein from New York's famed La MaMa theater, and though at the end of the day I decline his invitation to join the workshop, I meet fellow students Paul Reubens and Laraine Newman. To them, cabaret theater is the mother lode, and they're out to create characters and sketch comedies. Of course, this will lead to Gary Austin's Groundlings

Theatre and Reuben's *The Pee-wee Herman Show*. Laraine will go on to *Saturday Night Live*.

I'll eventually get to comedy, but first "a very long distance out of my way to come back a short distance correctly."

* * *

I MAY NOT BE DOING COMEDY through a cabaret workshop, but I haven't lost my sense of humor. I just keep it to myself.

CalArts has very long doorless halls. If I know that people are a certain distance behind me, I will turn a corner and then run as fast as I can to reach the end of the hallway, turn that corner, and quickly disappear. Those people who are behind me enter the hallway and wonder where I have gone. This trick of mine gets me dubbed "the phantom." People walking past me whisper, "There's the phantom."

One day a guy asks me straight out, "Are you the phantom?"

Straight-faced, I tell him, "Please don't tell anybody or I'll lose my power."

* * *

IN MY OWN ENSEMBLE, one of the MFA projects is to dismantle *The Bacchae* and look into the spirit of Dionysus.

I'm fascinated by the paradox of Dionysus, the god of the Greek theater—his two faces, tragedy and comedy, such opposites forming the whole of man; the "person" who seems to be behind words, or all the plays themselves. Humans in the midst of contradictions, a coming and going, entrances and exits, life and death, to find peace within the two, the great tension of opposites, promoting the stumble, the chaos in life, one's Bacchae. I am all into this, coming onto it for the first time. Wow!

To me, this is why The Beatles were sitting at the feet of Maharishi Mahesh Yogi, to "come together" within oneself—to become "whole." It's part of the cultural revolution at hand, this wanting a sense of wholeness; it's the basis of a cosmic consciousness movement. In music and art, in politics and on posters. "Make love, not war." "Smile on your brother, everybody *come together.*" Get "whole," don't break humanity apart!

It's on the streets. It's all over CalArts. It was the predominant conversation of the day, and I was listening to it. Trying to understand it all.

* * *

I'M VERY ACTIVE AT CALARTS. Sam Woodhouse, who's in the master's program for directing and will go on to create the San Diego Repertory Theatre with his partner Doug Jacobs, another MFA student, asks me to star in his thesis production of E. E. Cummings's Dada play *Him.* What a romp through the absurd, through open-ended imagination! And Paul Reubens asks me to play his spouse in a short student-directed film. It's a comedy. What else?

I gravitate to Allan Kaprow, who is teaching in the art department. He is the father of performance art and creator of the "Happenings." I once saw Allan leading a group of high school students touring the school across the quad near the cafeteria, except the students could move forward only by stepping on each other's shadow, awkwardly making their way to lunch. That was Allan, turning a campus tour into "a Happening."

A prevailing question throughout a whole generation of young people was, "What's happening?" Kaprow makes it fun. Later, through C. G. Jung, I will come to realize the value of moving through one's "shadow" to get to where you need to go.

* * *

FOR OUR MFA ENSEMBLE, we mount a production of *Major Bullshot-Gorgeous,* a comedy by the Roman playwright Plautus. After having been in the bowels of *The Bacchae,* the tragedy of *The*

Trojan Women, and the Dada insanity of *Him*, I am ready and eager to step into a comedy. We use a new translation by the lauded English poet Paul Roche, who is with us throughout the play as we mount the show and who tries to give this play, written almost two thousand years earlier, a timeless relevancy, pointing out scenes that he thinks "have been a joke since the time of Adam" and remain funny to this day.

Funny all this time? Well, the cast and I will ham up the play to fill in the gaps. Roche is a poet-scholar, and it's here that I begin to see the difference between the two.

"If ever a truism was self-evident," he says, reading from his introduction to the play, "it's that laughter keeps us sane." We have this quote printed on the show's program, but I don't necessarily agree. To me, it's more about what one thinks is funny and believes is sane. People laugh at the downfall of others; how "sane" is that? Dante's *Divine Comedy* lampoons the folk that he thinks should be in hell. And for Lenny Bruce, laughter didn't lead to sanity. It led to his arrest, time in jail, and eventually his overdose.

If anything, comedy and laughter is anarchy. It upsets formality. It breaks things up. It's Dionysian where Pentheus is torn to pieces. It's Laurel and Hardy wrecking your house.

* * *

SOMEONE IN CLASS SAYS, "Ignorance dampens wisdom." I imagine that ignorance is an empty cup, and you fill it up with whatever seems wise to you. This might be another truism that's self-evident, but I'm only twenty-two and just waking up, just starting to fill my cup. These CalArts teachers with some wisdom in their cups have ignited in me a voracious appetite to know, to get in on what's going on.

One day I come across a weird book in the CalArts library, *The Secret Teachings of All Ages* by Manly P. Hall. I am instantly enthralled by the alchemical images, Kabbalistic diagrams, Pythagorean numbers, and geometric symbolism. What is this stuff? Artaud was into what he called an "alchemical theatre," a language of "the double," a unique language "halfway between gesture and thought." You mean "halfway between" body and mind? What's in the middle of the two?

Is there some centering point between the two that is behind all that I do? Is this what people call God or all the other names for it?

In my dorm room, *The Secret Teachings of All Ages* is always on my table. It feels holy to me, a gateway into something deeply significant, something that the text refers to as "the Mysteries." This isn't comical. No, this is not funny at all. The Mysteries are behind the laugh, somewhere below the surface of a joke. It's the ground underneath the house that holds us all up. It's on the other side of the line that I unconsciously draw around myself, perhaps to protect me from my own mystery. It's behind all of our ideologies.

To enter it is to explore my limitations, just how short I am from ultimate truth or the way of wisdom. To cross the line, buck up! I suppose it's the only way *to know* more.

Pushing boundaries and crossing lines are what make directors Jerzy Grotowski and Peter Brook hot topics on campus. Brook is doing some very experimental work. I saw his interpretation of *A Midsummer Night's Dream* at the Mark Taper Forum. Onstage, the actors perform in a large white box and fly in on red feathers. They wear enormous high heels. The whole play, usually fixed in a classical style, is deconstructed and reconstructed, suitably performed in a brand-new way. What a display of imagination!

As for Grotowski, I attend a lecture of his and ask him outright, "What is living death?" I am responding to theater designer Frederick Kiesler's radical 1926 declaration that "the theatre is dead." This supposition was and still is meant to be as startling as Nietzsche's argument that "God is dead." Grotowski speaks about "the holy actor," the one who is presumably alive, and so implies an unholy actor presumably dead. I want to know about this actor who is a living death. I'm for a living theater. Like Dionysus, the god of the

Greek theater, who is the god of a living theater? Who is the god of a dead one?

Grotowski speaks briefly about "the commercial theatre" differing from "a theatre of higher value." I'm confused by all this stuff. This rub about a commercial theater being less than a higher theater—does he mean a theater without a box office is more alive, far holier, like a holy anchorite out in the desert living without money? Isn't Grotowski selling a book, *Towards a Poor Theatre*? Is this book cheaper than all the other books?

* * *

I FALL IN LOVE WITH A GIRL in my ensemble, Cass. We often listen to my friend Phil playing his violin, something he does all over campus, positioning himself in areas where the sound reverberates and heightens the tonality of his music. One day, we don't hear Phil playing. What's up? Where did Phil go? A few days go by, and I run into him in the hall. He's very excited and swept up by a class he's been taking on Kabbalistic phenomenology.

"Yeah, what's that stuff all about?" I ask.

"It's everything," he answers. "Come to class. Dr. Hurtak will teach you."

I can't imagine fitting in another class. I'm so busy within my department. And as the lead in *Bullshot*, I have a head full of dialogue. Even more, I'm so in love with Cass. I must have time to see her. But I accept Phil's invitation. Let's see what "everything" is all about.

* * *

THERE ARE ABOUT EIGHT STUDENTS in the classroom including Phil, who gives me a look, like "Buckle up. You're in for it now." I take a seat ready to see what caused him to stop playing his violin.

Moments later, Dr. James Hurtak enters. A founding member of the school's critical studies department, Hurtak is a Fulbright Scholar, an ordained rabbi, and a brilliantly captivating speaker. He wears a dark blue suit, white shirt, and a black beret. He carries a brown briefcase with a few books inside. Seeing me in the room, he comes right over. "Welcome, Michael," he says. He tells me that Phil has spoken highly of me and that I'm a gifted actor.

Still standing next to me, he begins. He briefly mentions the divinity of the Torah and other parts of scripture containing "higher intelligence," a phrase that I will come to know well through his lectures. Then he hands me a Bible, *The Holy Scriptures*, as a gift to me.

I'm not Jewish, and this is my first time reading the Torah, but if Adam and Eve are the First Parents, then, as Hurtak puts it, we're all family from the same garden—Jews, Greeks, Romans, and everyone else—separated only by the names for God. I'm thinking we may be family, but we're still at each other's throat. I've read enough in Greek plays to see how "families" kill each other off. Even God kills off those he doesn't like. Though he created them in the first place, he ends up blaming them for being the way they are. They came from God, and now God kills off parts of himself? The whole thing bewilders me.

Still, over the ensuing days and weeks, I carry the Bible Hurtak gave me in my bag and read whenever I have the time. Hurtak advises me to highlight the sections in scripture where the prophets, like Ezekiel, come into "higher intelligence," where they receive their "assignments" directly from Yahweh. I interpret this "higher intelligence" as a kind of inspiration bestowed upon an artist to do great works. I'm captivated.

Finishing the short run of *Bullshot*, I latch onto Hurtak and his extensive knowledge of ancient Middle East cultures; Egyptian, Phoenician, and Babylonian mythology; the mathematics in pyramid building; Hinduism, Buddhism, and Chinese philosophy; Western metaphysics, Hermetics, Gnosticism, alchemy, science, physics, and cosmology. He is a trove of knowledge—knowledge

114

thousands of years old—and I want to hear it all. Every religion in the world speaks of these things: all the prophets, the sages, the best of our lot, they had their connection to some holy, holy. A God or "higher intelligence." I want that!

Soon sections in my Bible are a sea of yellow and as the semester ends, I am falling under the hypnotic sway of Hurtak's fascinating lectures. I'm becoming susceptible to his thinking. I'm a follower, and I'm starting to lose myself in him. Maybe like my grandmother losing herself in some kind of "higher intelligence" that takes her away. Or am I looking for my Father in a box and he's not really there?

* * *

IT MAKES SOME SENSE that I'm so interested in Dr. Hurtak showing me the great Jewish prophet Ezekiel receiving from the "Father" the intelligence that helps him build a temple, or an idea that gives him a sense of order. At twenty-two, I am seeking order, wholeness, an ethos that will support me as I come into my manhood and meet the world.

It's about this time that my mother contacts me and says she has a large envelope at her house for me. Inside is a short note from my former army buddy Howard Ransom. It's paperclipped to a script, *The Hope House* by Sgt. Howard Ransom. The letter also includes a quote from scripture: "Rejoice in the resurrection." And then, "It Will Be Done!"

V-Corps insignia

Howard.

The script isn't like anything that we had first submitted. It doesn't matter. Howard is putting together his ethos, meeting the world through the army. Right now, I'm not sure what my script is all about, but I'm working on it.

My interest in acting is still on, even though, like Phil, who stopped playing his violin, right now I only want to hear more of Hurtak's rap. The effect this man is having on me is incredible! So, taken up by his material, I'm looking for a role to play in all of this. It's a huge script; I'm steeped in the psycho-philosophy of the Mysteries, all of which stands for some kind of "Life-process" behind the individual. For now, I feel akin to the prophets in scripture who are hooked up to this Life-process as some kind of holy, holy that speaks to them, gives them an orientation to follow.

At this time, I had a dream where I was holding some crystals and heard a voice say crystals are the blood of the prophets. In ancient Greek theater, a thespian was "of the gods" like a prophet is from God. What speaks through an "inspired" thespian? I sense in ancient times, theater was sacred, far more than it is today. It was more of a place for oracles, or "the gods," the "holy" to appear. Grotowski was speaking about the "holy actor," trying to rediscover such a "thespian." What creative process is needed to channel the "holy"? Where does this "holy" come from? For now, I feel like Howard rejoicing in a resurrection, like I'm coming out of a dead theater for a living one.

And I'm so in love with Cass! I'll put everything aside to be with her. For how long? Again, it *feels* like "I'm on a long drive to come back a short distance correctly." I need a long drive to think things over. A holy, holy sensation is on me. I've got an "assignment" from "higher intelligence" to figure it out. The *will* of something is moving me along. I'm not in complete control. Like breathing, it's being done to me.

Sometimes, Hurtak holds classes outside in the hills just behind the school. As his followers, we meet at night to meditate on certain star patterns and constellations. "Kadosh, Kadosh adonai…" we pray. Seemingly out of nowhere, a large fireball suddenly appears, zooming toward the earth, and quickly burns out. Whoa! To Hurtak, it's a sign—a sign from above that we've been acknowledged. Soon, I'll figure out that all kinds of "space trash" comes into our atmosphere and burns brightly as it falls to the earth. So I'm not sure about being "acknowledged."

Still, I'm riveted when Hurtak speaks of the sage or a "man of light" receiving vital information for a better life. Guided by an interest to know what's behind my interest, now in the hills behind the school, I wonder if certain star patterns and constellations really alter people. I invest this with my attention. Are they filling me up with what they're thinking? Or is it my thinking? Where does thinking come from? The stars? What's the message? Space trash? What's this stuff thinking about?

"Hi, Michael, we know you're thinking about what's behind our form of light. You want the message in all of this? Coming down to earth. A falling down to earth and burning out."

Falling down to earth... Didn't the dark son of God end up this way? Who am I rebelling against? The Life-process?

I'm tired and head back to my dorm room. I need the comfort of my Posturepedic. I'm still on the lookout for the soulless man who may be lurking about to get me. Where is my soul in all of this? What's a soul anyway? The "Life-process" or the natural world itself? Probably one and the same.

One day, Hurtak shows me a photo of the Mojave Desert and a stretch of ground, like a landing field, where what he calls "high-frequency vehicles" (UFOs) appear.

Supposedly, the vehicles are similar to "the throne chariot of God."

"You've seen these things, Jim?"

He maintains that they're out there.

CHAPTER 11

Zapped

I miss Cass so much. She graduated and for the summer has gone to Tufts University to do repertory theater. She will only do one play, she says, and then come back to me. We can't be apart for long.

In the meantime, I head out to this landing site for "high-frequency vehicles" in the Mojave Desert with my friend Jack, another student from Hurtak's class. The whole place belongs to George Van Tassel, a former airplane mechanic turned ufologist who claims that numerous encounters with space beings inspired him to, among other things, build an edifice for rejuvenating the human body. He calls it the Integratron. The specs for it were given to him by "higher intelligence."

He's been working on it for years. It stands at one end of his property, a round building with porthole-like windows running around the rim of its dome. It looks like it belongs in a low-budget science fiction movie. He also maintains an airstrip he built for space intelligence that he says land and take off here. He's close to Hurtak, and we have heard about how the Integratron spins and

can adjust frequencies within us to reduce "negative entropy," not only reversing the aging process in people but also "aligning them to higher intelligence."

We set up camp on Van Tassel's property and then look around. In one large underground room he has radios and electronic equipment with large antennas that rise from the ground like spindly cacti. The whole place is eerily apocalyptic.

"Do they come here?" I ask.

"All the time," Van Tassel says.

He tells me that he's being closely surveilled by the military for breaching their security by receiving "higher intelligence." Some of his mathematical knowledge corresponds to rocket launch systems and military tracking devices, he explains. But he emphasizes that what he does is for the welfare of man and not war-related or designed to destroy in any way.

"Man uses nature's laws for destructive purposes," he says. "The reason higher intelligence is here now is to counter man's capability to destroy the planet."

Sounds plausible.

That night Jack and I camp out near the airstrip. The desert night sky is fabulous. Debris from outer space falling into our atmosphere, these sightings thrill Jack. Just a few weeks ago he saw a Cessna at night and was convinced it was a high-frequency vehicle. I knew it was from the Van Nuys airport. I said so, but he disagreed. He thought we were being "acknowledged." So be it. How many centuries of this, where man is taken up by the supernatural, standing dumb before Creation, attributing so much of it to gods or spirits or some unseen hand behind it all, that's making us accountable, to wake up to some right in ourselves to make our short lives better again?

I tremble before the vastness of this night sky. I can only love and die, I tell myself. Just love and die.

We don't see any high-frequency vehicles that night. Before the early morning light, I tell Jack that it's all a lot of imagination.

"But one thing for sure, it's all alive, Jack. This universe is living through us. The whole thing is a high-frequency vehicle!"

This is as far as I can go with Hurtak's "higher intelligence." For now, I'm so in love with Cass. I miss her so much. I can only love and die.

I feel like my love for Cass is a counterweight to my soaring interest in Hurtak. Love will keep my feet on the ground.

* * *

WITHOUT CASS AT CALARTS, the school feels empty to me. Like Phil who stopped playing his violin, I don't feel like acting right now. My hair is growing out. I'm still processing the Mysteries.

Me at 22, ready for my contact experience.

Phil has gone home, and I heard that his parents will not allow him to return to CalArts; they think he's been zapped by Kabbalistic phenomenology. I suppose so. I can only hope he'll resume playing his violin again.

As for me, I still read *The Holy Scriptures*, and continue to do so to this day, the very book that Jim gave me, almost all highlighted in yellow by now.

* * *

Cass returns and misses me as much as I miss her. I have another year before I graduate. I decide to finish it at Evergreen State College. The school is so much cheaper than CalArts, and Uncle Sam will pay for it all, and there I can work with author-artist José Argüelles and his visionary work while looking into Eastern philosophy, Western mysticism, and reading the collected works of C. G. Jung. Jung will become my handrail supporting me through all of this. And so, Cass and I take off for Olympia, Washington.

On the way, we stop to visit Hurtak and his new wife, Desi, in Los Gatos. Desi is a critical studies grad from CalArts but now a part of Jim's "phenomenology." She's a bright woman and carries her own experience and what "cosmology" means to her. She's right on for Jim, grounds him in body and soul. I like her immediately.

Jim is establishing the Academy for Future Science at the Los Gatos "Cats Estate," built in the early 1900s by the poet Erskine Scott Wood. Two nine-foot white sculptured-cement cats flank the iron entry gates opening onto a forty-two-acre estate with an outdoor amphitheater and hundreds of ancient oak trees. It's a sanctuary so unto itself—such exclusive architecture, imported materials from India and China—and the grounds include the best of the Santa Cruz Mountains: springs and creeks, and chaparral for food and healing used by the native Awaswas for ten thousand years.

On Friday nights, Jim speaks outdoors in the amphitheater on the property, drawing crowds of seekers touched by the cosmic spirit, not on drugs and all that fortifying crud, but more natural seekers like myself seriously looking into this cosmic consciousness scene. Thousands of young people who have "tuned in and dropped out" are just wandering around hitchhiking or walking up and down the California coast, stopping off in Big Sur and Esalen, a center for tuning up one's "human potential" before moving on. Everybody is zapped by some kind of spiritual life. Some inspired by Timothy Leary's *Starseed* movement, or Baba Ram Dass's *Be Here Now*. And the "Oneness" teachings of Swami Satchidananda, or the Zen Buddhist thinking of Alan Watts. Also, "Living Love" from Ken Keyes, and the "Communication" work by Werner Erhard.

Up at the Cats, people are coming in with Albert Einstein's *The Theory of Relativity*, the works on the spirit of Maitreya by Lama Govinda, and the way of "transformation" taught by Elizabeth Clare Prophet. The "Esoteric Christ" is big, promoted by Madame Blavatsky's successor Annie Besant, and the spiritual works of Jiddu Krishnamurti. The beat just goes on and on. Everybody is into some kind of spiritual scene to meet the times.

Most of "the seekers" have at least one of these authors in their backpacks. I have mine, Hall's *The Secret Teachings of All Ages*. It's

to the point where seek-
ers are asking one another,
"What's your cosmology?"
To be hip is to be aware
of what you're doing with
your spiritual life. The
"hippy" is the person who
is into a genuine spiritual
experience. These are the
folks who usually come
around interested in what Hurtak is teaching at the Cats or his
Academy for Future Science—East/West consciousness, prophe-
cies for our time, and the way of "higher evolution." It comes on like
a clarion call! Yeah, the beat goes on.

The amphitheater would have up to a hundred people on a Friday
night. And it's all free, folks. Hurtak wasn't selling tickets.

In the midst of all this, Cass and I take to an older couple, Ray
and Victoria, two psychology grads from San Jose State University
and now living with Jim and Desi. With them we get into psychology and "couples work." Jim and Desi give us the lower level of the
house to live in. And so, for nearly a year, we become part of a small
"spiritual" commune of eight people—three couples and two single
artists, both very talented graphic designers from CalArts who live
upstairs and contribute most of the artwork to Jim's books.

During the week, I take classes at West Valley College right down
the road from us, in philosophy, art, and astronomy. My astronomy
professor comes to Jim's lectures on astrophysics, and they get along
well. Jim is already booked at Stanford to lecture on cosmology and
future science.

Ray and Victoria live in a guesthouse on the property. In the
mornings we would always get together and talk about dreams over
hot cups of Pero. To us, the "high-frequency vehicle" is the unconscious psyche. For now, an *inner* "vehicle" to get carried away by.

This dream psychology is all new to me, but the dreams do provide some insight into me and Cass being together. The two of us marry at the Cats with Ray and Victoria by our side, and then Cass and I head north to Olympia.

* * *

To AVOID NONRESIDENT TUITION, I have to establish residency. I live and work in Washington for a year, loading and unloading seventy-five-pound sacks of material used to make plastic industrial-grade piping. I feel I'm readying myself to return to school, being mentally alert, healthy, fully embodied through manual labor; working right alongside some ex-Marines, I get the job done.

Cass gives birth to our beautiful baby girl, who we name Sophia after the Gnostic text *Pistis Sophia*. In the story, Sophia comes into the earth to express love and wisdom, and our daughter is, indeed, the love and wisdom, the Greek's *philo-sophia*, in our lives.

Once I'm back in school, I find out that José Argüelles isn't returning for the year, focusing instead on his public meld of art and activism, like the launch of the first Earth Day, so I enroll in philosophy classes. I take an art class in which I create large, colorful geometries inspired by Argüelles's book on the mandala. It's clear now that I am "centering" myself through circles and symmetries.

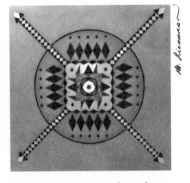

The art teacher is impressed and wants to seek a commission for me to create a large mandala for the school's clock tower. I do a sketch but then decide to move on. Doing it right would take so much time, scaffolding and so forth, and I just want to graduate and get back to acting. I feel the pull of the theater.

I set my sights on auditioning for the Seattle Rep and perhaps joining the Empty Space Theatre, where I once saw a first-rate production of Peter Handke's mystifying *The Ride Across Lake Constance*. As we settle into our cozy Seattle apartment, I go to work for American Building Maintenance, a graveyard shift in a twenty-story office building, cleaning eighteen public restrooms, which I do immaculately. I get into the alchemy of it, turning the stinky bathrooms into sweet-smelling, thoroughly clean commodes. I do everything the job requires perfectly.

On my first work night, a few hours before my shift is over, I tell my boss that I'm finished and he doesn't believe me. After checking it out himself, he's shocked. I think the guy doing the job before me was slack and had the boss thinking that it took a whole shift to clean all these bathrooms. I have the honesty to let him know I'm finished. What other work is there to do? He gives me more bathrooms. I'm up for it.

After two weeks of the cleanest bathrooms in town, he wants to teach me how to shampoo rugs and strip and wax linoleum floors. This is a promotion. Within a month, I'm given a three-story office building with eight offices to clean, requiring rug shampooing and the nightly waxing of the hallway floors. I'm making pretty good money. In the meantime, I find out that the Empty Space Theatre is disbanding. Then, for whatever reason, my audition at the Seattle Rep doesn't come through for me. I'm bewildered because I thought I was right on with my performance. So be it.

With no prospects for acting in Seattle, the city feels a lot farther away than Shasta Community College. It's time to start packing. Cass's parents live in Coronado, San Diego. She would love to see her family with our daughter, Sophia.

Also, my former classmates at CalArts, Sam Woodhouse and Doug Jacobs, have started the San Diego Repertory Theatre, which they will preside over for forty-five years. I can work there and check out the grad school at the UC campus in San Diego. Michael Addison, the former head of the theater school at CalArts, is now running the UC drama department. My prospects are solid.

I give a week's notice at my job.

"Boy, I hate to lose you," the boss says. "Is this about money?"

"No. We're going to San Diego. It's closer to family and friends. We have a baby, you know."

My last night on the job, I shampoo an office carpet, leaving in the nap the design of a mandala. A lovely concentric in the middle of the room. A perfect job. My work as a "maintenance engineer" is complete. The next day my family and I head south to sunny California.

CHAPTER 12

The Ha-Ha Returns

The drive down the West Coast is full of thrilling seascapes and frustrating car trouble, but things settle down once we're in San Diego and plans unfold.

Michael Addison discourages me from pursuing the MFA program at UC San Diego. "You don't need it," he says. "You're way ahead of the program here. You don't need to write papers. Work with Sam and Doug at the repertory company. They need good actors."

Indeed, Sam and Doug come through, and I'm set to play several characters in a production of *A Christmas Carol*. I also enroll in a one-year certification program to become a Montessori teacher. In just a year, Sophia will enter the toddler program at the San Diego Montessori school, and I want to be there for her.

Cass lands a full-time job in the automotive department at Sears, where she quickly becomes their top salesperson. The older salesmen don't like it. They see her as "equality bullshit." They believe she's there only because Sears has to hire women. "What does a woman know about cars and tires?"

A lot! She knows her department. She's an educated woman; she can get things done. To boot, Cass is pretty, and the men coming in to buy automotive stuff, they want to go to her. Also, women coming into the automotive department, many with shopping lists from their husbands, go straight to Cass. They feel more comfortable being helped by a woman.

The only time we hit pause is when Cass's father, a retired air force colonel and devout Christian Scientist, loses a painful battle with cancer. At the end, he puts down his religious books and stops listening to his tapes and spends his final days on a morphine drip, which induces a recurring vision. A luminous crystal ship is waiting for him, he says. A vehicle from God to take him home.

"It looks like it's all set up well for you," I say.

"It is," he replies.

I am struck by the way Richard emptied himself out to be available for entering the ship. He returns to *zero*. I did this when I went into the army. I emptied out, gave up my stuff for "another lifetime." All his books cast aside. The ideologies gone. He just laid on his bed and stared up at the ceiling, looking at the ship ready to take him away. In a few days, he passes.

* * *

SOON I AM COMFORTED THROUGH A DREAM. In it, I see a clown holding the globe of the earth, and the face of the clown is my own. To hold the earth, to be of the world, I *feel* I should drive to LA and start working in the comedy clubs. I am the Fool, the ha-ha soul, the clown at large.

My nights in the comedy clubs are about to begin. It's the same feeling of anticipation and readiness that I used to have when Ed Begley Jr. and I would perform at the Troubadour. In fact, that morning, after having had the dream, I get a call from Ed! Haven't seen or heard from him in years!

"I hear you're down in San Diego and finished a play there," he says.

"Yeah. It went well," I say. "I'm also becoming a Montessori teacher."

"Incredible," he says. "I'm married. I have a six-month-old daughter."

"I'm married too. I've got a year-and-half-old daughter."

"Amazing. Look at us!"

"Ed, this is so fortuitous! I just had this incredible dream and now you call! You remember our days as goofballs at the Troubadour?"

"Definitely!"

"Ah, yes, the Fool that I am. I'm going to start working in the comedy clubs."

"Yes, you have to come to LA and do that!"

Hearing from Ed again, this is a sign to me. Our early days together, nine years ago playing around in the comedy clubs, how easily I took to it. And now the dream. There is the Fool, the ha-ha spirit that will bring me into the world. Yes, I hold the earth, the world, and it will come to me through comedy.

* * *

I HAVE A FRIEND WHO I WORK WITH at the San Diego Repertory Theatre, an actress named Caryn Johnson. She's living nearby with her daughter. I tell her about my plan to start playing open mic nights at the Improv and the Comedy Store in Hollywood. She's been thinking of going to New York to build a one-woman show. She already has a few funny ideas for it. We both encourage each other to go. And both of us will do well, she as Whoopi Goldberg and me as Cosmo Kramer.

It starts with a dream, a vision. It always does. Then you chase it. Let the chase begin!

* * *

I START DRIVING TO LA every week to play open mic nights. I feel right at home. I record each set. I usually go on around midnight and only for five minutes. In both clubs, I wait for hours until it's my turn to perform, which lets me absorb the atmosphere and all the acts. I see established comics at their best and their worst, breaking in material, living and dying in front of the crowds like surfers making the wave or wiping out. The whole scene is alive with laughter.

The world of show business is also there—agents and managers watching their clients and scouting for new up-and-comers. These brokers come with the turf, like remoras or suckerfish, attaching themselves to the biggest, hottest, funniest fish in the room.

Budd Friedman, the owner of the Improv, moves me to the top of the open mic list. It's my start. I play around onstage, improvising for the minutes I'm given, and then I'm out the door for the long drive back to San Diego. There is a lot for me to do at home. Cass has work in the morning, and I take care of Sophia. I'm also after my certification as a Montessori teacher and about to work part time at the school my daughter will attend.

I can't mingle after a show. I just don't have the time. I usually keep to myself anyway. This is about to change as a few comics take to my sense of humor and usually come in to watch my set. I'm about to become a real part of the scene. One night, Budd catches my arm as I head out the door.

"Michael, where are you off to in such a hurry?"

"Hello, Budd. I have a long drive home, and I have work in the morning."

"I'm putting you down for Tuesday, Thursday, and Sunday nights at eleven. See you then," and he closes his big red calendar book.

I have just become a regular at the Improv! Soon, I'll go onstage four times a week around eleven thirty for a fifteen-minute set. I belong to comedy. It's all the motivation and encouragement I need to move to LA. I pass on the Montessori certificate.

Cass is supportive. She relocates to Sears in North Hollywood. We transfer my daughter to a Montessori school in Sherman Oaks, and I enroll in a bus-driving school in Van Nuys. My experience in the army following tanks in my cracker box assures me that I can drive the big Eighty-Eights. In a few months, I complete the course, get my license, and am hired immediately by the Buckley School in Sherman Oaks. Picking up kids in Encino and Bel Air in the morning and taking them home in the afternoon leaves me with time during the day to rest up for the late nights at the club.

There are other perks too. I offer a dime to any kid on my bus who can write a good joke for me. One kid says, "A guy walks into an antique store and says, 'What's new?'" The joke probably came from a Dixie Cup, but I pay up and drop it into my act.

* * *

THROUGH ED, I MEET JEFF GOLDBLUM and Bruno Kirby, and the four of us are often together. Writer-actor-comic Janice Fischer, who's part of a wild, free-form comedy group called the Village Idiots, also runs with us. As does Ed's buddy, actress Cindy Williams, who's making $85,000 a week as one of the stars on the hit sitcom *Laverne & Shirley*. One night she takes us all to a fancy dinner at Chasen's restaurant in Beverly Hills. I choke when I see the bill. It's $125. That's my monthly rent!

* * *

AFTER TWO MONTHS AT THE IMPROV, I catch the attention of Charlie Joffe, one of the most prominent managers in the business. Everyone except me knows that he handles Woody Allen, Billy Crystal, and the hottest comic in the club scene, Robin Williams. "You're very funny," he says to me one night as I come offstage.

"Thank you." I am on my way to the door.

Jay Leno nudges me. "That's Charlie Joffe," he says. "He's got his eye on you. Stick with him."

Three weeks later, Charlie asks me over to a table and wants to talk. I knew this was coming. He's in the room every time I perform.

"Everything you're doing up there is uniquely funny. All the characters, big laughs."

"Thank you, Charlie."

"Come out from behind the characters and let the audience see you once in a while. They want to see you."

"I'm afraid of that."

"I know you are, Michael. So is Robin. You're going to have a career, and it will call upon you to be yourself. You need to be there for that."

"It may not be very funny," I add.

"As long as you're authentic, it will be endearing."

* * *

I CAN SEE MY LIMITATIONS as a comic. I'm not that great. Better, well-seasoned comics hone their acts at the club. They are consistently funny and far more authentic in revealing the intimate details of their lives and their hang-ups through fault-finding confessions. To be so revealed, so "authentic," this is hard for me to get to, to be seen onstage, all out in the open as myself. At this point, I'm coming to the audience through characters and routines. Before I can step out as myself, I have to accept that I'm a "character actor" and stand by this. It can be just as "endearing," don't you think, Charlie?

Well, I do. But coming out as myself, sharing the person behind the mask, will take some time to get to. Actually, a long time. All the way up to the writing of this book.

* * *

CHARLIE IS AROUND A LOT and suggests that I work the Comedy Store too.

"Budd expects loyalty, Charlie," I say. "He doesn't like his regulars working at other clubs in town."

"Robin plays everywhere. You should too."

A time is set in the Original Room of the Comedy Store for Mitzi Shore to see my show. It goes well. So now I'm a regular at both the Comedy Store and the Improv.

Between the two clubs, I'm working every night. At the end of my show, I try to meet the audience as myself. I emerge from the characters and all the fanfare of my show and sincerely thank the audience for coming out. It's just a moment, far from "letting the audience see me," but for now, the audience is laughing and this is big enough for me.

But not everyone is happy or amused. There are nights when I'm all over the room, looking for laughs in all the wrong places. One time, I pick up a woman's purse and sift through it. When some pills in her purse accidently fall to the floor, the woman gets anxious and rather loud, says, "I need my medication! My medication!"

She sues the Comedy Store, and Mitzi has to cough up twenty-five hundred bucks. It results in a rule for all comics in the club: do not touch the belongings of anyone in the audience. Robin and a few other comics working the room often grab stuff from the audience, snatching their jackets or hats and using them to go into character. All that stops.

"Way to go, Richards," Robin teases me.

* * *

ONE NIGHT, A FIRE BREAKS OUT at the Improv. I'm onstage performing at the time, wearing a bathrobe and slippers and puffing on a big cigar, playing a redneck character who complains about the kids today. "I killed people! I was in the war! The problem with the kids today is that they never killed anybody!" The barbed rant is intended to be ironic—what good are kids who want peace and love?

Then I begin to smell smoke, and it's not coming from my cigar or my fault in any way, which it could have been. Just to show you how far out I can get onstage, one night, when a bit I was improvising didn't get a laugh, I told the audience I was going to sacrifice myself to the comedy gods—and I did! I lit my tie on fire and just stood there having no idea how I was going to get out of this. As the fire spread to my coat and appeared on its way toward my face, Jay Leno rushed onstage and doused me with water. I thank Jay for that! He must have had a great punch line, because the audience roared. Great! My sacrifice came through, but tonight is different!

The lights in the room come up and the hosting comic, Jack Graiman, comes in and calmly asks everyone to evacuate the building.

The club really is on fire, and it's too big for anyone to put out. All of us head down the hall and through the dining-bar area of the club and out the front doors. Outside, I turn and look back at the club. The roof is on fire. Flames leap in the air. I'm still in my bathrobe, standing in the street, watching the flames, when a car pulls up fast and club owner Budd Friedman jumps out wearing his bathrobe. We stand next to each other, a fine-looking couple. Fire engines arrive. One parks in the alley, and water shoots out of a hose into the flames. The others spring into action out front. They are now the show. We have become the audience.

Nearly half the club burns down before our eyes. The showroom is mostly destroyed. In the aftermath, Budd manages to keep the club open by converting the dining room into the showroom. There are stairs in there that lead up to the offices, which are now burned out. During my act, if something I try out doesn't go over too well, I go up there and lower a garden hose through an area of open ceiling, imploring the audience to stay calm and take turns breathing through the hose until we can get a full rescue team down to them.

The space is now a very small, intimate room to work. It only seats around forty people, but the regulars keep working there. Franklyn Ajaye, Billy Crystal, Bruce Mahler, Richard Lewis, Paul Reiser, Jay Leno, Barry Marder, Bill Maher, Paula Poundstone, Greg Travis, George Wallace, Robin Williams. The place is always at capacity. Sometimes, to help Budd out, Leno will climb on a ladder to change a bulb or Robin will be out front on the sidewalk performing for folks who can't get in.

* * *

I FIRST SEE ROBIN WILLIAMS perform at the Improv in 1980. He came swooping in, the great eagle that he was. The voices, the accents, the characters, the one-liners between bits—rapid fire. What a set, so spontaneous! I hear he is going to do another set that same night at the Comedy Store. I jump in my car and drive over there. I assume that he is going to repeat most of what I saw at the Improv, but no, he does another thirty minutes of material I hadn't seen before. I think most of it is off the cuff. Over an hour of comedy in one night, and here I am trying to get twenty minutes together. I am humbled.

As I get to know Robin, he shares a concern that he could dry up. I can't see that happening. He always carries a lot of material, funneled through an array of characters well positioned to fly in all directions. When he has a set together, he leans over and says, "My pockets are full." Time to unleash. He is bestowed, graced by the gods with a lot more than most of us, and his pockets were large enough to hold as much as he did.

Though he is made of the same flesh and blood as the rest of us, and suffers as we all do, I never regard him as human. To me, Robin's talent makes him transhuman, more spirit than body. His talent is prodigious, of the gods, too much for us mere humans to comprehend. Every time I see Robin, he seizes the room and destroys the place with laughter. No comic can easily follow him. Holy! Holy! What just came through here?

He once called Jack Nicholson "the Buddha of showbiz." I see Robin as a Maitreya, a laughing Buddha, an evolved master of the ha-ha! I am a mere follower, a babe in the woods. I love him from a distance. Any closer and I dissolve into his presence.

* * *

FOR SEVERAL WEEKS, I don't book myself in the clubs on Friday nights. There's a teacher in town named Joseph Campbell who is giving three lectures—one a week on three consecutive Fridays on the "Hero's Journey." I had read an article on him in the *LA Weekly* and thought he was right on, that all of mythology throughout the world is in each and every one of us. For me to stop the comedy for three Friday nights, well, I *felt* I had to meet this guy.

This series of lectures, held at St. Timothy Catholic Church in Westwood, is open to the public. A five-buck donation gets me in. I'm not familiar with his books yet. Only a few people show up for the series, no more than fifteen, but I can see that he doesn't care how many people are in the room. He only needs a few who are interested to light his fire.

I instantly take a liking to him. He is so informed and so easy to listen to, one of the best teachers I've ever encountered. He takes the most complex ideas from psychology, philosophy, science, and religion and brings it all home so clearly. A ten-year-old could understand this man. It will be eight years later that filmmaker George Lucas, who has based his *Star Wars* epic around the ideas of Campbell, using his book *The Hero with a Thousand Faces* to plot the story, has Joseph and Bill Moyers put together a series of interviews for a program called *The Power of Myth*.

But in 1980, as I sit through those three lectures, I know none of this. All I know is that this guy is on and knows mythology through and through. His application of psychology to the basis of religion and myth is fresh and, for me, downright insightful. He is no ordinary teacher. I thank him personally after each lecture. We hang out a bit and I talk about career, my dream of the clown holding the globe of the world, and now "being in the world" as a comic in the clubs. I am sure he will understand how inspired I am, and he does.

He speaks of inspiration, the archetype of the Fool, the clown myths, namely the Pueblo clowns (the "sacred clowns") or Tricksters, who actually made comedy out of eating dog ca-ca "to prove how durable their stomachs were," to eat the "urine and feces of

136

the world," namely the "shadow" running through everything and making it funny.

When I say goodnight, Joseph raises his hand and gives me a lion claw sign. He sees me as a young man entering the world with all my might. Hunt well. Bring home the meat. He is a wise old hunter saluting my soul.

* * *

ONE NIGHT AT THE IMPROV, producers John Moffitt and Bill Lee see me perform. They approach me as I'm leaving the club. Right on the spot they offer me a TV show called *Fridays*.

"We want you for our show."

This is certainly good news, perhaps the proverbial big break, which should cause me to at least pause and ask what show and why me, but I'm heading for the door, as always, and already hearing my alarm clock going off in a few hours.

"I'm sorry, I have to get up early tomorrow morning. I drive a school bus."

They laugh. They think I'm joking, but once I'm out the door, they realize I'm for real.

"Did he hear what we just said? We just offered him a TV show."

They repeat this to Budd, and he tells them that I really do drive a school bus and that I always leave like that, and they should talk to Charlie Joffe.

Later the next morning, after I'm back from my route, Charlie calls me.

"Michael, you got an offer for a show on ABC, an hour-long weekly sketch comedy show called *Fridays*."

"I don't think I can do the clubs and a sketch comedy show every week," I say.

"Why don't we set up a meeting and you hear them out and see how you feel."

"Where do we do this?"

"I have an office, Michael."

"You do? And all this time I thought you were working out of your car."

"I do that too."

"So, do you want to handle all of this, Charlie?"

"I already am."

* * *

THE OFFICES OF ROLLINS, JOFFE, MORRA, AND BREZNER are located in the Producers Building at Universal. Their hallway wall is decorated with headshots of their only clients: Woody Allen, Billy Crystal, Robert Klein, Dick Cavett, Melissa Manchester, David Letterman, and Robin Williams. Soon they will add Jim Carrey, Jimmy Brogan, and me.

I arrive carrying a Mead college ruled notebook. This is my first official business meeting since I left San Diego for LA six months ago, and I want to be ready to take notes. Charlie's longtime partner, Jack Rollins, works out of New York and won't be part of the meeting, but I meet Buddy Morra and Larry Brezner, both of whom I've seen watching acts and schmoozing at the Improv. They work with Charlie here in LA. They're a family.

We meet in Charlie's office, which doubles as a conference room. He comes in and, like his associates, he is upbeat and ready to go. These guys love meetings. Everyone's happy. Offers are fun. We take our seats in the office. John Moffitt and Bill Lee haven't arrived yet. It gives us time to get a game plan.

"Let them pitch the show," Charlie instructs. "It's just a pitch. You don't have to swing."

"I shouldn't beg?" I say. "I'll do it! I'll do it! Please let me do it!"

"We'll do the begging," Morra says.

There's laughter. Spirits are high. A few minutes later, John and Bill arrive and are brought into Charlie's office. They're feeling good too.

"Congratulations, you've got a go for the show," Charlie says, taking the lead. "Tell us how you see Michael in all of this?"

They lay it all out: I'll be part of a seven-member cast. They think I'm perfect for the show. They love the characters they have seen me do in my act.

"Yeah, I need to write them all down, keep track of them," I say.

"Michael has a notebook for all his characters," Charlie adds, pointing to the book in front of me.

"Do you write your act?" Bill asks.

"Yeah, I do it all myself," I say. "Everything."

"So, you've got a writer with his own characters," Charlie says. "And a performer. All in one."

It doesn't take long before Charlie has them agreeing to a writer's salary and that I have full ownership of my characters. This is on top of the performer's salary I'll get for being on camera. He wraps up the meeting.

"The performer's salary can be discussed if this is something Michael wants to do," he says.

I get to sleep on it. Whew! This is show business! John and Bill leave, and we're by ourselves now.

"Sketch comedy," Brezner muses. "Michael can do characters. I really like the premise. Plus, Bernie Brillstein is behind these guys. It's like a West Coast *Saturday Night Live*. ABC is into it. It could work."

"You can do this show or work on your stand-up," Charlie says. "You're only seven months into doing your act. Another six or seven months could be good for you."

"Charlie, I'm not really a stand-up comic," I say. "I'm an actor. Sketch comedy is a good format for me."

"You've got all your characters in that book?" Morra asks.

"Here?" I tap on my notebook. "I don't have anything written down."

"What's in there?" Charlie asks.

"Nothing." I quickly finger through the empty pages. "I brought it along to take notes."

They break out laughing.

"Oh, they think I've got all my characters written out in here."

"Don't worry about it, Michael. You're the character they want," Brezner says.

"A bunch of characters," I say.

"A bunch of characters," Charlie concludes.

I sent over a gift to Charlie for putting together my deal. A copy of C. G. Jung's book *Psychology and Alchemy*. Inside the book, I wrote a thank-you note for securing my deal. Once he got the book, Charlie called me and was touched by the concept of turning a deal, a client's career, into "gold."

CHAPTER 13

Fridays

J ohn Moffit and Bill Lee continue to assemble the *Fridays* cast and writing staff. Their process is relatively fast. Bruce Mahler, a regular at the Improv and probably one of the best prop comics going, and Mark Blankfield and his wife Brandis Kemp, fresh off *El Grande de Coca-Cola*, are among the other comic actors who land the gig. I'm told that the producers are also interested in a stand-up from New York who's performing at the Comedy Store. Some of us go together to watch the guy's set.

"Do you know Larry David?" Bruce asks.

"No, I've never heard of him," I say.

"He's very New York. A regular at Catch a Rising Star. They brought him out here for the network."

"Wow. They flew him out. He must be good. The network? Did the network come out to see you?"

"They know who we are. We're local."

True. As a regular, everybody knows who you are. You don't really break in an act to be seen for the first time in LA. There's always someone who's someone in the audience. That's Hollywood. If you really want to stay under the radar, you work after 11:00 p.m.

Larry's showcase is at nine thirty. That's close to bedtime for the suits. After ten thirty, you better be hotter than the sun for them to be there.

I don't like to watch another comic just before I'm going on. Later, I will find out that Larry shares that dislike. It's one of the first things the two of us will talk about as we get to know each other. Watching comics before I perform can trigger insecurity. I might start second-guessing my act. You can get sprayed by the last comic, especially if he or she killed. If I've got their act in my head, I'm in trouble.

So I head into the room when I hear the emcee about to introduce me. I come on as if I'm the only act of the night. I'm fresh, ready. Giddyup!

I don't tell jokes. I go broad, get physical, do faces, characters, anything to get the laughs. I'm simply a young knockabout clown.

I have never felt like a stand-up comic, but I do try to play within the format. Still, if you're showcasing, you do not want to follow me, because I can upset the room by tilting it into the big and bawdy. Character comics like Andy Kaufman, Jim Carrey, Howie Mandel, Sam Kinison, or Robin Williams can rip up the format and carry the audience away. If these guys were on before you, cancel your showcase.

Larry needn't worry. He's going up early. The "knockabouts" come later.

I'm sitting in the back with Bruce Mahler and looking forward to Larry's show. John and Bill are in the room, of course, with *Fridays* co-producer Jack Burns, and they're chatting it up with two executives from ABC as if they're all family. Jack is in his element. He was once part of a hot Vegas comedy act, so he's comfortable in a club. His comedy partner Avery Schreiber was sort of a mentor to Eddie and me at the Troubadour.

Then it's time. "Let's hear it for Larry David!"

Larry walks to the stage. He's funny looking. That's a plus in my book. I like him already. He has long, frizzy hair and wears a baseball jacket, looking like he's taken the Second Avenue subway to Hollywood. He's not smiling, doesn't seem happy at all. In fact, he's annoyed. He's playing annoyed. He starts out in character, complaining about lawyers. A lawyer said something to him the other day that ticked him off. "All of 'em, the whole profession, stinks!"

It's not just lawyers, though. He seems disdainful of the audience, as if he is bothered that he has to be there and has to talk to us. *Why do I have to make you laugh? Can't you find something funny on your own?* It doesn't seem like he's joking. He has no punch lines, only punches. It's like we're catching him mid rant. It's sort of funny, but also unsettling, which is the way Larry works. He's playing a guy on edge. He wants you on edge. This amuses me. He's pretty good so far.

Suddenly, Larry stops talking, looks across the room, sees something or someone that bothers him, says, "Fuck it!" and walks off the stage and straight out the back door. No explanation. No discernable problem. Just "Fuck it!" and the guy with the frizzy hair and baseball jacket is gone.

Everybody sits in silence, waiting for an explanation or another version of the ride to kick in. Surely there's more. I wait for Larry to return with a hilarious punch line. Jack and Bill look at each other, trying to figure out what is going on. That strikes me as interesting. They have never seen this before? There's some uneasy seconds before the emcee rushes up to the stage and introduces the next comic. Maybe it's Larry again? Brilliant. He'll come up as another comic, wearing a hairpiece, doing another voice, or he'll run back in and apologize, explaining he had to put money in the parking meter. But no. Larry doesn't return. This is not a put-on. There's no comeback. Larry just said, "Fuck it," and that's the show.

I think Larry told me later that he didn't like the way the audience felt. He's like the Soup Nazi. If he doesn't like the audience, "No comedy for you!"

John and Bill have seen Larry when he's on, and since they flew him out here, they arrange for another show the next night. I am working at the Improv so I don't see it, but he must have been at his best because he gets the job as a cast member and a writer. Well done, Larry! A master of his domain.

* * *

ONCE THE REST OF THE CAST and writers are assembled—a group that includes Rich Hall, Melanie Chartoff, John Rourke, Darrow Igus, Maryedith Burrell, Bruce Kirschbaum, and Larry Charles— Jack Burns organizes a comedy lab in one of our large production offices. Jack was a Second City guy who loves comedy ensemble work. He takes on multiple roles as the show's script supervisor, writer, cast member, announcer, and part-time producer. For two weeks, he gives us different improvisational exercises, including one that poses an interesting challenge: "Play nothing." How do you play doing nothing?

Just before my turn at playing nothing, unnoticed, I go out the door and drive home. That's my spin on "nothing." When I return, I play that I never left the room. When I am questioned about leaving the workshop, I take the position it never happened. "What are you talking about? I did nothing. Nothing happened."

Through these odd, challenging daily improv sessions, we get to know each other's strengths and styles. Everyone is quite good, and I'm happy to be among them.

* * *

FRIDAYS DEBUTS ON APRIL 11, 1980. I think I can speak for everyone involved when I say that making a weekly one-hour live show means hardly having enough time to finish anything. Sketches are pitched at the start of the week and assignments are handed out. Everybody is gripped by the same questions and concerns: What sketch am I doing, will I be funny, and how much of me is in the show?

A ticking clock hangs over everything we do, but mostly a sense of competition. The two opening sketches and the musical guest are basically the show. Everybody wants to be at the top of the show. Rewrites and line changes go right up until we are live, particularly after dress rehearsal. Hopefully you'll remember your lines. I don't read off cue cards—I have to know my lines to stay in character. Line changes all the way up to camera time is always a threat to my memory, but I come through.

I launch a character named Dick, a Vegas swinger with a very goofy swagger. The antithesis of Andy Kaufman's lounge singer Tony Clifton, Dick is an early incarnation of the "hipster doofus" in Kramer. Dick debuts in the second episode of *Fridays*,  bringing home a date—played by Brandis Kemp—after taking her to the Sizzler. Once in his apartment, Dick changes into a silk bathrobe, makes drinks, recites poetry, and dances his date onto his leather sofa.

I attend to every little detail in creating the sketch. The anxious moves that Dick puts on his lady friend, a clumsy, overbearing seduction—all of it causes the lady to flee from his apartment. The sketch gets lots of laughs, and so "Dick" becomes a recurring character.

Midway through the first season, I bring out another character, "Battle Boy." I play a kid who loves war and sets up battles with all his army toys and blows them all up. To present this character to Bill and John, I ask our art director to get me a thousand pounds of dirt. The unusual request prompts a few questions, but soon I have an enormous mountain of dirt on a special stage that can handle the weight.

I dig tunnels, make forts, burn toy soldiers, blow everything up! Like Dick, Battle Boy becomes a recurring character throughout the show's three seasons.

* * *

JACK BURNS THINKS WE'RE HITTING the mark, that the show's take on war, politics, drugs, and sex is cutting edge, exciting, raw, and dangerous. Musical guests like the Clash, Devo, Warren Zevon, and the Plasmatics compliment the radical vibe.

We bring in weekly guest stars, and none makes more of an impression on me than Shelley Winters, who may not seem new or cutting edge on-screen but behind the scenes she's no one with whom you want to tangle. In a well-written piece by Larry called "Frieda Mueller, Art Agent," Shelley plays an agent to famous artists. Larry plays Van Gogh and Blankfield is Toulouse-Lautrec. Demanding from day one, the two-time Oscar-winning actress doesn't realize there are going to be line changes as the sketch is sharpened and revised all the way up to camera time on Friday night. During rehearsal on Thursday, she sees that she has more lines than the day before, and she's not happy about it.

After counting the number of words, she calls her agent and instructs him to ask for more money. I am easily within earshot of her conversation. She doesn't care. "If they want me to say more god-damn words, they have to pay me more fucking money," she says.

I don't know where that request lands, but she agrees to continue rehearsing the sketch. However, about halfway through she stops as if something else is bothering her, something unrelated to the lines she has to say. I can't figure out what it might be. She looks at me, then Larry and Mark and everyone there. She looks pained, like she's just sucked on a lemon. Then she cries out, "My God, why is everybody on this show so fucking ugly?"

I say to myself, "God, she's right. We are ugly. We're all just a bunch of freaks. These freaky, unknown, crazy comic actors." It's as

if Shelley has found herself in hell, her version of hell being sur-
rounded by ugly people. I can hear her thinking: "I'm Academy
Award–winner Shelley Winters! Where is Robert Mitchum? Paul
Newman? Sidney Poitier? Even Ernest Borgnine—where the hell
is he?"

* * *

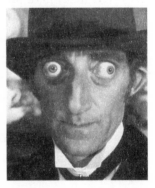

THE MOST FUN I HAVE with any guest
star on the show is with Marty Feldman.
We're always messing around backstage.
He loves physical comedy and goes hard
at it! In a sketch routine, Marty instigates
a pratfall where he and cast member Mark
Blankfield will throw themselves through
a large door window. This is a last-minute
idea. Except for the construction of the
door window to come apart as they crash through it, there's no padding on the floor to break their fall, and Marty lands hard on his side.

It's done live on air, of course, and it gets a huge laugh. I watch
from offstage and am not surprised that this forty-seven-year-old
star of *Young Frankenstein* and *Silent Movie* can throw himself
around like that for a laugh. He's a true knockabout comic. Without
padding, it's rough-and-tumble comedy.

"Are you all right?" I ask Marty afterward.

"I can't remember," he says, with eyes bulging like a pinball game gone tilt. "When are we going to do the sketch?"

Sadly, Marty dies of a heart attack shortly after his appearance on the show. Of course, I think of how hard he hit that floor. That should have killed him on the spot.

* * *

OF ALL THE SHOW'S GUESTS, Andy Kaufman's appearances give *Fridays* a real buzz of unpredictability. You never know what Andy is going to do.

Andy doesn't work with cue cards. I'm the same way. The only time I use cue cards on *Fridays* is when I dump them in front of Andy during the opening sketch of the show that airs February 20, 1981. The episode is instantly infamous for what appears to be a fight between me and Andy, and the show cuts to commercial.

What never gets out, though, is the challenge Andy poses the entire week, starting on Monday when he won't come out of his dressing room for the writers meeting. The reason? He is doing Transcendental Meditation. He won't come out until he's finished. He's actually transcended the writers meeting.

Overall, we have only so much time to create and rehearse the sketches, and as I said, it's never enough time.

By Tuesday, Andy hasn't approved any script for himself. So people are getting uptight with him. In confidence, Andy tells me that he only wants to do a sketch with me. He gives me his telephone number and tells me to call him if I have any ideas.

That evening I call him, as instructed.

"I have an idea," I say.

"Great, let me hear it," he says.

"Well, you know that character you do, Tony Clifton?" I say, referring to his aggressive lounge singer character, who he swears is not him but another person.

148

"Not you too!" he yells. "Fuck you!"

And he hangs up.

I call him back without getting an answer, and he refuses to speak to me throughout the week. If he sees me in the studio, he turns and walks the other way. Midweek, Jack Burns tells me they've come up with an idea for a sketch with Andy that will open the show. Andy and Maryedith Burrell and Melanie Chartoff and me will be a foursome dining at a restaurant. Each person will get up from the table and sneak off to secretly smoke a joint in the bathroom. Upon returning, we will show the effects.

The sketch reads funny. On its feet it's hilarious. Andy is still ignoring me.

At dress rehearsal, always with a live audience, the sketch kills.

I know something here: the night before the show, Jack gets me alone and tells me—and only me—that live, on air, during the scene, Andy is going to break out of the sketch. The other actors will have to deal with it as it happens. Andy did say that he wanted to do only one sketch in the show, and he wanted it with me. This is it. Well, I've got an idea of what to do, so I'll keep it under my hat until then.

Doing the sketch live, even from the top of the scene, Andy isn't saying all his lines. I'm not sure if he's breaking out now or what. When Andy takes his turn coming from the bathroom "high," he finally breaks from the script announcing he can't play a stoned guy. Maryedith continues laughing both "high" in character but also at our predicament, stuck without a sketch. I finally make my move: I walk off the set, grab the cue cards, and drop them on the table in front of Andy. The audience roars. Andy responds by throwing a glass of water at me. Melanie plays along and dumps the bread basket over his head and throws butter in his hair. He gets angry and tries to put the butter in her face. As they argue, I turn offstage to camera. "Cut out," I say in mock distress. Seeing Andy's aggression toward Melanie, I try to calm him down as Jack Burns rushes in to go for Andy. Now the crew comes in to break up the fight while Mark Blankfield continues to calmly wait tables. He's brilliant. "Cut out! Cut out!" I urge. Jack yells out, "Bobby, go to commercial!" End of sketch. Commercial up.

Everyone around us thinks the whole thing was real. Backstage, Andy is playing upset. He's trying to apologize to everyone. He's crying, tears and everything. "I'm so sorry!" He's just great. The crew wants to beat him up! "It's was a live show and the jerk stops doing the sketch!" He did, didn't he? Well, that's his genius at work.

* * *

As FRIDAYS COMES TO AN END after its third season, I offhandedly pitch an idea to John Moffitt: a TV version of *Waiting for Godot* where I want to do the play in the Mojave Desert near a freeway off-ramp. John ran it by someone at HBO, and they're interested. "This can happen, Michael." I envision Andy Kaufman playing Lucky, the actor Divine for Pozzo. I'll play Vladimir, Jim Carrey as Estragon.

Before the offers can go out, though, HBO needs a deal with Samuel Beckett. The network writes him a letter. Beckett responds with annoyance and puts an end to this project. "If I intended to have my play set in the California desert under a freeway, I would have written it that way! Absolutely not!—SB"

Considering the rejection, God knows what Peter Brook would have done with *Godot*. I suppose something more outlandish than the large white box for a stage with incoming red feathers. Whatever. I need to move on from *Fridays*. I just want to read for TV, film, and stage. Billy Crystal did *Soap*. Robin, though he's still in the clubs, is doing *Mork & Mindy*. I have no interest in returning to the comedy clubs. But Charlie is big on it and feels that's what I must do to stay alive in this business.

"You don't want to be relying on an agent to keep you going," he says. "Get your act together. It got you *Fridays*. Stay with the act. We'll get you an agent, but for now, get back to the act."

CHAPTER 14

The Real Don Johnson

I'm back in the clubs. On my first night at the Comedy Store, Robin Williams comes over. "I thought you were dead," he says, implying that unless I'm working out in the clubs, I'm not alive. Robin says nothing about my work on *Fridays*. I know there wasn't a lot of heat from the show. As Charlie said, "*Fridays* really didn't do anything for you." More than likely, Robin didn't watch the show, and if he did catch a few episodes, it was clear from tonight that I didn't make much of an impression on him.

It doesn't matter. *Fridays* was a good school for training. I have no regrets about doing the show. It was more of the clown holding up my world. Robin's juice is from the clubs. It's the clubs or bust for him. It's his lifeline. I get onstage, but I'm not hooked up to it anymore. After *Fridays*, I'm emptied out, back to zero. I cling to my past as a knockabout clown. I don't want to be there, but I keep going in at night "to stay alive."

Charlie and Robin put a whammy on me. I'm dead if I don't stick with stand-up. I can't shake them off. So I push myself to get back into an act and spend the next few months working four nights a week. Two nights at the Improv and two nights at the Comedy Store Annex in Westwood.

I'm miserable.

* * *

I'M ALWAYS OFF THE WALL going for the bizarre, and here I stay under the radar working late nights because I'm going further into the strange and out there—I'm just all-out nuts onstage. I don't want anybody to see what I'm doing. For a lot of it, I'm going in without an act. It's just free fall and whatever happens. One night I go on and just eat watermelon and that's my show. Fifteen minutes of this, I burp, and it's goodnight.

Most of the characters I conjure up don't want to be there, just like me. They're angry and rowdy. They screw around with the audience and scream. What? I do a lot of screaming! My shows are like experimental theater. Like Peter Handke's *Offending the Audience*, it's my "anti-play." There are some laughs, but not a lot of joy coming out of me. It's dark. A clown in the night.

I'm not the only one screaming onstage. There's a young comic fresh off open mic night who watches me rant. He screams too. He's angry onstage and doesn't give a fuck about it. He scares me. I think he's crazy and I'm heading in the same direction. He gets a few spots very late at night, usually in the morning hours. Somebody tells me he's "the sweeper." He clears the room so they can close the club. One night he comes over to me after I've done one of my offensive sets getting minimal laughs. I'm in the corner of the club, slumped in a chair. He tells me what a pleasure it is to watch me work. He thinks the two of us are the only comics doing anything funny. He only makes me feel more desperate to get out of the clubs.

His name is Sam Kinison.

One night I hear that he told the audience he wasn't really a stand-up comedian but rather a guy just off the street who intended to make a name for himself. Then he pulled out a gun, a toy gun, but only he knew that when he pointed it at the audience. He definitely swept the room. It makes me think: He's pretending that he's a guy out to shoot everybody in the room and he's watching me? I got to get out of here. This is getting too big and scary. And then I have a dream where Sam and I are standing together. There's yelling going on and this causes the American flag to rip in half. No good. I don't want to work in the clubs right now.

* * *

I GET A CALL FROM JIM CARREY. I wish I could tell him about *Godot*, but alas. He's with Charlie too, and he's upset with their management. His show *Duck Factory* didn't get picked up and he's concerned, not about the fate of his show but what the network said about him. It's got him in a tizzy. They told Larry Brezner that the faces Jim makes are "too big and scary."

"What did Larry say?" I ask.

"Larry agreed with them!" He then told Jim to lighten up making faces, don't make so many faces.

"But you get laughs making faces. That's one of the reasons you're starring in their show," I tell him.

I wonder what Charlie has to say. He's probably in New York with Woody.

Doesn't matter. Jim is going to dump these managers. He wants to move on without them. He's not messing around.

I'm shocked by what he's told me. Jim always gets big laughs making faces. It's clear that the network doesn't know what to do with him, and Charlie and company have just lost sight of a great talent. This causes me concern. If they are this unsympathetic with Jim, they can be wrong about me staying in the clubs. It's decided. I just need to get out and read for parts. I'm not going back into the clubs, Charlie. And as much as I would like people "to see me," to be more "authentic" as you put it, right now, acting, playing whatever "character" I can step into, is all that matters.

* * *

"Charlie, you gotta help me get an agent," I insist. "I have to get out of the club scene for a while."

Charlie feels my plight. And so, with Morra his associate, the two of us go to see this agent at ICM, one of the town's major talent agencies. Morra tells me that most of these agents are always blowing smoke up your ass, so we'll hear the agent out, and then you tell him what you want. I intend to do just that.

So there we are in the office with the agent, and he's putting on the Ritz.

"You heard of James Caan?" he asks.

"Yeah," I say.

"He's doing a new movie. I think you'd be good in it. You and him together."

He's definitely blowing smoke up my ass. Yeah, James Caan is waiting to work with me, right. How about Brando?

I have to get to the point with this agent. Can you send me out for guest spots on TV? To my relief, he sends me out that week. It's a guest-starring role on *Cheers*. I read for it and land the part. I'm with ICM. Now I'm on track with an agent.

* * *

FORMER DIRECTOR OF *Fridays* Tom Moore, who came on board in our last season when poor Jack Burns was derailed by a cocaine problem, gives me a great part in the farce *Wild Oats*, which he's directing at LA's Mark Taper Forum as part of the Olympic Arts Festival. Gordon Davidson, the artistic director of the Center Theatre Group, also offers me two roles in a West Coast premiere of Arthur Miller's *The American Clock*. Arthur is there for this. He talks to us about the play and makes a few line changes. He never says anything to me about my performance, and I take that as a good sign.

* * *

MY AGENT SENDS ME OUT for a number of shows, all guest-starring parts, and I land them all. Being on a soundstage or in a theater suits me. I really do feel much better here than in the comedy clubs.

* * *

EVERY ONCE IN A WHILE when I am between work, I feel compelled to retreat from everything and head for the hills nearby. Sometimes I feel like I want to wander around the earth with just a knapsack and sleeping bag. I feel a strange pull to tramp. I will take long walks through the Granada Hills up to the top, where I have a panoramic view of the San Fernando Valley on one side and the Mojave Desert on the other. I know the boy in me or the soul in me is hiking to the top of Baldwin Hills.

These walks have the same urgency. I am aligned with the north–south axis of the earth, with the sun rising and setting east to west. This orientation secures me. It feels holy to me. This is enough. I can't go any farther. I draw the line. If it were not for my wife and daughter, I would cross the line and tramp the world. This nudge to drift can pester me. It's got to be my grandmother. I too am touched by what caused her to wander away. However, I know I can make it home. I will not lose my way.

* * *

I HAVE A DREAM:

I hear some odd music playing in the distance. I walk toward it and come to a gate, which I enter and find myself in an area of brush and trees. The gate closes behind me. I continue to follow the music. I see in the distance a cabin with a porch and the people who are creating this music. I want to be with them, to be closer to this enchanting music that they are playing.

But as I get closer, the music becomes louder and chaotic. It's not music at all. It's utter chaos. I see the people, and they are dirty and sick looking. I am horrified. The sound they are making is only a maddening noise. I must get out of there fast or I will become one of them.

I quickly turn around to make my way back to the gate. I am terrified that the gate might have locked behind me. If it doesn't open, I will not be able to return. I'll have to remain with these deranged people, and I will become mad myself. But I reach the gate and to my relief the latch opens. I'm able to get out of there. I find myself standing on a parade float wearing a beautiful gold watch and waving to thousands of people so happy to see me.

I don't always know the meaning of my dreams, but when I wake up from this one, I know the gold watch and the waving to thousands of people represents a career success. But the dream is also a warning. It would be a mistake to wander away from my acting career. I must stay put in my community.

Maybe later I can pursue a spiritual life, a retiring into the Mysteries, into the earth that I'm holding, like the clown that's still holding me.

For now, I can't cross the line.

* * *

To STAY IN LINE, I decide to change agents for one who will send me out more. There's always something going on in movies, television, and the theater, I tell them. I want to work all the time. That's my gold watch. They're on board. Within days, I'm sent out to read for a part on *St. Elsewhere* and I get the role. It's a three-episode arc and pays well. I buy myself a gold watch.

From then on, I work constantly, racking up credits on *Scarecrow and Mrs. King, It's a Living, Hill Street Blues, Sidekicks*, and the miniseries *Fresno*. I also land co-starring roles in two movies, the whacky comedy *Transylvania 6-5000* and the British satire *Whoops Apocalypse*, in which I'm given the Peter Sellers–like opportunity to play six different characters.

* * *

My AGENT'S BIGGEST CLIENT is Don Johnson, whose TV series, *Miami Vice*, has rocketed from ratings hit to cultural phenomenon, and while I'm finishing *Whoops Apocalypse* in Florida, he sets it up for me to meet with producer Michael Mann. I go in wearing a dapper suit from one of my characters in the film.

Michael doesn't have a script for me now, but he does have an episode coming up that he'll put me in. So, without a read, I'll be guest-starring soon on an episode of television's top-rated series. Done. I fly home. Take a walk in the hills—keep "in line." Wait a few weeks for *Miami Vice*.

My episode is titled "The Fix," and I'm cast to star as a bookie fixing basketball games. I have multiple scenes, lots of dialogue, and presumably a hip wardrobe. By the time I take an early evening flight to Miami, I have memorized all my lines. The show is big. Let's get it done! Arriving that night at 11:00 p.m., I check into the beautiful art deco hotel room they reserved for me. A script is slid under my door with a call sheet for seven in the morning.

With an early call, I want to get a good night's sleep, but I quickly look through the script to check my lines and…what?

Almost all my dialogue has been changed.

Never mind the jet lag. I'm awake now. I have new lines to memorize. When I think I've got them down, I look at the clock. It's 1:00 a.m. That 7:00 a.m. call time hangs over me. I really should get some sleep now. Six hours will have to do. I'm better with eight hours, but I'll get by.

Once in bed, though, I can't sleep. I keep going over the new lines, my character, my wardrobe, what I'll look like. Most of my new scenes are on a yacht now. That's quite a change. And I like some of my old lines better. Why did they change them?

It's 4:00 a.m. I'm badly jet-lagged. I can't sleep and I'm so anxious about work. I keep going over the lines. I flub some. I don't know them well enough. To change the lines the night before and with an early call—shit!

At 5:00 a.m., even if I could sleep, how am I going to work with only two hours sleep?

By 6:00 a.m. I'm a mess. I'm thinking of a conversation I once had with actor Harry Dean Stanton. He was sick with a bad flu on his first day of shooting the movie *The Black Marble*. He told me that he used the flu and played the character sick. It worked. Can I play my character exhausted, just fried without sleep?

Half an hour later, forget it. No sleep. I get up to shower. The phone rings. Dripping wet, I answer it. The driver is in the lobby to take me to the set. I'm tired and look done in. Well, this is my character.

At the set, I'm told we'll start shooting two scenes on the yacht in an hour. I'm directed to makeup and hair. "Please give me your best at makeup," I say. "I didn't sleep last night."

Then I'm off to wardrobe, mumbling my new lines, looking as if I'm talking to myself. I try on various silky shirts and pants that they pulled for me. The assistant director pops in and says they're moving fast and will be ready for me sooner than expected. "Thirty minutes, Michael. Have you had breakfast?"

"No," I say, more focused on zipping up my pants. Ugh! Then the zipper catches on the material. I work to get it undone. "Can I get some scrambled eggs and toast? I'm really jet-lagged. I didn't get any sleep last night."

"That's no good," he says. "You want a cup of coffee?"

The zipper frustrates me.

"I don't know. I don't drink coffee. What's with this damn thing?" Finally, I zip the pants up. "Jeez!" I sit down to rest. I'm tired and cranky. No sleep.

"So, you just want eggs and toast?" the AD asks, trying to keep things moving forward.

"Yeah, thanks."

Wardrobe is finally set. They're going to iron my clothes and bring them to my dressing room when ready. I head there now. On my way, someone on the crew recognizes me from *Fridays* and goes on about how much he loves *Saturday Night Live*. It makes no sense. I tell him that I'm zonked, that I didn't get any sleep last night.

"Have a Cuban coffee," he says.

"Yeah, the AD thought I should have a cup of coffee."

"No, no, not regular coffee, a Cuban coffee!" he says. "It gives you way more energy. We're on location sometimes at four in the morning. We have to drink it. It's how we get things done. I'll get you one."

"Okay."

Nice guy, I think. He's off to the food wagon.

I reach my trailer as the AD arrives with my eggs and toast.

"That was fast," I say.

"They're still figuring out the lighting. Relax. It'll be a few minutes."

"Thanks."

I sit and wolf down my breakfast anyway. I go over my lines again. I think I got them. Maybe I could sleep for a few minutes. I lie down and feel a snooze coming on, but wardrobe arrives, and they're banging around hanging up my clothes. Then the crew guy arrives with the Cuban coffee. A small shot of this stuff in a little paper cup.

"Here you go, Mike."

"So, this'll do it, huh?"

"Oh yeah. It's like an espresso. It'll give you the energy you probably need."

I'm a health food guy, I tell him. I don't usually drink caffeine.

"I don't drink much of it either," he says. "But this gets you going. It works."

The AD appears. "About fifteen minutes, Michael."

I swig the shot of Cuban coffee, stand up, and dress for my scenes. I hope this Cuban coffee gives me a boost. I'm fading.

Within minutes, I feel a surge of energy. I'm wired and ready to go. But after an hour goes by, what's going on with this production? The AD returns and says there are delays. They're going to pick up some scenes from the previous day. "They'll get to my scenes on the boat after lunch," he says. Really? I could have slept, but now I'm all hyped up on the Cuban coffee. It definitely has me awake.

By eleven the buzz is wearing off. I'm tired but still unable to sleep. I get an early lunch hoping I can snooze for an hour. The AD orders me back into hair and makeup for a touch-up. They're going to shoot the yacht scenes after lunch. Tired, and with my energy level falling, I go back to the truck and get another Cuban coffee. I'm back up—and ready. However, lunch ends and another hour goes by. More delays. The schedule goes back to some exterior shooting on the dock outside the yacht. They don't need me yet. It's 3:30 p.m., and I drink another of these supersonic coffees.

Around five, the AD says they're changing my scenes to a night shoot with some shots on the deck. They need to relight the yacht now. Sleeping now is out of the question. There's nothing I can do except stay ready. That means more Cuban coffee.

I begin to notice a change in me. I start talking louder, my hands are quivering, and my movements are slightly exaggerated. They call me to the set, a multimillion-dollar yacht that glistens in the lights from being polished all day. I'm playing opposite NBA legend Bill Russell. I'm told he just got here. What? I've been here all day! This makes no sense. He only has a few lines.

I didn't know it was going to be Bill Russell. I see him bending down low to clear the height of the opening to enter a large lounging area on the yacht. He's so tall. Too tall? Inhumanly tall? I've never been near a professional basketball player on a glistening yacht.

I haven't slept in twenty-four hours. My nerves are up. Don Johnson will be here soon. I'll be meeting him. I remember *Fortune and Men's Eyes*. He's come a long way from that play back in 1969. Fifteen years ago! Now he's the hottest actor on TV! I remember that Don Johnson look-alike who picked me up on the highway and had me almost undress in his attic apartment. He could've easily been Don's double. I bounce from Don's double to Artaud's "Double," the other side of myself. It's a line I shouldn't cross? Artaud crossed it and went mad. What's moving me from one side of this boat to the other? Cuban coffee. Somebody is showing me around. My blocking, the thought of Don Johnson, my lines, I'm trying to cross over to my character, I'm unraveling.

I can't remember a single line of my dialogue! Panicked, I think momentarily about writing my lines on the floor with some chalk or something, if I even knew where the camera was going to be. The caffeine in my body is taking me down.

A woman asks if I want to go over my lines. She seems kind, and I want to cry, "Help me!" But I manage to hold it in. I'm grateful she's here. "Yes, please get me through this," I say.

"Sure," she says.

She's an angel.

"Thank you for being here," I say—or think I say. I don't really know what comes out of my mouth. My speech is slurred. I'm shaking. I ask the woman to get me some chalk. What? I start crying involuntarily. I ask her to help me. I'm having a severe reaction to the coffee. I can't stop shaking. I'm on the floor. An ambulance is called. I'm spinning. The EMT arrives.

"What'd you have to eat and drink?" as he takes my pulse.

I mention Cuban coffee.

"How many did you have?" he asks.

"Eight," I say. "Maybe more."

"All today?"

"S-starting this morning," I stutter.

He's a smart paramedic. He's seen this before with Cuban coffee. "You're having a caffeine reaction," he says. "Only have one, maybe two of those things per day. What you did is like drinking thirty cups of coffee. Your blood pressure is 182. Really high."

They strap me on a gurney and take me off the boat. On the way, we pass Don Johnson. It's the first time we see each other. Though I'm unable to speak, I try to convey to the show's star that I am coming apart. I'm trembling. It's Don Johnson! I shake even more furiously. Anxiety. Fear. Caffeine. Embarrassment. I can't stop it.

"What's with this guy?" Don says.

Someone tells him that the medic said, "He's high."

I try to explain. This time words come out of my mouth: "I'm not doing this. I can't get away from it. It's all over me." What I say doesn't make any sense to Don or me.

"He's on drugs, right?" Don says.

No, I'm at the end of my line with Cuban coffees. Be merciful. Don is perturbed. We have to shut down the shoot. As I'm taken away, I hear him snap at someone. "Is this my agent's guy? Get him on the phone!"

It's a while later, and I'm in my hotel room. A production assistant has brought in a large bag of oranges. My agent is on the phone, asking what happened.

"I had a bad reaction to caffeine," I say. "I just have to eat oranges, a lot of vitamin C."

"A reaction to caffeine? How did that happen?"

"I drank these Cuban coffees. I didn't know that each one is like four cups of coffee."

"How many did you drink?"

"I think around seven or eight, around thirty cups of coffee."

"Jesus."

"I was jet-lagged. I was trying to keep up my energy."

"Don called, and he's chewing me out for getting you on the show. He thinks you're a drug addict and messing everything up."

"I don't take drugs. It was a caffeine reaction!"

"Right. I told him you're into health foods and yoga."

"What did he say?"

"That's even worse."

The next day on the job, we get it done. In my final scene, my character is shot to death. I imagine Don loved that scene. That's a wrap! Don left the set before I am able to explain what happened last night. I regret we didn't talk.

Maybe... get a coffee?

CHAPTER 15

The Truth

Before the *Seinfeld* pilot, I star in three pilots: *Herndon* (1983), *Help* (1984), and *Slickers* (1985). All three are offered to me. The second pilot, *Help*, is retooled and called *Marblehead Manor*, and NBC airs twenty-four episodes in the 1987–1988 season.

Though I didn't find my niche in the pilots, I am able to do some physical comedy in *Marblehead Manor*. The producers welcome it, and the writers serve me well. The work I do provides a segue into the character of Stanley Spadowski in Weird Al's film *UHF*.

It's summer 1988, and I'm set to head for Tulsa, Oklahoma, for the next six weeks of shooting when out of the blue half my face freezes up with Bell's palsy. What causes this kind of paralysis is a mystery, but it looks like I'll have to back out of the film. I call Weird Al, and his response is classic. "Now you can play Stanley with half your face not working. You'll be funny. It'll be great."

Right. Like Harry Dean Stanton with the flu. It's all part of the character now.

When I get to Tulsa for the shoot, Al is eager to see my face, but the palsy has gone away. He's actually disappointed. Then, he lights up. "Maybe it'll come back!"

On the set one day, Kevin McCarthy asks me who I trained with as an actor. Does he think I'm a crummy actor? Aside from attending an acting class at Valley College and a year at CalArts, I've had no formal training. He invites me to the Actors Studio. "We'd love to have you!"

As I imagined it, their "Method acting" using "affective memory," basing your character in real experience, was derived from Stanislavski, and, well, his book on character building went over well with the general granting me permission to be a colonel everywhere I went.

"I'm up for it, Kevin."

"See you then."

After I am back, *Marblehead Manor* is canceled, which would ordinarily free me up to attend the Actors Studio, something I look forward to. But pilot season is also beginning, and I need to put my time and energy there. I think it might be good for me to drop into the comedy clubs to loosen up and get ready to read for comedy pilots. However, just as I'm about to call Budd and Mitzi to get myself back in the lineup, I have a dream that shakes me up. In it, I'm onstage at a comedy club and I'm screaming at the audience. When I come offstage, I see Robin. I'm ashamed of my performance and so disappointed in myself.

"Did you see all of that, Robin?"

"I did," he says.

"I don't know what's happening to me," I say. "I'm just so angry onstage."

He nods in agreement. "You need to go into analysis and deal with your mother."

* * *

Wow! I don't usually have dreams that are so direct. This one, though, hits home, rattling around in me for days. Dealing with my mother—is she the source of my anger? My mother not wanting me? Just bringing me home as a baby to be a prop for her mother so she'll "stick around"? And what's up with her stories about my father, lying about his death, avoiding most of my questions about him? That does anger me. Who was my father? And what were they like as a couple?

When my mother was pregnant with me, she must have been highly agitated. She was going to get an abortion. Then she was going to put me up for adoption. She, in fact, didn't bring me home after she had me. She didn't want me. My anger must be deep, pre-natal—a developing fetus, affected by my mother's feelings, that I'm just a problem to get rid of. I think of Metzger's interest in the *person behind words*. There's me within my mother before I was born. What's behind that?

Unwantedness.

And when the gods are disliked and ignored, they come back in a rage.

* * *

I DON'T WANT TO GO INTO THE CLUBS anymore. I'm interested in this dream with all that anger and screaming and Robin recommending I deal with my mother. I want to look into this.

I start working with Dr. Robert Stein, a psychiatrist and also a Jungian analyst who studied with Jung himself at the C. G. Jung Institute in Zurich. Back at CalArts, it was Jung's book on UFOs, *Flying Saucers: A Modern Myth of Things Seen in the Sky*, that helped me to see "high-frequency vehicles" as something within myself, to identify the "unidentified flying objects" as "contents" coming from the deepest recesses of myself, namely, the unconscious.

In my sessions with Bob, it's not just the personal mother that's taken into account but also my unconscious life, sometimes called the Great Mother from which we are all born. Freud and Jung were exploring this "Mother" as the subconscious or unconscious psyche within us all. For them, dreams and fantasies were routes to enter this unconscious realm.

All along, I haven't gotten into the things that bother me with my personal mother. With her, there always seemed to be little going on between us. It was like she was in her room and I was in mine. She was not affectionate. She never hugged or kissed me—not even when I was a child. It was Ma who held me all the time. Still, I did feel my mom's love for me. We were in this life together, looking over at each other to see if we were still there. Maybe we were looking past each other, hoping to see my father, both of us for different reasons.

I suggest bringing her into some sessions with me. I have never been able to take things up directly with my mother. She isn't that open about most things and, as I have seen over the course of my life, questions about my father only upset her. I can only go so far before she becomes a mess, occasionally to the point of losing control of her bladder. Perhaps Robert could help open her up in ways that I can't.

But he nixes the idea, knowing that my mother will never make the deep inquiries into herself. He thinks taking her into the unconscious psyche could trigger a psychotic break. She could get overwhelmed the way Ma did. It's up to me to go to my mother and keep it all aboveboard.

* * *

Soon I am at her house, having a variation of the same conversation we've had since I was a little boy curious about my father. Now I'm in my late forties.

"Mom, I want to get my dad's death certificate."

"Why do you want that?"

"Well, he died in an automobile accident in Arizona. I want to know more about this. I can start with the death certificate."

"I don't know what to tell you," she says.

"About what, Mom?"

"About this death certificate business."

She tries to avoid me, doesn't want to talk about it. I persist. She's getting agitated.

"Why does this upset you so much?" I ask.

She's not talking.

"Mom, did my father die in a car accident?"

She can't remember. She doesn't want to talk about it.

She doesn't feel well. She's off to the bathroom.

That's all for now.

* * *

I TRY AGAIN A FEW WEEKS LATER.

"Just tell me, Mom. How did my father die?"

She can't remember now.

I persist. "Did my father die?"

Finally. "No. He didn't," she says.

"No? You told me he died in the war, then a car accident. Come on! What's going on here?"

"I didn't want to upset you."

"It's less upsetting that he died in a car accident instead of the war? It's still death."

"I don't know if he's alive anymore," she says.

"So he's alive somewhere?"

"I don't know."

"So he wasn't born in Arizona. You made that up?"

"I think he lived there. I can't remember, Mike."

"Why did he go away?"

"He just wanted different things."

"Like what?"

"I can't remember."

"Did he want to get married?"

"I don't think he wanted to."

"So you broke it off?"

"Yes."

"Because he didn't want to get married?"

"Yes."

"And then you find out that you're pregnant."

"Yes."

"And you don't know where he is now?"

"That's right."

"So he didn't know you were pregnant?"

"That's right."

"And his name is William Richards, right?"

"I think so."

"That's the name on my birth certificate."

"Yes."

"So that's his name?"

"Yes."

"So my father is still alive?"

"He may be, Mike. I don't know."

Well, I want to know. I hire a private investigator to look into what information I have on my father, his name from my birth certificate, his life in Arizona, and where he lived in Los Angeles in 1948.

* * *

WITHIN A FEW WEEKS, the PI contacts me. He has found a William Richards who was born in Arizona and lived in Los Angeles in 1948. He's alive. He lives in San Diego of all places. I lived and worked there before I came to LA to work in the comedy clubs.

"William owns a tree nursery in San Diego," he informs me. "I called and checked it out. He's usually at work in the afternoon. He lives in Escondido. He wife passed away last year. Two daughters, grown. No criminal records."

"So, he's a good guy?"

"Looks that way. I've got both addresses."

"My dad owns a nursery and he's down there in San Diego. Amazing!"

"You should go to this nursery and see what you think."

"It could be somebody else?"

"Maybe. You'll know if it's him. Don't call him directly; you may spook him. Just go to the nursery like you're a customer. You want me to go with you?"

"I'll go on my own. I just want to make sure he's there when I arrive."

"Call and inquire and leave it at that. Don't talk to him on the phone."

"Right."

* * *

I CAREFULLY CALL THE NUMBER and ask if William Richards is there. Not yet, I'm told, but he'll be there after lunch. Great. I get in my car and drive two and a half hours to this nursery in San Diego. I walk in and ask for William Richards. A young guy watering plants in containers points to my dad standing out back holding a clipboard near a row of large boxed citrus trees. As I walk toward him, I see a short man with wispy red hair, blue eyes, and a fair complexion. I know this isn't my father. I speak with him anyway. I open up and tell him why I'm there, and he listens attentively. I can see he's disappointed for me.

"I'm sorry I'm not your daddy," he kindly says. The man is decent.

"Thanks so much for hearing me out," I say. "Do you mind if I take a Polaroid?"

"Go ahead."

* * *

I DRIVE BACK TO LA, straight to my mom's house to show her the Polaroid of this William Richards.

"Is this my father, Mom?" I ask.

She looks at the photo for a few moments.

"I don't think so, Mike."

"Of course it's not my father," I say in a raised voice. "Unless he changed the color of his eyeballs from brown to blue, his hair from brown to red, and his skin... He's nearly an albino!"

"Well, I didn't tell you to go down there and see this man."

"He's the only William Richards that fits the information you gave me!"

My mom pauses and stares at me. "Mike. What do you want from me?"

"Mom, you're not telling me the truth."

Silence.

"Why are you're lying to me?"

"I made the name up to put a father's name on your birth certificate."

"Why would you do that? I'm running around out here looking for someone with a fake name? Wasting all this money!"

"Well, you wanted to do it!"

"I went on what you told me! Now the name is fake? My name Richards is fake? Your name Richards is fake!"

"Mike, I don't know what you want out of me."

I scream out, "I'm trying to find my father!"

Silence.

"I don't remember who he was," she tells me.

"How can you not remember the name of the man who got you pregnant?"

172

"We separated. He went away," she says.

"What was his real name, Mom?"

"I can't remember."

Lying about his name, his birthplace, his occupation, how he died, and how she can't remember, I blurt out, "Just tell me and stop fucking around with me!"

No good.

My mother doesn't swear and with me standing over her at six foot three—she's only five foot two—well, I am an intimidating figure, that's for sure. Standing there in the living room, raising my voice in anger and swearing too, I'm sorry to say, this upsets her. She's off to the bathroom again. My poor mom. So, here's my "anger" and dealing with my "mother" correlating to the dream. Through the bathroom door, I tell her that I'm sorry this is so upsetting and leave for home.

* * *

LATER, SHE CALLS TO TELL ME that her brother Mike is coming over to talk to me. My uncle doesn't come around that often, and when he does it's not to see me. I have never had a relationship with this man. During World War II, he was a sergeant stationed in Italy as a translator. He speaks fluent Italian. He rarely visited Ma in the sanitarium despite my mother's pleas to do so. My mom told me that my grandfather used to hit him for getting into trouble all the time. I don't think Ma had it in her to intervene. Maybe that's why my uncle never had much of a connection to her.

He arrives that afternoon and suggests that he and I go to the corner restaurant, Bob's Big Boy, for a talk. Between the ages of eleven to fifteen, I ate dinner at Bob's, always by myself, three or four nights a week, because my mother was too tired to cook. (We usually ate Swanson TV dinners.) I was such a regular at Bob's that when I sat down at the counter, my meal—the Big Boy Combination

Plate—would automatically arrive without me ordering it. The waitresses, my surrogate mothers, knew what I routinely ate for supper.

My uncle and I sit opposite each other in a booth. He doesn't know that this restaurant is an extension of my house. It's like we're sitting in my dining room. He starts by telling me to lay off his sister. He speaks to me as if I'm some creep who's hassling her. What does he know about my father? Nothing. He's not interested in the past. "Just grow up and get on with your life," he says.

He's getting me angry. I walk out and head for my mom's house. I arrive there just as he pulls into the driveway. My mom appears at the screen door and meekly asks if everything is all right. Her brother gets out of his car, clearly pissed off. I ignore him and turn to my mom. "Why are you hiding behind your brother now?"

Bam!

My uncle slugs me hard in the face. My mother screams, "No, don't hit him!"

Her brother can be a tough guy. A hundred percent Italian who could get in your face, but a smart guy who loved mathematics, which he taught in high school. He's good and bad. I'm getting his bad side. You would think that he could be a good teacher here, handling me as he would a troubled student. You don't hit your students!

I shake off the blow and say, "Well, that's what your father used to do to you."

The idiot wants to hit me again, but my mom anticipates it and tells him to stop. He turns away and walks toward his car. "From now on, you'll call me Mr. Nardozza!" he yells. Suddenly, rage surges through me. I come close to picking up a brick from my mother's planter and throwing it through his windshield. It's the only time in my life that I have ever felt such a strong urge toward physical violence.

My uncle roars off in his car. My mom sees that he's of no use. What now?

* * *

I FOLLOW MY MOM INSIDE the house. I know she has never gotten along with her brother. My mom took care of their mother, did everything for her, and was peeved that her brother did nothing.

As sick as my grandmother was, before she lost her grip on things, I'd like to believe that she was holding on to me to keep herself with us for as long as possible. So why slug me, Mike? Presumably, I'm the one who kept your mother around for as long as she could hold on. Do you resent me for that? Or did you want her to go away earlier, or hold on to you instead of me? Whatever. Just leave us alone.

Tempers run short with the Nardozzas. I'm touched by this too. I have to work on my temper. It's tough with their blood running through me. And what about my father's blood? Or the blood of humanity coursing through me? Well, that's certainly a bigger family issue.

"Let her cover the mark as she will, the pang of it will always be in her heart."
—Nathaniel Hawthorne, *The Scarlet Letter*

Please tell me, Mom. What's the real story with my father?

My mother and I sit quietly with each other and then we finally talk. She tells me that she didn't want to have sex with the man whose name she never knew. The man pushed himself on her. A twenty-six-year-old Catholic girl who gets pregnant against her will in 1948, few wanted to come to her aid. Getting pregnant out of wedlock was seen as the woman's fault. Only other women who were in the same situation, like the gal who went to Mexico for an abortion and died there, offered sympathy.

Some would say that she shouldn't have been there in the first place. To cover up, to alleviate the guilt, even the "sin," my mother wanted both she and I to look legit. She gave us the name Richards. She invented a husband who dies tragically. She's a widow. I'm a boy now without his father. The incident was so traumatic that for most of her life, she was always guarded around men. She didn't trust them. She never married. I think her brother saw me as the offspring

175

of a man who raped his sister. A dirty, secret thing she carried and had to attend to, something bad and unwanted.

Dodging my questions about my father was my mother's way of protecting me from how ugly that incident was for her. *Yep, he was a good, loving man from Arizona who was innocently killed in a car accident or died heroically in the war.* Oh, my sweet mother. I am so sorry. I just didn't know.

Now I know as much as I need to know about my father. I know the truth.

As much as I had trouble finding God in Catholic school, I am pleased that the archdiocese insisted that my mom give birth to me, that she had enough trust to follow their guidance.

After all, here I am!

CHAPTER 16

Stella!

Still between projects and without any pilots yet, in early 1989, I intend to take Kevin McCarthy up on his offer to work at the Actors Studio. Class will be good for me. I crave the rigor and thought of study. I call the Studio and am told that an audition is required. Oh, it's a tryout? I recall Kevin's invite, "We'd love to have ya!" Really?

Though I'm taken aback at first, I figure, okay, I'll audition and get in. Auditions are not for another month. Fine. It'll give me enough time to memorize something from *The Zoo Story* by Edward Albee. That'll be my audition piece.

In a session with Robert, having gone over my interest in the Actors Studio, he mentions having read about the acting teacher Stella Adler, who is now in LA with her school, Conservatory West. "Why don't you look into this," he says. "See how it feels."

Absolutely. I head on over to check it out. I meet Stella's partner, Joanne Linville, who teaches several courses, including advanced technique, all of which lead to Stella's master class. Joann is about to

177

start a cold-reading class, ways to get at dialogue for the first time. I go ahead and register for it. I've got the time.

While I'm there, I meet a student of Stella's, a guy named Ben, who's in his sixties and seems like he'd make a good Peter in *The Zoo Story*. I don't really know this guy, but I ask him if he'll play the part for my audition at the Actors Studio. He winces and looks away.

"I'm with Stella," he says, sounding apologetic.

"I know. I'm just looking into the Studio. I've been invited by an actor I know there. I just want to check it out. See what they're made of. I'm going to be working with Joanne in her cold-reading class."

"If you're accepted at the Actors Studio, will you go?"

"I don't know. I'm in Joanne's class now, and I'd love to work with Stella."

"She's the best."

"Right."

"Okay, I'll do your audition. I've never been to the Actors Studio. I don't really act that much. I just love being around Stella."

He tells me he once did a few small parts in old TV shows but doesn't have an agent anymore and doesn't care to get one. He's not seeking a career. Acting is more of a hobby for him. He's retired and likes doing scenes with Stella's students. He's been around her for years.

"Great."

Within a week before the Actors Studio audition, Ben and I rehearse a few times. I handle most of the lines, and he's fine with what he's doing. It's just a five-minute scene. This will do. My time is suddenly an issue, as I'm also mulling over a sketch idea playing a *Fridays* character with Jay Leno for *The Tonight Show*.

* * *

THE AUDITION IS SET FOR ELEVEN in the morning. We get there at ten thirty. I want to run lines and get it done. Ben has to fill out a required "scene partner" form, which he thinks is unnecessary since he's not the one auditioning.

Other actors are there to audition, something that I didn't know about. It's sort of a cattle call. I'm a bit perturbed when we're finally called in at 11:45. I'll use it for my character?

There are several people sitting at the top of a small grandstand facing a compact stage area. They ask us to provide a little background about ourselves. They start with Ben. He tells them that he's simply my scene partner, enjoys acting, and that he works with Stella Adler and just loves her. My turn. I tell them about *Fridays*, guest-starring work, films that I've been in, and that I'm about to do *The Tonight Show*. I've had no formal acting training, I add. I just want to join the Studio to study acting.

"Great. What's your scene?"

"I'm doing a scene from *The Zoo Story*."

"Perfect."

Ben is already seated, and I pace for a moment before launching into the piece. We go along pretty good until we get to a point when Ben is supposed to take out a pipe, cueing me to say, "Well, boy, you're not going to get lung cancer, are you?" But Ben doesn't take out his pipe. He has forgotten. After an uncomfortable couple of moments, I stop the scene. Critical business has been forgotten.

"I'm sorry," I say.

I lean into Ben. "You forgot to take the pipe out."

"Oh, I'm sorry!" he whispers. "Should we start over?"

"Can we start over?" I ask the moderators.

"Go ahead, please!"

I'm thinking this thing is botched. We begin again and complete the scene. I'm not thrilled that Ben forgot the business with the pipe, but whatever. He isn't the one trying out. I think I did a good-enough job. Why does it have to be perfect? I'm there for training.

* * *

In the meantime, I start memorizing "The story of Jerry and the dog," the long monologue from Albee's play. I want to perform this someday for Stella Adler's master class. But I put it down for the time being when the script for the NBC comedy pilot *The Seinfeld Chronicles* is sent to my house. My agent says the network has asked me to audition. The character is named Kessler. I don't know, Kessler seems marginal. There's a lot of talking in these pages and not much for this Kessler character to do other than go into Jerry's apartment and ask, "Got any meat?"

But Jerry Seinfeld is funny, and he wrote the pilot with Larry David, my old *Fridays* cohort, who I know is funny. We'll see.

* * *

A week later, I run into Ben at a health food store. It turns out he was accepted at the Studio!

"I wasn't even applying, and they accepted me," he says. "How did you do?"

"I haven't heard from them," I say.

"You're kidding. Maybe they got their wires crossed and they think I'm you."

"You mean they mixed up our names and numbers?"

"Yeah."

"I don't know."

"Well, I'm staying with Stella," he says.

"Maybe I should go to the Studio as you, Ben."

"No, you're better off with Stella."

"I think you're right."

* * *

At Stella Adler Conservatory West, I tell Joanne about the outcome of my audition. She used to be a moderator at the Actors Studio and assures me that I'll be much better off with her and

Stella. She invites me into her advanced technique class. Do I have to audition? "Don't be silly," she says. "Just come."

The very next day I go in to read for *The Seinfeld Chronicles*. Within weeks I get the part and shoot the pilot. My feeling about the character and the show hasn't changed from when I read the script. I don't know where any of it is going, and I didn't reach the character. But at this point it's out of my hands.

* * *

THE SEINFELD CHRONICLES AIRS on Wednesday night, July 5, 1989, less than two and a half months after we shot the pilot.

It does all right in its time slot, finishing in second place behind *Jake and the Fatman*, and though it musters some positive reviews from critics, I hear it scores poorly in test screenings and the network hates it. So be it. I'm not thinking about a pickup. I'm focusing on other work. *UHF* opens on July 21. Reviews are mixed, but the *Washington Post* calls me "the funniest thing in the movie." I'm now in Texas to work on the feature *Problem Child*, starring John Ritter and his future wife, Amy Yasbeck, who play parents of a terribly unruly kid. When I'm back in town, I figure I'll land another pilot.

But I get a call from my agent that takes me off that merry-go-round, at least for now. NBC has picked up *The Seinfeld Chronicles*.

"Really? A full season?"

"No, four episodes."

"A four-episode pickup?"

"Yeah. They're not sure about the show. They want to see how four episodes does with an audience."

A four-episode pickup? It's unheard of in the annals of television.

"Well, it's a good start," I say.

"How so?"

"We're already unique."

PART 4

Giddyup!

CHAPTER 17

The Shortest First Season in the History of Television

Before the show goes into production, NBC wants changes. At first the network asks for a total makeover. What? I find out from Jason that they wanted to recast the show altogether, nixing him and me—everyone but Jerry. He got this scoop from George Shapiro, Jerry's manager.

So, why are we back?

I take it all on the chin. Why am I back?

I must be on a wait-and-see list. My insecurity from the pilot is reactivated. I didn't think that I was very good as Kessler. Now I could be cut at any time. All Jerry has to do is lock his apartment door and Kessler is out. Or they could say he moved or got evicted or committed.

Buck up! If the four-episode pickup is a wait and see, at least it will give me more time to develop the character. Right on!

Speaking of characters, NBC also wants Jerry to have a steady girlfriend. They believe romance and relationship comedy will rate. But that isn't the show Jerry and Larry have in mind. Larry and Jerry don't have girlfriends. They are men who hang out with each other at the club as stand-up comics, fraternizing with other comics, most of whom are guys like them who are usually perplexed by women. No, there aren't any ongoing relationships with women in their real lives and so there won't be any on the show.

This is a show about Jerry and Larry—channeled through the character George—and an agoraphobic mooch who lives across the hall from Jerry.

Jerry and George will talk about their lives in New York—the problems, irritations, and eccentricities of two friends navigating real life—and every so often Jerry's weird neighbor will pop in for some meat. But there isn't going to be any hugging or kissing on the show, period.

Larry says as much to the network, and Jerry backs him up. Done. But wait a minute.

It's clear to Larry and Jerry that they do need an ongoing woman character in the show. George and Jerry do have stories to tell about failed dating and wayward sex. Consequently, it's fairly easy to give in to the network and pitch the idea of Jerry having an ex-girlfriend who can stand in for all of their ex-dating experiences, all the conflicts and confusion from their attempt at relationships. The ex-girlfriend can be a friend who is around to discuss their relationships as they see them, invent them, or screw them up.

There are other changes. The show is no longer *The Seinfeld Chronicles*. Now it's simply called *Seinfeld*. That works. It's clean, simple, and to the point—the way Jerry likes things in real life. Also, my character's name has been changed to Kramer from Kessler. Larry's New York neighbor Kenny Kramer has signed off on using his last name? I don't know. To me, it's simply a rebirth. I have a new name. I'm leaving Kessler for a new character and a better performance to come.

I'll fill out the character so Larry and the writing staff will have more to go on. Larry will see this new, improved character Kramer better than ever and write him more substantially into the show. Or will he if I don't have a ponytail? Ha! Stop complicating things. For the most part, it's all about getting the laughs. I'll do just that. I'll change my approach from a slow-moving Kessler to a more ramped-up Kramer. Okay! I'm up for the four shows! Giddyup!

Oh, something else. Kessler's dog is gone. In the pilot, my first entrance was preceded by a dog, who ran into Jerry's bathroom. "He's getting a drink," I quipped. It was a line that I improvised. Now that we're back, I can do more with that dog. I'll bond with it, actually have the dog live with me, train it. We'll become a kind of comedy team. It's the only question I have for Larry right now: "What about the dog?"

Larry shrugs it off. "Too much of a hassle." Absolutely true! I'm way too rambunctious. In the pilot, no one expected that unreliable pooch to enter and then run into Jerry's bathroom or, really, right off the set! My throwaway line was covering the dog's erratic exit. As W. C. Fields once said, "Never work with animals or children."

I was going to live with the dog? Enough! I've got more to do improving this character. Suddenly, I get a feeling for Kramer's disposition! If I can't have a dog, I'll *be* a dog! This is how the new character will start off. I'll play the guy as a dog coming into Jerry's apartment as playful, friendly dogs do, a dog spirit bounding through the door, sniffing, curious, wondering what's going on in here. What's everyone doing? What's everyone talking about? Who wants to play? Where's the meat? Let's eat!

* * *

THE MOST SIGNIFICANT CHANGE involving the pickup is the addition of Julia Louis-Dreyfus to the cast. I'm told about this before we go back to work, and since Kessler/Kramer is supposedly a shut-in and I didn't have any scenes with Lee Garlington's waitress in the pilot, my reaction is more of a curious bystander: Oh, the other girl's not with us? Who is Julia going to play? I'm told she is Jerry's ex-girlfriend.

Oh, okay. She's the one. Hmm. Maybe I'll start taking her out. Kramer's got the hots for Elaine. She's fine. You don't want her, Jerry? Step aside! Down, Kramer. Sit!

I saw Julia a few times on *Saturday Night Live* and thought she was charming, very charismatic. She can easily play close to herself. She's very appealing, and indeed, I like her right off the bat. I meet her for the first time in the studio lot when I'm walking toward our soundstage.

"Julia?" I say, pulling up alongside her. "I'm Michael."

"Hi."

My first impression is a good one. She has a spark.

"So, you're with us now."

"Yeah."

Her smile. Her eyes. She's animated. And she's wearing black jeans and cool cowboy boots.

"I like those boots," I say.

In fact, I *love* that she's wearing cowboy boots. We need a lady who can stomp about in boots and keep things in line around here. Julia has her character Elaine wearing boots for a while, and I play Kramer as a friendly dog coming into Jerry's apartment. We're working it.

* * *

THE FIRST EPISODE WE SHOT, titled "Male Unbonding," has several storylines. Jerry is trying to break up with a friend he no longer likes, and the woman George is dating doesn't want to see him anymore. Also, Kramer has an idea for a new business: a make-your-own-pizza chain. The script was written before Julia was cast, so she has only one scene that has been hastily rejiggered to include her as Elaine.

From the first table read, she makes it clear that one scene ain't gonna cut it. She wants her share of lines, some equality around here, boys. I think of Cass when she was in the tire department at Sears. Julia knows her department well. She's not going to let the boys run off with the show. She's wearing her boots! She spent three years on *Saturday Night Live*, and, from my experience doing a live late-night sketch comedy show, I know the competition that occurs between cast members trying to get their share on the show.

Not that we have or will have that issue. But you must stay in the face of the producers and the writers and make sure you're in some of the best sketches. It's about being in the show and not just of it.

How am I fitting into this show? I'm playing broad and everyone else is playing close to themselves, and they're all so good at it. At this point, I don't care if I have only one scene. My aim is to get to Kramer, make it funny, go home, and get ready for the next episode. I'm thinking that the show is going to be like *Bosom Buddies*, always starring Jerry and Jason. I'm meant to be a minor hand in this, a supporting character with one or two scenes.

This will be okay for now. I want some time with Kramer. I don't want the focus on this show. I want to be under the radar while Kramer and I get to know each other. We need some time together.

* * *

I HAVE SEVERAL SCENES AS KRAMER imagines building his empire, Kramerica, one pizza at a time. This is rather symbolic—building up my character as Kramerica, "one pizza at a time," one scene at a time, one show at a time. Given the minimal attention Kessler got in the pilot, this is an improvement, and when the cast gathers to read through the script, as we will do before every episode for the next nine years, I see that Kramer also attends a Mets baseball game with Jerry's friend.

Interesting.

So, Kramer does get out of the apartment building. There's a world out there for this character to get into. Now that we're back, aside from the dog, which I have internalized, I haven't talked to Larry about Kramer. I simply note here, in this first episode, that Larry does see Kramer in the outside world. This is a heads-up. Kramer can definitely go places.

I'm into backstories. It helps me to put flesh on the bone, bring a character to life. Larry isn't thinking about Kramer's—or anyone else's—backstory. He's not thinking about Kramer all locked up with agoraphobia. That was an amusing thought not to be taken literally. Ah, but when you're working with Michael Richards, it's all relative.

I'm not going to ask Larry about Kramer's backstory. He doesn't have time for that. He's not thinking about the actual life of a character as if he's doing Chekhov or Ibsen. Kessler was agoraphobic in the pilot and now he's at a Mets game? It doesn't make sense. To whom? That was Kessler. This is Kramer. Two different backstories and more to come.

I create backstories to feel the character as an actual person with ground or life under his feet. I have something to stand upon. Working in this way, it can be other people who think he's agoraphobic. He can use this in some way. Kramer is a clever man. How else can he survive in New York City without a steady job? Do you know how much an apartment can cost in the city? A lot. How does Kramer really get by?

In Kramer's imagination it's anything he wants it to be. He goes for what he thinks is best until he changes his "imagination." He's mercurial, a trickster, the Fool's fool. Anything goes. He's unpredictable, unidentifiable. *Kramer lives through his imagination.*

At Conservatory West, I discuss this with Joanne Linville, not Larry. In the work she and Stella do, they emphasize using imagination. A Method actor playing someone in prison will go to prison, spend time there, talking to other prisoners. But Stella believes the actor can use their imagination to find these things within themselves. Draw on your imagination. Okay. Reality is three-dimensional. The fourth dimension is imagination. Kramer is imaginal, full of a lot of make-believe. He's truly the "fourth" among Jerry, Elaine, and George.

Kramer does indeed light up a room. He's not dark and withdrawn, stuck in the building. The phone rings when he's in Jerry's kitchen. Kramer pulls a cordless phone out of his pants pocket. "Hello, Kramerica Industries." Kramer's running his empire from his apartment, from the phone in his pocket. He imagines that it is a low-cost business that he's running so efficiently. As an actor, I'm playing that there is no Kramerica. This business is all in Kramer's "imagination." He's so into it. He doesn't know it's his imagination at work.

Yep, this character is kinda crazy, isn't he? A schizophrenic? Quite possibly. A dog at heart? Why not? It makes him lovable. Look at the episode from this standpoint: The character is living through his imagination. A kind of Walter Mitty. He's anything he wants to be. This makes him rather interesting to watch. Who is he now?

* * *

KRAMER PITCHES THE BUSINESS to Jerry and George. Make your own pizzas. George is skeptical. Of course he is. George is grounded in facts and logic. One could say facts and logic are causing him a lot of misery. Kramer is the antithesis—a man not bound by facts or logic. He's bound to open-ended imagination. He believes in imagination and all the real that comes out of that! In his imagination, he's going to work. Inside himself, his pocket, or outside in the world, to whoever he's talking to, it's all the same. A lot of make-believe going on.

Elaine says that Kramer's pizza business is a good idea. This endorses his conviction that he is indeed a part of the world and here to present a great idea for all—to make your own pizza is to make up your own life!

It's not just pizza. It's self-reliance, a "declaration of one's independence."

* * *

NBC SETS UP A PHOTO SHOOT without including me. The call sheets go out only to Jerry, Jason, and Julia. I catch wind of this and believe the writing is on the wall. I'll finish the remaining shows and that'll be that for me. I intend to make the best of my time here. I'll make comedy with what they give me. I'm going out funny.

I'm told it was a mistake, but make no mistake, they went ahead and did the shoot without me. The show is a threesome. I'm up for finishing the four shows and adios.

I'll make being on the show a personal quest. Let's see what I can do with the material I'm given. One line or a hundred, I'll try to get the laughs with what I'm given. Above all, stay close to Kramer. I'm giving birth here, but I'm not sure if I can deliver in time. I'm insecure because of this. The threesome is born and being raised. What does that make me? Stillborn? Still being born? We'll see.

The next episode is "The Stakeout," which formally introduces Elaine as Jerry's ex-girlfriend and makes it clear that they're still intimately and awkwardly involved in each other's lives. I'm only in one scene, but I like the scene. I'm in Jerry's apartment, helping his mother play Scrabble against Jerry. I work the scene. I create some business; I sneak a peek at Jerry's letters. I help Jerry's mom compose her word. I'm into defending the nonword "quon." I want her to win. I like Jerry's parents. I like family. I'm a family dog. Jerry's parents like and accept Kramer. I like Kramer too. I feel comfortable with Kramer. He puts me at ease. I see how endearing he is. The show needs his homey spirit. He's family. A dog sleeping at their feet.

In "The Robbery" and "The Stock Tip," as in the previous episodes, Kramer is written very light. I do what I can to bring him to life. I go over each script with Joanne. I've got Adler's most advanced techniques for character work behind me. I work to make every line jump. I apply backstory.

I begin to choose specific clothing for Kramer: old shirts and pants that he's worn for the past twenty-five years. I change into some of Kramer's old clothes every day when I'm on the set, including table reads and rehearsals. I don't come in as Kramer for a few lines and one scene. I'm with Kramer the whole day through. Walking around the soundstage, outside on the lot, I'm Kramer wherever I am. Jason and Julia think I'm nuts. Well, this can work for them. They think Kramer is off course anyway.

I can feel the K-Man is a-coming. The more I'm in character, the more comfortable I get with a Kramer who is fully engaged, a dog with his ears up. He can hear through walls. Still, because I haven't arrived yet, I do feel short of the mark. I'm trying to get to Kramer as fast as I can before I'm cut from the show, before another episode gets by me.

* * *

"It's just a fucking TV show," a prominent TV actor once said to me.

This actor can play so close to himself brilliantly. How do I play close to myself? I have no self to rely upon? This makes me nervous when I'm outside of character or outside of a persona, the mask that I wear. It's like I don't have a Michael Richards to play? I don't know who I am? For "a fucking TV show"? It's a whole lot more. I'm creating Kramer from the ground up—ticks and mannerisms, the whole shebang.

Still, I do get intense about it. Something is going to come out of this, a character called Kramer. But he's not here yet. I'm not here yet. This is unsettling to me as I go before camera. I'm not yet Kramer, but I'm no longer Kessler. I'm in the middle of it all. "To be or not to be."

* * *

I AM INSPIRED BY THE GREAT FOOL Charlie Chaplin. For so much of his childhood, he lived on the streets. By the time he was fourteen, his mother was in a mental institution and his father was gone. His brother Sydney tried to look after him. It's easy to see how Chaplin's Tramp character came about. He really was a little tramp on the streets for many years. Watching *The Kid*, I see truth: that's Chaplin living on the streets, artfully dodging the orphanage truck, hustling and relying on his wits to get by.

How all that loneliness led to the creation of the Tramp is obvious, but how all of Chaplin's comedy came about is just extraordinary. For Chaplin, comedy occurs out of suffering just as out of tremendous loneliness the whole world can be there for you. Like Chaplin as a kid, I was on the streets a lot, almost always after Ma went to Norwalk. I thought my father was dead, my grandfather was gone, my mother away working. I was left to myself, but guided by an intuition. I trust in it. I know something is going to come out of this—just as it is now. The character Kramer is coming. I can *feel* it. Like a whole world upon me.

* * *

I GO TO MY DRESSING ROOM and lie down. Relax. It's all coming as it does. I'm made for this. I wouldn't be on this show if I wasn't made for it. Seemingly, I made this happen, yet it's happening to me. I'm in character for it. I'm playing myself through character.

It's hard for me to take it lightly. I want this character Kramer to come through and get the laughs. I brood. I suffer from taking the work so seriously. I haven't gotten it right yet. I'm not satisfied with my work. I remember reading that Chaplin shut down production for a week to figure out a funny way to fall down some stairs. A week to fall down the stairs, to create the best way to make it brilliantly funny. He took the making of comedy seriously. Red Skelton prepared so many pratfalls, right down to stuffing towels and newspaper down his pants to cushion the fall. It takes work to "make 'em laugh."

Rest up. Just relax and be cool. Serenity now.

* * *

THE FOUR SHOWS—TRULY THE SHORTEST first season in the history of television—start airing on May 31, 1990, and go through June. By this time, the network's regular fall-winter shows have aired their season finales and gone into reruns, and *Seinfeld* is dropped into the slot after *Cheers*, NBC's top-rated sitcom even in reruns. *Seinfeld* benefits from this lead-in; our four shows average nineteen million viewers. Is that enough for a full-season pickup?

I have faith—faith in the work, and I have work to do. There's more of Kramer to come. I'm "the fourth" to round off the show. We're doing *four* shows. We'll all be together soon. I can *feel* it.

The four of us to form a whole.

195

CHAPTER 18

The Ah-Ha

I pick up the phone one day and hear an upbeat voice belonging to a guy who can probably count all the bad days in his life on one hand. It's Jerry Seinfeld.

"Michael!"

"Jerry."

"How are you?"

"Good."

"What are you doing?"

"Hanging out with Kramer. I still haven't found his shoes yet."

"Ha ha! Good. We may take the show over to Fox. How would you feel about that?"

I tell Jerry that I am on board for whatever he and Larry believe is best for the show. I know things are going to get better. I know the whole show will pull together soon. We need more time doing the show, and we're going to get it. NBC is on the fence about the show, he says. Fox is up for it, so NBC better jump off the fence and commit to a pickup or the show goes elsewhere.

It's midsummer 1990—about a year since the pilot aired—when NBC finally decides that *Seinfeld* has too much potential to let go. TV critics are nearly unanimous in their praise of the show (the *LA Times* says it "blows up a gale of wit and freshness" and "is just the kind of amusingly off-center comedy now missing from NBC's lineup"), and research shows that the coveted eighteen to thirty-nine demo have a fondness for Jerry, George, Elaine, and Kramer. The network orders thirteen episodes.

This is good news, but thirteen episodes is not a full season or a full vote of confidence. It's a noncommittal commitment. Jerry is thrilled, but his excitement is countered by Larry's anxiety about having to write that many episodes. Even after more writers are hired, including Larry's pal and our fellow *Fridays* alum Larry Charles, his concerns are understandable. It's hard to write thirteen episodes and even harder to make them exceptionally funny.

I know of only one person who doesn't worry whether they have it in themselves to perform, to deliver, to get the laughs, to win the race again and again: Jerry Seinfeld.

Aside from my intuition that we'll all come together soon, Jerry knows we're going somewhere with the show. The pickup is going to happen. He doesn't call it a feeling or an intuition. Jerry simply says, "I know." How does he know? It's his superpower. He knows.

I always enjoy being around Jerry's kind of confidence. I stay away from him when I am suffering doubt. It's about this time that I decide to keep my crap off of people. I can whine and it does nobody any good. Every time I feel short on character or not being attended to or written light, I keep it to myself. We're a team learning each other's moves and how to play together, and one day we'll be wholly contained as one of the best ensembles in television history.

This is something none of us see at the moment. But like me, Jerry knew that we weren't done with the show. We were funny in the first four episodes, and we will get funnier in the next thirteen and more after that if we are allowed to keep at it.

* * *

THAT SUMMER, I'M IN STELLA ADLER'S master class. She's hard on students. Raises her voice, challenges their acting. "I don't believe you!" "You're faking it." At her age, she slams her hand down on her table. "Don't kill me now!" And the heads roll. There's blood in the room. I saw a student break down crying and head for the door. Stella is tough. Whew! To paraphrase that prominent actor, "It's just fucking acting!" No, it's hard work. Good actors make it look easy.

I finally present my monologue from *The Zoo Story*. Right off, Stella wants to know where I'm coming from. "You don't just walk onto the stage and begin! Where have you been?" I get it. Again, backstory! She brings it home for me. From this day on, I will never enter Jerry's apartment without knowing where Kramer has been. I come in alive and touched by "where I've been" and also "where I'm going" when I head for the door. It's not always in the script. It's backstory. Done.

* * *

IN EARLY OCTOBER, THE FIRST SCRIPT of this new second season is sent to my house. When "The Ex-Girlfriend" arrives, I have economist E. F. Schumacher's book *Small Is Beautiful: A Study of Economics As If People Mattered* in my hand. I can relate some of Schumacher's ideas to character development; small details enhance the bigger picture, giving size to the whole character.

Nothing is small. I can take small and make it into laughter. I start with the way I look, the manner of my dress, my hair, the character's presence. Laurel and Hardy had a look; Mr. Hulot, a look; a returnable character on *Fridays* had a look. Thinking like this anticipates the work ahead for Kramer. Kramer emerges from small, as in infancy, and will get bigger with more work to do on the show. Small can be beautiful. One funny scene with Kramer at a time.

* * *

SINCE THE SHOOTING OF THE FOUR SHOWS, most of the time I am hanging out with Kramer. We go shopping together for clothes. We're not waiting to hear that the show got picked up. We know.

I figure Kramer doesn't get out much to shop, so I hit several vintage and secondhand clothing stores in Hollywood, looking for clothes from the '60s, the time when this character had clothes bought for him. I pick up a few colorful shirts, some well-worn slacks, a pair of classic high-top Converse shoes, and a pair of old leather shoes. This will serve as my wardrobe.

It's a start, and it begins to bring Kramer around for me. The character likes to dress well.

We shoot "The Ex-Girlfriend" in mid-October. I have a scene in which I emphasize to Jerry how great the cantaloupe I'm eating tastes, and it's cheaper than at the market. When Jerry says he doesn't go to the bodega where I get my fruit because it's farther than the grocery store, I say, "You can use my shopping cart."

Of course, Kramer has his own grocery cart! I love the detail. I wish I had put a shopping cart outside Kramer's apartment door. You'd always see it out there when Jerry's apartment door is open, always calling to mind Kramer's grocery cart. To Kramer it's like a fancy sports car parked out front. It's these small details that make for a whole character.

The next week we shoot "The Pony Remark." In it, Jerry thinks a remark he made to an older woman at a dinner party about "hating anyone that ever had a pony when they were growing up" might have upset her and contributed to her unexpected death the next day. In the opening scene, though, before this story gets going, Kramer enters Jerry's apartment and says he's "changing the configuration" of his own apartment. He's getting rid of all his furniture. "What're you doing?" Jerry asks.

"Levels."

"Levels?"

Multiple levels, I explain. With carpets and pillows. Like ancient Egypt. As I say this, my hands are illustrating this change, proof that this is not empty fantasy to Kramer; he has a picture in his mind that stretches from  the time of the pharaohs to the present day, from the pyramids to his apartment across the hall from Jerry's. The intensity in my eyes conveys that this is what Kramer really sees. He's a visionary.

Working with Joanne to visualize or see what I am talking about is a must. I *see* the carpet, the pillows, the fabric with images from ancient Egypt. This is how that intensity in my eyes comes about. As broad as Kramer could be, we must believe he is a real person, an eccentric for sure, but a person you could meet on the streets of New York. There has to be an intensity in the eyes of the character. This is life. This character really sees life and lives it the way he does. Kramer is always on an adventure. His excitement for life should amuse us. He's a dog too. He picks up on scents, and there he goes.

* * *

I'M IN THE WORLD, holding the globe, making laughter. We got the pickup. Kramer is on the ball. I'm in the show, one scene or two, small is beautiful, until the first week of December where I'm nothing at all. I am at the table read for "The Chinese Restaurant," an episode that shows Jerry, George, and Elaine suffering increasing frustration while waiting for a table at a Chinese restaurant before seeing a movie.

A few things about this episode are different from all the others we've done. First, it takes place entirely in a Chinese restaurant.

There are no scenes in Jerry's apartment. Neither are there any sub-plots. It's just the three of them waiting for a table.

The biggest difference, though, is personal and embarrassing for me: I'm not in the script. No one has given me a heads-up. As Jerry, Jason, Julia, and several guest actors read through the script, I sit at the table without uttering a single word, and this is because not a single word has been written for Kramer.

I have no idea that NBC disliked the script when it was first submitted, and executives pushed back so hard that Larry threatened to quit. Jerry intervened, and naturally, he backed Larry, and that's the reason we're pushing ahead with this format-busting episode. I wish I could have participated in this unique effort. How about Kramer just walking by and banging on the restaurant window to say hi? Anything, but don't send me home for the week with nothing.

Larry sidles up to me after the table read and says this won't happen again, I'll be in all the shows hereafter. So be it.

I use the time off to attend to the end of my marriage. My wife has told me that she is in love with another man. Stunned and distraught, I move out and get a small one-bedroom apartment in Sherman Oaks. My daughter is in high school, and I feel so far removed from her. Hopefully, I can buy a house and have her live with me. But not being in the show this week tweaks my insecurity again. I can't help feeling dispensable, imagining the end of the show for me altogether, a small player who's not so beautiful anymore.

Wow! After almost twenty years of marriage, I'm alone in an empty apartment determined to get on with my life, to buck up. Larry did assure me that not being in an episode this week won't happen again. I know he's a man of his word.

* * *

FOR JERRY AND LARRY, the show is shifting into a place of self-awareness and confidence. They are bending the format for sitcom television. The characters are fresh and set in New York, and as

Larry makes clear, there will be no learning, no cute redemption les-sons at the end of each show. It's a hardball life in New York, and we'll get the laughs from there. This is the uncompromising sensibil-ity of someone who earned his stripes doing many years of stand-up comedy in New York clubs.

I know Larry from *Fridays*. Leave him alone and let it get done. I also know that he'll let me do my thing. I was cast for it. I will give them an eccentric next-door neighbor.

Seinfeld has moved to Radford Studio Center in Studio City, shooting on Stage 19, the original location of Mack Sennett Studios in 1928. I'm very big on entering the shadows of this history and hopefully adding to it. I'm cut from the same cloth of the knock-about comics. A plaque outside the stage door memorializes the special place this stage holds in show business history. Beautiful! Our production and writing offices, including the office Jerry and Larry share, are a short walk from the stage, close to the studio cafeteria.

As Jerry and Larry settle into their new home, they push their desks together so they face each other much the same as they did it when they created the show, the two of them talking about the insignificant stuff that most of us walk by barely noticing, which is everything for two stand-up comics-turned-show creators and pro-ducers in constant search for material.

Their time is completely consumed by production meetings, rewrites, rehearsals, tapings, and editing shows. I'm rarely in the offices, but occasionally I visit Larry Charles in his, which is right next door to Jerry's and Larry's. Charles is a wonderful freak, a savant of sorts, a fellow I love to get philosophical with. He's also a mystic of sorts, deeply soulful, heartfelt, and witty. He's the only person around who will talk with me about psychology, scripture, or creation myths in general.

Like me and Larry David, he's an alum of *Fridays*, a talent rising from the smoky swamp of that show's writers room. I wrote at home. He loved being down there "in the pit" holding his breath. He has long hair, a long, sizable beard, and a disheveled, heavyset look, a self-styled hipster freak who knows comedy. His office is a mess. Papers cover every square inch of the floor; it's not even visible, yet he knows where every page on that floor is. He's organized. Everything is a mess that's in order.

"You want me to clean up?" I kid him. "I can clean it all up. I used to be a janitor."

His sense of order draws me to his office. I don't share much with others on the show about my process or my personal life for that matter, but I feel comfortable with this guy who's got sandwiches and papers and shit on every available flat surface. (Jerry's office, by the way, is spotless. His major concession to decor is a rack for tiny model Porsches. The pictures on the wall behind his desk are also of Porches, and they will get larger and glossier as the show goes on.) For Charles, his comedy emanates from New York. He studied at nearby Rutgers and set out to perform comedy in the city. Writing suited him better. He loves watching an actor lift his writing off the page.

Like me, Charles is the offspring of Priapus. We love the freakish. The mess he cultivates in his office is indicative of the place from where all comedy emanates—the irrational. He can sit amidst it and feel the funny rising from it; he sees order in chaos, the rational in the irrational. I can stare at it and see the same thing. I'm at home with this man. Kramer loves him. And Charles understands Kramer.

I tell him that in Kramer's "imagination" he can play characters. He can pass himself off as a psychiatrist, a doctor, a politician, or a movie star.

So Larry Charles writes "The Statue." Jerry finds a porcelain statue in a box of his dead grandfather's belongings. George broke one just like it as a ten-year-old boy and has been sad about it ever since. Kramer and George tussle over it. Kramer relents, go ahead, take it, and Jerry says he can have it.

Then the statue goes missing after Jerry has his apartment cleaned by an actor friend of Elaine's. When it turns up in the apartment the guy shares with the author of a book Elaine is editing, Kramer goes undercover, dressing up in Jerry's grandfather's old suit and hat and posing as a hard-boiled Joe Friday–type detective. He barges into the guy's apartment, orders him to "make love to the wall," and steals the statue back. George is ecstatic to have it back. "I don't know how to thank you," he says.

Kramer says he'll think of something, slaps George on the back, and the statue flies out of his hands and shatters on the floor.

The episode is as tightly written as an O. Henry story, and the scene featuring Kramer playing a cop is not just his breakout, it is also my breakthrough. Kramer is now playing a character. He can become characters. I do the scene in one take. I nearly tip over a lamp with my bag, but the camera pans up in time as the lamp starts to fall out of frame. If it had fallen on camera, we would've had to do the scene again. But all is good—I hope. I turn to director Tom Cherones. He reads my mind. "It was great!" he says. "We got it."

* * *

KRAMER PLAYING CHARACTERS is one thing. Now setting up Kramer to do funny, not just say funny, is the next step. It comes in the episode titled "The Revenge." In it, Jerry and Kramer seek revenge on the owner of their laundromat, who Kramer believes stole money from his pants pocket. Written by Larry David, it includes a second storyline in which George quits his job after he's told he can no longer use his boss's bathroom (Larry once quit *SNL* but then returned the following Monday as if he didn't quit).

In the script, I have a lengthy monologue about the laundromat where Jerry and I have returned to confront the owner. I explain to Elaine and George how we exacted revenge. This is the first extensive piece that Larry has written specifically for me. It's one of those big speeches that normally go to Jason or Julia, but now, in our twelfth episode of season two, I have one of my own. I'm grateful, but I'd rather act it all out than say it.

To me, the scene can be much funnier if I am actually staggering around the laundromat with a forty-five-pound bag of cement while Jerry tries to distract the owner from noticing what I'm up to. Here is the opportunity Uncle Milty told me about—to say *and* do funny at the same time.

But Cherones shakes his head.

"We don't really have time," he says. "And how are you going to do that in front of a live audience?" This is one of the reasons why dialogue-driven shows, mostly sitcoms, do not do comedy routines. They're simply seen as extended stage business that's time consuming, only slows the dialogue down, and sometimes costs more money to stage. Back before this, when talkies came into vogue, Buster Keaton, who is purely physical and all about stage business, was always asked to speed it up, keep the dialogue going. There was no room for physical comedy. On the other hand, I do believe that the success of *I Love Lucy* had much to do with the physical comedy that Lucy injected into the show.

But before I respond to Cherones, Jerry steps in. He says we'll shoot what I'm up to, the entire scene, business and all, and it'll be a "playback" on the house monitors for our live audience. Jerry gets me. As he once said to the network, "We're doing a comedy here." I know the laughs will be with us. We're set to shoot tomorrow afternoon. I've got to get it together.

I lay out the scene. A set is built. I stage all the business where Kramer struggles with the cement bag and pouring the cement into the washer. I know exactly how I'm going to move. We shoot the business with the cement—me stumbling over chairs, tottering under the weight of the bag, banging into a wall of machines, dust flying all over me—in one take. It's one of my favorite scenes for the entire run of the show.

The footage is edited into two parts. One is a cutaway to another scene, then back to me putting the cement in the washer. It works. Action speaks louder than words. I'm *doing* funny rather than saying funny, though at the end, standing there in front of the laundromat owner, my clothes and face spattered with powder cement, I have the closing line to cover my outrageous behavior: "I didn't know it was a full box." Huge laugh.

These two episodes marked the beginning for Kramer as a "character actor" and "the doing of physical comedy" right here on the Mack Sennett lot.

It's these two episodes, which we shoot back to back at the end of January and mid-February, that have a profound effect on me and I'd like to think the show as well. Until now, I've played Kramer a bit slow, like he's still locked up in the building or himself and a couple steps behind everyone else.

But now Kramer is unleashed. He's out of the building. I'm given the green light to run. I shift gears. I play him as if he's a few steps ahead of everybody. The shift is immediate. Kramer slides in or is propelled by the force of his "kavorka," pushed into the life he so imagines to be true.

* * *

AT THE END OF FEBRUARY 1991, we shoot "The Deal," the ninth of twelve episodes to air that season. It's Elaine's birthday, and while Jerry overthinks and ultimately botches her gift, Kramer gives her exactly what she wants along with a beautiful card, which she reads out loud to him and Jerry. It's poetry. Elaine is touched. Kramer turns to Jerry and grins. "Yeats."

The audience loves it, and so do I. It's a prelude to Kramer as the hipster-hearted doofus. He is deep enough to know and understand the great Irish poet.

"*Come Fairies, take me out of this dull world,*" Yeats wrote, "*for I would ride with you upon the wind and dance upon the mountains like a flame!*"

I feel Kramer is out of the "dull world." He's now lit up by his imagination. He is a dancing light. And I am upon his mountain so oriented through the character. Giddyup!

CHAPTER 19

The K-Man Cometh

The last episode of season two airs in mid-May 1991, and we do not have to wait long before NBC picks up the show with a full season order of twenty-two episodes. We're set now.

I spend the summer in Stella Adler's master class and work closely with Joanne Linville and a handful of her best students to launch an experimental lab at Conservatory West. I direct Megan Terry's *Keep Tightly Closed in a Cool Dry Place.* I should have acted in it. My direction is more of how I would play the characters. It's a trap that actors can fall into when they direct. Timothy McNeil, a very gifted character actor who's been with Stella for years, is marvelous in the play, along with David O'Neill. It's the same with the talented Mark Ruffalo, who is as good as he is but was once told by Stella not to get rid of his day job.

Brion James and John Ritter are also in Stella's master class. Brion's great line in *Blade Runner,* "Wake up! Time to die," has me gushing when we meet. What a villain! He's even better doing Chekhov. His best friend is comedian Tim Thomerson, who I saw on TV back in San Diego before I left for LA to work at the Improv. To meet these people is a kick for me. John and I did *Problem Child* together, and he worships Stella. He attributes his ability to do comedy to her techniques on building character, the look, movement, the voice, all grounded in backstory, legitimizing the "intention" of character. Paul Reubens was certainly in on this when he created Pee-wee Herman. We talked about it often.

Joanne's advanced technique class helps me unleash Kramer. Now, with a twenty-two-show pickup, she and I have a full *Seinfeld* season to work together. Each week we meet and go over the script, inventing backstory. The K-Man is as real as you and I.

At a secondhand clothing store in Venice, a guy has tipped me off to a vintage clothing shop in Santa Barbara that he thought might have more shirts from the late '60s, some jackets, and stylish old pants. At the time, nobody is interested in this stuff. It's not considered vintage or hip. It's not in demand by anybody—except me. I buy up whatever I can find. Kramer is still wearing the clothes he wore twenty-five years ago. For Kramer, it's cheaper this way living in NYC without a steady job.

At the shop in Santa Barbara, I find a few shirts. They're perfect. The owner catches my excitement.

"You like these?" he says.

"Yeah, this is the stuff I'm looking for," I say. "Do you have more?"

He disappears into a back room and returns with three boxes of Town and Country shirts still wrapped in plastic. They're brand new, in pristine condition! I buy all of them, seven brand-new shirts from the late '60s, for fifteen bucks. Yep, this is the way Kramer would shop. Kramer's pants—quality, cotton-cuffed trousers—also come from the used clothing stores, at five bucks a pair. However, I'm having a hard time finding his shoes. Old Converse tennis shoes doesn't feel right. It'll come.

For me, the shoes are the most important item of a character's ensemble. To be in the characters shoes—to be worn every day of rehearsal—this is a quirk of mine that I must attend to.

I finally come across a pair of '70s Doc Martens at a shop on Melrose Avenue. They have two pairs, and I quickly buy them both. I'll wear these same two for the duration of the series. They are black with nine white stars around the front of the toe on each pair (which will seem oddly significant down the road, as the show will run for nine seasons). At the studio, I black out the stars and begin the ritual of putting one pair on for every rehearsal as soon as I arrive for work. I save the other pair for showtime.

During rehearsal, along with the shoes I usually wear one of Kramer's shirts. Sometimes different shirts, as I try to find the one that feels right for the scene. This goes for jackets too. Throughout the week I pick through my stock for the right color of shirt, pants, and jacket, a combo that links Kramer to the world around him.

All this prep has kept me busy. But by the time we regroup on Stage 19 for season three, I am ready for adventure, and so is Kramer dressed for it all.

* * *

In "The Truth," the season's second episode, Kramer is dating Elaine's roommate, and Elaine is put off by the wild, uninhibited sex taking over her apartment. She's especially upset that Kramer walked into her bedroom and saw her naked. When she squirms uneasily in front of Jerry, wondering how life can ever be the same, Kramer stands up and offers to take off his clothes so she can see him in the raw.

The studio audience screams when I stand, unbutton my shirt, and whip off my belt, insisting I want her to see me nude too! It's a defining moment, a declaration that Kramer has no problem with the body as it is. He's the opposite of George, who is jammed up, frightened by sex, and unable to escape his mother's shadow. Kramer is a man of nature. Why stay so covered up?

If Kramer walks into a room and notices a woman there, he holds up and looks at her. I do it regardless of whether it's in the

210

script. Women are lovely to look at. It's Kramer's way of paying a compliment. Later in the episode, just before we shoot a scene where Kramer dances in the living room with Elaine's roommate, Larry slips up behind me and whispers, "Just do a little Dick here."

Larry is referencing my character from *Fridays*.

"I can do that?" I ask.

He gives me a little Dick-like expression. It's a green light. Another piece of this character comes together. Kramer is very comfortable with sex. Thank you, Larry.

* * *

My wife and I agree to a divorce. It seems to have come on me so fast, though one could argue that nineteen years isn't fast. I try to work things out on the phone, but it becomes a discussion for lawyers, and I don't know anything about lawyers. The situation sends me spiraling downward. One night I'm at Jerry's apartment in North Hollywood. Who better to turn to than Superman? But I'm too down even for Jerry. After a while, he gets his best friend, comedian Larry Miller, to come over, and together they try to cheer me up.

Jerry is concerned and, having little to no experience in a long-term relationship, especially marriage, he calls his manager, George Shapiro. I don't know what he says to George, but George moves in, which is what good managers do, and he sees that I'm a mess. He sends me to a top divorce lawyer.

Within days, the lawyer has me opening my own bank account and buying my own home. I really don't have much money for this. The house is run down and filled with the stench of all the cats and dogs that lived there. It used to be a nice house, but not anymore. With the help of a VA loan, zero down, after taking possession of the key, I let myself inside and I'm so overwhelmed by the mess that I sit on the filthy living room floor and cry. The place needs a lot of work. So do I, to catch up to myself—now clearly on my own.

One of the crew on *Seinfeld* recommends a contractor. He is a true artisan who can do just about anything, and that's what I need. And not just me. My sixteen-year-old daughter is living with her mother, and I want to fix things up so she can feel at home here too. The house is symbolic of all that's going on: I'm coming into Kramer, the show is coming into itself, I'm coming into a new phase of my life, I'm coming into this home, wanting to make it a real home, and eager to include my daughter.

Finally, the divorce papers are signed, and our marriage officially and legally ends with *Seinfeld*'s twenty-third episode, "The Parking Garage." With the papers signed, I'm feeling a bit lost, not sure where I am. Is it an accident this happens the same week I'm at the center of an episode about not being able to find my car in a parking garage? It wasn't planned, but the universe is full of signs that can tap you on the shoulder and say, "Hi, we're synced up," which is another way of saying we get along.

* * *

"The Parking Garage" is an inspired piece of writing from Larry David. In it, Kramer drives Jerry, George, and Elaine to the mall in New Jersey, where he purchases "the world's cheapest" air conditioner. Afterward, none of them can remember where Kramer parked his car. For the show, a large parking garage is built in our soundstage. (Interestingly, the network doesn't object to setting the whole episode in one set—here, a parking garage—the way they did "The Chinese Restaurant.") What's certainly good is that we're all in this show, this situation together, but each of us is serving a converging storyline. This is a complex shoot and done without a live audience. A lot of stop-and-go pickups; cars, camera angles, posted signs are constantly changed to give the effect that we're on different levels of a parking garage. The shoot goes very late into the night, three in the morning!

Kramer wants to find his car and go home. The sight of Kramer carrying this heavy box around the garage, straining to keep it in his grasp—who hasn't carried such a box of burdens?

No matter how organized or together we think we are, we're always in a fluctuating state of lost and found. We're always confronting problems and looking for the way out of here.

How funny is it that Jerry and George get snagged for trying to pee. There are no bathrooms down there, but they gotta go. What are they supposed to do? How many times have I been in New York, walked into a store, asked if I can use the bathroom, and been told no? I'm in the epicenter of civilization and I can't even take a piss! It doesn't make sense. It's not meant to. It's irrational.

Two things about this episode: I want some real weight in the box so that I really would tire of carrying it by the time we find the car. The other thing is that when we finally find the car, I chuck the box in the trunk, but I accidentally slam my face on the box. It's a real accident. My lip instantly swells. Julia starts to go up. She's holding it back. I can feel the laugh trying to get out of her. It should come out of her. Elaine would laugh! I continue to play it as Kramer. The four of us get into the car—and as written, the car starts and I'm supposed to back out and drive around in a circle, get disoriented, and ask, "Where are we?" But the car won't start! This is a God-given rewrite, the universe syncing us up to a better ending.

The four of us do our best not to laugh, but I think if we did laugh it still would have worked. The best we can do is laugh out loud. After everything we've been through, we're still stuck in the garage! It's just perfect.

* * *

SEASON THREE IS NOT WITHOUT its growing pains. "The Pen," which is all about Jerry and Elaine visiting Jerry's parents in Florida, is the second and only other *Seinfeld* episode that doesn't include me. I accept this with an equanimity that I didn't have last season when we did "The Chinese Restaurant." I'm more confident of my place in the show now. But Jason threatens to quit after learning that he's also not in the episode. He's furious. Well, it's his turn with it. I go home to put carpet in my daughter's new bedroom.

In his defense, I understand why he reacts this way. Jason came onto the show with the most confidence of anyone. He had won a Tony Award on the New York stage, not an insignificant achievement, and until the table read for "The Pen," he has assumed that *Seinfeld* is a buddy show, starring him and Jerry. But this business breeds both massive egos and incredible insecurity, and this episode is one of those ego-jarring wake-ups. With a simple shift in writing, the show could be about Jerry and Elaine, and NBC executives would love to have another Sam and Diane are-they-or-aren't-they-type romance in prime time.

But none of us needs to worry. Larry and Jerry don't have any such changes in mind. Larry is merely pushing the boundaries of the sitcom format, as he and the show's writers will continue to do as they gain a deeper understanding of the characters and the potential the show gives them to write about life.

That's really the story this entire third season—a show coming into its own. In "The Library," Larry Charles takes a simple plot—Jerry is fined for not returning a library book he checked out in 1971—and develops four intricate, interwoven storylines: Jerry's got this overdue book, Henry Miller's *Tropic of Cancer*; George's old gym teacher, who got fired for giving him a wedgie, is now homeless on the library steps; Kramer seduces an Alma Winemiller–like librarian who writes sensitive poetry; and Elaine uses said poetry to impress her boss. This is my *Summer and Smoke* episode. Kramer's kavorka is substantiated, and "Alma" is gratefully liberated through sex.

In "The Alternate Side," Kramer gets a one-line speaking part in a Woody Allen movie shooting outside the apartment building, and that line results in the show's first oft-repeated catchphrase, "These pretzels are making me thirsty." And, of course, Kramer imagines himself an actor, and the bug is upon him.

Then, in "The Fix-Up," Kramer is given a bag of brightly colored condoms, which he brings into Jerry's apartment, eager to share. Jerry's too practical to go for the bright colors. "No thanks." Kramer offers the bag to Elaine—"Go ahead, take half." She recoils in disgust. "What, am I, a hooker?" George takes one—only one—and shrugs, "It could happen."

Bull's-eye!

The comedy is coming through the characters! We know who these people are and how they behave. Kramer is being advanced, a real presence now among the other three characters. He's no longer just Jerry's crazy neighbor. He's part of the antics and often the ringleader. In the show's thirty-third episode, he hands out condoms. Of course, with Kramer, in the end there's a catch: in this case, the condoms are defective.

Regardless, his potency is coming through. "What are you going to do with all of them?" Elaine asks, referring to the bag of condoms. Kramer only needs to smile and say, "Well…"

The K-Man cometh. My entrances are their own event. At the top of the show, our live audience has to be told to hold the applause when Kramer enters. As much as I appreciate the recognition, waiting for the applause to end just throws off my tempo and holds up the action. I've got to slide into the scene, keep it moving. Although Kramer entering the room could easily imagine an audience applauding now that he's "an actor" and worked with Woody Allen.

* * *

LIFE IS A SERIES OF ENTRANCES AND EXITS, starting with the miraculous first and the inevitable last. Kramer is on it. To facilitate his entrances, I sand down the soles of my Dr. Martens so they're as smooth as bowling shoes and add a touch of silicon spray to give them even more slide.

When I burst through Jerry's door, I'm bringing stuff into the room. This character is a live wire. This is why I've got that "fourth" camera wide on me in every scene. I don't always know how the physical comedy will come off or where it's going to go. Nevertheless, I do prep work to catch it. Take "The Subway," another episode from Larry Charles that tracks the four of us on the subway. Jerry meets a nudist; George encounters a hooker who handcuffs him to a hotel room bed and robs him; Elaine is on her way to a lesbian wedding; and Kramer gets a tip on a horse race.

The interior of a subway car is built on the set, demonstrating the show can do anything and go anywhere now. The choreography behind the comedy can be quite intricate. For instance, setting up a bit with Tom Cherones for one scene in which everyone entering the train and going for a seat is coordinated with Kramer rushing for his own seat and losing out. I work with the extras; my moves are entirely dependent on their moves. It's marvelous how well coordinated we get. Together, we really catch the scene. It's another one of my favorite episodes with Kramer.

* * *

AFTER THE TAPING, we have our routines. Jerry, Jason, and Julia go to Jerry's Deli in Studio City for a late-night meal and decompression. I don't want to hang out in a noisy restaurant, and I'm not that keen on the food, especially late at night. I just want to go home and take off all my clothes and light a fire. On the day after our tapings, I'm always in my swimming pool for about thirty-five minutes, sitting in a patio chair secured at the bottom of the deep end, a diver's regulator in my mouth, breathing through my ScubaPro tank.

Ah, the quiet, the stillness, the way of the water all around me is a reboot. I inhale, and slowly exhaling I empty out—let it all go so I can fill up again. Inhale and let it out, entrances and exits.

* * *

IN OUR FINAL EPISODE OF THE SEASON, "The Keys," Jerry takes back the keys to his apartment from Kramer, who strikes out for new adventure in LA. "You're really going?" George asks. Kramer points to his head. "Up here, I'm already gone." It's a line that sums up the psyche of Kramer. From within him he's already there, where he would be outside of himself. He gets there fast through his imaginal life. He's not angry that Jerry has asked him to return his keys. Nor is he crazy. He knows that when one apartment door closes, another door will surely open. And then he's gone. To catch up to where he went. Giddyup!

* * *

THE NEXT TIME KRAMER POPS UP isn't in Jerry's apartment. He's onstage at Carnegie Hall in New York. Jerry's headlining two nights in the fabled old theater, and he has asked me to open for him. But not in the traditional way of an opening act. "Just go out and fool around for a few minutes," he says. "They'll love it." We know that Kramer has become quite popular. To have the K-Man there with him for such a gig, well, I'm delighted to be a part of Jerry's big night.

I said I don't have any material. He said, "Just go out there, something will happen." And it does. I come out onstage carrying the mic on its stand like one of the crew. As soon as the audience recognizes me, there is a huge applause. Wow! This house is up for a show. Just about any move I make gets a laugh. I glance curiously at the audience, as if confused by their presence or bewildered by mine, and I get a big laugh. I play with this for a few moments, making subtle faces. More laughs.

My routine is brief. I don't speak a word. It's all business with that mic on a stand and the long cord running to it. That long cord, which runs offstage to I don't know where. I pick it up and whip it about. I am trying to straighten it out, to get everything set up for Jerry. I manage to get tangled up in the cord, tripping and flopping about until I'm on the floor with the microphone stand all over me. Big laughs. All knotted up, I awkwardly make my way to the wings and exit. Applause.

Jerry comes out and takes center stage. Applause. I appear at the wings and take a bow. Applause. Now Jerry has the house for an hour. Standing ovation.

Kramer comes through the door and gets it on whether it's Jerry's apartment or onstage at Carnegie Hall. I don't need to think too much when Kramer is on. This character has become a ride that I'm holding on to. He just takes ahold of me and we're off. Everything is up and at 'em, a Giddyup! This is where his heart is. He's the heart of my clown, the best that I can be in this world.

The same can be said of the show.

All of us came together as a force of nature, a great ha-ha event that we all marveled at. Someone once said that "God moves in mysterious ways." I'll second that.

CHAPTER 20

The Hipster Doofus

The green bike that appears on Jerry's apartment wall midway through season three is a Klein—a Klein Rascal. It's there because of me.

I have been a fitness devotee since walking into an aerobics class at Jane Fonda's studio a few years before *Seinfeld*. Jane taught the class every now and then. She was really into it. It wasn't just a business. The class attracted its share of stars: Rutger Hauer, Lesley Ann Warren, and Garry Shandling were regulars. It could be a bit of a scene, but the workout was where it was at. Advanced aerobics was hard-core. People didn't finish the class. I never gave in. I went four or five times a week for a ninety-minute routine. Everything in the room was loudly amplified: the teacher shouting moves through a microphone, the loud rock music. I will say that after months of this, the sound from it all grated on my nerves.

I might've quit if the schedule hadn't changed. A few times a week the studio introduced Bikram yoga. Everyone gave it a shot. It was more rigorous than advanced aerobics. There wasn't a lot of running around, throwing your body about, or loud music. Instead, we quietly stood in place, stretching while holding difficult balancing poses, called asanas, and on the floor too, all-out stretching, then headstands and backbends, and it kicked everybody's ass. I would finish class in a pool of sweat and I hadn't moved a few feet from where I was standing.

Within a month, everybody who was used to aerobics ran back to that. I was the only one left. They canceled the class. So I went off looking for another place to do yoga.

Iyengar yoga was it. It's even more rigorous. A whole lot of attention to the positions. You use blocks and straps for alignment, and a "sticky mat," the first time I ever saw one, to maximize traction for increasing the stretch. You're also taught ways to breathe. Breathing correctly is a must or you'll never make it.

Backstage, Jerry notices me stretching, holding a standing position, and asks what I'm doing.

"Iyengar yoga."

"Why?" he asks.

"I stay flexible, helps me stay strong," I say. "It's a great workout. I just do the exercises to stretch out. It keeps me nimble, agile, better at physical comedy."

Jerry is intrigued and wants to know where you go for this stuff. Though he's a practitioner of Transcendental Meditation, he wants to learn yoga. I tell him about a small group led by Eric Small, a certified Iyengar teacher who works out of a well-equipped studio on the property of his magnificent mansion in Bel Air. I know Jerry will like the environment at first, but then he'll probably be on his way, which is how it goes. After attending a few classes, he's out of there. He's not the kind of man to follow some yoga teacher. He's holding his show, that's his asana, and he's holding it very well.

I don't stick around the class for much longer either. Once I learn the poses, I start doing them on my own. This is supposed to be the goal anyway, to "have your own practice" and go from there. I get mellow at the bottom of my pool or up in the mountains above the city, where I sit still with the sun. I also pedal my mountain bike along the trails around Topanga. I commute to the studio almost daily on my black twenty-six-inch Klein mountain bike. I started riding a year ago after my car was stolen. I figured I wasn't supposed to have a car; I'd just ride my bike everywhere. I'm close enough to the studio.

That lasted a few weeks until I came to my senses. You need a car in LA. Done.

So now I understand why my car was stolen. I was supposed to buy a new car! I was upgrading thanks to the show. But I still love riding my bike and continue to take it to the studio, always arriving there feeling up and ready, and also using it to cruise around the lot between the soundstages and throughout our stage area saying hello to everyone.

I used to geek out about my bike's Deore XT components, Bulls-eye front hub, titanium bottom bracket, Mavic headset, Ritchey seat post, Onza bar ends, and Panaracer Smokes. Now, I just pedal to get there. I'm not into all the "stuff" that a bike can be. My legs are the best thing going.

Before we go back for season four, I ramp up my cycling to get in peak shape for the new season. Endurance is crucial over the course of twenty-two episodes.

This summer, a few of the younger guys on the *Seinfeld* crew, very serious cyclists, are preparing for the infamous Kamikaze race down one of the more treacherous ski slopes on Mammoth Mountain. I train with them, doing twenty-, thirty-, and sometimes forty-mile distance rides, as well as strenuous shorter stints on the fourteen-and-a-half-mile Bulldog Loop in the Santa Monica Mountains. This is hard bike riding. No bullshit.

When it's time for the Kamikaze, we check into a little hotel in Mammoth. Early the next morning, we get our bikes and head for the slope. People are already taking practice runs, flying down the trail at thirty miles per hour! I see guys wiping out in a jumble of twisting limbs and bike frames wrapped in a cloud of dust. Two ambulances at the bottom of the trail are kept busy. I'm reminded of the summer I was an ambulance attendant just after high school and worked the weekend motorcycle races. I got twenty-five bucks for each person I took to the hospital. It was a bloodbath. In a weekend, I'd cover the cost of new American mag wheels for my Chevy.

Before my practice run, I imagine the ambulance drivers on the mountain: "Do we get a bonus for bringing in the dude from *Seinfeld?*"

To check it out, I go down the course at half speed. Whoa! This course is dangerous. You could fly off the trail into the treetops. Every bone in my body shakes and vibrates. I'm not even sure if my bike is going to hold up. A few riders have brought extra bikes to replace cracked frames. I've just got one bike for this. Is my frame already cracked? I don't have a working crew to check it out like some of these sponsored racers have. After another run, picking up speed to qualify, I come to a stop on flat ground. What the hell am I doing here?

I catch my breath and coast over to the booth where various trophies and large ribbons are displayed. I want to see what I'll get if I place. An official there shows me the prizes that go out to the division winners. "That's it, an acetate ribbon?" I just came to my senses. I've got to be back on the set in two weeks for the fall season of *Seinfeld.* I can't afford to get hurt. And this Kamikaze run for a blue rosette ribbon ain't gonna cut it. "Are they real gold, Mike?" I hear my mom say.

I watch my buddies and other riders take to the slope. It's a hairy event for them all. My bike is on its rack, and I'm in good shape ready to head home.

* * *

I CAN SENSE THE PROMISE of the new season. There's momentum, energy, and anticipation. *Seinfeld* has become something people discuss at work. Around the water cooler, it has risen to event status.

In addition to ratings, its eight Emmy nominations acknowledge the show's artistic success, and though *Seinfeld* wins only two statues at the event in early September (one for editing and the other for writing), everyone knows the show is coming into its own. We're about to hit our stride.

The new season opens with "The Trip Part 1" and "The Trip Part 2," a double episode in which Jerry gets booked on *The Tonight Show* in Los Angeles and takes George with him to look for Kramer, who's somewhere in Hollywood working on his acting career. Because Julia is nearing the due date of her first child, Elaine is not involved. This never hits me as I'm out on location shooting exteriors around Los Angeles. How Julia did our show with a baby in her dressing room, she was working harder than us all!

During rehearsal, I'm screwing around playing Kramer as an acting teacher through my old *Fridays* character Dick. I'm ad-libbing about colors and emotion. It cracks Jerry up. "We have to put that in the show," he says. The scene is set up backstage. I improvise the whole thing with Kramer lecturing a group of acting students about his technique. "I work with color," he says. "Imagining color, then finding the emotional, vibrational mood connected to color." The students listen intently. "If you look through my scripts," he continues, "you'll see that all my lines have a special color. I don't memorize language. I memorize color."

Suddenly, Kramer is the teacher, telling millions of people that each person has their color and they need to find their color. I playfully borrowed this from color psychology, that each color can symbolize a state of mind. Red is anger. Yellow is happiness. Blue is sadness.

Goethe once said, "The highest goal that man can achieve is amazement." Well, Kramer is certainly expressing his "amazement." A few episodes later, he tells George that he has to listen to his little man. "The little man knows all," he says. Kramer is now Neal Cassady to Jerry's Jack Kerouac, divining a rhythm, keeping the beat, providing narration, expanding minds.

He's the Fool and the philosopher. Either he's onto something or he's full of it or both. Whichever it is, it's amusing, and his students are paying attention.

The next two episodes, "The Pitch" and "The Ticket," take *Seinfeld* in a meta-direction few shows besides Garry Shandling's *The Larry Sanders Show* have ventured (a show I guest-starred in satirizing myself promoting *Seinfeld*). Having Jerry and George pitch NBC a show about nothing goes beyond the crafty inside joke they intended and knew they could return to all season. It's the key to greatness. Just as I have asked myself who Kramer is, now, in these early weeks of our fourth season, Larry and Jerry and the writing staff are asking that same question of the show itself. How did it come to be? Let's let the audience in on it.

Socrates said, "To know thyself is the beginning of wisdom." To know thyself—and make fun of thyself—is the beginning of comedy!

* * *

SEINFELD'S RATINGS CLIMB EVERY WEEK. What do people see in this show? What do they like about George, a wimpy mama's boy? Why do they love Elaine, who tries at everything but never quite lands it? Is Jerry that interesting? They struggle and flail, cheat and lie, stumble over their biases and insecurities, rationalize their faults and screwups, and fail to learn from their mistakes. And Kramer? Only he among them is free of neurosis and able to revel in his passions, ideas, and sexuality. But he's also perfectly imperfect, and everyone knows it except him.

"You know what Kramer is?" Larry says to me one day. We're idling backstage, and he looks at me like he's just had an epiphany.

"What?" I ask.

"He's a hipster doofus."

Yeah, I think. That's exactly who Kramer is.

Larry has caught up and figured him out. America, it seems to me, was way ahead of us. *Why was Kramer so popular?* This little show that is cleverly described as the show about nothing is, in fact, about everything. And Kramer is into "everything." Come to class. Dr. Kramer will teach you. Who hasn't thought about pirating cable? Who hasn't eyed those empty handicapped parking spots? And condoms? Well, some are defective. That's life.

And there's something else in this life that hasn't been played out on TV. And in "The Contest," this subject will be a groundbreaker, earning Larry David an Emmy.

"My mother caught me," George says.

At the table read, Jason's delivery is perfect. Jerry is already cracking up.

The premise is as simple as it is brilliant. After George admits that his mother caught him, Jerry, George, Elaine, and Kramer make a bet to see who can go the longest without "gratifying themselves."

The word "masturbation" is never mentioned in the script. And the need to be clever and coy as we check on each other's status leads to the show's most popular catchphrase: "master of your domain."

"But are you still master of your domain?" Jerry asks Elaine. "I'm queen of the castle," she says. "And you?" "Lord of the manor," he replies. By the time we shoot the episode, we can tell where the laughs will be. But none is bigger than when Kramer, just after seeing a naked woman in her apartment through Jerry's window, shortly returns to Jerry's apartment, slaps a bill on the counter, and declares, "I'm out!"

The audience goes wild. Not only is the audience in on the joke, but they are also hip to the whole gestalt. Kramer doesn't give a damn about the bet. He has no guilt. Some urges are too strong to resist. Some you don't want to resist. It's what makes us human. Indeed, before leaving Jerry's apartment again, Kramer warns Jerry and George, "Watch out. She's gonna get you next." That's life. She's the wild card, the highest trump, the irrational that declares you're out.

* * *

THE NEXT WEEK'S EPISODE, "The Pick," is another one of those shows whose storylines are rooted in cringeworthy reality. Jerry is dating a Calvin Klein model—that is, until she thinks she sees him picking his nose. Kramer takes Elaine's picture for her holiday card, which she discovers has inadvertently exposed one of her nipples to everyone on her mailing list, including her ten-year-old nephew and her coworkers. And George sees a therapist in the hope of dealing with his breakup but spends his first session trying to unzip his jacket.

Amid all this, Kramer realizes that Calvin Klein has stolen his idea for a fragrance that captures the scent of the beach. The new Calvin Klein scent is called "Ocean."

This storyline ties back to an episode the previous season in which Kramer pitched his idea to a rep from Calvin Klein.

Before the table read, Larry says he has a question for me. I see the twinkle in his eye and know something's up.

"Are you okay doing a scene in your underwear?"

Kramer will jump at this!

I'm walking around in my underwear on prime-time television in front of twenty-five million people? Let's break some ground! "Count me in!" I say.

Kramer's popularity has really taken off. The audience wants to see more of him, and when Kramer meets with Calvin Klein, they get an eyeful. Walking in angry, outraged, and determined to reap the millions due him, Kramer is quickly taken in by the smooth fashion mogul, who compliments his attitude and physique and overall look. Flattered, Kramer has a whole different connection to Calvin Klein. He's been seduced. As I turn to sit down, I stumble slightly, a choice I made to emphasize the shift in Kramer's mindset. And because it's funny.

In the next scene, Kramer is modeling Calvin Klein underwear for Calvin and two of his associates. Besides gray socks and my Dr. Martens, all I'm wearing is a tight pair of white Calvin Klein cotton briefs. "His buttocks are sublime," one of Calvin's associates purrs. I understand why Larry asked if I would be okay with this. The full gig is on display: my bottom, the bulge, everything. It's pretty heavy for network television. In early Greek comedy, funny characters did wear enlarged dildos. Well, it's all part of the Fool's kit. I'm into it.

For me, it's sublime. While rehearsing on the Calvin Klein set, I notice that one of the corner walls is curved, and it gives me an idea. When we shoot the scene, I strut about in my underwear, then stop to pose by the wall. Leaning into the wall's curve, I purposely slip and tumble to the floor. I know I have the fourth camera shooting wide for exactly this, from head to foot, "full gig" and all. The pratfall is right on. So is the laughter.

After the scene, Jerry's in front of me, grinning and shaking his head in admiration. "Michael, where did that fall come from?" he says. "From the cosmos," I say.

The episode airs on December 16, 1992, and soon after a gift basket arrives for me full of Calvin Klein cologne. Each episode thereafter, Kramer always wears Calvin Klein cologne. I smell great. He earned it.

* * *

By February 1993, *Seinfeld*'s ratings have almost doubled since the show was moved to Thursday nights from Wednesday, and I've got a lot of show to work with. The demands of a new show every week are consuming and exhausting. But I do need to get out a little bit. For my health and sanity, I realize a personal life is necessary. I date and hang out with women who are fun to be around. After two decades of marriage, though, this is all new to me again, and I must be careful who I bring into my life.

My daughter is about to graduate from high school and still needs me around. I'm all there. Also, I don't want to mislead or hurt any of the women I'm seeing. I want to have fun, but I try to make it clear that I'm not keen on getting into a relationship after my marriage blew up in my face. I like going out to great restaurants, but the show's popularity can turn something as simple as pulling up to the valet parking into a scene of excited fans and aggressive photographers.

I try to avoid the paparazzi. A recluse by nature, more comfortable sitting at the bottom of a swimming pool than walking a red carpet, I'm interested in craft, not celebrity, but the two are often interrelated, aren't they? I'm not going to pull myself apart over this. Fixing up my house and a great Italian dinner with my daughter does it for me. On weekends, I like to go to antique stores and flea markets. I'm always shopping for Kramer, always on the lookout for interesting clothes, stuff for his apartment, or interesting things for my house.

One of my favorite finds for Kramer is a shirt that has Shriner hats on it. I'm into the Shriners (I'll become a member), something I discovered through my love for Laurel and Hardy's classic film *Sons of the Desert* and my great admiration for Red Skelton, who was also fond of the fraternity and its Royal Order of Jesters. I think I wear Kramer well. I think we wear each other well. It's hard to tell the difference. Wherever I go, I'm Kramer to everyone. "Kramer!" they exclaim. "Look, it's Kramer!"

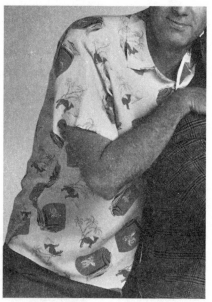

My Shriner shirt. Whoever has it now, may the kavorka be with you.

He's like a "high-frequency vehicle," a contact experience, and I've been taken up by him. I'm on board. All is well.

* * *

228

When we moved into Stage 19 on the Radford Studio lot, Jerry, George, and Julia chose dressing rooms on the second floor just outside our stage building. They were considered more desirable because they were large and have greater privacy. One smaller dressing room was on the first floor; that's the one I wanted. To me, it was the best of the bunch, with a large picture window, a big shower area, and a small outdoor terrace where I have a little sky and can sit and watch some of the cars and people going by. The decor is simple, with a few personal touches, most prominently a tinted, antique-looking illustration from *Marblehead Manor* of a butler tripping, the tray he's holding coming apart in midair.

Jerry has Superman. This butler is me. It's the pratfall holding its own, my own, doing physical comedy on the show, tripping up Kramer for a laugh. During rehearsal one day, I sketch a pratfall.

One day, I'm sitting on my terrace and Phil Hartman spots me. He honks the horn of his '63 powder blue Ford Thunderbird that he has restored and is driving through the lot to probably show it off. I would. It's just beautiful! Phil and I met through Paul Reubens when they were putting together the original *Pee-wee Herman Show* in 1981, and we became friends. His car is in mint condition, and he is beaming from behind the wheel. He loves the good ol' days when a car had steel to it instead of all the plastic in cars today.

"Hi, Michael," he says.

"The car," I say, nodding in appreciation. "I see it."

"It's nice, isn't it?" Phil says.

"It's you," I say. "It's beautiful. It's totally you."

Phil pitches me on partnering with him on a bit for a network special celebrating Bob Hope's ninetieth birthday, and I agree. The special is full of hilarious clips from Bob's long career in movies, comedy, and entertaining US troops. My pal Jay Leno hosts. Johnny Carson makes his first television appearance since retiring from *The Tonight Show*. Ginger Rogers blows kisses. Milton Berle quips, "Bob, I hope you live as long as some of my material." George Burns, then ninety-seven, takes a seat next to the man of the hour. "Bob, together we're one hundred eighty-seven years old," he says, "and we're doing something better than anyone else in show business. We're sitting down."

Phil and I play two Civil War soldiers who were in Gettysburg the first time Bob performed for the troops. We arrive in our costumes and stay in character at all times. I suppose both of us are more comfortable scoping out the event this way. We are nuts, and though we are youngsters compared to the old guard of entertainers present that night, Bob Hope's generation, everybody loves us. Phil and I are  of the up-and-coming generation, solid in television, he from *Saturday Night Live* and me through *Seinfeld*, and both featured in two films this year, *So I Married an Axe Murderer* and *Coneheads*. We're whoopin' it up!

And we're working. That's what much of this is about, right? For Bob Hope, George Burns, and others like them, it's the fact that they're still working. Our script is awful, but I keep in mind Jack Burns telling me that committing to the material gets you 70 percent there. Phil is also in on this. We ham it up, and the sketch does well. At least 70 percent, maybe more. My best to Jack Burns.

* * *

"The Junior Mint" is the twentieth episode of the season, our six-tieth overall. Jerry can't remember the name of his new girlfriend, and Elaine's formerly fat ex-boyfriend is in the hospital, awaiting a splenectomy operation. Jerry and Kramer, invited to view the surgery, watch from an observation deck above the operating table, and Kramer accidentally drops a Junior Mint into the patient's open body cavity. The operating room is a big set, and the scene requires camera positions that we can't set up for a live audience. So we shoot the scene without an audience as a playback. Which is fine by me.

A live audience can be terrifying. I am so aware that they are there! I get the job done, but I hate dropping a line in front of them. That just gets back to being on the stage. You never let the audience see you mess up, even a little mistake. You cover any way you can, enough that only the cast knows you went up on your line. Doing *Fridays* live, I was always nervous that I would flub a line on national television.

I think I'm more relaxed shooting without an audience. I can drop a line and pick it up on the next take. I can also play more with the acting and especially the stage business. Doing physical comedy, it's a plus to do retakes until you get your best. Having spent most of my career in front of an audience, it's not hard for me to feel their presence even though I'm shooting a scene without them. With or without an audience, I can feel the laughs within me. I generally know if a scene is funny.

I also know when the dialogue or the business is short of the mark. I'll punch it up, and with Kramer that's easy to do. I've got faces and body movements to go on. Even nonverbal utterances, like Kramer's quirky sounds, can button up a scene. Sometimes I will do some business in a scene and then flub the line at the end of it all. That entails redoing some of the scene for the audience. But the thing is, they're not going to laugh as loud because they have already seen the business. So on the second take I have learned to do the business that I have in the can a bit differently to get another big laugh.

Then I've got two takes in the can. It's like hitting a three-pointer in basketball and drawing the foul. You get to take another shot, and it becomes a four-point score. Like a foul, I try to turn flubs into points.

Wayne Knight, who plays Newman, is just good at what he does. We're always hanging out, appreciating that we're creating comedy in Mack Sennett's original soundstage. You know how Newman goes into rages, how Wayne blows up his face all red as if he's about to explode? Well, creating that kind of performance takes a lot of energy, and like Oliver Hardy, Wayne's weight plays into making it so damn funny. But I think Wayne does more takes than all of us, especially when Jerry is around.

Jerry is his best audience. He always busts up. Sometimes Jerry will slump to the floor from laughing so hard at Wayne's delivery all puffed up, purple in the face.

I once said to Jerry, "Don't go up on Wayne's take. He'll have to do it again. You'll kill the man!" Wayne actually said he didn't mind going out that way. That's commitment!

* * *

BY THE MIDDLE OF THE FOURTH SEASON, all this "show about nothing" is adding up to many things. Jerry, George, Elaine, and Kramer have evolved to the point that each character has their own storyline. We're also shooting more exteriors outside the stage without an audience. The hours are longer, but I don't care. It makes for a better show. The commitment to quality keeps going up as it should when thirty million people are watching us each week.

It does put more pressure on us, but all of us have been around the block. Nobody is on this show who doesn't have years of experience. Still, servicing a megahit show with just four days to put it up on its feet is a fast-lane operation always checking for quality control. The pressure is on Larry David and the writing staff to write episodes that measure up to the previous weeks.

Two words are circulated that capture how far we've come, what *Seinfeld* has become—cultural phenomenon. All of us are wrapped up in it, leaning into our talent, but Larry must deliver to meet so many expectations. This is a man who folded at the Comedy Store one night and then came back the next night and blew everybody away. He's got the stuff.

This isn't about writing well or good writing. It's about great comedic writing every week. It's about servicing characters played by actors who are looking out for them, making sure the dialogue is right.

Which comes first, the character or the writing? I suppose they are of each other. The great comic actor Sid Caesar admitted that the pressure of doing *Your Show of Shows* drove him to drink—and he had great characters and Carl Reiner, Mel Brooks, and Woody Allen on his writing staff. So, what happened? It's that pressure of keeping character and writing together, that they continue to sustain the best that you can be. If it falls short, the cookie crumbles. But I'll never drink or do drugs because of it.

Our staff is top notch and includes Larry Charles, Peter Mehlman, Bruce Kirschbaum, Elaine Pope, and Andy Robin, who wrote "The Junior Mint."

All are sharp, precise, gifted writers. But it ain't easy. Every pitch has to go to Larry and Jerry. Every script, no matter who's credited, passes through Jerry and ultimately Larry, the one head to hold it all in. Writers are hired and off the show in weeks. Larry has no stomach for firing writers. Jerry is the ax. He loves to chop the fat off the meat. He's the butcher. You want your meat lean and tender? Jerry is the man to go to. I see great comics who write their own material hired to write for the show, and they're out in a week! Jerry "knows," and so we're all eating the best of cuts.

Much of this comes to me secondhand, because I am tunnel-visioned on my own job. During the week, I often sit in a chair behind the set with my eyes closed, trancelike, stewing over my lines. Everyone knows it's my chair, my process, my time. No one bothers me. They can feel my intensity. I am visualizing each scene where I can heighten comedy, speaking to the lines, are you going to work out or not? If a line continues to rub me in the wrong way, I'll let our director know. I never take it up with Jerry and Larry directly. I don't need to.

In the evening I usually get new pages based on my concerns, new lines to play with. These changes were always better than what I had before.

We get to the point that after a run-through, we all know what has to be changed and none of us needs to say anything. The new pages arrive that night with changes better than ever. We're all on the same page! The character and the writing are working together.

* * *

DURING REHEARSALS AND CERTAINLY BEFORE CAMERA, I lie down on my dressing room floor and visualize my scenes. Every move in detail and more—my imagination adds more. This can result in something I do that wasn't done in rehearsal. I save it all for camera time, especially anything physical. I want to keep that fresh. I go over my dialogue, visualizing what I am talking about. If I'm talking about a street in the city, a car, a person, a piece of fruit, I see it. I *imagine* the person, place, or thing in different settings. I *feel* what I am talking about, the mood behind my lines. I watch my body, how I'm moving, how I'm standing, sitting, what can be funny about it? I remember the scenes. When I step in front of the camera, I'm on "all levels," or as Robin used to say, "My pockets are full."

* * *

ONE AFTERNOON, AS I AM WALKING across the studio lot, I am stopped by a woman calling my name. After introducing herself, she offers a generous compliment of my work and asks why I didn't apply for an Emmy nomination the previous year. What? Before I can tell her that I have no clue as to how such things work, she tells me that everyone else on the show applied.

"I didn't know I was supposed to apply," I say.

She tells me she's on the board of the Television Academy and involved in the nominating process, and yes, she explains, it all begins with an application. "You fill out a form and send in your reel and an eight-hundred-dollar application fee," she says. "We love you. We missed you this year."

When the time comes later in the season, presumably, Castle Rock submitted applications for Jerry, George, and Julia, as they did the previous year. For whatever reason, they ignore me again. But this time I'm hip to the process and on it myself. I ask one of our film editors to cut together my scenes from "The Junior Mint" episode into a single presentation that I can submit. He knows how to do it. He does it for the other cast members.

I like his edit. Each scene with Kramer works. It's got a good arc and a nice payoff at the end. I write the check and send it off to the Academy. Done.

* * *

We close the long season with another epic two-parter. In "The Pilot," Jerry and George get the go-ahead from NBC to cast their pilot and make their show. They have a week—their show imitating their life.

Since the move to Thursday nights, the show is pulling in even bigger numbers and becoming arguably the hottest, buzziest show on television, though Larry David's script on the origins of this show makes such success seem like a recipe for disaster, the kind of thing likely "to curb one's enthusiasm," if not worse. It's quintessential Larry David thinking, an illuminating window into his recognition of the irrational, stumbling through fear, his concerns about ability and "know-how" diminished through insecurity and worry.

Consider this: moments after getting the call that the pilot is a go and Jerry telling him that he's going to be successful, George is in session with his therapist, worrying about all the good things that might happen to him.

"What if the pilot gets picked up and it becomes a series?" he says.

"That'd be wonderful, George," his therapist says. "You'll be rich and successful."

"That's exactly what I'm worried about," he says. "God would never let me be successful. He'd kill me first. He'll never let me be happy."

"I thought you didn't believe in God."

"I do for the bad things."

Unlike George/Larry, Jerry is unfazed by the pilot and the potential that might follow. The Jerry on TV is just like Jerry in real life. Elaine must fend off the advances of the network's president, who is obsessed with her. (That's fiction, by the way.) And Kramer, in an exaggeration of NBC's initial reservations about me, is denied the opportunity to audition to play himself. "You aren't an actor," Jerry tells him. Undeterred, he shows up anyway, under an alias, but not before they see numerous other would-be Kramers, including one guy who is, indeed, a better Kramer than Kramer himself.

That so-called better Kramer is played by actor Larry Hankin, who was one of the actors that auditioned for the part when I did and was, I think, their second choice. In fact, during a break in rehearsal one day, he looks at me and says, "If only you had dropped dead, I'd be where you are today." I understand. "Probably so," I say.

Parts 1 and 2 of "The Pilot," teeming with all these inside jokes and self-inflicted barbs, fills the 8:00 to 9:00 p.m. hour before the *Cheers* series finale on May 20, 1993, and pulls in over thirty million viewers. It's a huge number. *Seinfeld* is now part of the cultural fabric, the very success George/Larry dreaded and Jerry accepted as inevitable. Somewhere out there, and loving it, is Kramer. He has emerged as America's most beloved hipster doofus, a character who defies the gravity of normalcy that plagues his friends.

CHAPTER 21

....

And the Emmy Goes to...

Toward the end of our summer break, the Television Academy announces the Emmy Award nominations. *Seinfeld* is nominated in multiple categories. Jerry is nominated. Julia is nominated. Jason is nominated. And...so am I. My phone rings with people calling to congratulate me. My mother. My daughter. My friends. A few gift baskets arrive from NBC, Castle Rock.

"You're going to win," someone tells me.

"Honestly, I feel like I've already won. The four of us are all nominated. We're together as an ensemble. One, two, three, four. We're whole. What could be better?"

I mean this. One, two, three, four. We're united!

* * *

THERE IS STILL WORK TO BE DONE. It feels so good to be back inside Studio 19. Everyone is up for the show. I'm so at home in my dressing room. I lie out on the floor just imagining a great year ahead.

238

One, two, three, four. We're united! I anticipate all the great work to be done over the next nine months.

Our first episode back is "The Mango," a show about orgasms and impotence that delivers a water cooler moment when Elaine admits that she faked it with Jerry. What he thought was her big O was in reality, as Shakespeare put it, much ado about nothing. "You faked it?" Jerry asks. "I faked it," Elaine says. "The whole thing? The whole production? It was all an act?" She nods. "Not bad, huh?" Then Kramer chimes in. "You know, I've faked it."

This is the kind of moment when *Seinfeld* is at its best. Honesty. To be revealed, naked before each other. I am this and you are too. Confessions. It's the little things we hide. We make nothing out of it, yet it's everything, the biggest part of ourselves that we conceal. Kramer saw me naked! Don't fret about it. I'll join you. I'll get naked too. You'll never be left alone, our friendship is an all for one and one for all.

The truth is, "I faked it," says Elaine. Bravo! It's not a show about nothing. It's a show about truth. I think the truth comes out well through Kramer, as is so indicative with his line to a self-conscious girl in "The Nose Job," the ninth episode of the third season:

Kramer: "Well, you're as pretty as any of them. You just need a nose job."

Elaine: "Kramer!"

Kramer: "What? What?"

Elaine: "How could you say something like that?"

Everyone in the room is shocked by Kramer's remark. But he's right. The truth is as big as the nose on your face. Shape it anyway you like, but you're going to have to deal with it, bring it all out in the open. That's Kramer. He's usually the opener. He cuts through the crud, jumps right over the fence, and gets to the truth. He's hip, but also a doofus lacking tact.

Man! How many times I get hit with the truth. It can be so upsetting, But, well, it's just how it moves us along. Truth is after us. It's nice to be wanted.

* * *

On September 3, 1993, I'm onstage at the MTV Video Music Awards, presenting the silver Moon Man statue for Best Alternative Video. My daughter is of the age where this is a big deal—and culturally, very little is bigger. I simply accepted the job so I could take Sophia to the show. She's tuned into what's going on now in music. For me, I'm listening to John Cage, who is fascinated by sound in general. Of course, it's debatable whether Cage is actually making music but, whatever. He's my kind of character.

Attending the music awards, when I'm out of character, without Kramer's bravado, his on-the-nose remarks, I'm shy and rather concealed. I'm an introvert. I hang back. I'm wearing a face of some kind, but I'm not truly authentic. I'm a mask. No one knows this, not even me.

Supermodel Cindy Crawford hosts the preshow, and backstage is a party with Kurt Cobain and Courtney Love, Neil Young and Michael Stipe, Peter Gabriel and Lenny Kravitz, and a Who's Who of hip and hipper. Sting and I take photos. Cameras flash. Everybody is leaning in on everybody for a shot. Everyone seems so comfortable, so at ease with their "little man" or inner woman. They belong. They're really interested in one another. They appear to be for each other. And me? I say hello to my old pal Whoopi Goldberg.

"I'm in a daze," I say, thinking maybe she'll understand and clue me into her secret for handling this kind of thing so effortlessly.

"Have fun," she says.

How do you do that? "Have fun." Don't take this event so seriously. But I stand in awe of such talented, successful people. I suppose if we were working on something together, that would break the ice. Well, we're all together for this music award show. So, "Have fun." But I just don't want to fake it.

Before announcing the nominees, I ad-lib a few words about being here—a meta-reference, observing being "here or there?" A mental puzzle that finally leads to Nirvana winning for the video

"In Bloom." Dave Grohl carries Kurt Cobain piggyback style up to the stage. They're having fun! Krist Novoselic says his thanks for the group. Amid the hubbub, I hand the envelope announcing the winner to Kurt and suggest he may want to keep it. I know I'll keep mine if I win an Emmy.

"Thanks, man," he says, folding it in half and putting it in his pocket. We lock eyes. We're all in a daze. Fame is swinging us about.

* * *

TWO AND A HALF WEEKS LATER, I'm at the Emmy Awards at the Pasadena Civic Auditorium. With eight total nominations, *Seinfeld* is represented by the cast and Larry David and several writers. I walk the red carpet with my mother and my then girlfriend, Ann, a steady hand who's at home in this kind of scene. As an actress, she toured the world with Liz Taylor in the play *The Little Foxes*. She's also more extroverted and genuinely open to people. It's a circus of photographers and reporters asking questions, and it just makes me nervy. What's my problem? I'm an introvert and I'm standing in one of the most extroverted events in the world! I'm being pulled out of myself to face all kinds of people, trying to be as genuine as possible, but I'm all jammed up inside. I can't say what I mean. I'm tongue-tied. I can't have fun, Whoopi!

I think I'd rather be lying on the floor of my dressing room channeling the life of Kramer. I'm contained by Kramer. In a character, I'm in armor. I hear Charlie Joffe's warning to me, "You're going to have a career, and it will call upon you to be yourself. You need to be there for that." How prescient.

On the red carpet, I tell the interviewers that I'm delighted to be there and part of a cast who all received nominations, plus Larry, who is up for writing "The Contest," and the show itself is nominated for Best Comedy! With the press, I'm repeating this over and over again. It seems like I'm reminding myself where I am. "Being here or there," it's this mind puzzle again. Right *here* on the red carpet I'm trying to play a guy at the Emmys who genuinely knows where he's at and having fun, too.

I'm not sure if I'm coming across. It's an incredible event for me. I want to fit in. I should. I'm continually told by the interviewers that I've been nominated for an Emmy. They press me for my feelings about it. "I'm part of an incredible ensemble. We're all in on this together!" And nothing could be better than the four of us nominated? What could be better is if I were actually enjoying myself. Oh, come on! "Have fun!" Nope. I'm close to being overwhelmed and fainting.

We're told this show is being broadcast in eighty-five countries and is expected to have a worldwide viewership of more than five hundred million people. "Have fun!"

I have zero expectations of winning in my category, Outstanding Supporting Actor. With Jason as one of the nominees, I'm quite sure that he'll win. He was nominated the previous year. This is his time. He's brilliant in the show, and I think most everyone in the Academy would agree.

When our category comes up, Jay Leno recites the names of the nominees: Rip Torn and Jeffrey Tambor from *The Larry Sanders Show*, Michael Jeter from *Evening Shade*, Jason and me. There's a brief pause while Jay rips open the envelope. "And the winner is..." I'm waiting to applaud Jason but instead hear Jay say, "Ah, my old buddy Michael Richards."

What?

I walk up to the stage and give a little Kramer move on the last step. Kramer got me up here, and he hands me off to Jay. I feel safe with Kramer nearby and for the moment next to Jay. He saved me that night at the club when I lit myself on fire. I'm on fire now. Jay? I grip the Emmy to hold me up before I fall down. I thank my daughter, my *Seinfeld* peers, my mother, Ann, and "my mentor" Robert Stein. Without anything prepared, I keep it brief, but as usual, I leave out a lot of people who should have been acknowledged, namely Joanne Linville, my acting coach, and George Shapiro, who advised, "Don't get too thin, eat!" I can look too thin on camera and off—in life. Eat more of it! Eat from the "Tree of Life" and "have fun!"

Standing before the world, a clown holding the globe of the earth. I'm on the float going by, wearing a "gold watch," waving to millions of people.

Leave it to Larry to come up with the line of the night. After winning an Emmy for writing, he quips, "This is all very well and good, but I'm still bald." It's true. We're still the same person wherever we are. Tomorrow morning, we'll be back on the set. Party over.

But there's no denying this night is a special one. Late that evening, amid all the glitter and congratulations, it's my mom who makes me feel like a winner. As we walk to the Governors Ball, she grabs my arm and gasps, "My God, Mike, there's Angela Lansbury!" I awkwardly introduce her to the legendary actress, who offers a charming hello and says, "You must be proud of this talented son of yours!" My mom couldn't be cuter as she says, "Oh, I am. I am."

I sit her at a table with my Emmy while my publicist, Elizabeth Much, leads me away to meet people. Before disappearing into the crowded room, I glance back and see my mom put her hand on the statue. It's as if she's receiving it, and the way she looks at it says everything I couldn't. "Is it real gold, Mike?"

* * *

WHEN WE SHOOT "THE PUFFY SHIRT," I can't resist watching two pros work, Jerry Stiller and Estelle Harris. This will be the second episode of season five, and Stiller has joined the show as George's father, Frank Costanza, who was originally played by John Randolph in one brief scene the previous season. Estelle plays George's domineering mother, Estelle Costanza. They are brilliant together.

Written by Larry David, the episode is a classic and one of Larry's admitted favorites. In it, George, who's broke and out of work, moves back in with his parents, and Jerry agrees to wear a puffy pirate-style shirt (designed by Kramer's low-talking girlfriend) on *The Tonight Show*. George also becomes a hand model, Jerry utters an oft-repeated and recycled line, "But I don't want to be a pirate," and there's even a "master of my domain" reference that prompts George to confess he once won a contest by holding out the longest.

The treat for me, though, is watching Jerry Stiller. This is the first of his twenty-six appearances on the show, and we quickly become very close. I like the way he is so methodical in his approach to work. Like me, he keeps to himself during the week. When we cross paths backstage, I give him a little nod of recognition that lets him know that I know that he isn't just walking around aimlessly, he's working, thinking, processing, creating.

I see him sitting backstage on the couch behind one of the flats. He looks like he's sleeping. I know otherwise. He senses my presence. One of his eyes opens. Then the other.

"You see it all, don't you?" I say.

"I'm trying to look at me," he says.

"I know what you're doing."

"I know you do."

During the scene in which Frank and Estelle and George are eating at a restaurant, Frank pulls a silver dollar out of his pocket apropos of nothing. While Estelle asks George why he doesn't want to take a civil service exam—"You get job security and a paycheck every week," she says—Frank starts talking about the silver dollar collection he had as a kid. The incongruity of this long-married couple is beautiful. But I can see Stiller start to go up on his line. He's holding the coin.

"I couldn't see myself spending one of these," he says, reaching for his line, on the verge of forgetting it. "I got some kind of ah-ah-ah-ah..."—he shuts his eyes and reels it in—"phobia."

There's a huge laugh. Stiller has been doing comedy so long even a near miss is bound to come out funny, and it did, which is why I am out there watching him.

Two years later, we share a scene in the episode titled "The Doll" in which we're playing pool in a tiny space at Frank and Estelle's house. By this time, Frank and Kramer have established a closeness that George only wishes he had with his daddy. The scene is sprung on us, and there isn't time to do it in front of an audience. Director Andy Ackerman puts it to us, "Do something on the fly. I have to shoot it now." Jerry Stiller throws me a look, like, "What are we going to do?" I simply say, "I'll shoot, then you'll shoot."

We trade antics shooting the ball. My turn, your turn. We lay the whole thing down in about ten minutes. We're so in sync. It's a beautiful ballet of funny. Afterward, Stiller says to me it was the best time he ever had making comedy. I treasure that compliment.

What a team of semiregulars we're assembling on the show! I adore Liz Sheridan and Barney Martin, who play Jerry's parents, Helen and Morty. Wayne Knight is just perfect. Danny Woodburn is a gem. John O'Hurley is uniquely wonderful, Richard Fancy as Mr. Lippman just solid, Ian Abercrombie as Mr. Pitt gets the laughs, and Phil Morris as Jackie Chiles, should have his own show!

Veteran character actor Lawrence Tierney delivered a riveting performance as Elaine's father in "The Jacket." He made an impression by actually swiping one of the butcher knives from Jerry's kitchen and later mentioning in his tough guy persona that he knew how to use a knife. He was spooky. Jerry never had him on the set again.

For a long time afterward, Larry and Jerry hung that over all of us. "If you aren't good, we're going to invite Lawrence Tierney back."

* * *

THOUGH I EXECUTED A MAGNIFICENT PRATFALL off the couch in "The Bris," it's not my favorite episode. The rabbi is loud and mean and way over the top. It's written that way, but it causes me to reconsider how loud Kramer can get, or mean, or way over the top. I'm just checking in to make sure I'm on the ball. Something I do often, but this show is a time-out that has Linville and I assessing the character. We both agree to stay true to backstory to "keep that intensity" in Kramer's eyes. The K-Man's "pockets should stay full."

In "The Sniffing Accountant," Kramer is out to bust the accountant as a cokehead. It's a comedy of errors that had me guzzling a glass of near beer and smoking a cigarette at the same time. It's "over the top" but still fits into the scene. The burp in the outtakes is real.

How to be "over the top" and "fit into the scene," this is always a tussle with me. I keep my feet on the ground through backstories, but I also feel the spirit of comedy pulling me along. But I have to shape it. Sometimes I'm on the fly and it works out, but most of the time I've got to visualize, take the time to "see me" doing the comedy beforehand and then to make choices. In the moment, especially through rehearsal, I'll get ideas, a way to go, but to put it all together, to make sure I'm not too over the top, I lie out on the floor a lot to see what I'm up to. I'm watching the show before it becomes a show. I can usually tell if it's going to work.

Gratefully, it's organic and all rather spontaneous. Still, it feels otherworldly, and I know I'm not in charge of it all. It plays me. I'm in its show. I'm the creator being created by...what? Ah, this is a mystery. It keeps me rather humble and somewhat insecure. I hope "the show" keeps coming to me.

In "The Non-Fat Yogurt," Larry gives us a script that is uniquely *Seinfeld*: Jerry, George, and Elaine discover a nonfat yogurt they love is really a fat-filled sham, and Elaine and Kramer get mixed up in New York's mayoral race between David Dinkins and Rudy Giuliani, who tapes a guest spot in New York the morning after he wins the actual election.

Rudy wants in on *Seinfeld*. We're New York! *Seinfeld* is truly New York! And Kramer is, well, as I said, "Every wild, weird, and goofy thing going on in New York City is running through this guy's hair."

In "The Stand-In," Kramer is hired as a stand-in on *All My Children*, where he befriends another stand-in, a three-foot eleven-inch-tall actor named Mickey, who is played by Danny Woodburn. George refers to Mickey as a midget. "It's little person," Mickey snaps. Hearing that Mickey is concerned about keeping his job because the kid for whom he doubles is growing, Kramer encourages his new pal to wear lifts. Though this is verboten in the little people acting community, Mickey does it, but is caught "heightening" and ostracized by his fellow little people on the show. Mickey takes out his anger on Kramer, slamming into him and knocking him over. I have some body armor made for this slamming, a special jacket with a steel plate in it to protect my back as I go over backwards, hitting the floor hard with all of Danny on top of me. This is in addition to the kit bag I keep stocked with elbow and knee pads, hip girdles rigged with plastic shields, a butt pad—stuff I routinely wear under my clothes to protect me from all the pratfalls and bumping about I do on the show.

Danny and I have natural chemistry on and off camera. Immediately after he plows into me, and despite the fact that I'm wearing a back and neck brace custom-made for this stunt, he looks down at me flat on the floor and asks, "Are you all right?" He means it. "Yeah, I think we nailed it," I say. That's still not enough for him. "Are you sure you're okay?" "You heard that audience, Danny. We nailed it." That's fine for them, but he's looking at me with such concern. It causes me to ask him how he's feeling. "You okay?" "I'm fine if you are," he says. His concern for me was so genuine. That's Danny Woodburn. This man has heart.

Hanging out, I tell Danny about my experience working with Billy Barty on the movie *UHF*. Billy was a well-known actor and activist, and I loved him because he was as big a character as they come. After a day of shooting, a few of us went out one evening, including Billy. We had a limo with booze, and Billy got smashed. I don't drink, but I'm hanging out with green tea and still made the mistake of calling Billy a midget. He suddenly jumps up. "We're little people," he declared. "I started the Little People of America in 1957. Don't ever call little people midgets!"

Billy was so damn likeable that I didn't mind being corrected with such intensity. I even thanked him. He was too soused to hold on to a grudge or much of anything else. When we got back to our hotel later that night, I opened the limo door and Billy literally rolled out of the car, his body rolling alongside of me like a ball, straight up to the hotel entrance, all three feet nine inches of him tumbling along like that. It was weird and wonderful.

When I tell this story to Danny, he looks sad that Billy behaved that way. I try to make up for it by telling him I corrected a couple of our writers talking about having funny "midgets" on the show. "I told them it's 'little people,'" I say, adding, "So I got that right." Danny laughs out loud. "What does it matter?" he says. "You can call me a fucking Martian. I don't give a doo-da." A very open-minded man. He and Billy together would have been a hoot.

* * *

"The Conversion," the eleventh episode that season, is another gem that brings out the best in Kramer and resonates more with me than anyone might suspect. George attempts to win back his girlfriend by converting to her Latvian Orthodox religion. When Kramer waits there one night to pick up George, he crosses paths with a beautiful young nun who likes him. "What do you mean she liked you?" Jerry asks after I blow into his apartment with one of my longest skids across his threshold. "*Liked* me," Kramer says.

The message comes through loud and clear. "I have this power," he explains to Jerry and George, "and I have no control over it." That power is called *kavorka*—Latvian for "the lure of the animal." Indeed,

Kramer is a magnet for women. "They will do anything to be possessed by you," says the priest with whom he meets. Ah, the "lure of the animal," the erotic vitality within us! I feel this kavorka, this great Eros as relatedness coursing throughout everything. I'm feeling this, particularly in relation to women.

I go on Howard Stern, and all he wants to know is how much I am getting. You're probably getting a lot! He senses my kavorka. He's very intuitive. I'm not that comfortable talking about my sex life with him and his listeners. Howard knows this too and enjoys getting at me anyway. I'm impressed. It's the sort of thing I do to myself all the time—always probing, looking into my stuff. It's what I do with my analyst, Robert. Of course, that's all very private, isn't it? With Howard, though, it's a bring it all out in the open so we can see, too. It's his job to be a snoop. He's very good at it. I'm sure if he wasn't a radio host, he'd be a very sharp psychoanalyst.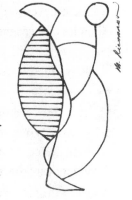

Sex stands behind creativity, culture, the whole of our species. But how to sublimate such energy? I'm up for it. Otherwise, I'm going to go apeshit chasing every woman I see. So, lifting my urges, my horny desires, this almighty Pan, I'll say, we can have some fun together, but I do need to put my hairy-legged friend on a leash. My humanity, chasing after goals, inventions, the building of our civilization depends on this.

As a professional Fool, I'm Kramer considering the "levels," configuring my apartment, getting the place in order; through the clown, I hold my world together, and for the most part, I'm sublimating.

My kavorka, this almighty Eros, a magnetism that joins the coming and the going, the entrances and exits, Kramer has it all. He slides into Jerry's apartment as a force of nature, to live, to be involved, to Giddyup! He's life incentive. How many people have told me so? Kramer's ha-ha has pulled them through. So nice to be a part of it all.

* * *

ROBERT, MY TRUSTWORTHY ANALYST and friend, is diagnosed with incurable cancer. It takes him quickly. Nothing I do will pull him back. It doesn't work that way.

Here again, as I watched Cass's father, Richard, pass, I meet Thanatos, the force of death that cuts the fat off the meat—how lean we all get.

Robert is emptying out. Letting go hurts. Family, friends, humanity, one's gathering must go.

The time I spend re-collecting myself, developing consciousness, now dying, seemingly a loss of consciousness, where does it all go now?

What we bring into our lives, upon death is it all forgotten? It comes and goes where? Consciousness into unconsciousness, the land of the dead, but there, dreams are always alive. They come and go like everything else, but I can't say they are forgotten. They continue to live in a mysterious way. Robert comes around every so often. In my dreams, he's still very much alive.

I've come to remember a few things from him. Everything I am is everywhere else. It's living through the whole of Nature. None of this goes away. It just changes for the time being.

For now, I stand upon a float waving to the viewers watching each episode of *Seinfeld* go by.

CHAPTER 22

The Celebrity

It's January 1994, and NBC sends Jerry, Jason, Julia, and me to Florida as the star attractions of the biggest conference for the television industry's station owners, affiliates, marketers, and programmers. Like an excited group of sixth graders on an overnight field trip, we are ferried by limo to the airport, where we board a private jet. Except for the pilots, flight attendant, and table teeming with sushi, crackers, cheese, beverages, and other tidbits, we are the only passengers on board. How luxurious. The network is giving us the works.

Regardless, I still travel with my own stash: apples, peanut butter, romaine lettuce, hummus, soy milk, and granola. I'll take their crackers with my peanut butter, their vegetable rolls with my hummus, and a few cheese squares with my apples.

But this truly is the way to go. All of us know the heat is on! No way NBC is flying us private unless we are red hot. On the flight, I sit next to Julia. With her, I feel like brother and sister, and our conversation makes the time pass quickly.

It's early afternoon when we get to the hotel, and I'm in my room only a few minutes checking the view out the window when the phone rings. It's Julia.

"Can you believe this room we're in?" she says.

Happily married and happy to be a mom, Julia is a down-to-earth woman with the same openness and accessibility off camera that she has on it, a quality that masks the privilege and wealth around which she was raised, but I recognize the tone in her voice. She doesn't care for her room. She knows what a great room is all about. In short, she's got taste. I haven't even thought about mine beyond the fact I have a window that doesn't look out onto a parking lot. But I take a moment to survey the room. I notice the furnishings are older and "the bathroom is sort of gunky," which I mention to Julia. I want to support her.

"Yeah, Michael, the bathroom," she says. "A shower curtain?"

"Yeah, I got one too," I say. "The zigzag pattern on it is sort of cool."

She laughs. "This place is a dump!" she says.

I'm thinking of Bette Davis in *Beyond the Forest*, and how Bette hated that film and wanted out of it.

I'm talking to Bette Davis.

"Where else can we go?" I ask.

"I'm calling Rick Ludwin," she says, referring to NBC's head of late night and early backer of the show, who's still our go-to exec, "to see if we can get something better."

"I'm right with you. Let's get something better."

If Julia thinks it can be better, I'm in.

After we hang up, there's a knock at my door. When I checked in, I asked the person at the front desk if I could get my tuxedo cleaned and pressed before tonight's event. The young man at the door is there to pick it up. He assures me that it will be back to my room and ready by 5:00 p.m. We're getting picked up at 6:30 p.m., I tell him. Because I'm nervous about handing it over, I emphasize that I really need it by five.

"I'm wearing it tonight," I say.

"I understand," he says. "You'll have it in plenty of time. I'm such a fan."

"Thank you."

"Make sure to have it back."

"No problem, Mr. Richards, don't worry."

I'm relaxing when Julia calls back half an hour later. She says that she was offered another room, but she hates the whole hotel.

"You didn't like the other room?" I ask.

"They're all the same," she says.

I shouldn't be laughing, but I am. I come from humble beginnings on La Brea and Crenshaw. I know the hotel isn't the Four Seasons, but it's clean, the TV works, and it's free. "It's all free, Julia! And we got the private jet going home." Julia gives in, and we end up laughing at ourselves. Everyone should be imprisoned in such squalor. She hangs up in a good mood, saying she has to start getting ready, and I look at the clock radio and see it's five o'clock. Where's my tux? I'm still asking that question fifteen minutes later. I call down to the front desk and am told not to worry.

"But I'm leaving in one hour," I say.

"Not a problem, Mr. Richards," I'm told.

"But the guy said—"

"It is on its way, Mr. Richards. Don't worry."

So, not worrying, I take a quick shower, still admiring the zigzag pattern in the shower curtain. Twenty minutes pass without a knock on my door or a phone call. I'm waiting now wearing my black socks, underwear, and a T-shirt. At six, I call back down to the front desk. I'm told my tux will be here any minute.

"We're so sorry for the delay, Mr. Richards."

At six fifteen, I'm on the phone again with the guy.

"Where is it?"

"We're trying to reach the driver."

At six thirty, I'm frantic. I call downstairs.

"Listen, I don't have my tux and I'm being picked up any minute now!" I say.

"Oh yes, Mr. Richards," the guy says. "There's a problem."

"There is? There wasn't a problem when I called fifteen minutes ago. And the four times before that. And now you're telling me there's a problem? What's the problem?"

"The van with the tuxedo went to the wrong hotel."

"The wrong hotel. When will it get here?"

"In about forty-five minutes, Mr. Richards."

I hang up in a silent rage.

Within a few minutes, our driver calls my room. He's waiting downstairs ready to take us to the NBC event. I call the desk downstairs and explain my dilemma. There's nothing they can do. I'll just have to wait for the tux. Now I'm Bette Davis.

"What a dump!" *A fucking shower curtain!* How dare they. And my tux! Which has apparently checked into another hotel without me!

Okay, that's it! Five minutes later, I step out of the elevator and into the lobby wearing the hotel bathrobe, cinched tight. It's terrycloth white with the hotel's name inscribed on it. Underneath, I have on my underwear, plus my black socks and dress shoes. I join Jerry and Jason and Julia, all of whom are waiting for me near the front desk, dressed in appropriate elegance for a formal occasion. Their heads turn in disbelief as they check out my ensemble.

"This is how I'm going," I say loudly. Then to the personnel at the desk, "I'm wearing your crummy hotel robe to one of the biggest events in the city, and I'm going to tell everyone there why I'm wearing it. This place is a dump!"

Julia steps toward me with a worried expression on her face.

"What are you doing?" she says.

"I'm going to the event," I say. "I'm going to tell everyone there this hotel lost my tuxedo!"

"You can't go like this," Jerry says.

"Of course I can, because THEY LOST MY TUXEDO!" I yell.

"Just put on your regular clothes," he says.

"I'm not putting on my regular clothes," I say. "That's worse. I'm going to tell everyone what happened to me and TO NOT STAY AT THIS HOTEL! Come on, let's go."

"You're going like this?" Jerry asks.

"Absolutely!" I head for the car.

At this point, Jerry just sees the humor in it all. Julia is laughing too. Jason shrugs and moves on. He has always thought I'm out of my mind.

I blurt out one final solo, "The place is a dump!" and we're off. I'm really pissed. Just out of mind with anger!

* * *

INSIDE THE NBC EVENT, which is gorgeous and teeming with women in gowns and men in tuxedos, I stand out in my bathrobe and shiny shoes, puffing on my cigar and apologizing for my appearance. But no one believes me. Everyone thinks this is a brilliant gag beautifully performed by yours truly. People are genuinely amused. Seeing me irritated and all hyped up, they see me as Kramer.

Indeed, Warren Littlefield, the president of NBC, comes up to me and whispers, "The robe idea. You're a fucking genius." Then he walks away. During dinner, I sit at a table with Jerry, Jason, and Julia, and at one point, each of us is introduced. One by one, we stand, a spotlight shines on us, and there's applause. Except when it's my turn, I stand to an applause with some laughter. I'm on to it all and so I play it up. "You think this is funny? You can all go to hell!" They roar with laughter. So here I am, Michael to myself and Kramer to millions. Once fuming with anger and now Kramer is getting laughs. The worst leads to the best. I couldn't have planned it any better.

Then Warren is onstage, standing behind a dais, talking about the upcoming prime-time lineup and the success of *Seinfeld*, when he's interrupted by a loud knock on one of the doors in the back of this enormous conference room. It's followed by another, more forceful knock. Someone opens the door and a man enters and stands there, holding my tuxedo wrapped in plastic on the hotel hanger. It couldn't have been timed any better. I jump up from my seat and shout, "Finally!"

The whole room explodes in laughter. It's beautiful.

But it's not the end.

After I change into the tux—most everyone there liked the robe better—someone from one of the Florida affiliates tells me that the hotel I was denouncing is owned by the mob. "You really gotta be careful," he says, adding a half chuckle. "You're in Florida." Though I shrug it off, about twenty minutes later, two guys straight out of a casting call for Italian hoods sidle up to me and one of them says, "Mr. Richards, we're from the hotel that lost track of your tux. We understand you have a problem with the service."

"No, it's all worked out," I say. "I got my tux. Everything's fine."

They shake their head.

"Mr. Bianchi, who owns the hotel, hears that you feel the hotel has not treated you as it should," the guy says. "Come with us. He wants to speak with you. He's in this room over here."

"That's all right," I say.

They don't move, "Please, come with us," and I realize the invitation is one I can't refuse. Mr. Bianchi is also straight out of central casting. Silver-haired, relatively short, wearing a customized tux that's perfectly tailored with diamond studs. "I wasn't able to get my tux earlier, but it's not a big deal right now," I say. He wears the disappointed look of a man whose finely tuned machine has failed him. "Something has to be done about this," he says softly.

Suddenly, I'm very sorry that I told multiple reporters that his entire hotel should be torn down. Given the boss and his two goombahs on either side of me, it seems a little extreme.

"I think I overreacted," I say.

"I don't think so, Mr. Richards. I'm going to do something for you now. It's how I do things. You're staying here tonight," the boss says.

"I'm giving you the presidential penthouse for as long as you want to stay." This man also owns this hotel!

"That's very generous and unnecessary," I say.

"I insist," he says. "My associates here will escort you when you're ready."

I pass this development along to Jerry, Jason, and Julia, who are getting ready to leave the event and return to the "dump." I explain that the owner of the hotels wants me to stay here. They're giving me the five-thousand-square-foot penthouse.

"They gave you the penthouse?" Julia says.

"The entire top floor," I say.

"I can't believe this shit," she says. "You're really going to stay here?"

"I don't think I have a choice. Those two guys, they're my chaperones," I say, gesturing to the heavies waiting inconspicuously nearby.

Jerry laughs. "Well, we're going to leave now. Hopefully we'll see you again."

"Really? You think it's safe?"

Jerry is enjoying this. "I don't know. You'll have to find out."

"I can't believe you pulled this off," Julia says.

"Everything just fell into place," I say.

"We'll see you tomorrow morning. You did good tonight. Everybody loved it."

Jerry gives me a hug. "Good night...or goodbye."

After they leave, the two "escorts" want to take me upstairs to the penthouse. It's a Kramer-esque moment. Standing between them on the elevator, I hear Jerry's voice in my head: "Hopefully we'll see you again." These guys are going to push me off the top of the building! Sure enough, once inside the massive penthouse, they want to take me out to the balcony. "We want to show you the expansive view," not to mention the drop down to the ground! Yeah, it's quite a height, about twenty-five stories. I'm handed the keys and they leave. Whew!

The place is like a palace, with its own top-of-the-world outside swimming pool. There's a landing pad for my helicopter. I take a swim. Sit in the jacuzzi. Order some chicken soup and crackers. I sit by the helicopter pad looking at the views and taking in what happened this evening. These wonderous moments where the ha-ha comes through like a Holy Ghost, it's a godsend. This evening at the hotels, delaying my tux, the robe, the cigar, NBC and their affiliates, the way it all came about, just perfect. It all came through on its own. This feels religious. It has a holy, holy to it. Underneath these stars, a living universe, I think of Ezekiel receiving a scroll from God, giving him what he needs to get a mighty edifice built. For me, just a comedy routine will do.

Here I am on the roof of this remarkable penthouse; from this evening's comedy of errors, God certainly has a sense of humor. Looking up at the stars, wondering about godsends and inspiration, keeping all that night sky in place all around us, I call this a divine inspiration, the kavorka luring the animal that I am into the cosmos. It's what makes a fabulous play, assists us with the ball, leads me up for the shot that makes the hoop. The whole of the universe is on this team. It includes us all. I have a faith in this. I feel the holy, holy is everywhere. Symbolically, it's the dove upon the Christos, the calling of Muhammad, the Shekinah of the prophets, what gives them ultimate direction. It's the Greek Dionysus of theater, the entrances and exits of us all. It's India's Atman, Buddha's Mindfulness, China's Tao, the great Siberian spirit in Russia.

I call "inspiration," this kavorka, by all kinds of names. It's simply "God" for all, the Creative running throughout all. It's my clown holding the whole world. I see it to believe it. I know it as performance. All of us are in the show. It's utterly magic, a mystery that comforts me.

What a wonderful evening. How all of this fell into my lap. Everyone had a good time. Still, I felt bad that I went off on the hotel and embarrassed the owner.

Mr. Bianchi is an honorable man. Mistakes happen. What a comedy of errors! In the morning, I take a swim and have my breakfast. The owner has a limo waiting to take me to the airport.

Jerry and Julia are standing around by the plane.

"So?"

"Well?"

I try to look blasé.

"I don't know. There were five bedrooms, and I didn't get a chance to sleep in all of 'em."

* * *

OBVIOUSLY I'M NO LONGER LIVING a normal life anymore. I'm a TV star, a marquee name, bold type in the newspapers, and in Hollywood that's royalty. There's no waiting in the line when I go out. I can get a table at the hottest restaurants without a reservation. Welcome, Mr. Richards.

One weekend I agree to meet a buddy of mine at a nightclub on Sunset Boulevard. I'm not a regular at these places, and he's going on about "having fun," meeting the gals, and all that hoo-hah. So I'm open for it. Door security recognizes me from the show, and the red velvet rope at the entrance is unfastened, allowing me to pass right through.

Inside, the club is packed. People stand around, the pounding bass of loud music shakes the floor, and colored ceiling lights whirl about. Right off the bat I think that I'm going to get a headache in here or permanent eardrum damage or both. Will I ever be able to memorize my lines again? I should have brought some earplugs, or I could have stayed home and read Joseph Campbell. But come on, Michael, live a little. Yeah, let's check it out, says my kavorka.

A few days earlier, I had a dream that I was riding around in a red Ferrari with Silenus, and we were drinking liquor from a silver flask. Silenus was the Greek god of winemaking. He was associated with Dionysus. Oh, my old friend from CalArts! In philosophical

alchemy, the grape is transformed into wine, a kind of transubstan-
tiation, moving the body into spirit, this evening, sex into caution.
Beware. As I'm standing there in all the noise, I think of Ulysses
on his ship with crew. They put wax in their ears, while Ulysses ties
himself to the mast to avoid jumping into the sea and swimming
to the sirens whose song will lure them all to the rocks and destroy
them. Who's telling me this?

Music is cranked, the sound is deafening. What kind of "siren
song" is this? I meet up with my buddy. He has to shout to be heard
over the music.

"You made it!"

"Yes, I did!"

"I've got a table reserved for us! Come on!"

He leads the way and we get about ten feet before he starts shouting to some woman he knows.

"Is that the table over there?" I ask.

"Yes!"

"I'll meet you over there!"

"Right!"

I head over to the reserved table. Everyone is noticing me. I'm
a celebrity. I don't get out much, and I'm not comfortable being
gawked at. Several women are sitting at a table next to us, and the
girl closest to me is cute and probably (and correctly) thinks that I
am thinking she's cute. They always know. Built-in radar. Still, she's
distant, but I kiddingly ask her, albeit with a straight face, if she
could see if the club could turn the loud music down. She doesn't
laugh. She thinks I'm serious. "I'm just kidding," I say.

She relaxes and smiles to let me know she gets the joke. We start
talking, and it turns out that she recently broke up with a drummer
from a famous rock band. I remember the group when they debuted
on *Fridays*. She can see that I'm uptight in this environment. It's
hard for me to hear what she's saying shouting at each other over
the music. I'll never get used to this, yet it sort of amuses me. I can
imagine Kramer being in this loud joint all night and then the next

day still shouting when he talks to people. He's deranged from the pounding music.

The gal wants to go outside and get some air, and she asks if I want to come along. Sure, I'd love to breathe again. It's not only too loud in here, but it's hot and stuffy too. I follow her as she slowly makes her way through the crowd to get to the door for some fresh air. I imagine I'm following a guardian spirit to get me out of this crowded den of people. She's taking me to paradise, simply fresh air. Lead on.

We're now standing on the crowded sidewalk along Sunset Boulevard. Loud motorcycles pass by. They grate on me. Still, here I am with this lovely angel. She's very beautiful. I'd like to kiss her.

Now the games begin. Another gal comes up to me and asks if she could talk to me in private. About what? She introduces herself as a script reader at some agency I've never heard of. This is another cute gal—clearly a lovely siren that I'd love to wrap myself around. I'm curious to hear what she's talking about, so I follow her to some area along a black brick wall. The wall is ominous enough. She's as equally sexy as the smoker seeking fresh air. Yeah, I'd like to kiss her too.

She says she knows that I'm on *Seinfeld*, thinks I'm incredible, but doesn't know why I'm wasting my time in this club. I should be at home reading some of the amazing film scripts that she reads, scripts that she knows would be perfect for me to act in.

I ask her, "Why are you here wasting your time and not home reading scripts?"

She laughs. "To meet you," she says.

She's seducing me. I want to kiss her. I try to break the spell. "Well, I'm very focused on the show these days," I say. "I don't have a lot of time to read film scripts or set them up somewhere."

"You could set up a film when you're on hiatus," she says. "I could help you with that."

This girl should be my agent. Probably what she's out for, but I'm not thinking about my career right now. I'm just a guy now.

She knows this. She is a late-night angler who has a fish on the line. I know this too, but my instincts are dulled by her slinky slip dress and my imagination. She comes right out and asks me if I want to go to her place. She's had enough of the noise. This gal doesn't beat around the bush. For most men, a dream come true. I'm sensing a fatal attraction, and I'm up for it. Suddenly, I'm antsy to pee and tell her I'll be right back. Oh, how romantic. Will I go back to her place? I want to be with her. When I come out of the bathroom, she's right there.

"Hold on," she says.

She enters the woman's bathroom. Yes, how romantic. I lean up against the wall for some support and inner counseling when I hear, "Hello, Michael." I turn to see that the man leaning against the wall next to me is Bruce Willis. "Hi, Bruce." I'm surprised he knows me. This is the magical world of celebrity: everybody knows everybody even though we've never met. The two of us stand there for a moment, me and the star of *Die Hard*, watching the nightlifers roam about looking for anything that will keep them in place. I'm in place with Bruce now. It feels right to be here.

"Bruce, did you see that woman that I was just talking to?"

"Yes, I did."

"She wants to take me home. She says I should be reading film scripts, that I'm wasting my time here."

"What do you think?" he asks.

"She's lovely."

"Yes, she is."

"She's a siren."

"Yes, she is."

"She is?"

Bruce is silent with that Willis grin of his. He's a Silenus, a lot wiser than I am.

"You have to be careful, don't you?" I ask.

"I'm always careful."

My night lady comes out of the bathroom. She wants me to follow her to her place in North Hollywood. I've got Bruce's remark coursing through my head: "I'm always careful."

We walk out of the club together and once we're down the street, I decide to be careful and tell this woman that it's late and I need to get some sleep.

"You can sleep at my place." She takes my hand.

"I won't sleep with you around me."

"So, what's wrong with that?" She presses her body to mine.

"I'm tired. I need to head home."

She backs off fast. Weirdly, her face turns angry.

"You're blowing me off?"

"No, I'm just heading home to get some rest," I say.

"I'm trying to help you," she says, raising her voice. "I'm giving you my time and now you're blowing me off?"

"We were just talking."

She suddenly gets vicious, very ugly.

"Hey! I don't just talk! I'm serious about what I say. I don't fuck around, asshole!"

She walks away in a huff, leaving me shaken. I go to my car parked a block away, expecting her to jump out from the shadows and do me in.

I head for home. Glad I had a moment with Bruce. I'm a bit wiser trying to be careful.

* * *

I'M DRIVING HOME IN A WHIRL, sizing myself up. I got married when I was twenty-two years old! Just before this, I didn't have lots of flings, or girlfriends.

I was faithful in my marriage. I'm forty-two years old now, divorced, and I just gotta get into where I'm at now. I can't stay contained in a relationship or get into another marriage, just you and me and no one else. I stayed inside a marriage for twenty years! The love rising and then setting like the sun. "Love and die."

Yeah, I'm back where I left off at twenty-two, then, or now, grounded through my love for Cass, hold me to what is real! "Love and die." Married and divorced! I'm in the graveyard. But I just got a heads-up from Bruce. Be careful. I'm all for that. Be true unto yourself. I'm all of this.

So don't kill me now, honey.

* * *

How I BEHAVE AROUND OTHER CELEBRITIES...well, I'm usually shy and awkward. Later on, I'll do my usual reflecting and learn something about myself, something I can use later on to get through the big world of showbiz. I'm fine when I'm working, but hanging out in the green room I'm not that relaxed.

Back when I was on *Fridays*, Billy Crystal invited me to his house for the afternoon. He was a guest on the show, and we got along well enough in the clubs. He was with Charlie, our manager, and so we were in this business together. Arriving, his wife told me to make myself at home.

"Really?"

"Absolutely."

So I went out to mingle with people standing about and chatting near the pool area. I think I needed a laugh, or to entertain them, but I was also uncomfortable being in a star-filled social situation and wanted to get out of there. I don't know what compelled me, but I put my hand in the pool water. It was heated. Nice. With my clothes on, shoes and all, I dropped into the pool and sprawled out at the bottom of the deep end. Able to hold my breath for well over a minute. I was down there for a long time.

It was the kind of thing that people would brand an attention-seeking stunt, and maybe it was my awkward version of an icebreaker, but the truth is I liked it better down there than with everybody up on the patio. Not knowing it at the time, this was a case of being acutely introverted and unusually awkward around people, especially extroverted celebrities, including Billy, who, despite all we had in common, I still found intimidating. Eventually I bobbed to the surface, turning over slowly to see faces—famous faces—staring at me. Oh, back to all this now? I wished I'd had a tank of air. I would've stayed down there for an hour.

Tom Poston was the first to say something.

"Are you all right?" he asked.

"Fine, and the water's nice," I said, dripping wet after climbing out of the pool.

Billy tossed me a towel. He wasn't mad or anything. But I think I made people uncomfortable. I'm just not a mingler.

* * *

ONE TIME WHEN JERRY was on a talk show, he was asked what kind of comedian I am. He said I was "a natural." I took his response to mean that I've got a flair for comedy and I'm also a natural oddball.

* * *

CARRIE FISHER'S HOUSE is on Coldwater Canyon in Beverly Hills, and it's the green room for Hollywood's Who's Who. The actual house boasts a pedigree that includes Bette Davis and famed costumer Edith Head. It's a Spanish hacienda that Carrie describes as rustic country, though you only need to take a few steps inside to see it's uniquely Carrie, filled with French antiques, folk art, and fanciful collections that have colorful backstories. However, it's the people who regularly gather at her home that give it that truly special aura of remarkableness. Carrie's open heart and magnetism drew the most exciting talent to her door like a Hollywood Gertrude Stein.

One night, I'm walking down the hall to Carrie's den. Along the hallway, people are seated on the floor, lounging against the wall. I hear someone call out, "Hello, Michael." A voice out of nowhere, like the voice of Bruce Willis, a call to know thyself. It's Elliott Gould.

"Oh, hi, Elliott."

We've never met before. But we know of each other in this celebrity salon.

"You're great on the show."

"Thanks."

"Enjoy it while it lasts," he says.

That remark hits me hard. Is he putting me down? At the time on *Seinfeld*, I knew I wasn't coming to an end. But then I know he's been around the block a few times. He's come to so many endings and beginnings with his career. The man's giving me a heads-up, I think. But do I look like I need a heads-up?

How impertinent. I'm just walking down the hall minding my own business. Is Elliott envious? Is he thinking, you're not going to be a big shot forever? Am I acting like a big shot? Actually, I fall over myself in the presence of stars. I was recently invited to play cards with Mel Gibson on Friday nights at his house. I declined. There's no way I could go. I can't sit around with Braveheart. None of these people are normal to me. Like Robin, they're deities, the most outstanding among us.

Elliott has quite an impact on me. The remark was on me for days, actually for years. It's supposed to be, because it's a remarkable thought. Enjoy it now, because you're dead tomorrow. Big stuff. Lighten up and enjoy myself. Yes, you're right, Elliott. Thanks for the message. Like everything, you're a godsend.

* * *

AT THE END OF THE HALL, I bump into Albert Brooks.

"You're great on the show," he says.

What's he going to tell me next? I beat him to the punch.

"Enjoy it while it lasts," I say.

Albert is upbeat and into enjoying life.

"Have you bought a great house yet?" he asks.

"Yes, I did. I'm fixing it up now," I say.

"I just bought a wonderful place up on Mulholland."

I'm thinking I'm not up that high. I'm certainly humble after Elliott's remark. My house is at the bottom of Coldwater, a block south of Ventura Boulevard. A lot cheaper.

I go on about how much my house means to me and my daughter, a home that centers us in every way. This inspires Albert to gush about his house and how his house centers him too. Ed Begley Jr. appears, and he and Albert know each other.

Albert invites us to see his house.

"I'm only fifteen minutes from here," he says.

"Let's go."

Ed and I follow Albert to his great new house. During the drive up Coldwater to Mulholland, I'm continuing to mull over Elliott's remark. "Enjoy it while it lasts." It's hard for me to just "enjoy." I'm always tussling with life.

Bruce told me to be very careful. Elliott is telling me to enjoy it while it lasts. In other words, live. Live WELL! Once it's over, that's it. It doesn't come back again. Enjoy it while it lasts!

Albert turns down a long driveway to his house. I follow. We hear the fading in and out of a dog barking menacingly. We get out of our cars, and with each step we take toward the house, there's more dog barking.

"What is that?" I ask.

"That's my dog on the watch," Albert proudly says.

I heard the barking along the driveway, but this is clearly a different dog barking than the one I heard a moment ago.

"It sounds like a recording," I say. "You got something rigged up? Speakers in the bushes?"

Albert unlocks his front door. A dog doesn't appear. He turns off the barking sound, which is part of his security system. He's disappointed.

"How did you know?"

"I can still tell the difference between animal and machine," I say. "There's hope for me yet."

"God," he sighs, clearly pained by my reaction. "I want my money back. I paid a lot for this system."

"Just get a real dog," I tell him.

Albert whines, "I should, shouldn't I? I'm a fake. This isn't good."

He's genuinely concerned. This always makes me comfortable, people who don't fake it.

His house is a large one-story, with beam ceilings and stone. It's rustic and modern, Beverly Hills and the Valley divided by Mulholland Drive. In the living room, enormous bay windows look out onto a forested backyard, tennis court, and pool. Nature and culture combined. The place is comfortable, a retreat oozing serenity.

"Very nice, Albert."

He's excited about the place. "Look at this!" He leads me to a small room and quickly flips on the light revealing a large treadmill facing the wall. "I run miles on it. It's got all these speeds. You can set it to go uphill, up a steep incline. Try it."

I get on the treadmill and get it going.

"Crank it up a little bit," he says.

Albert leans in and gives me more speed. I can't resist doing a routine. I pretend that I'm losing control. Half of me is in the air and I tumble well, right off the treadmill, but my foot slams into the wall and puts a hole in it. And cut! But the hole in the wall! I apologize profusely.

"Albert, I'm so sorry. I'll pay whatever it costs to fix. I know how much you love this new house."

"No, it's fine. As long as you're okay."

"No, I'm not! My back and neck, I'm gonna sue you!"

"Really?"

"No, I'm kidding. It was fun. I love your house, Albert!"

Later, I hear that Albert drew a circle around the hole and wrote, "This hole was left by Michael Richards."

* * *

BACK TO CARRIE'S. Liza Minnelli is there, and Sean Penn, and they want go to another party nearby. We quickly drive over there. On the porch there are a few people, but it's getting late and the candles are burning down. Sean is reciting some of his poetry. Liza is close by. I like her.

I saw her in Vegas doing a show. I was a guest of hers and sat in a large, curved booth for such people. I think her promoters arranged it. She sang to me. She's very sweet. After the show I told her so. She gave me a mighty hug. Unknowingly, my heart is not developed enough to be so easily affectionate, so sincerely kind and lovingly connected. I don't know Liza yet. I stand so far outside her. Just meeting her, any woman right now, I'm back to being a very young man. I'm single again. I'm really only twenty-two years old. I'm where I was when I first met Cass. I have no experience dating, being with the other woman. I'm awkward and shy. Unless I'm performing, well, I've got no character to hide behind.

Liza is a woman of the world. All that great showbiz behind her. What a remarkable upbringing, and possessing her own talent too! She's fascinating. We're standing on the porch together. Sean's voice is louder, giving size to his words. I enjoy his intensity. He's definitely into words, trying to bring himself out from behind them. I was just as possessed at CalArts; in Deena's class, trying to get at something through words, that something being myself, my heart. Hurtak became my language for a while. His words leading me along until I was taken up by "a living universe."

And now? I sense it's love that gets us out of words. But all the falling down that goes along with it—love brings us together and takes us apart to see what we're made of. "Enjoy it while it lasts."

* * *

ONE NIGHT JERRY AND I GO OUT to an Italian restaurant in Beverly Hills. It's a rare night out together. Ordinarily our shooting schedule doesn't allow for such socializing, but tonight—it's early enough. We're out for enjoying a good meal. We're doing well. This is a small celebration for working together. Who's sitting at the corner of the bar with the restaurant phone in front of him? Tony Curtis. He looks as if he's running the place.

A few minutes later he comes over to our table. I stand to greet this man and introduce him to Jerry. To Jerry, Tony is an actor, a celebrity in Hollywood. To me, Tony is a star in *Some Like It Hot*, one of the greatest screwball comedies every made, and, of course, other classic films. To me he's a definitive Hollywood star, and he does have our respect.

"Congratulations on the success of your show," he says.

"Thank you." Jerry is reserved. I'm not sure why. He has a sixth sense. He seems to know where this is all going. Overall, I'm just happy to be in the presence of Tony Curtis. Naturally, I'm a bit awkward but in awe of the man. Tony appreciates this. He wants to do something in return.

"So, what are you two gentlemen up to tonight?" he asks.

Kiddingly, I say, "Ah, Tony. We're just two lonely men unable to find the ladies in our life." Jerry and I are definitely single.

Tony lights up. "You're looking for cookies?"

"Oh, yes! The cookies." I turn to Jerry. I'm becoming Kramer. "Cookies, Jerry."

Tony says he'll be right back.

I gush about Tony. "He looks great for his age! I hope I look that good when I'm older. That open-shirt look of his, very sexy. That's Tony Curtis!"

Jerry is calm and amused. I suppose he sees me as Kramer in the coffee shop.

"We ought to get him on the show," I say.

"I'm sure that's what he's thinking."

"Yeah, he's working the room. He's slick. This beautiful-looking man is working it. Look at him, Jerry, over by the bar on the phone. This place is his office. He's doing business making big showbiz connections. Jerry, he's coming over here!"

"Just relax."

"Relax? It's Tony Curtis!" I say.

Tony is back. "I've got it all arranged."

"What's that?" Jerry asks.

"Cookies. I called Hefner at the mansion. It's all set."

"We'll go to the mansion?" I ask.

"Yeah, everything is arranged."

"For cookies," I say.

"Yes." Tony is on it.

To Jerry, "Let's go over there and check it out," I say.

"We're not going over there," Jerry exclaims.

"It's cookies, Jerry." I'm giddy and just letting Kramer have his. "Tony's got cookies for us!"

"We're not going there for cookies," Jerry says.

"Do you know where the mansion is?" Tony asks.

"Yes, I do," Jerry says.

"You guys work it out. I'll be over here if you need anything else."

"Thanks, Tony!"

Jerry is shaking head. "Cookies."

"What an episode this would make," I say. "Tony comes into Monk's and lays this on us. He's got cookies for us. Cookies, Jerry! Kramer would be thrilled! Maybe it gets into a whole sting thing with cops after us all, and Tony's hiding out in your apartment! Elaine is mistaken for a cookie, and George sees Tony hiding out in your bedroom, in your bed, under the covers, and thinks you and Tony are lovers."

When we leave, Tony is at the bar talking on the phone. I wave goodbye. He waves back. What a guy! I go on about a Tony episode for days, and Jerry thinks it over. He sees the humor in it all. "Jerry, we can call the episode, 'The Cookies.'"

From then on, whenever I come through with a piece of business or a delivery that buttons up a scene well, I will sometimes turn to Jerry and say, "Cookies!" This keeps the work fun. I so love making my pal Jerry laugh!

CHAPTER 23

Cosmo

Though it doesn't happen often, Jerry and I come across each other in our cars on Coldwater Canyon driving to the studio, and so, game on: whoever can get to the studio first is the winner! This is all-out street racing up to 100 miles an hour down Ventura Boulevard.

That's right. The stars of America's top-rated television show have no problem—or common sense, for that matter—engaging in such a sport. Jerry and I are perfect examples of how easily grown men can turn into competitive street racers in production cars that are designed to go over 170 miles an hour.

It's truly indicative of our lives in the fast lane. For men who love high-end performance cars, this occasional outburst of speed is inevitable. Each day Jerry drives one of his treasured Porches from a collection that began years earlier but is expanding at a more rapid pace with the success of the TV series. On the days that we challenge each other, we're usually in our fastest car.

This is serious stuff. Jerry has gone through the Porsche racing school. He wears driving gloves! He's McQueen doing his best driving at Sebring.

I only have two cars: I rebuilt another '56 Chevy Nomad just like the one I had in high school, and a new Mercedes S600 coupe with a V12 engine that leaves the pavement in flames. The only other person I know with a car like it is Jim Carrey. One fine summer day, he was visiting Nick Cage, another street racer with a penchant for Ferraris and Lamborghinis. Nick is off the chart with cars that can easily go over two hundred miles an hour! Jim had his S600 parked next door to my place in Malibu. I see him on the balcony at Nick's.

"You're not making any more of those scary faces, are you?" I ask.

He makes a "scary face," the kind that has put him at twenty million a picture.

"I see you got that S600," I said.

"It goes so fast," he said, flashing me a wicked smile.

"Doesn't it!" I said, grinning back at him.

There's no way my muscle cars can beat a twin-turbocharged Porsche 959 with a trained racer like Jerry, sportin' his gloves, putting his behemoth through the paces along Coldwater Canyon. But I'm an old hand at street racing since my days in high school. I weave well through traffic, plus I'm insane. Jerry is trained. I'm naturally gifted and fearless when it comes to street racing. There are dangers. Harrison Ford's character, Bob Falfa, in *American Graffiti* messed up and turned that beautiful car over, but he did it while racing without any traffic around. How do you mess that up? For me, it's the worst scene in the movie.

On a street like Ventura Boulevard, you race in bursts. There's traffic. The only reason I beat Jerry isn't so much about the burst as it is the weaving through traffic. Here, we're surging to eighty miles an hour but only for a short distance. Then you're back at sixty, sometimes forty. Porsches burst well, but again, I'm a weaver. They don't teach you street racing on a Porsche training track. That's more about straightaways and curves, not dodging cars, buses, bikes, and people using the crosswalk.

Then we're on the lot. We pull into our parking spaces, get out of our cars, wipe off any dust.

We're cool and composed. Just two colleagues heading into the office.

"Michael."

"Jerry."

Have a nice day.

* * *

THE PORSCHES THAT JERRY DRIVES to work every day are immaculately washed and detailed. One day, that "phantom" trickster at CalArts comes upon me. As I leave the production offices, unseen, I watch Jerry pull into his parking space. After getting out of his car, he stops to admire it. Then, before walking away, he sees either a smudge or a speck of dirt and he rubs it off before going into the building. Typical Jerry behavior—very exacting, into the details, going for perfection.

Now Jerry heads upstairs to his office. Knowing the first thing Jerry will do when he gets to his desk is look out the window at his beautiful Porsche, I hurry over and quickly place a leaf on the hood of his car, then step out of sight. Sure enough, a moment later, he comes downstairs, removes the leaf, and heads back upstairs. I repeat this one more time, a few more leaves this time scattered across the hood. I must be careful that he doesn't catch on that this is a prank, a distinct possibility since his car isn't parked under a tree.

But Jerry appears again and removes the leaves from his car. He walks around the car, looking it over. Then he glances around. I can see the gears turning in his head. The only leaves around are on the lawn by some bushes. There's no wind. Something weird is going on around here. He heads back upstairs. I can't do it again. He'll know it's a prank.

I'm imagining that he's mulling over the supernatural—a curious mystery that he will have to keep to himself. This is the part that amuses me the most. Otherwise, people will question his sanity.

Of course, I don't say anything when I see him on the set. I'm hoping he will confide in me. I am prepared to invent a story that every so often there are twigs on my car too, even though there are no bushes or trees around. It's gotta be birds, Jerry. I consider putting a leaf on his car every other day, but I let it go, knowing this will only agitate him, or worse harm him the way kryptonite weakens Superman, and I don't want to upset him. A week later, I'm talking to Jerry and feign that I'm annoyed with twigs always ending up on my car when there are no trees around. Isn't that weird, Jerry?

He says nothing about the leaves on his car. He's either forgotten or he doesn't want to discuss the paranormal. I bet it's the latter, and because of that I intend to put a few leaves on his car the next day. But my conscience gets the better of me, and that afternoon I tell Jerry it was me who put those leaves on his car. He busts out laughing. "And the twigs on your car, you made that up?" he asks. I play it straight. "Oh, no, that really happened. That's something that I don't want to talk about."

Overall, well-engineered cars are symbolic of the way Jerry engineers the show. Looking at a Porsche, he will point out all the little details—a certain curve to the car, doors, handles, hood design, the undercarriage, the screws…even the placement of screws. He's the same way with the show. Word by word, script by script, screw by screw, attending to all the details necessary to get the laugh. Along the way, a leaf now and then won't hurt.

* * *

LIKE JERRY, I AM ALSO AN AVID COLLECTOR, but my pursuit involves books. I initially set out to purchase first editions of any classic novel and then went on to collect the complete works of early nineteenth-century American literature from Washington Irving to Mark Twain. As long as *Seinfeld* continued, I started collecting English literature, European literature, the Greek and Latin classics,

Chinese and Indian philosophy, and the collected works of Russian writers. And of course, Yeats.

* * *

THE OFFICE JERRY AND LARRY SHARE is large and immaculate—large enough for Larry to have laid out a putting green setup. When I'm up there, I often see him practicing his putts. Larry's enthusiasm for golf was given to Kramer. There are a number of scenes where Kramer is all-out for golfing or throwing his bag and clubs to the floor and just giving up. That's all Larry—win or lose, he makes a golfer out of Kramer.

As a result, I get invitations to play in celebrity golf tournaments, but I'm not a golfer at all. One time I am at a hotel in Hawaii and a group of golfers invites me to play with them. I like that word "play." I tell them that I have my own style for playing the game and that I'm very good. "Well, join us!" they say. I do. My style is that I don't use a club. I throw the ball. I only use the club when I'm in close range of the pin.

And here's the thing: I have a great arm. I'm very accurate. So after a few holes, this group of golfers wants me out of their game. We laugh it up for a few minutes, but they clearly want me to go. Eighteen holes of this? I'm glad to be on my way.

But Kramer into golf, that always makes me laugh. The game that Larry loves so much, I think of it as his rec-reation time through Kramer. Of course, Larry would never tolerate nixing the clubs for throwing the ball. "Come on! Have some respect for the  sport!" Okay, you club the ball for me. I'll bebop about in that golf cart. To me, the cart is the best piece of equipment for that game.

In the episode "The Marine Biologist," Kramer's golf practice on the beach causes a Titleist ball to end up inside a whale. It sets up the character George beautifully with a confession brilliantly performed by Jason. From the blowhole of the whale, George retrieved the ball. I get the blow line, "Is that a Titleist?" A golf ball like a Jonah in the whale, only when it's out of the great beast do things get back on track.

* * *

BECAUSE OF THE POPULARITY of Kramer, late that summer, I am sent to Florida to meet with NBC affiliates, to say hello to everybody, and cheerlead for the network. I'm in a hotel that overlooks Disney World. My room is a one-bedroom suite with a well-appointed, sizable bathroom that I know would earn Julia's approval. I sort of liked the shower curtain better.

I'm in the room for half an hour before the hotel's manager calls. He upgrades me into their finest. It's a mind-blowingly luxurious suite with a sweeping staircase, a two-story domain with roughly three thousand square feet of living and entertaining space. There are two large, fully stocked liquor cabinets nearly floor to ceiling that look as if they were lifted from the VIP room of a Miami nightclub. They light up beautifully and have an adjoining bar area, stools and all, that could easily sit fifteen people.

It's a lot for one person. I have a huge terrace with spectacular views of Disney World below. Wow! I have three large bedrooms upstairs. It's not as sprawling, but still, this suite is as spectacular as the penthouse given to me the last time I was in Florida. What an upgrade! I call the manager to thank him. "Enjoy! The hotel board loves you on the show. You're their favorite character. Let me know if you need anything." Wow!

It's early afternoon, and I go for a walk. While I'm out, I run into a few people connected with NBC and affiliates from around the country. I have no idea who they are, but they know Kramer. They're happy to see the "K-Man!" They congratulate me on my second Emmy nomination.

At the early evening event for all the affiliates, I shake hands, pose for photos, and say a few awkward words about the joys of doing *Seinfeld* and working for NBC. Really, it's all a lot of hard work but I stick to a joyful theme. I really don't know why. I should say I'm busting my ass on this show and I'm just a vessel for this wonderful character coming through. That would have been a heck of a lot more interesting. Oh, well. From the event, my plan is to head back to my incredible room. Before leaving, though, I get into a conversation with one of the affiliates, a woman named Theresa who remembers the night I wore the bathrobe and how funny that was. I tell her about the penthouse I got that evening and mention the suite I have now is equally amazing. I invite her and two of her girlfriends, also affiliates, to stop by and take a look. "It's incredible," I say. "Room 2000."

Around eight the doorbell to my fabulous suite rings. It's Theresa and the ladies! Her two associates. "Please come in!" They are in heaven as I show them around. There's a phone call. It's for Theresa. A few affiliates that she knows are wondering if they can stop by. "Sure!" I say, "Have 'em come up." Four people now arrive who told others that this is where they're going for a drink. Word spreads that the scene for the evening is in suite 2000. Kramer's throwing a party. I'm about to live joyfully as all of this is coming through me like Kramer does. Joy arrives to get the party going. Giddyup!

The phone rings again. "Sure! Have them stop by!" Theresa wants to help me host these people. "It's the kind of work I do," she says. She's an operational manager from some TV station in Maryland. "I'd appreciate that. Thanks, Theresa." The doorbell rings. A group of five enter, and Theresa greets them and then returns to let me know who they are. "Great, sure, come in! Come in!" I'm delighted that everyone is enjoying my incredible suite.

My guests graciously thank me for letting them drop by. I tell them to make themselves at home. I ask Theresa if we should serve something. "We could offer a glass of wine," she says.

"I suppose so." I eyeball the liquor cabinets. "We've got plenty."

Theresa offers wine, and everyone is thrilled. The phone rings, the doorbell rings, the party is on.

"Shall we serve champagne?" I suggest.

"That would be wonderful." Someone asks if they can make a drink. "Absolutely! Anybody else?"

"I'll have a gin and tonic."

"Kramer, you want one?"

"No, I'm fine. Help yourself."

Within an hour and a half there are well over a hundred people in my suite—and more coming. Theresa hosts it all with assistance from a girlfriend who attends to the phone calls and people at the door. "Is this the Kramer party?" "Come on in!" The girl introduces each person. *Now presenting the king and queen of WMAQ-TV in Chicago!* The affiliates are roaring with laughter. What a party! I'm playing at extroversion. I stand around drinking Perrier water and talking to everybody. I even wear a hotel bathrobe over my clothes, which everybody howls over. "Oh, yes! That night in the robe and you had a cigar! My God, you were hilarious!" Some guy offers me fine cigars. I puff on my cigar with all my affiliate friends.

Their good time is my good time in my magnificent suite! The terrace is full of people, who periodically toast Kramer! It's all rather fun, and I'm happy to share what I have with everybody, but by 2:00 a.m., I'm exhausted and need to call it a night. I ask Theresa if she can wrap this all up. Within fifteen minutes everybody is gone. I stand there alone, surveying the scene. The place is a mess. Most of the booze has been consumed. What just happened?

When I check out, the manager asks me if I enjoyed the suite. I sincerely thank him for the upgrade with some guilt. "I sort of left the place a little messy," I say. "I had a few friends over." He says, "It's our pleasure." Is it? I say nothing about 125 people in my upgrade drinking up all the booze! I suspect it was over twenty-five bottles of champagne from one cabinet alone. The other cabinet was full of hard liquor, wine, beer, and soft drinks. Most of the bottles have been opened. I think everybody left plastered. I had a few friends over, all right.

"Please stay with us again," the manager says.

"Really?"

I'm thinking that NBC is going to get billed for all of this. No good. I just lived it up. "Enjoy it while it lasts." I sheepishly tell the desk clerk I opened the liquor cabinets. I pull out a credit card. Should I pay for this?

"No, I see here that this is a corporate reservation. NBC is taking care of all your expenses."

"Yeah, but all the liquor... This suite too?"

"No, that was an upgrade at no extra cost."

"Really?"

He doesn't account for the liquor.

I leave for the airport figuring the hotel or NBC will eventually send me an astronomical bill. Whatever. At the *Seinfeld* production office, I start receiving notes from affiliates all over the country, thanking me for throwing such a great party. NBC president Warren Littlefield calls. "You did it again, Michael! What a great idea to throw a party for everyone. Our affiliates had a great time with Kramer! Thank you!"

"Sure, Warren, anytime."

So, who paid for all that liquor? It wasn't NBC. It was comped by the owner of the hotel. Ah, who owns this hotel? Somebody made it right for me.

* * *

WE HAVE A NEW DIRECTOR, Andy Ackerman. This LA native wears a bemused smile reflecting his passion for comedy. Having learned the business from the editing room up, and in fact having won an Emmy for editing at age twenty-four, he has the same kind of presence as his mentor, the great and prolific director James Burrows, whom I met and loved way back when I guest-starred on *Cheers* and shot the pilot for *Marblehead Manor*.

Andy has directed a slew of TV comedies, including *Cheers*, *Wings*, *Suddenly Susan*, and *Frasier*, but *Seinfeld* is a big move for him. As far as I'm concerned, it's the right move. We hit it off immediately, getting so acquainted with each other through the first episodes of the season, "The Chaperone," "The Big Salad," and "The Pledge Drive."

These shows, and the rest to come with Andy, put us all in a good mood. He brings a great calm to the set. My groove with him includes a signaling; I can look at Andy and without speaking a word, he knows what I'm *feeling*. It's like a fast break in basketball—we know where the ball is going. He gives me a thumbs-up or he cocks his head and we do another take. He's with me. He's with everyone as we get the job done.

* * *

IN EARLY SEPTEMBER 1994, work pauses for the Emmy Awards. We were all submitted and we're all nominated. As we settle into our seats in the Pasadena Civic Auditorium, I'm thinking once again that Jason will win this year. I won last year. It's his turn now.

Between award presentations early in the show, Jason leads a song-and-dance number celebrating TV theme songs. He has the entire place singing along with him. He's amazing. That's why he won a Tony! This is his night! But then: "And the Emmy goes to… Michael Richards for *Seinfeld*!" Again? I'm shocked. In a kind of stupor, I head for the stage.

With the award in my hand, I barely say, "I don't know what to say." That's it. Nothing more. I can't speak. I look around, stuck in myself. I see Jerry in the audience mouthing, "Say something!" But I can't. I'm truly at a loss for words. I stand before eighteen hundred people in the audience, twenty-four million watching in the US, several hundred million worldwide, and I'm wordless. The audience begins to laugh. They think my awkward silence is a gag. "Thank you," I say, and I walk offstage. What have I just done? I couldn't speak. I said nothing. I couldn't speak!

"Brilliant!" says a producer as I come offstage. Laughing, he slaps my shoulder. "You're so funny. Congratulations."

He doesn't know what really happened. I know. Jerry knows. I caved in on myself. I was embarrassingly thoughtless for having forgotten to thank Jerry, Larry, Julia, Jason, our director, the show's writers, the network, the Academy, our membership, and again, Joanne Linville. I am mortified. Ugh! I blew it! I folded up. I died out there.

"Come out and let the audience see you once in a while." I just did. I was speechless.

I can barely walk right now. I have to sit down. I have to be quiet for a while. Again? So quiet, so speechless again? I'm coming apart.

I am ushered into the press room, where I stand, holding my Emmy, before the corps of reporters. I don't know what I'm saying or who the heck I am. I really should be by myself—maybe at the bottom of my pool in my weighted-down chair breathing through my Aqua-Lung.

I have just won my second Emmy. But the affair has frightened me. I have turned dumb and idiotic. I can't stand before this world outside of character.

I'm so sorry that I couldn't come out and meet you all! Say something! Dear holy, holy that holds this Creation together, as you take me apart, be gentle. Kill me softly with love. Let love be all there is. Perhaps someday I'll be able to speak to this world through love.

But first I need to speak to myself with love.

I come down hard on little ol' me for locking up at the Emmys. It's better to look into the lessons. I'm trying. Backstories aren't just about acting. What's going on in back of me is just as important. Whatever it is, I feel it's in back of everything. I'm not clear on this yet. Extroversion is at hand. Most of me feels like it's all "out there," pulling me out of myself to meet it all. It's a two-way street. An inner and outer that tugs on me, takes me back and forth like the tides of the sea, or the course of the seasons.

I live in a kind of fear of this. I'm not sure why. This upsets me. I'm not well. There must be something wrong with me. Why can't I thank people who I work with?

I stand so nervous before the world. Why do I fail to come out and meet others joyfully? I live split off, separated from my humanity. It's embarrassing me. The good side to this is that I am aware of it. I've got to go easy on myself. Take it one step at a time. It's all that I can do. Trust in "Thy Will Be Done." I'm a process unfolding.

It will be years from now until I know what is lacking. Facing the world out there, I'm just not coming through well. I feel so *unrelated*. I'm split off. From what just happened, I'm in the shadows. The shadow runs right through it all. It's always a day and night around here. The opposites tugging on me. I don't have much middle ground.

* * *

MAIL HAS BEEN POURING IN from fans asking to see inside Kramer's apartment—to see inside of Kramer. People want to know more about him. It's all about Kramer, the character behind his own mask.

What does Kramer's apartment look like? That's easy. Much easier than standing before the Academy and millions of TV viewers, facing all that on my own, outside of character. So, let's stay on Kramer. Just on Kramer will do.

How about Kramer's first name? People want to know Kramer's first name. They get their wish in our ninety-seventh episode, "The Switch."

It's late fall when this script by staff writers Bruce Kirschbaum and Sam Kass is ready to be shot. For a few weeks Larry and I have been thinking about names, but so far none have been close enough to the mark to even remember. In "The Switch," Jerry's girlfriend doesn't laugh at his jokes, but he's more interested in her roommate anyway. George, thinking his model girlfriend is bulimic, wants to enlist an older woman to spy on her in the bathroom. A matron to hand out towels.

Reluctantly, Kramer suggests his mother. She's a matron. "Babs?" says Elaine. The problem is, Kramer hasn't seen his mom for five years. "I don't even want to get into my childhood," he winces. "I'm still carrying a lot of pain." George and Kramer seek her out anyway, and when they find her laying out hand towels in the ladies' bathroom, surprised, she blurts out her son's name.

NBC promotes a full campaign on this. In the days and weeks leading up to the episode's airing, the network is deluged by calls and letters from people who can't wait and want to know Kramer's first name before the episode airs! A publicist says reaction hasn't been this big since Johnny Carson bid farewell to America's late-night TV watchers. And suddenly there it is, courtesy of Kramer's mother—"Cosmo."

Mystery solved.

Cosmo Kramer.

Even I don't know this until just before the table read when Larry quickly comes up to me and says, "I've got Kramer's first name. 'Cosmo.'" Without a second's hesitation, I say, "Absolutely! That's it!" It was close to Larry all along. Cosmo was the name of a kid who used to live in Larry's old apartment building, the same one in which Kenny Kramer lived right down the hall. That makes it even better. The name was right there in the building the whole time. It's cosmic, part of the cosmos. "I'm Cosmo, Jerry!" Kramer declares. "I'm Cosmo Kramer! And that's who I'm going to be from now on. I'm Cosmo."

There's a little ring of it in Johnny Cash's song "A Boy Named Sue." "My name is Sue! How do you do!" For Kramer, the disclosure of his name is a big "How do you do!" He's revealed to Jerry, George, Elaine, and the thirty million people who tune in to watch that night. Most significantly, he meets himself through his name. How do you do! My name is Cosmo!

My mama, Babs, is played by Sheree North, who I meet that week and regrettably don't spend much time with—other than when we're on set rehearsing. I can still see her sitting alone on the set. I should've kept her company. She's Kramer's mom. In the scene, when she hears Kramer say "Ma" and turns around to see him for the first time in years, well, Sheree's face conveys a lifetime of stories. Great backstories that could have been there for Babs.

Sheree came up in the old studio system. In 1955, she appeared on the cover of *Life* magazine billed as Marilyn Monroe's successor! She worked nonstop in episodic television.

My mamma Babs whooping it up in 1955.

I regret not doing more with Sheree. We followed through with everyone else's parents. It would've been interesting to have Babs around, maybe have her living in Kramer's apartment. I should've gotten the writers to think about that. Babs, I'm sorry. We should've gotten to know you more. Love, Cosmo.

* * *

THIS IS FOLLOWED BY "THE JIMMY," our eighteenth episode of the season and one of my favorites. Jerry, put under, gets molested in his dentist's office, and Kramer, his mouth numb and drooling after getting work done on his teeth, is mistaken for a mentally challenged person as he hails a taxi. The show is politically incorrect, but the climate was different enough then that Elaine responds to Jerry's concern that something happened while he was in the chair by saying, "So you were violated by two people while you were under the gas. So what. You're single."

Then Kramer ends up being serenaded by crooner Mel Tormé at an AMCA (Able Mentally Challenged Adults) charity banquet, where he's the guest of honor. Half my face is drooping from being punched before the event. I'm disheveled in my suit but smiling and trying to sing along. It's a classic case of mistaken identity. I've never heard Larry David laugh as hard. We do a couple of takes, and each time I hear him lose it. For me, Larry's laugh is the ultimate sign of approval.

A few weeks later, in the episode "The Fusilli Jerry," Kramer picks up new license plates. The DMV made a mistake. On his plates, he's the ASSMAN. So wrong and so funny. This plate will become one of the most popular show items to be signed by me for collectors.

The show's popularity is through the roof, and around this time huge brand deals come through for everybody. Jerry sticks exclusively to American Express. Julia is with Clairol, and Jason goes with Rold Gold. I got greedy. The money was so outrageous, I went with Clorets, Pepsi, Mercedes, and Vodafone.

* * *

In the season six finale, "The Understudy," Jerry dates Bette Midler's understudy in a new Broadway musical. There's a softball game in Central Park between Jerry's team from the Improv and the cast and crew from Bette's show. During the game, George slides into Bette at home plate and knocks her out. In a side story, Elaine believes the manicurists in her nail salon are making fun of her in Korean. But it's all about Bette, who lands in the hospital, where an overly solicitous Kramer serenades her with "Wind Beneath My Wings."

She is our most famous guest star to date, and from the moment she comes in for the table read, I make sure she's comfortable on the set. Welcome to *Seinfeld*! Welcome to Kramer!

All week I am like her brother, looking out for her and making sure she has everything she wants, which is what Kramer does for her in the episode. Really, I'm about as Method as you can get. I'm wearing Kramer's shoes. I'm taking care of Bette. But like Kramer, I love a diva. But overall, I'm in character! Where's Michael? Deep within Kramer or at home at the bottom of his pool.

* * *

One day, I'm visiting Jon Lovitz and Chris Farley, who have a friend's place just up the coast from me. Jon's got a cigar. "Michael. Michael. Nice of you to drop by," he says. Chris is like an overgrown ten-year-old kid. "Wow, wow, wow!" he says, leaping up from his chair. "I love you, man!"

"How're you doing, Chris?" I say.

"Bitchin'," he enthuses. As only Chris Farley can say it. And mean it. He is fun personified.

Jon provides me with a cigar. After a few minutes of puffing and small talk, I ask what they're up to. Chris bounds across the room and points outside.

"We've got an inflatable!"

I look outside and there's a fourteen-foot inflatable boat in the sand with what looks like a 20 hp motor on the back. That's a lot of power for a small inflatable. Any sizable motor on a small inflatable is tricky, and when captained by these two knuckleheads, it's downright nuts. Nevertheless, I'm game to give it a try. How can I resist? These guys want to play. I grew up swimming this stretch of beach as a teenager, when we'd ride over from the Valley and spend all day in the water. I'm at home in the depths and the big, wild pull of Mama Earth's surging sea. I still bodysurf all day when it's warm. I'm in.

"We're going to hit the high seas!" Chris roars. "Come on!"

Outside, we grab the inflatable and drag it into the water. Chris seems about as large as the boat. Jon and I are walking alongside the inflatable guiding it through the water with cigars in our mouths. I already know that none of this is going to work. John gets the motor going. Chris suddenly jumps into the boat. "Let's go! Let's go!" Seeing the propeller out of the water is all wrong. I yell, "Lower the propeller into the water!" Jon lowers it, then quickly jumps into the boat to work the throttle. I'm pushing the boat to get it into deeper water, nervous about the prop cutting me up. I don't want to be near the thing. The motor is in neutral. I see waves coming. "Give it throttle!" I yell.

The motor kicks in, and I jump into the boat. We're heading toward a swell. "Crank it!" I scream. Jon is still fussing with the throttle. "Crank it!" We're not going to make it. I bid my cuckoo bird cohorts farewell and bail before getting slammed by a wave, easily flipping the boat over from bow to stern, the worst way to go. I hope no one gets hit by the engine or the prop, which could cut a body in half. This is no good. A bunch of crazy, reckless Fools.

I pop up from under water and see Chris turning around in the water looking for the boat. It's upside down in white water moving fast toward shore. Jon is bobbing about disoriented, sizing up what went wrong. For me, it was getting in the boat with these guys! "Are you all right, Jon?" "Yes, the throttle was stuck." Chris is strong in the water and already heading in. His shorts are sagging, almost all the way off, and his butt is hanging out. He's whooping and hollering, "Whoaaaaaa!" He really is that guy. I call out to Chris, "Is that motor off?" He yells back, "Let's go again!"

Let's go again! Chris is a daredevil. So much fun. "And all the men and women merely players; they have their exits and entrances." I take my exit and drive back to my place on the coast. I make a smoothy, sit out on the deck with my lady friend, and watch the sunset.

Enjoy it while it lasts.

CHAPTER 24

Finding Home

Interesting adventures happen whenever I'm with my pal Ed Begley Jr., and this night is no exception. It's the end of September 1995, and I go with Ed to hang out at the home of Gavin de Becker, the security expert to the stars. I haven't met Gavin and don't know much about his line of work, but once inside his house off Laurel Canyon, I see my friends Jeff Goldblum and Peter Falk sitting with a few other people. All are talking about the subject that has a stranglehold on everyone's thoughts these days, the O. J. Simpson trial.

Both sides have rested their cases, and the gang here is going on and on about how the prosecution should've done this, the defense said that, the judge is wrong, the jury is tainted, and so on. I haven't followed any of it. In Stage 19, home to the *Seinfeld* set, staff and crew spend their breaks watching the trial on one of the monitors in the prop room backstage. I'm lying on my dressing room floor, probably going over things with Kramer, and don't know anything about the trial.

Clearly, I'm in the minority.

Here at Gavin's, everyone is a trial lawyer or thinking they could be one.

Then a shocker: the front door opens and in walk the people they've been talking about, debating, and second-guessing for months, the actual prosecutors, Marcia Clark and Chris Darden. I guess they came to hang out, too. The prosecuting team admits they're feeling down and disheartened about their chances of getting a conviction. Someone mentions vital evidence the judge threw out or didn't allow, and suddenly everyone has a strong opinion about it.

For a moment, it looks like real life is imitating one of our shows. You got Columbo, Dr. Ehrlich from *St. Elsewhere*, the scientist from *Jurassic Park*, and Kramer huddling with the legal team trying football great O. J. Simpson for murder. It's surreal, especially when Peter says he has to go but steps back into the living room a moment later with just one more question, as he usually does through his character Columbo, another question that usually leads him to solve the case.

After he's gone, Jeff does a dead-on impression of Peter, which makes the room laugh and lightens the mood, but these folks are very serious about the trial. I sit quietly wondering why O. J. isn't in an uproar over this trial, spending millions of dollars to defend himself while the real murderer is still out there, probably watching the trial on TV like everyone else right now. I would be in a fury demanding the cops find the killer, now! and way more outspoken about my kids needing me at home, instead of this bullshit trial for 252 days. I'm innocent! Get off my back! I'm not the killer! Yeah, I'd be saying this out loud every day!

They go on about DNA evidence proving O. J. was the killer, but this was thrown out of the trial? Is this so true, I ask myself, that the court allowed a proven murderer to get off? If so, where's your heart and soul defending someone that you know is guilty? That's just diabolical. To throw out the truth, to throw out vital evidence?

I'm peeling my orange and just listening.

I suppose the trial will have to occur in the afterlife, presuming that the weighing of the heart, or a judgment of the soul will, indeed, take place there. I suppose most of the people who do horrible things don't think so. There's a Bible in the courtroom. "Do you solemnly swear to tell the truth, the whole truth, and nothing but the truth, so help you God?" Yet some lawyers, despite seeing or knowing the truth, finagle a way to get it thrown out of the trial to win the case.

Poor Nicole and her unlucky friend Ron, who walked in on it all. Will they get justice in an afterlife? The group I'm sitting with isn't interested in this crud. They want justice now. The prosecuting team doesn't think justice is coming? I'm thinking now of Dostoevsky's *Crime and Punishment*. If guilty, will O. J. Simpson fester, as Raskolnikov did, and eventually admit to the crime? Will O. J.'s soul turn him in?

I wouldn't want that blood on my soul. You beat the rap here, but it's going to come up somewhere else and bite you in the ass. My soul turns me in on everything. I gotta be honest, take a hard look at myself. I'll drop everything I'm doing to get at the truth. Truth is all that matters. Am I being naive? I'm just sitting at de Becker's, eating an orange, watching my friends go on and on about the trial. I'm stuck on this: If truthful evidence is being thrown out by the defense team, why don't they have all the lawyers swear on the Bible? "Swear to tell the truth, *nothing but the truth...*" Am I being naive? Being a lawyer to fake out the truth, I give up. I'm going home.

* * *

WE ARE BEGINNING OUR SEVENTH SEASON, and with more than one hundred episodes having aired, people sometimes stop me and deliver lines from shows that ran years ago, expecting me to come in on cue with my line. "I'm sorry, I don't remember those lines anymore," I tell them. "How could you forget those lines? You were so funny saying them," they remark.

It does hit me that the show is going out to thirty million homes each week. People have their favorite episodes, and sometimes they know the lines of their favorite character for that episode. Incredible.

Here's the thing: I don't watch the show. I'm too critical of myself. I can always see that I should have done this or that, something that could have been better. I do the best I can each week and move on. So one of the reasons I can't remember lines from all those previous episodes is that I've never seen them. I just work on an episode and move on to the next one. Then it's down to the bottom of my swimming pool.

I'm sorry I let fans down when they want to do a scene with me. I'm amused when they know the lines and I don't. Sometimes they deliver the lines better than I do!

Bravo!

In early September 1995 the entire cast goes to the Emmys, and as always, I'm proud to be a part of the team. All of us are nominated, along with the show itself for Outstanding Comedy, Directing, and Editing. Jason co-hosts with Cybill Shepherd, and he and I are in the same category again—going up against each other. Maybe we'll tie. Has that ever happened before?

Oh well, at least we're all at the Emmys together. It really does strengthen us as an ensemble. We're all together in this, that's for sure.

None of us wins this year.

Frasier sweeps the night, and David Hyde Pierce goes home with the Emmy for Outstanding Supporting Actor in a Comedy. And he should win, he's so good. But does this mean that we're not as good as we used to be? These prize shows make me a little crazy. I mustn't take them too seriously, but at this point in the game, I do. I'm in a state of entitlement. Fame does this to you. Not winning always feels like losing. It's so easy to lose perspective.

It's hard on an introvert like me to be in the spotlight, to be recognized, and to be pulled into situations and shows where I am caught up in fanfare and winning. I know how this sounds. Poor me. But I'm really not comfortable with all this. I'm not out to be better than the other actor. It's enough to just work hard each week to bring as much of Kramer across as I can. I'm much happier when I am at home with my daughter, remodeling the house, and spending time with my girlfriend.

But crossing the line into my greater nature is not the way for me right now. Working from the outside in is the task at hand. My constant tussle between introversion and extroversion is on.

* * *

INTROVERSION! It will keep me from accepting a star on the Hollywood Walk of Fame. I turn it down. My star isn't important; I put myself down in this way. I'm back to something from the beginning of me that thinks I shouldn't be around. I should be excluded. No star. No acknowledgment for the work that goes into such an honor. I'm a put-down. I'm hard on myself. I'll continue in this manner and turn down two offers to host *Saturday Night Live*. I own my characters from *Fridays*. I could have done Battle Boy. I've got the kid's costume and boxes of army toys for some big battles. Nope. I shut myself off from it. I don't want to come out any more than I already am through *Seinfeld*. The whole of all this is nearly overwhelming.

Diane Keaton has the opportunity to direct a film through Spielberg's company, Amblin. She would like me to star in this film about a boy's dog being magically transformed into a man played by me. We get together and she actually brings a ball and throws it around as I go after it, jumping over hedges and running all over the place. It's all rather hilarious. I'm in form playing a dog running after a ball. Spielberg wants to meet with us at his office. He's up for making the film but no, not so fast. I have questions about the script. Spielberg says that my concerns will be straightened out as we proceed.

Sorry, I want to think things over.

What?

I think my way right out of the project and end up passing on it. Oh boy.

But I've got to cut myself some slack. I am already playing Kramer like a dog! I'm doing this on the biggest show on TV. I want to keep looking for something else.

This is understood, and Diane calls me several weeks later having been offered another script to direct, this one the movie *Unstrung Heroes*. The producers would like me for one of the parts. I read the script by Richard LaGravenese and like it very much. I go over the part with Joanne. I've got it. Diane and I go out for dinner, and she's like a manager. "You've got to face up to how hot you are right now. Get things in development!" I know *Seinfeld* is going to be around for a while. I don't feel like creating more work for myself, but I'll do *Unstrung Heroes*. This is one ball I will go after.

* * *

BACK ON STAGE 19. There are no prize shows here. This is the hard work of doing a TV show every week. Everyone is up for getting to it. This is what we're made for. Larry has written the first three episodes of the season. There are the usual hijinks: Kramer is involved in a dognapping that plays out over these opening weeks. In the fifth episode, "The Hot Tub," Kramer's imagination takes over again when he installs a makeshift hot tub in his apartment. For the shoot, the heater on the thing isn't working. The water is cold. The crew is concerned. But if this is the way it is, so be it.

"Let's just do it," I tell Andy Ackerman. "It'll be invigorating!" Being in cold water and acting as if it's a hot Jacuzzi, it's the actor's life for me! Stella would have applauded.

The next week we shoot "The Soup Nazi," which features actor Larry Thomas as an extremely temperamental purveyor of lunchtime soup whose customers willingly subject themselves to his strict code of behavior lest he bark at them, "No soup for you!" as happens to George and Elaine. Kramer, of course, is pals with him. "You suffer for your soup," he says, leaning against the wall and sipping straight from the container.

One thing about Kramer that comes through in "The Soup Nazi" is that he doesn't get into brawls. Kramer's tough, but he doesn't use his fists. Then how tough is he? Little Mickey will tear Kramer up if he gets out of line. Yet back in season two's episode of "The Statue," Kramer plays a cop who barges into a man's apartment and forcefully throws the man up against a wall to subdue him. Ah, but he's in character then. He's playing a tough guy. When two guys steal the armoire that Elaine had picked up on the street and asked him to watch, he doesn't fight back. Later, after spying the thieves on the street, neither Jerry nor Kramer have the *cojones* to confront them. But why fight over a piece of crummy furniture? Pick your battles carefully.

The little things in Kramer's life can trip him up. He goes down like most of us. The best of him is that he gets right back up, quicker than most.

Kramer has an innate understanding of suffering. It's all part of his hipster doofus image. He's the one who slides into the struggle and all the anguish to hustle up an outcome, something he's been dreaming about all along. He has his quibbles and skirmishes, like us all. When Kramer gets thrown out of the bodega where he gets his fruit in "The Mango," it's like being thrown out of Eden. "No fruit for you!" That's what happens when points of view collide, when God and Creation are at odds with each other. The flooding occurs. It's archetypal.

I've been thrown out of circumstances, and it floods me with remorse. Making my way out of it, the flooding subsides, and there's new ground to stand upon. Thank goodness for this.

* * *

IN THE REAL WORLD, a few shortsighted psychiatrists conduct a study assessing Kramer's mental state. Performing a lobotomy by getting rid of comedy all together, they diagnose Kramer as a paranoid schizophrenic. I wonder how they would have assessed the Marx Brothers, especially Harpo, or Chaplin's character the Tramp, or Tati's Hulot.

I suppose they'd suggest comedy in general should be put in a straitjacket. Were that true, what kind of world would we be living in? Serenity now.

* * *

BACK AT THE IMPROV, Charlie Joffe warned me, "You're going to have to come out from behind your characters."

This is the time to do it. Interviews, talk shows. I don't have to be Kramer or the clown all the time. But I'm not comfortable "being myself" in front of cameras. The format requires performing through set-up questions, and I feel hemmed in by it all. I usually hate myself after doing these shows. It takes me days to get over my appearances. And this digs into me while I'm doing *Seinfeld*; I'm distracted going over how lousy I was on these shows. We're not talking on these shows, we're, well, I suppose it's acting. It's acting, Michael! Well then, I'm a lousy actor! This kind of stuff is rattling about in my head. Magazines and newspapers are no better. I'm always quoted out of context and shaped as a kooky crazy man playing Kramer.

But then, who am I really? Kramer and the *Seinfeld* show, coming out publicly from behind all of this *just as myself* is yet to be seen.

Kramer is pure character. It's what I do, "character" acting. Thank goodness there was a place for me on *Seinfeld*. As light as I was written for, I wasn't sure if my character work would fit into the show with other actors playing so close to themselves. But then, how close am I to Kramer? I'm playing close to something here that's of myself. I'm eccentric. Touched by Ma, the queer side of life, the freakish. How else could I play Kramer?

I find my way home through characters. I'm certainly at home being an actor. Just not on talk shows! Ha. And behind all this? The natural world, the source of myself behind the cultural mask, but for now, I dare not "cross the line" into the other side of this nature. This is for later in my life. For now, stick to the mask! Stay in the world as much as possible, Michael. This is easy for me to do just attending to *Seinfeld* and a private life that I keep to myself.

At Conservatory West, my work with Joanne Linville and Stella Adler had me playing closer to myself, what we referred to as being "at zero." Doing scenes from Tennessee Williams, Chekhov, or O'Neill brings me closer to zero because the characters in the plays are quite human and deeply psychological. To play them, I have to find real emotion through myself. Stella always scolds actors for "bullshitting an audience." I don't want to be the one who causes her to pound her hand on the table and yell, "I don't believe a goddamn thing you're doing!" Either you get to zero or you'll get slammed.

I talked about this with Anthony Hopkins one day. He told me that he works with "nothing at all." He just learns his lines and says them as he does anything else. He doesn't act. What? He tells me that he just memorizes the lines and says them. He leaves it up to the audience to read into it. "Why should I do all the work?" he says. It's all rather incredible to me. He is a *naturally* gifted actor. I stand in awe.

Peter Sellers in the comedy *Being There* played character and still got fairly close to himself "at zero." Jacques Tati played character and was natural at zero without dialogue; his character Hulot never spoke. Physically, he could go broad, but inwardly, he was at zero, much like Keaton. Laurel and Hardy, they seemed to be at zero, even with their physical comedy, unlike the Marx Brothers, who joyously played over the top, though the zaniest among them, Harpo, brought it all down to zero through the harp.

The person behind the schtick, just coming out from behind a character, no acting, nothing fake, to be genuine, a Michael Richards without a mask, I've got a way to go.

* * *

In "The Pool Guy," Kramer gets a new phone number ("Too many chicks know my number," he tells Jerry) that is one digit off from Moviefone. Naturally, he begins dispensing information about the movies playing in theaters. He has the time, and he's all out for helping his fellow man.

The bit shows Kramer sitting on a sofa in his apartment—the widest glimpse into his lair to date—and I get involved in selecting the items, including his wood-paneled walls and the collection of fusilli displayed over his sofa. I even help design his red circular lava lamp. I am particular about the furnishings and other accoutrements in his place. I want them to be old and cheap, from thrift shops, but at the same time they need to be somewhat cool and collectible.

In "The Cadillac," an hour-long double episode, Jerry spends some of the large paycheck he got from performing in Atlantic City on a brand-new Cadillac for his father, Morty. We bring on veteran comic Sandy Baron as a board member from Morty and Helen's homeowner's association in Florida, and not only is he unimpressed by the car, but he also accuses HOA president Morty of stealing money from the board to get it.

Sandy is fun to watch as he throws himself into the part. The way he says the word "Cadillac"—"I don't care about a Cad-ill-ac!"—the word becomes the size of a Cadillac spit out of his mouth. This is comedy acting!

The most revealing line of the episode, though, belongs to Liz Sheridan, who plays Jerry's mother, Helen, when she tells her husband they can't keep the car. "I'm not letting him buy us a Cadillac," she says. "He hasn't got that kind of money." It's a funny line that reflects the shift in lifestyle afforded by success in show business and more specifically, the kind of success we are having thanks to the show.

Up until now, I bought a home through a VA loan, but now I own the house outright. I own a new car. I buy rare books. I travel. After every third show, we get a week off. I usually take a shuttle flight from LAX to Monterey, California, and retreat for several days at the Post Ranch Inn in Big Sur. The previous summer, I discovered the earthy joys and comforts of Italy, particularly the Amalfi Coast. I'm Italian and my family heritage begins in Potenza, where I have relatives not far from Positano and Ravello, my favorite places to stay.

Just above the little town of Ravello, an incredible villa called La Rondinaia has been built on a cliff one thousand feet above the ocean. It's an imposing landmark along the Amalfi Coast. Some locals told me that the villa belongs to writer Gore Vidal. I know he's a smart man—I've read some of his books. But to own that villa, wow, the man knows how to live well. I'm also told he bought it for

$275,000. That's it? Wow! He's meant to have it. It just comes with his particular genius.

I dauntlessly mention to some locals that if that villa ever came up for sale, I'd buy it in a second. It must have got back to Gore. Nearly ten years later, I get a call from Gore's Italian real estate agent. La Rondinaia is up for sale.

"Gore wants to know if you wanna buy it?"

"Sure," I say, ready to move in. "How much does Gore want for it?"

"Twenty-three million."

"What? That's too low," I kid. "How 'bout I give you thirty million?"

The broker is silent. I break in.

"In all seriousness, you're asking price is way more than I can spend to live in Italy."

A local hotelier eventually buys the villa for millions less and later puts it up for sale for close to what Gore's real estate agent had asked from me. Okay, Gore got it for $275,000. I should have countered at $325,000. Take it or leave it. I'm a busy man, Tommaso! Instead, it was, "Tell Gore, I love his home and fare thee well."

* * *

Jason is the first among us to buy a mansion. It's a beautiful home in Hancock Park, one of LA's stately neighborhoods of old money and stature. After Gore's house came and went, I muse about buying a bigger home in Beverly Hills, but having spent years putting together my modest Studio City house, I feel I've got the place I need for now. Some of it has to do with the fact that I'm just ten minutes from the studio. I usually ride my bike to work.

But now that a "shift in lifestyle" is upon me, and my daughter is covered and living on her own, I decide to get a realtor to look at the best houses in Beverly Hills. I thought of buying Brian Wilson's house in Malibu, which I had leased for a while. It was offered to me, and being near the ocean is always relaxing, but "near" is different than having the sea literally under the house each month at high tide. An infinitesimal shift in the earth's axis and I'm under water. So I pass on Brian's place.

A more immediate drawback is the traffic along Pacific Coast Highway. I don't like it. During rush hour, and on the weekends when it seems that all of LA is cruising the coast, it's too congested. So living out in Malibu won't do.

Growing up in LA, I always dreamed of living in Bel Air. Since I was eleven years old, I have told my mom that someday I was going to live in Beverly Hills. I grew up fascinated by the mansions and the maps to stars' homes. When my mom was attending UCLA on Saturdays to further her knowledge of medical recordkeeping, I'd have her drop me off in front of the *Beverly Hillbillies* mansion. That was one of my favorite comedies. An equally wonderful mansion was being built down the street from the *Hillbillies* mansion. Because construction was at a standstill over the weekend, I was able to slip through the flimsy chain-link fence and hang out on the building site.

I loved hanging out there. Security was minimal if there was any at all, and most sites didn't even have fences. This mansion under construction was the place. Every Saturday, I lounged around in my mansion, checking out its progress. I felt that my time in this place was all my own. There was no one around. I "lived" there until my mom's classes were over. She picked me up out front.

Sometimes I walked around in Bel Air, eyeballing the mansions, and sat on the curb across the street from homes occupied by the famous, including Lucy, Jimmy Stewart, and my favorite, Red Skelton.

Now I'm looking at homes in Beverly Hills with my realtor. I go into a number of them and see they've been remodeled and modernized with canned lights, new floors and tile, with the original kitchens and bathrooms torn out. I'm after the original glamour, older homes that have not been updated but are in maintained condition. A well-built Mediterranean mansion in original condition will do, I tell my realtor.

My search goes on for months. After looking at over one hundred homes in Beverly Hills, I decide I want to be closer to the ocean. Not on the beach, but close to it.

One weekend, Kenny Kramer is in town. He comes along as I check out a place for sale in Pacific Palisades. He's so easygoing, and I see why Larry likes him so much. It amuses me that I'm out here looking for a house to buy with Kenny alongside me. I'm waiting for him to take charge, or come up with a scam like Kramer would, but Kenny behaves himself. He was probably playing it cool. I'm self-directed, and he probably picked up on that.

At the end of 1995, I'm driving slowly down streets in Pacific Palisades, along a bluff overlooking the ocean. The area reminds me of the view I last had in Positano. Catalina Island sits in the distance the way Capri does outside the Bay of Naples. A cool wind blows. The air is fresh. The horizon is as far as the eye can see. This place has the feel of Italy. So many of the streets have Italian names. There are a few old Mediterranean-style homes in the Palisades, but not many. Back in the '30s, being out here was the boonies.

I drive each street looking for the older homes. I find two that interest me. They're mansions, and one of them is incredible. It sits on top of a bluff with unobstructed ocean views. It's clearly one of the first large homes built in the Palisades. I soon find out it was built in 1930. I admire these older homes the way Jerry does Porsches. Like his cars, these older houses are built very well. At this time, neither of these estates is up for sale.

For the heck of it, I leave handwritten notes in the mailboxes. "I'm not a broker," it says. "I'm looking for a house to buy, and this is exactly the kind of place I'm looking for. Please call if you're interested in selling." I sign the note with my name and number.

It turns out the best of the two homes is being leased by a couple who are friends of the owner, and they recognize my name. They take the time to get ahold of my agent at ICM to confirm that it's really me.

"Toni, would Michael Richards leave a tattered piece of paper in a mailbox asking to buy your home?"

"Absolutely."

The next day the couple call me. They're an upstanding, reserved family who are part of LA's old guard. Soon, I'll see that they have pictures of themselves with the Reagans. I'm sure they think I'm kind of tacky putting a note in the mailbox, which I am. They say that they told their dear friend and owner of the house that I wanted to buy the place. To their surprise, the owner said he would sell. He had only just come to this decision and thought it was rather fortuitous that I left my note in his mailbox.

"Would you like to see the house?" they ask me.

"Yes, I would," I say. "Do you know how much he's asking?"

"Well, you know it's a Paul Williams house," she says.

I think she's referring to the songwriter who wrote "An Old Fashioned Love Song."

"He built the house?" I ask.

"Oh yes," she says.

For a moment, I'm picturing the musician walking around with a tool belt and ladder, hammering two-by-fours and applying the plaster. My lack of reaction tells her that I don't understand the significance of what she said.

"Not the musician," she says. "The architect. Paul R. Williams."

"Oh. Does this house have the original kitchen and bathrooms?"

"Yes, it does."

I set up a time to see the estate, excited that maybe this will be my house. But what's a house like this worth?

I call my realtor to do comps of the neighborhood and immediately head to the library to learn about Paul R. Williams. A short time later, I'm thinking, Wow, how come I've never heard of Paul R. Williams? Because I'm ignorant. He was the first African American architect in Los Angeles, the first Black member to join the American Institute of Architects. More so, he's a brilliant architect, having designed some of the finest houses and commercial properties throughout Southern California. He's quite important.

* * *

A MEETING IS SET FOR ME to see the house in a few days. I continue researching Williams. I find a book that has pictures of the house in it. There it is! It's certainly a notable Paul R. Williams–designed house. It's just amazing inside. This house is going to be way out of my price range, I think. I learn more about the iconic buildings and homes that Williams designed in Los Angeles. Landmarks such as the LA County Courthouse, the old Ambassador Hotel, the Saks Fifth Avenue building in Beverly Hills, along with homes for Frank

Sinatra, Lucille Ball, and Cary Grant. Wow! When I was eleven, I saw those houses in Beverly Hills!

Williams is no ordinary architect. I read that his signature is glamour and beauty, but what I see is incredible genius at the core of his work. The design, the floor plans, the building materials, and sites are special. Both his parents died when he was very young, and he was put in foster care, and so I can imagine at least part of the drive behind his enormous creativity was a desire to create the home he wished he'd had.

I also learn that the owner, Charlie Hathaway, is another LA native who became a very successful businessman and developer. He owns the LA Athletic Club and started the California Yacht Club. He has recently sold the Riviera Country Club his grandfather started for well over a hundred million bucks! Now I'm concerned. How much is he going to want for this house? Actually, it's more than a house. It's a work of art!

I take my realtor with me when I see the house for the first time. I've told him to bring papers just in case. I may make an offer on the spot. Just from the pictures I saw in the book I know it's beautiful, and if the inside is all original, well, that's why I'm bringing a pen too.

The couple who are going to escort us through the house meet us in front. We walk along a columned outdoor corridor with panoramic views of the Pacific below. I'm holding my breath and listening to the sound of the surf. My realtor is a step or two behind me as I am led into the house. One step inside, I turn to him and whisper, "This is the house."

During the walk-through, I see all the original tilework in the kitchen and bathrooms. The house has dramatic whitewater views, glamour, and warmth. I can see where it needs wallpaper removed, hardwood floors refinished, some patching and painting, some updating, but the bones of the house, it's all here. I want to buy this house. But can I afford it?

And I'll only pay cash. I want no debt. No loans on interest. If I don't have the money for it, then I won't buy it. I will make my offer based on the comps. The trouble with the comps is that they're for houses far less in stature than this one. They are all from the late '50s and '60s. This house is from 1930. Comps can hardly hold up to the craft of this house and its location on a knoll overlooking the ocean.

The following day I meet with Mr. Hathaway at the property. All I bring is myself and a blank check. Mr. Hathaway is tall, athletic, silver haired. His handshake is as firm as his smile. He has owned this home for more than twenty years and raised his kids here. The place is filled with wonderful memories, he says. This is a happy home. He asks me to go through the house again while he sits outside and waits for me. I do just that.

The house looks better to me than the day before. I don't want to look anymore. I don't want to get attached. Most likely, Mr. Hathaway wants far more money than I can spend for this place. When I come out, he asks me to sit down and tell him what I think of the house. In all honesty, I gush, "It's magnificent. It's a masterpiece. I just don't know if I can afford it."

He smiles. "So, you like the house?"

"I do. Very much so."

"Make me an offer."

My realtor thought the house would go for more than I'm about to offer. I'm coming in low—but not purposely. It's all the money I have. So be it.

"I won't take a loan out," I explain. "I don't like living in debt."

Mr. Hathaway waits impassively. He's a much more experienced negotiator.

I mention the one and only number I can offer. It's all the money in my savings.

He takes a beat and trains his piercing eyes directly on mine before offering a smile and extending his hand. "Okay, it's yours."

I'm dumbfounded. After we shake hands, I write him a check on the spot. Done. We stroll along the walkway. He puts his arm around me.

"You know, Michael, I could've got a lot more money if I had put it on the market," he says. "But I want this house to be in good hands, and I believe you have the hands for it. It needs some work, buts it's all here. You bought a great house, Michael. Congratulations."

There's a chance the place will be a money pit, but I know better. I feel the greatness of the house, and know I'm going to have many happy years here.

"It's such a beautiful home, Charlie! Thank you."

"I have one request," he says. "Once a year, I would like to bring my family back here so we can sit outside by the fireplace and look at the ocean and get together like we've done for so many years."

"Absolutely."

Shortly after January 1996, the house is mine. I have stayed in touch and I am forever grateful to the Hathaways. They are always welcome in my home. Same for Karen Hudson, Paul R. Williams's granddaughter, who put together that book I first saw about her grandfather. She tells me it was his favorite house. The original plans came with the house too.

I hear Albert Brooks asking me, as he once did, "Have you bought a great house yet?" Now I can say, yes, Albert, I have. My La Rondinaia.

* * *

Julia had recently closed on her home in Pacific Palisades. I told her I had just written a check for a Mediterranean home built there in 1930 by a famous architect. What? Yeah, ocean views and everything! She shoves me like Elaine would shove Kramer. "Get outta here!"

Yep, we're both living in the Palisades. Because we are locked inside Stage 19 and intensely focused on playing these characters, we often overlook the changes happening to all of us in our lives away from the set. Julia has her first child. Jason has his. Larry is about to follow us into the Palisades to buy a house there too. Jerry is about to buy an apartment in New York in a building he's always admired since he was a kid.

* * *

BY THE TIME WE TAPE "The Friars Club," which has my most elaborate stunt to date when Kramer is thrown into the Hudson River (I actually sink to the bottom of a twelve-foot tank with forty pounds of weights strapped to me and people saying, "We can't have Michael do that," and me responding, "Of course I'm doing it; I have twenty years of diving experience"), I will have been in more than one hundred episodes since I broke down in Jerry's (real) apartment over my crumbling marriage and the divorce was finalized. There has been much growth and discovery and more to do. And at the bottom of a twelve-foot tank, it's a meditation for me.

The lives that come into our soundstage also have a profound effect on each of us. Late that winter, Marjorie Gross, one of the show's writers the past two seasons, begins to lose her battle with ovarian cancer, which was diagnosed about two years earlier. A longtime friend of both Jerry and Larry, she wrote on Amy Heckerling's breakthrough series *Square Pegs* and various other shows before landing on the *Seinfeld* staff, where she joined Carol Leifer, Elaine Pope, and Jennifer Crittenden in bringing a woman's point of view to our male-skewing show. These women are sharp and very talented writers.

Jerry makes sure a bed is put in Marjorie's office for when she's fatigued. Marjorie was always upbeat around me and everyone else, so I never thought too much about her battle with the Big C. Isn't that how it is? We're all so upbeat and forward-focused with our lives, doing this and that, going here and there, we don't think about dying.

One day when Marjorie was going through chemo, I see her come in wearing a baseball hat. "I have to say, I like the way you look without the cap," I say. Yul Brynner looks great without hair. A woman can too. Marjorie agrees. "It's everybody else that thinks it's weird," she says. "I wear the baseball cap to console them. I shouldn't. I'm really fine with the way I look." I tell her that she looks great—and she does. She's beautiful and upbeat.

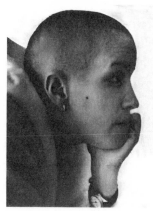

By midseason, Marjorie is writing her own last act. She is a brave soul who has come to terms with life. Death is as natural to her as the wind through the trees—a winter's breeze with jokes in the air. "I finally lost weight," she cracks. In April, she pens an article in the *New Yorker* about her illness titled "Cancer Becomes Me." Two months later, Marjorie passes away.

* * *

OUR SECOND-TO-LAST EPISODE, "The Wait Out," is the only time I am injured during the run of the series. It's one of my favorite Kramer episodes. George and his fiancée, Susan, cause another couple to break up, Jerry and Elaine eye the newly single twosome, and Kramer gets stuck in a pair of tight jeans. During rehearsal, as Jerry tries to wrestle the jeans off me, he grabs me wrong, and it tweaks my back on the edge of the couch.

"Uh, hold on," I say, gingerly getting to my feet and slowly unfolding my almost forty-seven-year-old body until I am standing straight up. "I got a tweak. I'll have to drink a lot of liquor now." We laugh. I get through the next day's taping without anyone knowing I'm worse for wear, the wearing of those tight jeans.

Ouch! When it comes time to shoot that scene, I'm in some pain, but it all worked out.

The tweak is gone in a few days. This is one of the great advantages of Iyengar yoga—I'm as flexible as a rubber band. I was certainly kidding about the liquor.

Then it's on to our seventh-season finale, "The Invitations." Written by Larry David, it finds George trying with typical frustration to get out of his wedding to Susan.

In the end, there is no wedding: Susan dies after licking 250 wedding invitations. When I hear that twisted turn of fate at the table read, I let out a big hoot. I know that Larry doesn't like the glue on envelopes. Chemicals. "Don't ever put your tongue on that stuff," he says. To this day, I don't.

* * *

WHAT I DON'T KNOW is that this season is Larry's last one. After this twenty-fourth episode of the season and one hundred thirty-fourth overall, he's done. I am not aware he's made this decision. Not that he needed to let me in on his thoughts. I'm sure he has told Jerry and the executives at Castle Rock, but he doesn't say goodbye or thanks or what a run, or anything like that to me or anyone else as far as I know.

His departure surprises me, and yet it doesn't. The pressure he has put on himself to come up with enough stories season after season and make sure they're funny is well known to everyone. It's a lot of pressure to stay fresh each week, all brand new and funny with another great show. Stress and strain is everywhere; the pressure on carbon to turn it into a diamond makes our show go round and around. If you're not under pressure, it supposedly means you don't give a damn. We all give a damn.

Episodes coming and going. So many entrances and exits. Now Larry is out the door.

The first time I ever saw Larry at the Comedy Store, he just walked off the stage at the beginning of his act. "Fuck it." He didn't feel right that night. I understand. Larry has wanted to quit the show before. At the beginning of season three, he said goodbye after getting notes from NBC executives. "Good luck," he told Jerry. "Fuck it." Then he comes back and he's better than ever.

Not only did he have the responsibility to make sure each episode was swingin', really swingin', as the show progressed, he had to serve characters who became stars themselves, servicing the nuances of that every week, in addition to the overall storylines holding everybody together.

The demand for excellence has come from every corner, not the least of which was his own. Larry wants everything right. Thank God for that. I'm reminded of Marlon Brando's response to someone asking why he didn't do theater anymore. "I can't get onstage and do that every night," he said. Getting stuck in the machinery of routine terrified Brando. Doing *Seinfeld* every week demands it.

For Larry, the routine ends. Enough. I assume he wants to get out for himself. Make it now on his own. Burn as a star performer through his own fire. He's got the stuff for it. He leaves with the writers knowing the characters. Just get the material close enough, and we'll run with it. Jerry knows this and no doubt is depending on this or bust. We'll see.

Good luck, Larry. Giddyup, Jerry.

....

CHAPTER 25

It's Go Time

In May, I am in Lake Tahoe to help induct Red Skelton into the National Comedy Hall of Fame. I do this for the producer George Schlatter, the creator of *Rowan & Martin's Laugh-In*, because I'm really into Red Skelton. This is a once-in-a-lifetime chance to meet my longtime comedy inspiration.

Red is the last of the knockabout clowns, and I see the toll this has taken on him when we meet the day before in the hotel-casino's art gallery, where he is hosting a show of his latest clown paintings. An accomplished artist, he sits in a wheelchair ("My knees, all those pratfalls," he later tells me), looking older but still very much like the entertainer whose sketch comedy show featuring characters like Clem Kadiddlehopper and Freddie the Freeloader ran on TV for twenty-three years!

I know all about Red. The music he's composed, the stories he's written, the movies he's starred in, his devotion to Catholicism, the way he closed every show by saying, "Good night, and may God bless." For me, it's like meeting Chaplin. We talk about our shared passion for clowns—Red has been into clowns since boyhood, his father was a circus clown, and he accepts the potency of my dream of being the clown holding the globe, the world that launched me into professional comedy.

At the banquet, I have some prepared remarks in my hand, but I set them down and offer a tribute that comes straight from my heart. I also recite a poem that Red wrote to his father when he was ten. George Schlatter, also a great fan of Red's, gave me the poem, knowing the impact it would have on the man of honor. Red never knew his father. His father died two months before he was born.

From his chair Red looks up at me. His eyes are filled with tears. What a moment! I start to get choked up myself. I didn't have a father either.

When I introduce Red, he practically leaps from his wheelchair, nine-inch cigar in hand, and walks to the podium. After the standing ovation winds down, he says, "Well, I can't top that. Good night." But he does. For the next twenty minutes, he tells jokes and stories that has the crowd in stitches.

The man is a marvel. When we were together earlier, I noticed that he was wearing a ring signifying he's a thirty-third-degree Mason. That's up there. Red is famously involved in Freemasonry, and I tell him that I've always been interested in Masonry. In my early twenties, I read Albert Pike's 1871 book, *Morals and Dogma of the Ancient and Accepted Scottish Rite of Freemasonry*. I explain my interest in Hermetic Masonry going back to philosophical alchemy and the Rosicrucian mystics. I also mention Manly P. Hall, the thirty-third-degree Mason who wrote *The Secret Teachings of All Ages*, the book I was so interested in when I was a student at CalArts.

Impressed by my knowledge of Masonry, Red offers to "introduce" me, and I'm delighted. Mark Twain, Oliver Hardy, Will Rogers, Bud Abbott, Don Rickles, Peter Sellers, and Richard Pryor were Masons. Through Red, I'm all for joining a fraternity that had such a funny crew, although I'm drawn more to what's called "Speculative

Masonry," the deeper "subjective" side of the craft, and the way it complements my interest in natural philosophy, earth science, and analytical psychology. I am not a deist, but my awareness and passion for Masonry and "Nature's God" registers with Red, and I am introduced.

* * *

IF ANYONE IS CONCERNED about entering season eight without Larry, I suppose it should be Jason. George has so much of Larry in him. They are symbiotic in that way. But I also know that Jason makes that character jump. From the day I saw Jason open up on the pilot, I thought he was sensational. Larry knew it too, and reveled in it. Jason could take Larry's dialogue and make it sparkle. He's a better Larry than Larry!

Jason's saving grace is that he has his character down. At this point, if any of the writers can write close enough to George, Jason will take it home. Julia and I have the same confidence.

And Jerry? He's Jerry. When we come back, the show doesn't appear to be any different without Larry's presence for the first time since he and Jerry created the show, and that's all to Jerry's credit. Larry set us up to cruise, and Jerry's usual attention to detail keeps the show running with the same attention he lavishes on his Porsches. There's not a leaf or a spot on them. It's a clean machine.

* * *

IT GOES WELL. Some of the shows get broader. Jerry and the writers are playing with the format and just how far we can go with the characters. This is somewhat intentional, but also what makes Jerry and the writers laugh. The spirit of the show carries us along. Sometimes we refer to it as "the beast" with a mind of its own. We're all on its back being carried along. Over a hundred people attend to *Seinfeld*. It's a big production. All hands on deck. And the wind is favorable. We open our sails and let it rip.

At its best, the show examines life under a microscope. Sometimes, as in this season, the microscope is not always there and we get an episode like "The Bizarro Jerry," in which Elaine's new friends are the opposite of Jerry, George, and Kramer, and Kramer starts working in an office where he just stopped in to use their bathroom. He doesn't really have a job there, but he "imagines" that he does. This is okay with the character Kramer. He's always passing through the apparent world into something larger and more exciting, breaking with reality, traveling to whatever "levels" of interest he's got going.

But for the others, who are usually grounded in the everyday goo of city life, the broad, otherworldly plotlines can only be played for laughs, somewhat against character. Not that this is bad. It's merely different. Our fourth episode, "The Little Kicks" is of this stripe because of Elaine's uncomfortably awkward dancing at her office party. The dancing is different and difficult for others to accept. It

appears "otherworldly," broad, and unacceptable. Differences upsetting the kettle, defying the ordinary way of doing things—this is our show to some extent. It always hinges on differences and is predominately unique, so signified by Elaine's extraordinary dancing. The show does indeed encompass the bizarre.

"The Fatigues" is another one of those bizarro episodes that's still very funny, but going, going, gone. Kramer hosts a party for Jewish singles and enlists Frank Costanza to cook. But Frank, a former army cook, hung up his apron long ago; he confesses to Kramer the terror he suffered in the Korean War that has kept him from standing above a stove ever since. "In my mind," he says, "there's a war that's still going on."

What left him suffering PTSD? It turns out he over-seasoned some Texas prime meat—"At least it used to be prime," he says— and "sent sixteen of my own men to the latrines that night." "They were just boys," he says. Kramer urges him to get back in the kitchen. "Two hundred Jewish singles need you," he says. "This is your chance to make it all right again."

Frank's army playback is on another planet. Only Kramer can go there. Like "levels," Kramer is multidimensional; disturbing playbacks are par for the course. "Another planet" is as close to Kramer as Jerry's apartment. He's also the humanitarian of the bunch. Jerry would lay a one-liner on Frank and be out the door. Elaine would find an excuse to leave. George would hold his head and not care at all. Only Kramer accepts the bizarre and brings reassurance to Frank that it's okay to be out of your mind. He'll help him deal with it. With Kramer as the bizarro leading the bizarre, it's a hoot to see the whole party utterly destroyed by Frank, violently overturning the food tables so under the spell of his playback from the war within him.

Overall, as bizarre as some of the episodes get, all of us are com-fortable in the craziest of unreal situations. The show is a machine, our "high-frequency vehicle." No one person is steering the ship on their own, but I have come to this place where, more than 140 episodes into this journey, I'm confident that Kramer knows how to drive. In "The Muffin Tops" episode, Kramer's "Peterman Reality Tour" has our man behind the wheel. It transcends the make-believe of television when the real-life Kenny Kramer starts his own tour of significant *Seinfeld* spots in NYC. And to meet Kenny is well worth the price of admis-sion. I recommend his tour. Tell 'em Kramer sent you.

* * *

IT's 1996. At the end of the year, I'm feeling that *Seinfeld* is going to end in a few years.

Julia has been thinking about this too, and with our contracts coming to an end, she's the one who comes to me and throws out a number. "We're not taking less," she says. It's the same number I have in my head, and with Jason in accord, we agree to go into this as a threesome, seeing strength in numbers, to keep this alliance together as negotiations drag on into what *Entertainment Weekly* calls "bare-knuckle bargaining" and raises a question mark over the show's future. It would be easier to break into Fort Knox than to get NBC to part with any of their profits.

They offer a slight raise far short of our asking and refuse to negotiate further. What? They call us "supporting actors," not stars, and say they'll replace us. What? They point to *Frasier* and *Friends* and *Suddenly Susan*, intimating that Thursday night can be strong without us. I guess this is the way business is done—"It's nothing personal, Sonny"—but this tactic of diminishing our contributions to the show pisses me off. I'm a flapper! The insult stings.

"Maybe we should go back and ask for double!" I say.

We do—and then some. Unbeknownst to Julia and Jason, I'm emboldened because I had asked Jerry straight out his opinion on what we were asking for. The man is one of our executive producers, a co-owner of the show, and most likely he's being kept abreast of the new contracts Jason, Julia, and I are asking for. It's in his interest to shrug and say he can't talk to me about it. Or shouldn't talk to me. Instead, when I say, "Jerry, do you think I'm out of line if we want this?" "Nope. Ask for it," he says.

"Yeah?" I say, suddenly turning into Kramer.

"Just get it," he says.

He knew the money was there.

* * *

I LIKE MY MOVES IN "THE CHICKEN ROASTER" episode where the chicken roaster sign outside Kramer's apartment window is having a traumatic effect on him. In one scene, the incredible light appears to be bending him backwards. This was one of Jerry's favorite Kramer takes throughout the run of the show.

Someone in postproduction added a buzzing sound (from the roaster sign) as I open the door to go back to my apartment. It's a nice touch to enhance my daffy reaction to such a light.

In "The Abstinence," I get a kick out of the way my makeup is done to show the moldering effects on Kramer of three days of exposure to heavy cigarette and cigar smoke after he turns his apartment into a club for smokers. "Don't look at me," I ad-lib to Jerry, referencing Anthony Quinn's *The Hunchback of Notre Dame*, after seeing my reflection in his toaster. "I'm hideous."

This was a scene we had to shoot several times because Jerry couldn't keep from laughing.

I love cracking him up off camera, but during a taping of the show I worry that we'll lose a vital take. I always stay in character. Mistakes can be "God's rewrite," making the scene even better, as in the episode "The Parking Garage."

* * *

In "The Little Jerry," Kramer purchases a chicken, which he names Little Jerry Seinfeld, so he can have cage-free eggs. But, as Jerry tells him, it's a rooster. "Well, that would explain Little Jerry's poor egg production," says Kramer. As scripted, that's the closing line to end the scene and get the laugh we needed, but I went further by holding up the chicken and taking a look at its rear end to see what I've got here. It got a bigger laugh to button up the scene.

This farm-minded idea in the middle of New York City, a chicken in your apartment for cage-free eggs, is something only Kramer would hatch. Not a bad idea if only he had gotten a hen, but still, keep the rooster because it takes two to make ends meet. The idea of producing your own eggs is a good one. This was one storyline I wish we had stuck with, that Kramer has chickens in his apartment named after his friends. "Pretty Elaine," "Funny George," "Hello Newman" would all be good egg layers. And with Kramer's shopping cart always parked outside his front door, well, the K-Man is coming through. Definitely.

Later in the episode, Kramer takes the rooster for a walk on a leash and goes into the bodega. The rooster goes on the attack when a guy comes in with his dog. The rest is improvised. I quickly pick up the rooster and shield it under my arm, then check out my bird to make sure it's okay. I find myself looking at its rear end…again. But this time, oh my God, where's its head? I do a flustered take, then turn the bird around discovering that its head is still with us. Whew! These little antics bring out the best in Kramer…and me.

But working with animals can be difficult, as W. C. Fields said. The chicken on a leash for a walk with Kramer down the street was nearly impossible to do. The chicken just wouldn't walk with me or at all. On one take I was pushing it along, which I thought would be funny, Kramer pushing the bird down the street instead of walking it, but even the push didn't last long, maybe just a few feet and then the chicken stopped and wouldn't budge. I could have pushed the bird along the sidewalk anyway, but I didn't want it to look like I was hurting it. We managed to get a bit of walking for the show but had to cut away as I entered the bodega.

By comparison, the monkey we used in "The Face Painter" did everything on cue, including spit at me—which was in the script! We shot the monkey scene in one take with just a few pickups for close-ups. W. C. Fields would have been delighted to have that animal on his set.

During a break, I'm sitting with Jerry and he mentions an upcoming script titled "The English Patient," which includes a character named Izzy Mandelbaum that was written for Jerry Lewis. Jerry tells me that Lewis wants $50,000.

"So he's going to be here?" I ask.

"We're not going to pay him fifty thousand dollars," Jerry says.

I look at him the way Kramer would, aghast.

"Are you kidding? It's Jerry Lewis!"

"Not for fifty thousand dollars."

"Think of all he had to do to become Jerry Lewis. Give him the fifty."

"It's not going to happen."

"Who's going to play the part?" I ask.

"We want a celebrity, but not for fifty thousand dollars," Jerry says.

"Jerry, let's bring in Tony Curtis! Cookies, Jerry!"

It's too late. An offer already went out to Lloyd Bridges. Just as good. I'm a fan. I was raised on *Sea Hunt*! Shortly, I hear Lloyd is, indeed, cast to play Izzy. Cool. I decide to call the production office and pretend to be Lloyd's agent. I'm going to leave a message for Jerry that Lloyd wants forty-five thousand for the episode or forget it. Jerry's assistant picks up. Better yet. After I start my spiel as the agent, she interrupts.

"Michael?"

I thought my voice for Lloyd's agent was pretty good. Not so.

"Do you want to talk to Jerry? He's on the set rehearsing," she says.

"Well, I'm glad Jerry's on the ball. Tell him to stick with it. Over and out." I hang up.

* * *

I LOVE KRAMER'S FRIENDSHIP with Mickey. These two always get into trouble, as seen in "The Yada Yada." In it, Jerry's dentist Tim Whatley is back, this time telling Jewish jokes, and George's girlfriend sloughs everything off by saying "and yada yada," and soon everyone is saying it. But as far as I'm concerned, the pièce de résistance is the trouble Mickey and I have trying to double-date two girls.

When the two of us barge into Jerry's apartment, we're at each other's throats, frustrated and trading insults arising from our inability to pick which of the girls each of us should date. Kramer can't remember their names, and Mickey doesn't know which one is his type. "Oh, everybody's your type," Kramer says.

"What the hell does that mean?" Mickey says.

"You've been married three times."

With that, Mickey loses it and yells, "That's it! IT'S GO TIME!"

And a fight breaks out. Mickey would hurt Kramer, but luckily the fight is stopped by Jerry and Elaine. I love it that Mickey can easily whip Kramer and is always all-out for a fight. He comes at you the same way Kramer comes through the door. The scene is everything I love about working with Mickey.

There's a scene in a restaurant where we meet the girls for dinner and wrestle each other for dibs on who sits next to whom. Danny and I improvise the whole thing, and I think it's among the best knockabouts we've done together on the series. It's this kind of stuff that I want to do with Mickey all the time. I was padded up for the tussle not sure how far it was going to go. Will we wipe out the whole table? I didn't want it to run too long or get too violent. Kramer tries to cover by being polite with the girls, and I love it that Mickey yanks him back down to the ground where they disappear behind the table. I fling my leg up to button up the scene. At the end of the episode, Mickey gets married to one of the girls.

Mickey's parents are played by Robert Wagner and Jill St. John. I had no idea the two of them were guesting on the show until they came in for rehearsal. Great casting! How much for the two? Fifty thousand? I was told that they were very reasonable. So be it.

* * *

IN THE SEASON EIGHT FINALE, "The Summer of George," George is out of work, Jerry is dating a waitress who has a live-in boyfriend, and Kramer finds himself having to fire Raquel Welch from a Broadway play for which he was mistakenly given a Tony Award. As our guest star, Raquel's sense of self and know-how is fun to watch. During rehearsal, she requests several wardrobe changes to go better with the color of the set walls and the lighting. Outfits were pulled just for this. Later that night, Raquel called and wanted her wardrobe changed to another color. With just a day to go before shooting the show, head of wardrobe had to go shopping for Raquel, and it took a day with all the tailoring. A few people insisted that Raquel was being difficult. Not me. I saw a woman who knows what works for her and what doesn't. She's certainly not shy about asking for what she needs to look her best. I was impressed that she had it all figured out! She also had ideas about where the camera should be for her close-ups, and on the angle of her face, her weak side, her strong side. I saw some eyes rolling, but I saw Raquel striving to look fabulous on the highest-rated comedy show going. Brava, Raquel.

* * *

WE'RE APPROACHING THE END of our ongoing contract negotiations. The press has been all over it. Will we get what we want? Or will the show end? The numbers are out there—not just the $1 million per episode we have been asking for and the network's hard-line stance against it, but also the $1 billion Jerry stands to make through syndication and the $200 million profit NBC makes from advertising. Just open the LA Times or Hollywood Reporter. It's all public, and it's mind-boggling.

As we reach the end of the season and just days before NBC's upfront at which they announce their next fall lineup to advertisers, we have to reach an agreement or say goodbye to the best job (and highest ad rates) on television. A meeting is scheduled with executives and representatives from all sides. Both Julia and Jason attend in person. I'm at home, like Kramer running "Kramerica" from his cordless phone, but this isn't in my imagination. This is really happening. My position is clear: stick to our number. I don't care about stock in NBC's parent company, GE (one perk the network is presenting). For me, I want the money.

After a few hours and numerous phone calls, I hear that they're done. They've reached an agreement on what NBC will later describe as a package that works for everyone. It covers two years. They just need me to sign off. It's short of our number—my number—but everyone in the meeting is all for "the package." Even as I agree, I know we could do better. Alas, our lawyers are happy with what we're getting. I must say, the package is a first of its kind. Soon, other acting ensembles on the network will get our first number. We weren't that far off. We actually set the bar.

* * *

FINALLY, IT'S SUMMER—and we're off. Julia is ready to give birth to her second child any week (it happens at the end of May). Baggy shirts and large coats have hidden her pregnancy all season. Jason and his wife, Daena, have two boys now, and he's looking forward to family time in his new home. Jerry has also given birth to several more Porsches. I recommend that he take a drive along scenic Highway 1 to Big Sur.

He speeds up there, gets out of the car, takes in a deep breath of fresh air, gets back in the car, and speeds back to LA.

"How long were you there?" I ask.

"About a minute."

"What?"

"I saw it. I get it. It's nice."

"You could have stayed at the Big Sur Inn."

"I could have, but I didn't."

"It's more about driving the Porsche than seeing anything else," I conclude.

"That's right."

Jerry has little time for a scenic drive away from the show. He sped up there and right back to his show. That's the beautiful view, the scenic in his life, the show! It's full time or bust!

Once, Jerry drives over to see my new house in Pacific Palisades. He looks at the view of the ocean, shakes his head, and says, "You're not going to get anything done here." It's far too relaxing for him. Gene Simmons also stopped by once. I had just come back from Bali and told him how much I enjoyed myself. "Traveling is a waste of time and money," he said. "I'd rather be working." Gene and Jerry would get along fine.

* * *

A FEW WEEKS BEFORE THE SEASON ENDS, Jerry and I are hanging out and I can tell that he is worn out. "I'm getting tired," he admits.

I knew what that meant. It was the grind of running the show, the wear and tear of doing it without Larry. Time was running out, and the best and most lucrative way to end the show was while it was on top. It'll make billions on its own. No need to work at it anymore.

I do *feel* the end of the show. I suggest we move the production out of LA and shoot the whole thing in New York City. It would be a new and different energy and maybe add another season.

"Does that inspire you?" I ask.

"I've thought about all that. A few years ago, yes, but not now. I don't have it in me."

Done. One more season and it'll be over.

I say nothing more to anyone. Jerry will say it when he feels the time is right.

CHAPTER 26

Have a Good Show

Time for season nine. The NBC fall promo boasts, "Now the three words you've waited all summer for—*Seinfeld is back!*" We've come a long way from our July 1989 debut, and I am able to speak and thank people when I pick up my third Emmy Award in mid-September. Still, I am uncomfortable. I still feel awkward and out of sync at these celebrity events, but I bring my mother and my daughter, and I am somewhat grounded around them.

Three days later I'm saddened by news that Red Skelton has passed away at his home in Rancho Mirage, California. His widow, Lothian, and I trade phone calls. She and her advisors and family have much of the estate to straighten out. Red had an eye and a penchant for collecting everything from fine art to cars, and when she mentions contacting Sotheby's to sell his library, I quickly say, "I'll buy his books. Just tell me what you want."

I hold my breath. How many millions will she want? It turns out that she has a rough assessment from an auction house. I say fine and write her a check. No dickering, no negotiation. Soon I am in possession of about three thousand beautiful leather-bound books, rare and in the finest condition. Not long after I finish building cases for them, Lothian asks if she can come by and see the books in their new home.

I show her into my library and watch her slowly walk about the place.

"I like this room very much," she says.

She gently runs her hand across a few leather-bound volumes that once belonged to her husband. I can see this is a way for her to feel close to him again. Later, once I begin reading some of these books, I will discover that Red often wrote short love notes to her that were tucked away in random volumes. When I come across one, I send it to her. It's as if Red is contacting her, letting her know again how much he loves her. I get to be the messenger.

* * *

IN OUR FOURTH EPISODE of the season, "The Blood," Lloyd Bridges reprises his role as Izzy Mandelbaum. Lloyd has a terrible time with his lines this go-round, and I think someone offers to put up cue cards. Lloyd scoffs at the suggestion. "I've never worked one day in my life with cue cards," he says. "I'm not going to start now." He's Izzy Mandelbaum! The man was US Navy diver Mike Nelson on *Sea Hunt*. As a kid I watched nearly every episode. I admire his mettle and pride. The man is an actor. Let him work!

Six months later, Lloyd passes away. When I hear the news, I think about my grandfather slipping me a pack of Life Savers and then he's gone. All this going away. "Enjoy it while it lasts."

That sentiment is something I have in mind when we shoot "The Merv Griffin Show" episode, one of my very favorites. The writer, Bruce Kaplan, came up with the whole story: While out walking together, Jerry and Kramer come upon a dumpster filled with what looks to Jerry like garbage. However, Kramer recognizes it as something more significant—the set from the old Merv Griffin talk show.

It's history. Kramer quickly hops into the dumpster, amazed. "Jerry, this stuff belongs in the Smithsonian," he says.

When I first read this particular scene, it reminds me of Neil discovering a bunch of Warhol's Brillo boxes in the dumpsters behind the LA County Museum of Art. The museum thought they were junk or that Warhol and staff just threw them out after his show. What those boxes are worth now—sweet.

Then there's Kramer's line about the chairs in the dumpster: "One minute, Elliott Gould is sitting on you, then the next thing, you're yesterday's trash." Any number of celebrities on *The Merv Griffin Show* could have been mentioned in the script. Richard Burton, Orson Welles, Sophia Loren, Ingrid Bergman...the list is long. It even includes Jerry, who was on the show in 1981.

For whatever reason, though, Bruce picked Elliott Gould. And so of course my brain zooms back to when I saw Elliott seated on the floor in the hallway at Carrie Fisher's house, looking up at me and saying, "Enjoy it while it lasts."

Seeing his name attached to this moment with the set in the dumpster, with the history that's upon all those chairs, including Elliott, I see he wasn't being glib. Elliott knew, "Enjoy it while it lasts," and at a time where I sense that *Seinfeld* will be folding up this year and worth far more than Warhol's Brillo boxes.

* * *

IT'S OCTOBER, AND WE'RE STILL in the early part of the season, having shot only about one-quarter of our episodes, and up until now Jerry hasn't said anything more to me about the way he's feeling about the show and how much longer we might go. There's been no follow-up on the comment he made to me the previous season about being "tired." Then one day when the two of us are by ourselves on the set at the kitchen counter, just as we were years ago when my hair was in question—it happens.

"I don't think I can go much longer than a year here," he says.

"It's definitely your call," I say.

Our ratings are as high as ever, which is really the best time for Jerry to end the show. Go out on top. Don't play past your prime. From the way NBC announced at the upfronts that we were coming back for one or two more seasons, I assume Jerry has it in his contract that he can pull the plug anytime. In fact, he does. A few weeks later he informs the network. This season is going to be the end.

NBC reacts as expected. They offer Jerry, who's already the highest paid TV actor in history, a reported $5 million per episode. Multiply that by twenty-four episodes and, well, that's a lot of Porsches. But Jerry declines. Why should he work so hard? Behind it all he's up for the syndication deals.

The news breaks the day after Christmas. "Seinfeld Says It's All Over, and It's No Joke for NBC," declares the *New York Times*, which calls the show a "cultural signpost" and ranks it *among the greatest comedies of all time*, alongside *I Love Lucy* and *The Honeymooners*. "To keep a show of this caliber at its peak has been a great undertaking," the network says in their official statement. "We respect Jerry's decision that at the end of this season it's time to move on." Jerry agrees. "I wanted to end the show on the same kind of peak we've been doing it on for years," he tells the *Times*. "I wanted the end to be from a point of strength. I wanted the end to be graceful."

For the most part it is.

* * *

IN ADDITION TO JERRY'S TEASE that the series will end with a special final episode, we still have a chunk of the season to shoot. Many of the remaining episodes—"The Apology," "The Strike," "The Reverse Peephole"—are already outlined and on the storyboard. "The Burning," our sixteenth episode, gives me one more chance to work with Danny Woodburn. Kramer and Mickey are hired to act out symptoms of diseases for medical students practicing their diagnoses.

At the hospital, they're handed assignments. Mickey gets bacterial meningitis. Kramer is given gonorrhea. Disappointed, he offers to trade with Mickey. "Sorry, buddy, this is the *Hamlet* of diseases," Mickey says. "Severe pain, nausea, delusions—it's got everything." But Kramer delivers an over-the-top description of a romantic encounter that left him with a burning when he urinates, and the next week, when maladies are assigned, Mickey is given cirrhosis of the liver and Kramer is assigned gonorrhea again. It's intended as a compliment, an encore performance. "I don't believe this," he says, upset. "I'm being typecast."

In an attempt to avoid this creative straitjacket, Kramer steals Mickey's disease. As a result, there in the hospital, Mickey decides it's go time again, and with no one to hold him back, he pummels Kramer. Stealing. Fighting over our stuff. It's a fool's gold.

And how portentous, this reaction to being "typecast." Not that it is a curse, but I will always be seen as Kramer. Anything other than Kramer probably won't fly.

The finale is several weeks off, but I think Kramer's actual goodbye—in terms of character development—comes in "The Wizard" when a production company buys the movie rights to Kramer's coffee-table book and he announces that he's retiring "from the grind." Jerry is astonished by the news and wants to know how much Kramer is being paid. (Actually, Jerry will be selling the rights to his show for the rest of his life. Kramer is cashing out too.)

To celebrate, Kramer has bought himself a gold watch. When I read this, I immediately remember the dream I had years earlier in which I found myself wearing a gold watch and waving to people as I stood on a float in a parade. Kramer gets his gold watch. Our lives intersect. He's got everything he's wanted. He's leaving the grind. He moves in next door to Jerry's parents in their retirement community in Florida. He clobbers old guys in ping-pong, dances one of the residents to her death, and runs for president of the condo association.

But after trying to buy his way to victory, things go haywire, and he loses the election to "the guy in the wheelchair." He heads back to

New York. It's a sly comment on the way retirement doesn't always live up to the hype. How will I retire? I won't be running for anything; I may be running away from everything. I've got my eye on the wilderness. I want to have a small stone cabin, take off the mask, read great books, and just sit with the land. It's sort of like Kramer, when he says, "Up here, I'm already gone."

* * *

THE LAST SCRIPTED REGULAR SEASON episode before the finale is "The Puerto Rican Day." The entire writing staff is credited. In it, the four of us—Jerry, George, Elaine, and Kramer—are returning to the city from a Mets game and get stuck in a massive traffic jam caused by the Puerto Rican Day parade.

We shoot it at Universal Studios, and aside from episode two, "The Trip," in our fourth season, "The Puerto Rican Day" looks and feels as if it's the largest undertaking in all our years of taking the show on location. Five days of blocking and shooting. An enormous production and in such contrast to the one little stage where we shot the pilot a decade ago. There are dozens of extras, a sea of cars, an army of trailers, and lots of people running around. It's epic—proof that *Seinfeld* is the most expensive sitcom going, going, almost gone. I expect to see David Lean directing, not Andy Ackerman.

Nine years ago, Kramer never left his apartment. Now he's at the center of New York. He's out there living through it all. But this character inadvertently causes some trouble in this episode.

A controversy erupts after the show airs. People watching react to the scene where Kramer accidentally lights the Puerto Rican flag on fire, then stomps on the flag to put out the flames. Seemingly insensitive, it's an accident that only a doofus like Kramer could create. Overall, it's an ultra-comedy of error, certainly not real politics.

When the dust of controversy settles, I'm thinking it over.

I'm troubled that Kramer, a kind of Everyman, can unconsciously set fire to a country's flag. Isn't that how it all gets started? Living so unconsciously, making erroneous assumptions, creating big mistakes, we set fire to ourselves through war? We try to stomp it out but just make things worse.

* * *

THE SECOND TO THE LAST EPISODE to air is a clip show celebrating the series' entire nine-season history, which doesn't affect our schedule, so we're straight from the long "The Puerto Rican Day" production into the show Larry David has returned to write—the finale. At the table read, no one mentions this is the last one. But everyone is there. All the characters from the past. Everyone will get their say. Will it go over?

The episode opens with Jerry getting a call from the new NBC president, saying they're going to pick up his and George's pilot to series. The show about nothing will be on the air. He offers Jerry and George the NBC corporate jet to anyplace they want to go. (The offer stems from our actual use of the NBC jet traveling about the country promoting *Seinfeld*.) On their way to Paris (promoting *Seinfeld*, we never went this far courtesy of NBC; usually, it was as far as New York for photoshoots and personal appearances), the plane experiences some issues courtesy of Kramer that force them to make an unscheduled landing in Latham, Massachusetts, where they are arrested for violating the town's Good Samaritan law. At their trial, every major character that's been on the show is brought back to testify against them!

The first fifteen minutes of the forty-six-minute show feature some of the sharpest writing the show has had all season, maybe in several seasons. Jerry and George start in Monk's, talking about ketchup and going to the movies. "You go, you sit, you eat popcorn... I'm sick of it," George says. Then George complains he wants his fifteen minutes. It's his shot at the unfairness of life. "Ah, quit complaining," Jerry says. "At least you have your health." George doesn't care. "Health isn't good enough. I want more than health…I'm sick of health."

News that NBC is picking up their show and guaranteeing thirteen episodes is unfiltered Larry David reliving his nightmares from *Seinfeld's* earliest days. "Since when do you know how to write?" George's mother chirps. "I never saw you write anything. I don't know how you're going to write all those shows. And where are you going to get all the ideas?"

"I don't need any ideas," George says. "It's a show about nothing."

"The whole thing sounds pretty stupid to me," his mother says.

The rest of the show is a kind of review or anthology of gripes from the second bench, all of whom show up in the courtroom. The conceit is clever, but I wonder whether it will hold up and deliver the kind of satisfying ending that fans want and the show deserves. Saying goodbye is never easy. We know this group will not hug or cry. It's not our ethos. Indeed, Jerry, Jason, Elaine, and Kramer are found guilty of criminal indifference ("They have quite a record of mocking and maligning.") and sent to jail, but that doesn't mean they can't get out, escape, come back. It doesn't seem like an end. It feels more like a revue than a show. It also feels like a great escape from jail to come. They flee to South America? This amuses me. The four of them living in South America now. We could do the show from there! No. Jerry would turn to ashes. And I'm getting close to "crossing the line" for the wilderness. I want to retire to the hinterland, the "land behind" the words.

The episode is a huge endeavor, and from the start, I don't feel right. For the first time in all the shows we've done, I can't function. There's too much going on. The little bubble backstage where I've always lived is gone. People are coming and going: the cast and crew, all the guest stars, the agents, managers, friends who come with them to witness the historic last show, and executives from the network or wherever, it's Grand Central.

Also, some press is here. A book on the finale is being put together. I'm on the set, and somebody is asking me questions to publish my take on photos for the book. I'm half in and out of Kramer. No good. I don't know who anybody is, and I don't have the time to find out. I'm on display instead of at work. No good. I let Jerry know that I'm half-baked out here. Efforts are made to keep the soundstage clear of people, but still, people are about. Whatever.

To keep the show a secret, scripts aren't being sent to us in the typical manner. I don't even see my pages most days. Stress builds up and a blood vessel breaks in my right eye, which makes me self-conscious about being in front of camera. It's really the first time since the pilot that I feel so off. The beginning and the end, a perfect circle. I'm standing in Jerry's kitchen with my eyes closed, trying to visualize the way I'm going to do a scene. I just got the "top secret" material.

"Michael?"

I open my eyes. It's Jerry.

"Just checking in," he says.

I roll my eyes.

"What is it? My hair? Does the network think it's too crazy?"

He laughs.

"I'm working, Jerry," I say. "After all these years, it doesn't get any easier."

Later, I'm talking to Larry and Jason stops next to us and grins. "This is classic," he says. "Larry incredibly tense but seemingly casual, and Michael suggesting some sort of alternate bit. One never relaxes. The other never stops looking for possibilities." This is true, and for Jason as well. But I'm still off on this show. I imagine I'm questioning how broad this hopping-around business of Kramer is as he tries to get water out of his ear. It's too over the top.

On the day we tape inside our soundstage (without an audience), I pause and stare at Jerry's apartment door. In nine years, it's never been painted or cleaned. It's full of scuff marks—most if not all of them belonging to me. It's one of the pieces of the set Jerry has said he's taking with him. So many entrances and exits. So many adventures, schemes, and situations springing to life through that door. So much kavorka! So much imagination.

Before each show, the four of us always gather just behind the set and wish each other a good show. We hold hands and say, "Circle of power. Have a good show." It's just a playful rite to affirm our bond, even though we're already bonded. For nine years, we have probably spent more waking time together on the set than we have at our own homes. When we huddle for the last time, there's still no hugging. But Jerry has tears in his eyes. "For the rest of our lives, when anybody thinks about one of us, they will think about the four of us," he says, "and I can't think of any people that I would rather be associated with in this way."

Hours later, it's finished. Finally, a few hugs. We take our bows. I hold a finger up to my mouth. A sign of silence—there will be no more words from this character. It doesn't mean Kramer has nothing more to say. Only that this wonderful hipster doofus who has spent nine years swinging into life will be quiet for a while.

Afterward, others linger, some, including Jerry, until the sun comes up the next morning. I'm long gone. I slipped out the back. The few things I had in my dressing room were already packed. I only took Kramer's two pair of shoes, the Doc Martens, so well suited for sliding into it all. Maybe I'll put 'em on again someday.

PART 5

You Gotta Listen to the Little Man

CHAPTER 27

The Flop

Near the end of the show, I asked Jerry, "What are you gonna do after this?"

"I can't wait to get back to stand-up," he said. "I miss it so much. It's really what I do, more than a TV show. And there's something else just as important. I want to get married and have a family. I'm forty-five, it's time."

Jerry knew exactly what he wanted. Which was so Jerry. It would only take a year for all of it to come about. Jerry would build his stand-up act. And always staying in shape, Jerry would meet Jessica at the gym. They would fall in love at first sight; marriage and family would follow. He would have everything he wanted.

It's amazing. When you're really open to something, it will happen.

What am I open to? Well, I need to get the *Seinfeld* finale out of my system. My work in that episode wasn't very good. I went too broad playing Kramer's irritation with water in his ear. What the heck am I doing jumping around like that? Come on, Michael, it's the end of the series. You completed 180 episodes. Let it go.

The problem is, I still care. Yep, for the sake of posterity, I do care. I suspect that *Seinfeld* will be watched for a long time hereafter. Well, I can't make every shot. This finale was a big curtain call for everybody. It was a good thing. Time to move on.

Three weeks later, I sell my house in Studio City and finally move into my new home in the Palisades. I'm running on empty now that the *Seinfeld* show is over. I'm not interested in any acting work right now, and without a character to play, I'm really down to myself. I want to be at home and read some of my books and chill. After a few months of this, I have the time to get into Freemasonry, to finally see what this fraternity is all about. The grandfather of C. G. Jung was a leading Mason—the grand master of the Grand Lodge in Switzerland, in fact. I'm uncovering a trove of Masonic symbolism throughout Jung's books on alchemical psychology.

I'm fascinated by all of it. On the back of a chair in our lodge are the words "KNOW THYSELF." From my experience in analytical psychology, it seems to be the most that a person can do.

I quickly pass through the front door of Masonic ritual and right out the back as a thirty-third-degree Mason. I head for the natural world outside of any organization. I feel most at home with Nature, as I did with my Baldwin Hills from the get-go, my primal roots, the place where I started as a kid and always felt at home. Outside of the actual lodge of Masonry, my "lodge" or temple is the earth. Symbols are secondary to what they point to. The "Master" in my "East" is simply the sun. To "know thyself," I embrace Nature as my Self. In this place I don't wear any club jackets. I'm emptied out. "Thy Will Be Done." So be it.

I'm certainly experiencing a withdrawal from nine seasons of *Seinfeld*!

I'm at the top of Granada Hills sitting with the sun.

I just want to sit with this for a while. It's rather heavenly, and I've got the time for it.

How lucky I am.

* * *

EARLY ON, AS *SEINFELD* WAS CATCHING FIRE, George Shapiro and Howard West wanted to handle me, but I turned them down. I knew that I'd be doing the show for years, and working after each season during my downtime was not a priority. Lucrative endorsement deals from major brands were coming directly to me. I handled it myself. Career-wise, I wasn't running ahead for more work to do. Working nine months each year on *Seinfeld* was enough for me. When my season break came up, I seized it. I read, traveled, and spent time alone in the mountains.

Things could've been different. Before *Seinfeld* wrapped, NBC offered me a new series in development called *Monk*. It was written with me in mind. The role of a quirky detective suffering from obsessive-compulsive disorder, this had a lot of room for subtle, character-driven comedy and was, well...*perfect* for me. But I was too up to my neck doing *Seinfeld* every week to give this new show a real look, so I turned it down. Without guiding managers like George and Howard, the offer became a lost opportunity.

Looking back at it all, Tony Shalhoub was just perfect for the part. I couldn't have topped the work he did. I really did need to cool out after nine seasons of *Seinfeld* instead of going after another TV series. I didn't have it in me to keep galloping along.

I'll lose sight of this realization after a year when idleness gets the better of me and I fear no longer working. For the time being, though, my drive for work has waned!

What's tugging on me to go elsewhere? The other side of my Nature.

* * *

I THINK OF MY GRANDMOTHER, how she drifted away from us. Am I drifting away from my community? I reach for a handrail. I seek out those thinkers, those writers who speak of the exodus. I read scripture, myths, and look into symbolic art. I have Goethe at hand, the alchemical writings of Newton. William Blake, Joseph Campbell, C. G. Jung. Their books are all around me. I must be careful. I sense a powerful spiritual life within me, but I can't go it alone. I'm not quite ready. I can't take off the mask, the actor that I am. I need this persona.

With Kramer, the hipster doofus is behind me, and I need help. I get a directory of agents from somewhere, and I look up CAA. That's where Jerry and Julia are. Yeah, I should be there too. I look at CAA's list of agents, and Rick Nicita is at the top. I call his office in Beverly Hills.

I suppose this is as tacky as putting a tattered note in a mailbox asking if you'll sell your house to me. But I got the house!

"Hi, this is Michael Richards from *Seinfeld*. Is Rick there?"

I'm on hold.

Then Rick is on the phone. "Michael Richards, what's up?"

"Well, I'm out here without an agent. Can you bring me in?"

He asks where I am.

"I'm in North Hollywood."

"I'll be right there."

"You don't have to drive all the way out here, Rick."

"Oh, yes, I do."

And he does.

When I see him, he wants to know what I'm looking for.

"I need an agent. Someone who can keep me in the world."

"Well, you've got one. I'm your agent. Welcome to CAA."

* * *

RICK FOLLOWS UP ON AN OFFER for me to play the character Micawber in a TV miniseries adaptation of Charles Dickens's *David Copperfield*. W. C. Fields played Micawber in George Cukor's 1935 movie. Fields was at the height of his popularity, and he simply played W. C. Fields in the part of Micawber and was brilliantly funny. I can't play Micawber as Kramer, though, and I am unknown as anything else, so I have to go at Micawber as an actor, which is what I want to do anyway.

I spend weeks working on an English accent. I shave my head to match a description of Micawber that came from Dickens's own pen: "He was tall and lanky with *a head that was as smooth as an egg.*"

The next couple of months I'm shooting in Dublin. Nice to be here away from LA.

For the most part, I'm working with English and Irish actors, but Sally Field is with us. She knits on the set while waiting to work. It's her way of staying relaxed.

Unlike the character Micawber, who was usually penniless, a scrounger and hustler, I can afford dinner at fine restaurants where I get into a routine of sitting by myself, absentmindedly doodling with a Rapidograph pen on my napkin. My doodles are complex abstractions. Like Sally's knitting, the doodles relax me while I'm unwinding from a day of shooting and waiting for my meal.

Quite calm from a doodle, my meal arrives. A toast! To my dinner, my part in *Copperfield*, my travels throughout Ireland, and the esoteric writings of Yeats!

* * *

BACK FROM DUBLIN, months have gone by and I haven't seen anything from CAA. No scripts, nothing in development. I'm thinking of Charlie, telling me years ago that you don't want to be waiting

345

around for agents to call. I'm going to have to get into this, but for now, my daughter is in Chicago attending DePaul University. Eager to see her, I head there for a visit. Maybe CAA will come up with something in the meantime. If not, then I'll get into it with them when I get back.

In Chicago, I always lease a white Lincoln Continental and cruise through the South Side. I love the "Continental" ride throughout the city.

I plan to take Sophia and a few of her university friends to see a movie, but first, we stop for an early dinner at an Italian restaurant that someone recommended. "The best in Chicago," he said. "For real Italian food, you go there."

It's crowded when we arrive and looks like we should've made a reservation, but the maître d' or owner—I can't tell the difference—eliminates our concerns. "You don't need a reservation! We know who you are! Get in here!" He exchanges some words in Italian with a few others—waiters, captains, busboys...the place is brimming with employees—and we are led over to the finest booth in the place. There are pictures of Sinatra, Dean Martin, and Tony Bennett on the walls, all of them sitting at this same booth.

"This is Frank's table!" the head guy gushes, kicking off what is an amazing meal with a generous serving of hospitality. We decline dessert so we can make it to the movie. As we wait for the bill, one of the guys comes over with a bunch of freshly baked bread in a bag.

"We want you to have some of our bread," he says. "Take this bread."

"We make our own bread here," another guy says. "That's what we do here. It's delicious. You'll love it."

"Fantastic! Sure, I'll take the bread. Thanks."

We get up and head for the door followed by waiters, staff, various restaurant people all thanking us for coming there. "You know you were sitting in Sinatra's booth," one of them says. "Always there for him when he was in town." Someone else hands me a card. "Let me know and you'll have your place here anytime." Another guy chimes in, "You're Italian. You're family here!"

"Where in Italy?" a big guy asks.

"Potenza," I say.

He says something to me in Italian.

"I don't speak Italian," I said.

"Come around more often, you will!" he jokes.

"You're gonna love that bread!"

"I'm sure! What a great meal. Thank you!"

Outside, I see two white limousines parked in front of the restaurant. A few families are getting out of them. Wives, kids, grandmothers. They spot me and get excited. I realize they are all coming to see Kramer. Some want autographs. Everyone wants to take a picture with me. I try to be gracious, but time is going by and we want to see the movie. I look at my watch. Another limo pulls up.

I imagine the guys in the back of the restaurant are calling home. "Kramer's here. Get down here now!" Finally, I say to someone, "We gotta go."

"Just a few more pictures," he says.

"I can't," I say more firmly this time. "We really gotta go."

He looks at me, and I see his entire face change. His expression goes from friendly host to Luca Brasi.

"I give you bread. You take the bread, and now you won't take a picture with my family?"

Another man steps in. "Angelo, behave yourself." Then he turns to me. "I apologize. He gets fiery."

"Oh, I'm sorry," I say.

An older man appears and speaks to Angelo.

"What are you doing?"

"He ignores my family. He wants to go now."

"No, no, Angelo, he's not ignoring. They have to go now."

"I give him bread and he doesn't take a picture with my family."

The older man snaps at him. "He's taking pictures with Vie and the family." Then to me, in a soft, controlled voice: "It's for the family.

They watch you all the time on TV. They get so excited. You're a big television star."

"It's okay," I say. "I'm sorry, Angelo. I'll take pictures with whoever wants a picture."

Forget the movie. I get into their excitement and leave it at that. Everyone gets their pictures, and I leave with several loaves of freshly baked Italian bread. All is well. But I learn something here. *If you take the bread, you will have to give something back.* Angelo made that clear. This lesson will come up for me again. Live and learn. *Vivendo si impara.* (I looked it up.)

* * *

COMING BACK TO LA FROM CHICAGO and the bread incident, several former *Seinfeld* writers who are working together contact me about an idea for a TV pilot. When I mention this to Nicita, he connects me with CAA's television department. They tell me to avoid getting into business with these writers. "They can't supervise a show," they say. This doesn't make sense to me. They were acting supervisors on *Seinfeld*. Jerry wouldn't have kept them on if they weren't good. More so, each of these writers has won an Emmy for a *Seinfeld* episode they wrote. What's going on here?

The writers tell me that they recently left CAA and set themselves up on their own at Castle Rock ("We didn't need CAA," they say. "We can produce our own shows.") and now they say the agency is against them for leaving. I don't want to be in the middle of a spat. I call Jerry and ask him about these writers. "If anyone can put a show together for you, it's these guys," he says.

I read some material they have put together. It's somewhat funny, but still short of the mark. "It's a first draft," they explain. "We just want to see if you're interested. If so, we can develop it for you. We'll produce it together." This is something to think about. Put projects into development like Diane Keaton once suggested. Okay, this script needs work. This is confirmed in a dream I have in which the

348

show presents itself as a Christmas tree with just a few bulbs on it and no lights. I tell this dream to the writers on the phone. The show needs some lights. I'm told not to worry.

"We can hire ten writers, and that's plenty of bulbs and lights to go on!"

I give them some notes and leave it at that.

* * *

MEANWHILE, ALL THIS TIME IS PASSING and nothing comes my way from CAA. And why isn't their television department supporting me on this proposal? They can still rep me and help me find ten writers and a director. I know they're feuding with these writers for leaving the agency, but does this serve me well? I'm thinking that my tree at CAA has few bulbs and no lights.

Or is it me? I worry that my tree is sparse and unimpressive to them.

"CAA is a factory, not a creative agency," the writers tell me. "They don't know what to do with you. Together, we have way more clout. We can make a pilot! Do it all on our own with Castle Rock and any network of our choosing."

The writers are right. I can do a pilot on my own. My lawyer can draw up a contract with anyone I choose. I don't need to produce with CAA's television department or pay them ongoing commissions.

It's just that the script I have in my hand isn't that good. It could get better, and these writers promise that it will, and I suppose it's better than waiting around for an agent to call. Let's see how it goes.

I call Nicita and tell him that I'm leaving the agency. I want to be on my own for a while. To his credit, he has the entire agency in for an all-hands-on-deck conference to show that the agency is behind me, including Mike Ovitz, who swears his support. Despite this, I still leave CAA and go with the *Seinfeld* writers to do a pilot that's "short of bulbs and lights" with no script to go on.

I'm holding on to *Seinfeld*, the writers with their track record, and Jerry's endorsement. For this, I bid adieu to one of the most powerful agencies in show business.

I was at the height of a popular TV show, and now I am about to crash and burn. How profound.

* * *

THE THING IS, I NEVER CONSIDER that this pilot project could become a show. I saw it as a pilot script "in development," and if it's good then I'll consider doing it. This is where CAA or George and Howard could've helped. And, creatively, I have no big ideas for a pilot of my own, nothing uniquely funny to go on. More so, I'm going at something here that I really have no energy for.

I simply miss the routine and security of going to work. I'm fifty-three years old. I'm past midlife heading toward my autumn years. I can feel some of its cool air upon me—I'm not really as ambitious as I used to be. I'm approaching a "to be or not to be" attitude toward work as an actor. Do I want to act or not? At this point, I don't need another show with all the time that goes into it. I don't know this yet. I sure don't know where this TV pilot is about to take me.

My lawyer sets up a pay-or-play deal for developing a pilot with NBC and Castle Rock. The terms are great. I'm swayed by the money. *I'm taking the bread.* I don't have anyone around me sounding a cautionary note. I had CAA. Did I listen? No. And I'm not really tuning into myself. Can I make this script funny? Just go on that! I'm looking into it. I don't want to be waiting around for an agent to call.

No one warns that I will have to give the network a show if the pilot is picked up. As improbable as it sounds, this never crosses my mind. At this point, the pilot is simply a "work in progress." It's just a pilot "in development." And if it is picked up, then it must be good, right? NBC doesn't want a flop.

Oh, really?

Folly is about to reign. Not only am I taking the bread, but I'm also about to eat it.

Perhaps it is a way of killing myself, to burn my bridges so I cannot return to the heave-ho of showbiz. To rip my persona off once and for all.

Where else should I be? Sitting on the top of Granada Hills? I mustn't cross that line to return to the other side of my Nature. It takes a death to do so. But then doesn't rebirth follow? No, no, I'm not up for it. I want to stay in the everyday world and work. Something in me wants to get anchored to a show. Yet, another part of me wants an exodus into the wilderness, the depths of my Nature. Is this a midlife crisis? In the middle of either being here or getting out. I'm back to my "to be or not to be."

Read the material the writers have given me. Can I make it work? Read myself. Do I have it in me to do another show? *A Christmas tree that has just a few bulbs on it and no lights.* There it is again!

* * *

THE NEXT DRAFT OF THE SCRIPT continues to have potential, but I think it's still bland, rather generic, and not freaky enough for my taste. It must have a weirder story. A touch of sci-fi, something otherworldly about my character, a self-determined freak who investigates situations in an unusual way. Unfortunately, I know the best hook for this is the one going for *Monk*. I'm afraid I missed that boat.

Bottom line, this pilot feels like a traditional sitcom, and we need something else, something different. To counter this, I want to shoot the pilot as a film, all on location. As a "work in progress" we decide to take it to the next level. Let's bring in the director Michael Ritchie. I'm a big fan of his movie *Fletch*, and I want that look; then we can cast the pilot and just shoot it. Presumably, I'll take it to the next level once I'm in front of camera. Since it's a work in progress, we'll also keep writing and modifying as we shoot. It's a way to get this thing on its feet to see what we're made of.

* * *

IT's A HARD SHOOT. Ten- to twelve-hour days for five straight days. I'm in nearly every scene and trying to watch the other actors to see how we're doing. This takes me out of my own character. I'm not used to working like this. But who is this character I'm playing? I don't know. I think I've got something going, but it's not as sizable as it should be. We're rewriting, rethinking throughout the shoot. I'm not inspired filming like this; there's no way I can do this week after week.

* * *

BY THE END OF THE SHOOT, the wind is knocked out of me. I've never experienced anything as grueling. Ritchie had his problems too, though it wasn't until much later that I hear he was yelling at NBC to stay out of his hair. There were shots that he wanted to get, and NBC just wanted him to move along. He told them to fuck off. The *Hollywood Reporter* goes with a story that I'm feuding with NBC. They have it all wrong and mix up Michael Ritchie with Michael Richards.

I'm so wiped out by the shoot that I don't care to straighten it out. Also, I don't want to put Ritchie on the spot by separating myself from him. I need him to edit. I'll be the fall guy.

I get the flu while the pilot is being edited, and I can't get out of bed. Ritchie does a great job putting the pilot together. I'm pleased with it. It's not particularly funny, but I think it holds up for what it is, a work in progress. As an on-the-air show, I don't think it's good enough. I'm already thinking of recasting and adding a few more plot points. Then I hear the pilot is being tested in front of audiences.

What? It's been less than a week since the show was edited. I'm barely out of bed and not at full strength. Things are moving fast. Too fast for me.

* * *

Rick Ludwin, who championed *Seinfeld* in its infancy, is now head of NBC's comedy development, and I'm in his office with my writers and Glenn Padnick from Castle Rock to go over the test results. Except there's not much to go over. The pilot didn't test well, and NBC wants to pass. Glenn doesn't accept this. He won't take no for an answer. He reminds Rick that the *Seinfeld* pilot also tested poorly.

I don't think his argument holds up. Jerry was an unknown when he made his pilot, so not testing well back then makes some sense. It's different with me. I'm very well known. If I didn't test well, this should be a heads-up. A year ago my film *Trial and Error* flopped. Yeah, my head's up.

Glenn is clearly distraught, as he should be. Castle Rock is probably shouldering most of the cost for this thing, including my hefty salary. He and the writers suggest reshooting some of the pilot. They can punch it up, they say, and make it better. NBC is open to it. I always thought this was a "work in progress," so I'm curious to see what the writers have in mind and head back home for bed.

Rick Ludwin calls the next day and asks how I am feeling.

"Shooting the pilot took a lot out of me, Rick. I'm sorry it didn't test well."

I tell him straight out that I can't do a weekly on-location film shoot. I mention a few scenes that could have been funnier, some recasting ideas, and a general openness to what the writers come up with.

"If that doesn't work, I'm still around, Rick. Maybe we can find something else to do."

"Rest up," he says.

I intend to do just that. I book a room at Canyon Ranch in Arizona for a week.

On the fourth day I'm there, my lawyer calls.

"Congratulations!"

"For what?"

"NBC has picked up your show."

"You mean reshooting the pilot?"

"No, the show's been picked up for thirteen."

* * *

I GET THE WRITERS ON THE PHONE. They tell me that they got the pickup by promising a whole new show. They are going to dump the film pilot altogether.

"No one will ever see it," they say.

"And what might the new show be?" I ask, wondering why no one bothered to tell me and what else is being promised.

"We're working on it, but it won't be a film shoot that wears you out. We promise."

"How do I know it's going to be any good?"

"We're going to hire ten writers. Lots of lights and bulbs! We'll brainstorm and come up with something that works. Sometimes on *Seinfeld* we would throw out a script for that week and write something else, sometimes from just a storyline scheduled for development. All the writers pitched in for that week's show. Remember that?"

"I do."

"We have a few months here, and with ten writers we'll come up with something great! NBC will hire the best to get a show off the ground for you. Trust us. We'll make this happen."

What is happening to me? Am I being used?

I get a call from my lawyer about leaving Canyon Ranch and flying to New York right away for press and the upfronts, where my new show will be announced. What? What about those few months we need for coming up with something great? We're moving very fast now. Even faster than before. "Not so fast!" is what I should be saying. Dumping the pilot and going to some other kind of show, a sitcom now because the film shoot busted my ass, just what is this new sitcom all about?

I call the writers again.

"This is all getting away from me! I'm going to New York to do upfronts on a show that I don't know anything about!"

"Just go on the premise of the pilot. We've got thirteen episodes. We're going to hire great writers. We're going to make this work."

They're elated. I can hear it in their voices.

I'm feeling sick.

"And I don't want to call this thing, *The Michael Richards Show*."

"It's a temporary title until we come up with something better."

"The name of the show is going out now," I say.

"We can change it later."

I remember an old Zen adage: "Better to see the face than to know the name." Yes, forget the name of the show. I need a face, a character, a show, and I need it now! What's this show about? The same premise as the film pilot. I'm a private investigator. The show will have a new supporting cast. Who are the characters? I don't know. Who are the actors? I don't know. What are the plots? I don't know. Who's going to direct? I don't know.

* * *

I'm sent to New York for a junket with the network affiliates and advertisers. The Upfronts! I should have told the affiliates my show is about a guy in a bathrobe who has a cigar and is wandering around lost in hotels. No one can find his tux. He's like Sisyphus. Pushing his rock from one hotel but then getting lost in the two hotels he just came from.

Then, all too suddenly, I'm onstage in New York, pushing my rock, standing in front of hundreds of people after being told to talk about the great NBC lineup—*ER*, *The West Wing*, *Frasier*, *Friends*, *Will & Grace*, *Third Rock from the Sun*. But I don't have much to say. I don't even watch these shows! I have no prep. No script. No jokes.

"And talk about your show, Michael." You mean the pilot? The show that tested poorly, that's so bad no one will ever see it?

I'm unable to say much. This is similar to the night I received my second Emmy and just froze onstage. I've got no character to hide behind. It's *The Michael Richards Show*! What character is this? I'm out here as myself? The horribly shy, introverted, meta-minded doodler now has to introduce the entire NBC lineup?

I'm so taken aback by it all. I imagine standing there onstage like Terence Stamp in Fellini's *Toby Dammit*, close to blurting out, "Why did you bring me here!"

But I know the answer to this.

I did this all to myself. This is my show. If only I could have written this all up as the show itself. This is the show, like Jerry and Larry talking to each other in the Korean market—just what we're doing now. This is the show! It's about everything that's about to befall me—a popular comic actor starring in a show that flops! It's called *The Flop*. I just didn't get it.

It's all a crapshoot, isn't it? Who knows who will come out of this alive. You're up one day and you're down the next. I have no idea what the hell I said about *The Michael Richards Show* that day. Hopefully, I bucked up and made it sound good. I really was among great company in that lineup, I later realized.

Still, I do remember feeling like I wanted to run off the stage and jump into my sports car and speed down the narrow unlit streets of Positano and finally right off an unfinished bridge where I lose my head. Nino Rota's "The Demon Child" theme comes up. Blackout.

It's *The Michael Richards Show*! Starring Michael Richards! I appear with jam all over my face stuffing "the bread" into my mouth. I can't talk, my mouth is so full. He's so funny! He took the bread! The fucking idiot took the bread!

* * *

THE FILM SHOOT IS GONE. We're in the studio. Four cameras. It's a fucking sitcom! With a director who I don't know. My character is named Vic Nardozza. The series is called *The Michael Richards Show*. I've lost complete control. The cover of *TV Guide*'s fall preview issue, featuring me, John Goodman, Geena Davis, and Bette Midler, announces us as the star attractions for this fall's TV comedy lineup. On the cover, I look like a heavy with a chip on his shoulder and a gun in my pocket. Sets are built. I have no idea who approved spending hundreds of thousands of dollars on sets for a script that isn't funny and will be thrown out that week for another script that's not funny. We haven't even had a run-through yet.

An episode is shot. I don't hear many laughs. "It's funny, Michael," the writers say. I really want to believe them, I really do. But I know we're not making it.

An NBC executive, a woman who I don't know, sees me off in the corner nearly in tears. "We have to get you a showrunner," she says. Is that all I need? A person who can run an unfunny show better?

Directors come and go. Castle Rock and the writers want to try them out first, pick one later. I have no one to depend on. Without a director assisting me with the material, someone who can truly signal to me that we're on top of it, a bridge from the actors to the writers, I remain headless and without real direction. Camera block all you want; you're still shooting shit.

A poster comes out advertising the show. "Meet a detective who doesn't have a clue"...as to what's funny anymore!

I try to buck up. I'll work hard to be Vic. I'll probably throw in a little Kramer, more like imitating Kramer. I'm sorry. I'm half in and half out of character. I'm me, or somebody named, The Michael Richards Show, and a Vic Nardozza doing comedy *imitating* Kramer. I'm all mixed up. The reviews are murder. I'm roasted alive. I'm dismissed as unfunny, thumbs down, over and out.

* * *

"No, it's funny, Michael."

Ignore the reviews, the writers tell me. It's funny! I do what I can with it. At run-throughs there are few laughs. It's just the writers laughing at their own writing. It's rather sad how they're bucking themselves up this way. I know it's not funny. I try to compensate by playing Kramer. It just doesn't fit with the normality of Vic Nardozza and Michael Richards combined. Going broad to get laughs with this combo is in bad taste. I've lost my head on a bridge to nowhere. Nino Rota reprisal up. Blackout.

My uncle Mike sends my mother an angry note, complaining that I am using his name—Nardozza—in the show. At first I think the show is so crummy that he doesn't want his name associated, but no, he just has it out for me. "That's not his name to use!" he says. "Tell him to find another name." Like me trying to find the name of my father. To my uncle, I have never been legit. He only sees me as the bastard child of a man who forced his sister into sex and got her pregnant. I am the rotten offspring, and my uncle hated me for it. "From now on you'll call me Mr. Nardozza!"

Well, Mr. Nardozza, I thought my mom would get a kick out of hearing her family's name on TV. It was for her. Really just a tribute to my mama.

I never hear from my uncle again. He dies three years later of colon cancer.

By the seventh episode, the show is so crappy, the ratings so dismal, the critics so bloodthirsty that I break down in a rage at a writers meeting. Someone is debating whether a countertop should be orange or gray. I'M DEAD HERE AND YOU'RE DISCUSSING THE COLOR OF TABLETOPS! I'm shaking. I'm coming apart. "But it's not funny! I'm not funny! I'm dead here!" Everyone just stares at me. They know it's true.

I just can't do one more crummy script!

"I think we're done here," Rick Ludwin says.

"I hope so," I say. "I hope the fuck so!"

I go home that night and call Stuart, a friend of mine. He's a psychiatrist. He's helped a lot of people in the business, and right now I
just need to talk to someone.

"Stuart?"

"Michael! How's it going?"

"Well, I'm sitting at home right now. I'm crying involuntarily. I
can't stop myself. My hands are shaking. You got a minute?"

* * *

RICK LUDWIN IS MERCIFUL ENOUGH to get me off the air. He saw
that I was really coming apart, physically and mentally. I feared that
NBC would force me to keep making these crummy shows. As long
as they had to pay, they might as well get some play. But they shut
the show down after eight episodes and pay me for the remaining
four. I suppose they sold enough advertising time to finally cut me
loose, or maybe they feared that I was so bad it could hurt the rest of
their lineup as well as *Seinfeld* in syndication.

Pull the plug! Get him off the air!

I am relieved. I'm through with it all. I never want to do another
TV show again.

The last episode airs on January 2, 2001. I feel like I stepped out
of the wreckage of a crash. I think I'm still alive. No, I'm dead. Gratefully dead. When I finally broke down at that writers meeting, what
they heard was a man screaming as he fell from a great height. I'm
sorry I was so loud about it.

I'd prefer to fall quietly like a leaf from the tree, down to the
ground, to the source of the tree in the first place. I'm simply reab-
sorbed into Creation. From high to low, everything back down to
where it was before.

For the next few months, I try to recover at home, at the bottom
of my pool. I can hear that prominent actor saying, "It's just a fucking TV show!" I'm trying to lessen its importance. I'm released from
it all. I've got my gold watch. I was on the float waving to all the

people as I passed by. This time, I feel regret, humiliation, and failure, but also, most importantly, relief. Relief saves me from despair. I no longer have to be in the show. I can go home. End of *The Flop*.

CHAPTER 28

Whirling

"Come, come, whoever you are, wanderer, worshiper, lover of leaving, it doesn't matter," says Rumi. "Ours is not a caravan of despair."

From visionary poets like Blake and Whitman and the poetry of scripture, Rumi is clearly right alongside. What always amazes me is that like Christ and the Buddha, Rumi never wrote a thing. Most of what we have of these men is through "imaginative interpretations" penned by those who supposedly heard what these preceptors were saying.

Rumi's poetry was written by diligent followers eight hundred years ago, and while I trust the words to be a faithful rendition, I can feel the numinous even between the lines.

With *The Michael Richards Show* canceled, I do not have agents and managers to console me and say buck up, we'll get you something else. Neither do I have family to cushion the fall. I have Rumi and his epic poem, *The Mathnawi*, telling me, "It doesn't matter. Ours is not a caravan of despair."

Rumi consoles me. He is my good friend keeping me company in the dark. My lights are out. I have no energy to turn them back on. I have power but no desire to use it. I prefer to sit in the dark and not see anyone right now. I won't answer the phone. It's just Rumi and me. The show had to end so I could be receptive to his wisdom. I feel my failings and those of all humanity: losing the game, scoring poorly, shut down and rejected. What a sublime feeling!

I come upon a tour taking place through Shambhala Travels in San Francisco to visit Turkey and some of the oldest Sufi monasteries. Sufism is derived from Rumi, as Buddhism is derived from Buddha or Christianity from Christ. These highly evolved men were conduits to the best parts of ourselves. And as I nurse the wounds of failure, reading Rumi, I come across a great line: "Bitter water and sweet water have (the same) clearness." To look into the two kinds of water, salt ("bitter") and fresh ("sweet"), the two signifying the opposites, both *Seinfeld* and *The Michael Richards Show*, through the "clearness" of the two, the winning and the losing, the coming and the going, the entrances and the exits, one side is not greater than the other.

The two—like night and day, comedy and tragedy, the rational and the irrational—share the same "clearness." I find this recognition comforting.

The tour will end in Istanbul with whirling dervishes, members of a Sufi order, re-creating the "whirling poet" Rumi, who, by accounts, clung to a pole in the ground and whirled about chanting his poetry while devotees recorded his words.

There is one more opening for the tour. I immediately book the trip, and in just a week, I am with a small group of Shambhala tourists in Konya, Turkey, the home of Rumi.

Though I am hurting from the bitterness of *The Michael Richards Show*, I'm feeling quite open, congenial, and inspired to move through things. I bond with the man conducting this tour and his wife. We are close, and apart from the group, the three of us visit several Sufi sites closed to the public. I notice the people at these sacred sites are reverential toward him. I assume they are just being friendly because of his authority as a tour guide. I don't have any idea until the end of our time together that he is a sheikh, one who leads whirling dervishes and a Mevlevi Sufi of high regard.

* * *

THERE ARE TEN OF US on the tour. We travel in a small school bus. Along the way, we stop in a town to hear a Sufi master speak. She has a sizable following. About two hundred people come out to hear her. We are behind an old Ottoman-style house in a grassy field with some outdoor chairs. Blankets are spread out. Most of the people sit on the ground. The master is on a small raised stage. I take off my shoes and socks to relax and stretch out, supporting my head with my hands, my legs and feet extended toward the master.

As I listen to her sermon, a follower comes over to me and whispers that my feet pointing toward the master is disrespectful. I immediately sit up. "Really? Why is that?" He tells me that the soles of the feet are on the ground, "close to the dirt, the low places."

"I was wearing shoes," I respond. "My feet are clean."

"The feet are below, heaven is above," he says.

He returns to where he was sitting. I sit up for about ten minutes and then I need to ask the master a question, but first I lie back the way I was before, with my legs and feet pointing in her direction. I raise my hand. She acknowledges me.

"I am lying here, my feet in your direction. Am I being disrespectful?"

She breaks out laughing. She's truly amused.

"There's no disrespect. Feet are lovely. Do you feel disrespectful?"

"No, I feel comfortable."

"Please. Be comfortable. There's no disrespect."

"Thank you."

I'm sorry I did that, but I was curious about the follower's reprimand. I'll do as I'm told to accommodate custom. But I'm also interested in a custom's significance. This business of the feet being low-down and not as high as whatever, I needed to follow up to see what the master had to say about it.

Regarding appropriate spiritual behavior, from now on, I think much of it is "in the eye of the beholder." As a kid in parochial school, I never liked enforced kneeling in the pews. After a while it hurt my legs. Why couldn't I just sit and "be comfortable"? I like this Sufi teacher. She's open-minded. Very cool.

Still, I am sensitive to tradition, so when in Rome...I do as they do. Feet up or down, you tell me. I want no trouble. I mean no disrespect. Besides, what's behind all the posturing, the words, the look of the place, the *feeling* it invokes is what I'm really after.

* * *

BEFORE THE LAST LEG of our tour to Istanbul, we head south to Antalya and the ancient Greek-Roman amphitheater in Aspendos. I am walking behind the site and away from the group when two young Turkish boys around eleven and thirteen approach and show me some trinkets they have wrapped in a towel. They're small bronze statues of a female figure about seven inches tall. They have about eleven of them. Each one is different than the other. They're quite lovely. I wonder who this "female figure" is?

They tell me that all of them are real, "very old, ancient." I'm thinking they're trinkets that they dirtied up to look old to sell to the tourists. Whatever, I do like the way they look.

"How much for all of them?"

"Forty dollars."

That's less than five dollars apiece. I like these kids and so I give them a hundred bucks for all eleven. I put the pieces in my day pack.

"We can get more," they say.

"Where do you get them?" I ask. "Who makes them?"

"They are under here. Down in the ground. Very old."

"You go underground and get this stuff?"

"Yes. We can bring you more."

At that moment, two thin black serpents, only about a foot long, appear. I stand there looking at them coming toward us. In spurts of energy, they dart about very quickly. I've never seen snakes move like this. As a kid, about the age of these boys, I caught snakes all the time in the wash area of Sepulveda Dam. I'm not afraid to handle them. The boys are frightened, though, and pull me back. They tell me that these snakes are dangerous. They bite. We all back off, and I leave for the hotel with my pieces.

It's a good thing. The snakes are *Naja haje*—the Egyptian cobra. Very venomous. An omen? Why did those snakes appear as the boys handed off those trinkets to me?

There's a young professor traveling with our group who teaches Byzantine culture at Cambridge. Back at the hotel, I show him the sculptures. He examines them carefully. "They could be genuine," he says. "This is bronze. A preferred metal for the Greeks and Romans." He gives me a short lecture and says there are many ancient sites still to be excavated throughout western Turkey, even an ancient amphitheater larger than the one in Rome. He thinks it's possible that the kids are digging down into these unexcavated sites, finding stuff, and selling it to the tourists.

But who are these women, I wonder, these female figures shaped in bronze? "Usually, a primordial mother goddess," he says. "The first mother," I muse. "A fertility goddess of the earth" is how the professor puts it.

I also tell him about the appearance of the two black snakes. "Rebirth, healing, or protection. That's how the Romans viewed snakes," I say. "These snakes appeared like protectors. They showed up just as the boys handed the pieces to me." I'm thinking like a Roman, that a situation can appear ordinary but may also include an "extraordinary" side, a hidden meaning containing an imposing fate. For Romans, as for many ancient cultures, reading the Fates bodes well.

Like most people, I usually enter a situation for what it is. I'm not so superstitious, but I pay close attention to the way I *feel*. For the ancients, without the Fates, you might as well be blind. Since the whole situation occurred behind a site well over two thousand years old, I'm up for the "extraordinary." What's more, I did indeed *feel* something portentous when the snakes appeared. It's a sense that always served me well on the streets as a kid living on Hauser and La Brea. I suppose today we call this intuition. Regarding the two serpents, to quote Shakespeare, "Something is rotten in Denmark."

The professor doubts that the two snakes are guardian spirits out to get me for taking their booty. From the look on his face, I can tell he doesn't want to talk to me anymore. I don't blame him. Bringing up the "extraordinary" perplexes him. It's just too out there.

He politely excuses himself to attend to his reading. I'm not offended. He lives on campus wherever he goes. To him, the way I imagine two snakes going about their business is just presumptuous, if not downright preposterous. Leaving his room, I see a dichotomy between extraordinary and ordinary thinking. For me, it's a play on two kinds of meaning, the apparent and the hidden, and these opposites are interrelated. Perhaps the professor is into the material world and I'm into the *feeling*, or the spiritual world. But it's not so cut-and-dried with him over there and me over here. Body and spirit are naturally connected. Like matter and psyche, or particle and wave, they are of each other. Ultimately, I'm grateful for his insight.

* * *

THE NEXT MORNING the group and I are at the airport preparing to board a shuttle flight to Istanbul. I've got my little statues packed in my suitcase. Armed soldiers with semiautomatic rifles stand around the place. I'm thinking about the two snakes. Our bags are scanned through a metal detector.

I'm not packing guns or knives, so I tell myself to relax. But then, before I can take my next breath, I'm ordered to open my suitcase. "Sure." They see the pieces.

My gentle-looking Sufi group is shocked to see me led away at gunpoint. Our tourist guide intervenes; they talk heatedly in Turkish. He tells me that I'm under arrest for smuggling antiquities. I just got bit by two serpents.

A lot of talk goes on. The phone rings. This is a big deal.

"Come on! If I was smuggling antiques out of the country, why would I have them in my suitcase going through a metal detector?"

I'm getting impatient.

"I'm a tourist! Tell 'em the kids sold me this stuff!"

The tour guide raises his voice. He doesn't want to miss our flight. Am I really going to jail now? It looks like it. Now I'm flanked by two armed guards—two snakes.

We make an arrangement: with the tour guide accompanying me, I'm to take the pieces to an appointed museum in Istanbul and leave them with the director, who will be expecting us. Thankfully, my tour guide is well regarded and has some pull to get these officials to whirl about him. I board the plane with the pieces. I feel like Indiana Jones.

If convicted of smuggling antiquities out of Turkey, it would be five to fifteen years in prison. It's *Midnight Express* for me.

I turn in the pieces at the museum, where they confirm that they are genuine antiquities over nine hundred years old. While I'm romping around Turkey, to think of those two boys crawling around in the ancient world is just incredible, and their voices, so ready and eager to go back centuries, are still with me. "We can get more!"

* * *

WE'RE IN ISTANBUL, and it's here that I learn our tour guide is a sheikh. As the head dervish, he's the director, the motivator, the inner guide, one's inspiration or "the touch" that sends the dervishes whirling, "the right foot is the wheel, the left foot is the pole," now in the round, as round as the earth turns around its pole. It's a beautiful show. I meet the dervishes later that afternoon, sitting around backstage like grounded pilots waiting for takeoff. A few of them smoke cigarettes. It doesn't affect their whirl or their meditation. What do you do when you stop whirling? Hang out. Wait until you whirl again. I don't feel like I ever want to whirl again. That was a long way to fall from being so high up with *Seinfeld*.

One of the dervishes asks me if I'd like to whirl. I see their show as Peter Brook's holy theatre. Their rite of man whirling around one's center, or one's sun; to me, aligning with Nature. For now, I don't want to be a performer. No more costumes, lights, and sound. I can't be a dervish, but I know their dance within me.

Later that afternoon, I walk over to the Hagia Sophia ("Holy Wisdom"), at one time the biggest Christian church under Constantinople, then later a mosque, and now a museum. Changing hands like this, I thank God it hasn't become a Walmart.

I see the professor there. This place is why he came on the tour. He's obsessed with Byzantine architecture, and the Hagia Sophia's heightened dome is the definitive feature of this ornate monument from Roman times. I can see that it's been redone over the centuries. At some point, its many windows were sealed, diminishing or shutting out the light that once filled the nave. The professor wants to know if the statues are authentic. They are indeed. I kiddingly add, "And so were those snakes."

I leave the professor to his ponderings but fail to ask about his interest in this architecture and how it stirs his soul. Having an open heart and fellow-feeling is not always with me. It's a shortcoming that limits my intelligence.

I'm interested in rotundas—the ocular opening, the appearance of light into a dark, enclosed place. To enter this light, I am revealed through light ☉! How else can I see? I feel the "extraordinary" coming.

* * *

AT THE FAR NORTH WALL of the Hagia Sophia, there is a mural I must see. It's the Virgin Mary holding the infant Christ. The great Madonna. Who are you? Certainly, a work of art, but tell me who you are before you became a Christian. Tell me just how "extraordinary" you are!

How the imagination works, how inventive YOU can be. I stand before the great Feminine. She is like a priestess at Delphi.

"Who are you?" I ask.

And so, I imagine Her telling me, "I am the earth. From the light in my core, I give birth to Consciousness, the round of the seasons forming the fourfold cross ✛ that you are. In my lap is the light of Wisdom."

I'm turning toward the earth to find some stability. I'm wandering, rather aimlessly. I'm outside of showbiz. I have no desire to work as an actor. I want something deeper in my life now.

It's a spiritual life, speaking to me through the Madonna and Child. She comes to me as the earth! I am a playful child, in the lap of the earth. I have to go on this. I am in need of this. Sit with the earth. Find comfort with the earth.

* * *

THE SHAMBHALA TOUR IS OVER, ending here in Istanbul. This evening, some students of the sheikh arrive from the States. They're here to see a few of the Sufi monasteries and take courses from their sheikh. He asks me to stay and join them for study. I'm grateful for the invite, but after my experience at the Hagia Sophia I need to put my thoughts in order.

I want to be free from the bitterness that brought me here in the first place. But I can't just snap my fingers and the night goes away. I don't want to wallow in this shit either. The best I can do is dress for the occasion. Find shelter—images and pictures "to know thyself." In the dark or the light, I just have to walk through it all for what it is.

From the dream of the clown hold-ing the globe of the earth, leading into my community with laughter, now the outfit is off. I'm in mourning, bare bones as symbolized through alchemy's dark of the sun.

I decide to wander about in Turkey for a few weeks, then head for Athens, maybe Crete and a few of the Greek islands. It's all on a whim. I'll simply wander for a while. Even sleep on the ground, close to the earth, rest, walk about, see what comes out of it.

I'm walking through the bitterness of a canceled TV show. It was a painful process that went lower and lower and then bust! The force of the irrational disassembling me week by week until I was canceled altogether. I was emptied out and continue to feel empty. This is a death.

I enter the next world where Rumi is my guide. Inspiration comes upon me. I'm with Sufis. I come to know their dance. Then, face to face with the Holy Wisdom of the Madonna and her Christos. Born through the earth, I've known you since I was a child in the Baldwin Hills. More recently, YOU became the kavorka, the Eros that brings about relatedness. I felt YOU uniting the bitter and the sweet, the high and the low, the light and the dark. YOU are the earth, the body that holds me in place. YOU are my rotunda. I gaze up at the light. I see Consciousness in this.

What am I now? Moods. Listening to my moods, my feelings, their personalities within me. I'm not so all alone. They guide me along. Wherever I am, just listening to the moods and how they feel me. In due time, inspiration will arise. To be inspired, this becomes a resurrection.

The next day I set off on my own. From Istanbul I go to Troy, where I tramp about for days with a knapsack of bread, peanut butter, apricots, and a thermos of water. At night, I sleep on the ground in a sleeping bag. It feels natural for me to walk along with the sun and the stars.

The "moods" circulating around the light of Consciousness. Some people call them angels.

Early one evening, I see a tattered paperback book in some nearby bushes. It is *The Last Temptation of Christ*. It's in English! I am curious to know what the last temptation is. I page through the book until I see that the temptation deals with death. "To know death." I'm on the ground in my sleeping bag with the dark closing in on me. I fear my death. I feel so vulnerable, so insecure. So forsaken. I need protection. I make my way to any hotel. I feel much safer in a room with a lock on the door.

To lock out death? I need to commune with you. I recall Castaneda talking about communing with death. I'm always dying from one moment to the next. Time moves me along. How can I escape this? With a lock on the door? I break out laughing. I am death. I can't get rid of this shadow. I cast it wherever I go.

I'm walking across the plains of Troy. There, I carefully plod through miles of farmland. At the site of Troy, I find most of it is still underground. A few low walls, some pillars, but for now just deep ditches and ramps. The site is clearly under early excavation and development. I can't imagine Virgil's poetic account of a huge Trojan Horse from anywhere around here. The thing isn't even mentioned in *The Iliad*, which is the first account of what supposedly went on here.

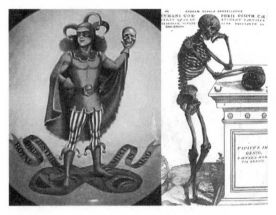

To contemplate the skull, my Golgatha, "Who among you can laugh and be elevated at the same time?"
—Friedrich Nietzsche, *Thus Spoke Zarathustra*

Maybe *The Iliad* was just a long tall tale. An "imaginative interpretation," more of a story to entertain, like Robin Hood or something.

This Trojan city-fort is miles away from the sea. However, it's said that the plains I was tromping through were once underwater. Where was the shoreline then? The camp of the Greeks? I don't see any Turkish kids crawling up from underground here. No trinkets from the underworld. No snakes to fuck me up at the airport. The entrance fee to Troy is sixty Turkish liras per person. About $3.22 in American money. Not bad. Kids under eight are free. My boys in Aspendos would be digging around on their own, then in the parking lot selling Helen's perfume bottles for forty bucks.

* * *

AFTER WALKING WELL OVER a hundred miles, I arrive in Athens. I get a hotel room, shower, and sleep for twelve hours. Revived, I go to the ancient Acropolis, where I stand ignorant of its significance. Just on its own, without my imagination lighting up the site, it feels like a graveyard, a cemetery spruced up for tourism. Workers on high scaffolding apply cement to the pillars supporting what? An ancient bureaucracy, a government building, a site for the gods? The hillsides in the distance look holier than this place. They are certainly more ancient.

I'm not on this carved-up hill for long. The wind is so strong that I want to leave. There is no place to sit or lie down for the night. Everything is forbidden. Gates and fences, guards and exit signs, tourists wandering around up here, blowing in the wind. Where will I sleep for the night?

I don't know where the home of Socrates is located. I read somewhere that he lived just outside the city. No doubt in the holy hills away from the polis and its commanding gods. Better to interiorize his spirit. The man's home is somewhere inside me.

* * *

My daughter is turning twenty-six and asks me to come home for her birthday. I don't know what else would have brought me back. I'm heading home, honey.

* * *

After I'm back in LA and just past my daughter's celebration, Andy Kaufman's partner, Bob Zmuda, calls and says he's thinking of me and wanted to check in.

"Are you around?" he asks.

"I am for now. I just got back from the other side of myself. Good to hear from you, Bob."

"I'm going to Burning Man. It's in the Nevada desert. Come with me. You'll love it, Michael."

I haven't heard of Burning Man, but after he explains it—a kind of *Mad Max* meets the Grateful Dead with costumes, nudity, dancing, art, and the burning of a giant effigy on the last night—I say, "That sounds perfect for me." Especially that burning effigy business.

Transitions. Moving from one body to the next, the dying involved, to burn away the old for the new. I think I know the rite.

"I'm with you, Bob. Let's go!"

Together we fly to some airport not far from this desert event. We pick up a rental car and head to the Burning Man camp. Arriving, I see an art car, a black Fleetwood Cadillac with a large black gothic cathedral with stained-glass windows built on top. What in the world is that?

There is an official theme to this year's Burning Man—The Seven Ages—represented by installations and described as "beginning with the cradle, where one could symbolically return to the womb and be reborn, the stages continued on through life to death and enlightenment." This part stands out: "Return to the womb to be reborn." And I will add, through the earth. I keep what this means for me to myself. Zmuda isn't looking for a retake. He's into altered normality, the freakish, the priapic that adds to the ha-ha. When he sees it, and he sees it often, he just bursts out laughing, "Michael, look at this!"

I love this side of Bob. He's a reminder of the Fool coursing through everything. It's all so irrational. For some, a madness that eats us alive like the warm human meat in the mouth of a maenad, or the great Kali that eats us all. It's simply time that devours me.

Forgive me. I'm still on the dark side, the flipside of doing well. I'm a burning man now burnt out!

Bob bursts out laughing. "You came to the right place! Everybody here is a burnout."

I'm thinking of CalArts, the guy at my door wanting his soul back. Where's my soul in all of this? I forget that my soul is everywhere. I forget! I forget everything that I am. I pick and choose from the "10,000 things" as referenced in Buddhism, differentiating this from that. Well, then, see what I'm picking out and discarding, how this stuff can form an identity that I get stuck in. It's probably why we have a Burning Man, to burn through identities, beliefs, roles that delimit us.

* * *

AGAIN, I SEE THE BLACK CADILLAC hearse with a cathedral sculpture rising from the back. I assume this dramatic-looking vehicle is part of my "Last Temptation." It's death's chariot. Like a "high-frequency vehicle" appearing to Ezekiel, I imagine  that this car has a "scroll" for me, something to tell me. It does. "Playfully," I *imagine* an image symbolizing the spirit of Asclepius, healer of souls. It is the caduceus, a healing staff from my underworld, the unconscious!

Oh no, not those two snakes again! Here, the snakes are far more significant.

After I'd finished my medical training in the army, I wore the caduceus insignia on my uniform lapel.

In the army, I wasn't versed in the mythological significance of the caduceus. It's amazing that thousands of years later, the caduceus continues to stand for healing. For me, the two snakes symbolize the opposites intertwining the earth's axis pole. At the top of the caduceus, the wings signify a movement through time—the earth rotating around the center of itself on its axis. So, this caduceus is associated with healing, "Well, hold onto the earth and one becomes whole." Like Rumi holding on to the pole and speaking about the virtues of wholeness, for me, the earth can provide wholeness by holding on to Her.

"Who does that char-  iot belong to?" I've got to meet the owner. Someone says, "Oh, that belongs to Rebecca. She built it." Who's Rebecca? Someone else points to an attractive young woman in a long, baggy black dress. "That's Rebecca."

We meet, and we're in sync. I tell her of my death through the show, and my love of Rumi to the rescue, my wanderings, and that I'm a ghost for now.

She knows the underworld, the unconscious realm, and the spirit of Asclepius! I cruise around with Rebecca for a while. Lots of jaunts out to the Mojave Desert. We sit content with the wasteland, the shadows, the dark before the light.

* * *

Toward the end of 2002, I've been offered the part of Jonathan Brewster in a West End comedy production of *Arsenic and Old Lace*. Jonathan is a whacky serial killer who is taken in by his two aunts. Unbeknownst to him, the two sweet old ladies are themselves killers. I haven't been onstage in seventeen years, and I like the idea of playing a kooky killer in a comedy, and why not do a play in London at the Strand? Cheerio.

Arsenic and Old Lace originally opened at London's Strand Theatre in 1942 and ran for nearly five years. Even when the Nazis were bombing London, the play was still performed. The house never closed. Well, then for the sake of posterity, I belong here with my funny portrayal of Jonathan Brewster. I spent a month and a half beforehand learning my lines, so on the first day of rehearsal, I'm off book. I'm ready to open. The cast—very fine English stage actors doing accurate Brooklyn accents—are superb.

My dressing room is a small cubby at the top of the theater, not one of the large rooms reserved for the leads close to the stage. It's been painted black for me. My makeup area is a shrine to death, with black candles, black prismatic crystals, a few animal skulls, and a small metal sculpture of the Grim Reaper sitting on a throne. I'm using "imagination," getting my spooky character into form. I'm sure Stella would approve.

The play runs for five months. That summer, American tourists coming to see Kramer instead get my weird portrayal of Boris Karloff, who had originally played Jonathan Brewster. To honor him, I have a black-and-white photo of Karloff's face in the corner of my makeup mirror. One night during our run, Karloff's daughter, Sara, comes backstage to congratulate me. It is all rather fun.

The dark comedy lets me unwind after being in my own dark for a while. It's a perfect venue for getting me back to the stage.

Tuckered out after doing the play, I retreat to a property I bought in the Sierras. The place is at 8,500 feet, with 3,000 acres of pinyon pines, several large springs, and open meadows with views of Mount Whitney, the tallest mountain in the contiguous US. I plan to build a small stone cabin in a rocky area overlooking one of the springs. Till then, I bunk in a mobile home that came with the land. I plan to build a large sun/moon wheel aligning through the earth, an ancient way of orienting oneself to nature.

But there is unrest in the area that affects the property. A dead rat taints my 3,000-gallon water tank. Somebody breaks into my mobile home and steals all my bedding and foodstuff. The police station is  twenty-six miles away, so what can they do? The Navy in Ridgecrest conducts a helicopter exercise over my property, dropping a flare that burns up and ultimately destroys 190 acres of ancient pinyon pines. It takes over a hundred firefighters to put the fire out. I thank them, but what the heck is going on up here?

I settle with the military, but regardless of the money they pay me, it can't buy the trees back to the way they stood for the past two hundred years.

A few weeks after this, someone steals the metal entry gate to my property! The lawless have the upper hand. I've had enough. I sell the place.

It's an inner retreat from now on.

Keep it simple. The earth is everywhere. Why try to own it? I should carry the "medicine wheel" within me and be oriented from wherever I am.

* * *

ENTER BETH. When the two of us meet at a Santa Monica café, I am having breakfast with friends. She walks in wearing a hoodie and carrying a backpack, sits at a nearby table, and immerses herself in a stack of books. One of my friends actually spots Beth. "Oh man, look at that. God, she's gorgeous." I tell him to go for it. But he's too timid to approach her. "Go and talk to her," I urge. The truth is, I don't want anything to do with women right now. But my friend says, "You go talk to her." So I'll show him how it's done, and I get up and say hello.

"Hi. Are you a student?" I ask. She is an actress with a very nice career going and also taking classes at UCLA and Santa Monica College. We end up talking for two hours! Oh boy. Here we go.

We date a bit, then she spends much of the summer with her family in Connecticut, and we talk on the phone all the time. We miss each other but qualify it by repeatedly telling each other that we aren't interested in a serious relationship. Why do we have to keep saying this to each other?

Something's up. Uh-oh.

At the end of 2003, I'm in New York starring in the off-Broadway production of *Trumbo*, a play about the blacklisted screenwriter Dalton Trumbo that his son adapted from his father's letters. It's a peculiar gig. A new guest star comes in each week. Christopher Lloyd preceded me, and Chris Cooper is set to follow. It turns out that Beth is back east that same week, spending New Year's with family, and we get together. We're so in love! We can't get around it anymore. We're a couple.

It's all about being in love.

....

CHAPTER 29

Not Funny

" **D**o you know who you are?"

It's an uneventful afternoon in early 2006, and I am walking through the parking lot of the Brentwood Country Mart when someone yells this question out to me.

At first I think it's a kooky fan or a person living on the street. Then I look up and see George Carlin.

"Do you know who you are, my man?"

"Well, you know, that's a very big question, George. I'm definitely looking into it."

Ever since *The Michael Richards Show* put my lights out, I haven't had much interest in showbiz. I did the play in London, but after five months of that, instead of going out and getting into other plays, I'm content hanging out with my library, reading a great deal, taking my daily walks in the mountains, and spending time with Beth. At fifty-seven, I'm somewhat retired. Unless a script comes along that lights my fire, I'd rather plow through the collected works of Victor Hugo.

"So, what's up with you these days, George?" I ask.

"I'm at the Universal Amphitheater this week," he says. "Come by and check it out."

I take up this master of stand-up, really, this Socrates of our time, on his invitation. For nearly ninety minutes, Carlin is onstage with his notebooks open on a nearby table. He is clearly breaking in an act. Unlike most stars appearing at the amphitheater with all they've got, Carlin uses high-end venues like this to work out material for his HBO specials. Before leaving the city and hitting the road, he does several more nights at the Comedy & Magic Club in Hermosa Beach.

"It's well managed," he tells me. "I can get some work done there."

George invites me to see his shows at the Comedy & Magic Club. George goes on early. He wants a sober room for a more honest laugh. Once again, he has pages of notes laid out on a piano bench right there beside him onstage. If not for his notes, you'd never know he is working on new material as he smoothly moves along from routine to routine. He has been doing this for forty-some years, and it shows. Stand-up is his domain, and he is truly a master of the art and in control of a very meticulous process for building an act.

Like Twain, Carlin is a social critic and part of the cultural fabric. He was the first host of *SNL* in 1975. Two years later, he did his first HBO special. He's snarky, rather brutal, pissed off or indifferent about a whole lot of things, even mean, tough-minded, and "fuck you!" I admire his strength. He's standing up to what he calls "the bullshit." Watching him, I begin to get the urge to get at stand-up again. I get offers for speaking engagements and appearances. It would be nice to have some comedy ready and take some of these offers. Yes, I stopped doing stand-up in 1988—eighteen years ago—because I didn't like my act, how I could get so mean onstage, screaming and expressing all my gripes about people and so forth. Then I had that very upsetting dream in which I saw Sam Kinison and me together causing the American flag to tear in half. No good. I took the dream as a warning. I'm just going to stick to acting work.

But hanging out with George has rubbed off on me. I remember the way Sam Kinison turned so much of his darkness into comedy. After all these years, I'm feeling that I want to start working on an act, sticking to it no matter how crappy it gets. Sam stuck to it for five years before getting to his diamond, sweeping us into laughter. I won't back off this time. No matter how dark it gets, let's see where the act takes me.

* * *

THE COMEDY & MAGIC CLUB'S OWNER, Mike Lacey, gives me all the spots I want. I do two shows a night, four times a week in the two rooms at the club. Mike records my sets and gives me the DVD before I leave for home. Within a couple of months, I have a fifteen-minute act that gets laughs and feels pretty good.

I come up with a plan to stay at the Comedy & Magic Club for a year, then hire a few comedy writers to come in and do punch-up. Mike is supportive, and after five months at his club, my act grows to twenty-five-minutes. Soon I receive a great offer to play Tahoe for a week. They're presuming I have a longer act. I could have whacked around on their stage and stretched the act out longer, but I want more material, and to be better, more developed, before I do a major gig.

So, no thanks. I'm not doing this for the money. It's about being good, really good. The offer tells me that I'm on the right track. If the light is bright enough, all the moths will appear.

To heat things up, I start playing the Improv, the Comedy Store, and the Laugh Factory. Being back in these clubs, I stake this out as a rebirth. I'm up on my feet, coming out of what I can do, which is make people laugh. Budd Friedman, Mitzi Shore, and Jamie Masada, the club owners, give me their full support. I do up to thirteen shows a week, unannounced, and always introduced as a surprise guest. I don't want people buying a ticket with expectations of seeing me. This lightens my load as I try out stuff to build up the act.

I record everything to review what works and what doesn't. I'm rather meticulous about it. But I seldom write out all that I'm going to do onstage. I go on with a few key words written on paper. The process generally makes me nervous because I'm always flying by the seat of my pants. I'm loose and all over the place. Many times, I'm not doing an act. I just improvise and play around with the audience. In this way, the act has a way of doing me. I go along with it and hope for the best.

The audience knows when I'm off book, and they love it. They can sense the danger. Most of the time I come through, and so does the audience. Their laughter, it's what keeps me going night after night. I've been known to bomb. I'm also known as an inspired Fool who makes people laugh. How else would I be a regular at every major comedy club in Los Angeles? How did I end up on the *Seinfeld* show to create one of the most eccentric, weirdly funny characters on television? It started at the comedy clubs. Bad nights were a part of it all—turning carbon into a diamond, and the pressure is intense.

And about my fame, well, none of it matters when you're working late at night in a comedy club. Fame goes out the door in just a few minutes. Actually, being famous, the audience expects more out of you! They expect you to be good and funny. Again, that's why I'm undercover, off the lineup, not billed on the marquee. I need time to fail, to screw up, to be unfunny. I'm building an act.

Since I'm not seen on the lineup, the audience goes crazy when I pop in. It's here that I see the level of Kramer's popularity, the impact this character has had on people. I'm grateful, but the first thing I've got to do when I get onstage is get over the bar this character has set for me. Usually, I do.

* * *

THE GIGANTIC WAVE that I rode as Cosmo Kramer—this incredible character—was one kind of phenomenon, but now, as I work night after night in the clubs to put together an act, building it bit by bit from fifteen minutes to thirty and eventually, hopefully, an hour or more, I am riding a creative force that brings about another sizable wave. But this one wipes me out late Friday night, November 17, 2006.

Earlier that evening I agree to appear on a talk show hosted by a former *Seinfeld* writer, one of the producers of *The Michael Richards Show*. It's an awkward interview, but it's a chance to button things up. I have regrets but hold no grudges, and I get through it.

After the talk show, the limo provided gets stuck in traffic on the way to the Comedy Store. What else is new in LA?

But I'm thrown off schedule. I'm stressed. I've got my act to do. When I finally get to the Comedy Store, they're running behind too. Okay. I work the Main Room, the largest of the rooms inside the club and where, supposedly, the best acts perform. I know the fame of the *Seinfeld* show is what enables me to drop in whenever I want as a "special guest." So be it.

My show goes well.

One down and now another show to do up the street at the Laugh Factory.

Beth picks me up at the Comedy Store and we head over. Backstage, I'm told they're also running a few acts behind and it will be about forty-five minutes until I go on. Oh boy, it's getting late.

Beth leaves me backstage and sits out front with friends to watch the acts. Since I'm always nervy before I perform, I go out the back door and take a walk into the residential area away from the bustle of the club and the traffic noise from Sunset Boulevard. From the talk show earlier, I've got the failure of *The Michael Richards Show* on my mind. But I'm not walking across the plains of Troy again. For now, on this walk, the cool night air from Laurel Canyon refreshes me.

After a while, I head back to the club to stretch out a bit: a few asanas for keeping the spine limber; I'm staying flexible for the pratfalls in my show.

What might I do tonight? I have options. As an opener, I could walk onstage and continue walking right off the stage, right over tables and into the wall, crashing to the floor, and then play with the disorientation. At fifty-seven, I can still knock about like I did when I played Kramer. Even then I was older, the oldest in the cast and nearing fifty when the *Seinfeld* season finale aired.

Just a couple of weeks before, Jay Leno saw me in Hermosa Beach and encouraged me to book special engagements in theaters and casinos. "Stay with it," he said. He was right. I've got a way to go, but I'm on it.

* * *

"IT'S GOING TO BE ANOTHER twenty-five minutes," I'm told.

I should eat something, but there's only bar food. Chips and liquor won't cut it.

I stretch out on the floor upstairs again and visualize my opening.

Some of the comics who have already performed are grumbling about the audience. They're like surfers watching the waves. It's gnarly out there. The water is choppy. The waves are breaking inside close to the rocks. The guy right before me comes offstage and warns, "They're edgy, all drunk. Good luck." Maybe so, but as Budd Friedman put it years ago, "Never blame your audience."

Finally: "Michael, you're up."

* * *

IT'S LATER THAN WHEN I NORMALLY GO ON. As usual, my surprise appearance has everybody going wild. It's going to be a great night! I walk onto the stage and right over a few tables, crashing into the wall. It's all fun ad-libbing with the audience. Just standing onstage with a mic, we're already past that and Kramer! See ya later, Cosmo. The audience is howling. I start up my material. They want to go where I go.

Let's go! I'm playing a dog on a leash restrained by my owner as I try to meet another dog. Because it's very physical, I can't really hear

the laughs. Just a lot of talking and commotion, especially from the balcony area of the club. I yell out in my bitter old "get offa my lawn!" George character I played on *Fridays*. "Shut the fuck up!" It's crude and fiery, and it gets a big laugh. The audience loves a confrontation. I'm unleashed. I've been here before. It's outrageous! Irrational! Part of the Fool's kit. Let's go wild!

I don't do this on the street. That's what's fun about a comedy club. Get crazy, go wild! You're not supposed to do this out in the real world. I'm being naughty, and the audience loves it.

Then I hear someone from the balcony area shout, "You're not funny. We don't think you're very funny!" The room stops. Glancing up in the direction of the comment, I don't know whether the guy has been there the whole night or walked in late, but I'm thinking it's him and his group who are so noisy, and his dig about "not being funny" hits me hard.

Of course, looking back at it all, I wish I had just agreed with him. "Okay, I'm not very funny for you tonight. Is there anything I can do? Wash your car, mow your lawn? I don't want you leaving here dissatisfied." Instead, I take his remark pretty hard. A solid punch below the belt.

Yeah, that was low, "You're not funny!" Yep, fighting words to a comic. How do I make this funny? It's a challenge. The kind of stuff that leads to becoming a seasoned stand-up comic, which I'm not. I'm in a stream of unconsciousness as we both blast each other. I actually think I might be able to tie it all up and make it funny in the end. Alas, I turn into that night's sweeper.

He went low and I went even lower. We both ended up at the bottom of the barrel.

* * *

THE WHOLE ROOM HAS BEEN LEVELED, shocked by my anger and foul language. I drop the mic and leave the stage.

Jamie Masada, the club owner, is standing right there.

"Where is that guy?" I ask. "I need to talk to him. This all went crazy. I want to make peace."

Jamie says the guy and his friends are gone. They were escorted out. They were given their money back and told to leave.

Then throw me out too! We were both in on this clamor.

I don't want it to end this way. I head for the entrance door of the club. I'll go outside and find him. Let's work through this. We can't leave it like this.

"Michael, they're gone! Just come upstairs and let it go." I'm at the entrance door. It's crowded. I was the last show. Everybody is leaving. A girl sees me, rushes over, and asks me to autograph her napkin. Her man pulls her away. "We don't want his autograph!" he says.

Yes, it was a very bad show. "I'm sorry."

* * *

UPSTAIRS WITH JAMIE. He tries to restore calm and put the situation in context by recalling past disasters at the Laugh Factory. Kinison once got in a fight with a heckler outside the club who was angry at him for making fun of Jesus. Another time, Carlin threw a chair when someone interrupted his act. What? Of all the performers to mention right now. Kinison sort of got me out of stand-up and Carlin inspired me to get back in.

Both these performers went through a rite of passage with the audience. Is this mine? Will I get through it? Will I hold on?

It's late and I'm worn out. I'm supposed to perform again tomorrow night.

"I'm a wreck over this, Jamie," I say. "I'm going to cancel tomorrow."

Jamie won't let me. Don't let this night beat you up. You have to keep working.

I remember my pact to keep at this act no matter how dark it gets.

* * *

Oh, what comes through so hard and fast! The funny and not so funny, the war of opposites right underneath me; all the devils and angels, all the peace and love and war and hate, all *within* me.

To make comedy out of it—to work an idea, to try out a character, to turn an ugly, nasty, dark situation into a laugh—I don't always succeed. The task is to stay with it, to hold out. Can I hold out?

"You're not funny." I had those words going on inside me often enough. He laid it out so clearly, so simply, my biggest fear—not being funny. Later, I'll come to realize that all of this, everything he said, is me. His voice is my voice. This is all ME going on. My inferiority sets in. My anger erupts. We put each other down. Who's going to come out on top? Anger is all over the place. I have to get through this. Can I hold out?

Many club nights, I went off on wordy tangents, moods, or thoughts on whatever was weighing in on me. It wasn't always funny. I'm on the lookout for comedy. Please come out from wherever you are. Sometimes there's a breakthrough. I'll get a bit out of it.

I'm mining for gold in the mud. It's dirty work. I'm in the mines. It's dark down here, and the air gets foul. Can I hold out?

* * *

THE FOLLOWING NIGHT I'm back on at the Laugh Factory. My show goes well. But there is a woman from one of the media outlets standing by as I come offstage. She wants to know how I plan to make amends for my racism once the footage of my act is shown to the country. Racism? Yeah, I said the N-word. And then some. What the hell's the matter with me? Anger. Anger was the matter with me. I fucked up. And I was never able to meet the man and work through what we said to each other. Footage? Was someone shooting me last night while I was performing? Who? No one had my permission to release footage of me and my work to the public. It's printed on the club's ticket: no photography, no recording of the show. And why is this reporter backstage? Who let her in?

On Monday I'm the biggest story on every news outlet in the country.

I don't have the mindset to stand up for my act, my process, the way I perform, or the unfunny that goes along with developing my act.

I have no defense.

I blew it.

"Never blame the audience."

But I did blame the audience, didn't I? I screwed up. But I'll go back to the rule. I won't blame anyone except myself for what happened. It's all me anyway.

* * *

LARRY KING FROM CNN sends a handwritten note to my house, inviting me to sit with him for an exclusive interview. "You can tell your side of the story now," he writes. The big media outlets initially released the footage of my act, got the whole mess out in the open for all of America to be in on, and now here's an outlet that wants me to show up on one of their talk shows to bleed in front of millions of people? I mustn't blame them. People are doing their jobs. I'm big news right now. They want to get in on it.

I don't respond to their offer. I don't know how to face the press. Somehow, I have to face myself first.

Jerry calls. He's scheduled to be on Letterman and suggests I conference in via satellite and apologize. Thank you, Jerry. I'm all up for this.

* * *

I HEAD TO CBS, where I will be beamed into Letterman's New York studio. There's no pre-interview, as is usually done on these host shows. I have no publicist, nothing written for me to say. I don't meet with a producer beforehand to go over anything. This isn't a performance. I'm raw. No mask. No makeup. No character to hide behind.

I sit in the corner of a room with drab green walls around me. There's a small camera set up in front of me. I'm all messed up, incredibly messed up. The first and last time I did Letterman was a few years ago, and I "wasn't funny." I wanted to be, but I just couldn't get there. So here I am, not being funny again. This time, dazed and in shock that the media has edited my far-flung act in a late-night comedy club and sent it out to Everywhere, USA, and the world. Here I am dead and all, waiting to go on national television where people can now look at Michael Richards, the corpse.

I've been dead before. I do not boast. In my dark, to follow its path, there is an orientation to this. I must trust in "Thy Will Be Done."

The *New York Times* reported that I looked like a "defrocked priest" giving my apology on Letterman. Various pundits and PR experts weighed in on the authenticity of my apology. I wasn't out to present the perfect PR apology-speech. I just spoke naturally from myself, from my heart as much as I could. I can only be for real, confess my anger, my lousy act, my upset over ugly words.

I hear in my earpiece: "How are you doing?" Dave asks.

"Not good," I say.

Dave asks me to explain what happened.

"I lost my temper onstage. I was at the comedy club trying to do my act, and I got heckled…and went into a rage. Said some pretty nasty things to some Afro Americans. A lot of trash talk."

There is laughter in the studio audience. Jerry shushes them. "Stop laughing. It's not funny."

Yep, that's right. "I'm not funny." Not funny enough at the club. And not funny in front of two of America's greatest funnymen sitting there, looking at the corpse that I am.

"Were you actually being heckled?" Dave asks. "Or were they talking and disturbing the act?"

"That was going on too," I say.

Laughter comes through my earpiece.

"I'm hearing your audience laughing. I'm not even sure this is where I should be addressing the situation…I'm really busted up over this. I'm really very sorry."

"Is there much more you can do? That you would like to do?" Dave asks.

"I just have to do personal work."

And that's it. My dream of the torn flag was certainly a foreshadow. My sincere apology for going through with it all. I have work to do.

CHAPTER 30

Heart-Work

Anger appears to get the best of me, but what is the best of me that rises out of anger?

Anger rips me in two. I see my flag torn in half. My anger has the strength to do this. For this, I'm grateful. I see where my work begins…again and again, like the seasons round and round, always of the light and dark. This is the sharp pointy world below, or the thorns of the moral world. Out of this, I head for the light to bloom through the heart. But first:

From the sharp pointy world below, rising up toward the sun, blooming before the light.

"I don't know what's happening to me. I'm just so angry onstage."

"You need to go into analysis and deal with your mother."

I call a therapist, Dr. John Dobbs, a Jungian analyst like my mentor Robert Stein, who passed away ten years earlier. Dr. Dobbs comes to my house at nighttime because this is a crisis. I am in a catastrophe. I'm coming apart after my apology on the Letterman show, as I should. I have to withdraw from the world. I have to go to the depths of myself, the call of the psyche, and back to the earth, the "Mother," the way of Her temperament within me.

Straight out, John asks me to come up with an image that can hold me together, to take my time, think about it overnight. But the image comes to me instantly. It feels so right. A silver heart that I have in my study.

This image of the heart is a conduit to an inner receptivity, "to know" the way of my turmoil and its tempering aim to make a better man out of me.

* * *

RIGHT NOW, I ONLY HAVE a few people in my life: a Jungian analyst and Beth. She is hit hard by the controversy but able to stand alongside me. She was offended by what I said, but, as she repeatedly tells me, "I know who you are. I've seen you step into stuff so many times while performing and come out of it with a pearl." For now, "It won't be for anybody but yourself." This is inner work. An exodus. She knows I'm going to be with this for a long time. All she can do is keep the media, the exploiters, away from us. She's out to guard our privacy.

Jason, Julia, and Jerry all reach out. I'm embarrassed, and I'm also concerned about the mess spilling onto them. They will have to comment. My loved ones will also need to deal with this. And I am touched by those who contact me with words of support—show-biz friends I've lost touch with over the years, old friends, and other celebrities who know what it feels like to be in the news unfavorably.

I know there is the competing feeling of disgust and concern when they check in on me, but still, like Beth, they know me.

Comics understand what happened. For some, it's mostly fodder for their late-night monologue. I am fair game. Public condemnation and humiliation are forms of justice.

Though I barely know Paula Poundstone, she invites me and Beth over to her house to hang out with her and her kids. She knows I screwed up but isn't going to hold it against me. She had her own bouts with the press and knows what I am going through. She's an angel keeping us company.

As for those friends who don't call, I think they'd like to help me out of the mess I'm in, but they don't know how to respond to what I said that night. I certainly can't explain my comedic process and how I cut loose on a comedy club stage. It will sound ridiculous and defensive. More so, the fit of anger and such ugly, racist words that came out of me were just too nuts to handle. I mean, I was having a hard time catching up to myself, and they certainly couldn't do it for me. The force of shadow that tripped me up, now in front of the whole country, was just incredible, nearly overwhelming. For most of them, they had to turn away and head for cover.

How my anger leveled the room, it was as big as my success on the *Seinfeld* show. I'm a sizable man. I can reach a lot of people, comedically, and now tragically. In the beginning, Carlin asked me if I knew who I was. At the end, Jerry asked me the same question: "Do you know who you are?" Well, I may think that I'm rather normal, but the reality is, I'm not. I don't say this out of conceit. Being of the extraordinary, I have a professional responsibility to keep my shit together. This is one part of me, but the way of the shadow, where it's taking me, I'm not sure where we're going. I'm so sorry for all of this.

Thank goodness it's not you.

* * *

THE CONSTANT REQUESTS FOR INTERVIEWS, I ignore. Looking at what is being written about me, there's no way I can read this stuff and openly respond. I can't fix things out there anyway! Someone recommends a PR crisis-management expert, supposedly the best in the country. Beth fields the call. This guy tells her it will take a couple of years for me to straighten things out and get my career back in order. "He doesn't care about restoring his career," she says. "He doesn't have a career to rebuild." She turns to me and silently asks if I want to get on the phone. I do, and the expert tells me that I shouldn't have apologized in the way I did on Letterman.

"What's wrong with the truth?" I ask.

"Telling the truth is not always the way you handle a crisis," he says.

What? It's all I know, the truth. I can't handle this mess without it. I must stay true to myself, true to my soul or bust. There's no way I want to spin my way out of this. I am not out for redemption or some comeback where I'm more popular than ever. And I don't want to do anything phony or inauthentic, like work in a soup kitchen in Watts, which the crisis PR guy also suggested. I just want to apologize, acknowledge what I did, and take stock of myself. This is about me and my shadow. What everybody else is thinking is unto themselves. The most I can do for everybody is go home and get my shit together.

* * *

THE PHONE RINGS. It's Frances Fisher, who is concerned about me and wants to help. We once went out on a dinner date and just spent the evening in her kitchen talking about life, spiritual matters, and the "all too human." On the phone she straight out says, "You need to get out of town, disappear for a while. I can help you with this." And she does. She knows of a spiritually minded friend living in Mexico who has a place where I can get some time alone. And so, with my silver heart and Beth's blessing, I leave the States for several weeks. Only Frances and Beth know where I am.

For the most part, I write in my journal and take long solitary walks along an empty coastline away from everyone. One day I find a paperback in the sand on the Upanishads that gets me interested in the author, an Indian who taught Vedanta in Los Angeles of all places. Inspired by the Vedanta philosophy, I make a note to check him out when I get back. I'm also inspired by the Mayan temples, these structures that are so orientated through the earth and its relationship to the sun. I'm seeking order to compensate for the mess that I'm in.

"I'm a loathsome, offensive brute..." and I can't look away.

* * *

IN MARCH, I VISIT THE ASHRAM east of Los Angeles associated with the teacher from India, a twenty-nine-year-old Hindu monk and self-described "enlightened Master and modern mystic" who wrote the book on the Upanishads that I found in the sand. Vedanta philosophy has some punch to it. I go to several events at the ashram. I love this community, the way they are uplifted by their spiritual interests. There's a family feeling, incense and flowers; everyone is Hindu and open-hearted through their faith. Their door is open. They take me in as family. I love the food, the study, the wisdom of their Vedanta. I'd like to meet their teacher.

That summer Beth and I are invited to travel with these families to Angkor Wat, where we are to meet their guru. Everyone in our group talks ecstatically about him, eagerly waiting to receive wisdom from their master. Beth and I are intrigued and share in the anticipation of meeting the man. Early in the morning on our first day in Angkor Wat, our group is directed to a certain temple site, and as the sun rises, there he is!

The guy is quite a character. He's a young Indian man, an engineer by training. He's now a headlining guru! He's got the bearing for it, the know-how, and the audience. He's such a colorful character with his long black hair and engaging smile, wearing his bright orange robe and carrying a trident! I can't worship the man, but I'm open to what he talks about. Most of it is based on Vedanta philosophy, and he appears to know his stuff. I just follow along and enjoy our time together in Angkor Wat.

The temples are aligned to the cardinal points! I've got my compass and contemplate the discovery of orientations. I'm considering the way of the earth/moon and sun incorporated in the building of these ancient temples, so similar in stature to the Mayan temples halfway around the world, both embodying a Perfect Nature sacred to the human soul. A line from Walt Whitman comes to me: "*That stellar concave spreading overhead, softly absorbed into me, rising so free interminably high, stretching east, west, north, south—and I, though but a point in the centre below, embodying all.*"

In the "centre," my heart open to uniting the differences, the opposites, and to see that all sides are within me.

* * *

ONE MORNING IN ANGKOR WAT, an American reporter shows up at our hotel. Somebody from the group tells me that he's looking for me. I find him in the lobby and walk over to him.

"Do you want to take a walk to a temple site I know of and get your story?" I ask.

"I'd appreciate that," he says.

His article is decent. Appearing in the *Los Angeles Times*, it reveals that I'm attending to a "spiritual life." I suppose so. It's the only place for me to go. It's been with me for a while. A "spiritual life." I've "crossed the line" now to get there.

We tour Angkor Wat and several areas of Cambodia, and then Beth and I go on to Thailand, where I purchase an engagement ring with two stones, a ruby heart and a sapphire heart, sitting side by side. We are to rejoin our friends in India for the Hindu pilgrimage Char Dham, but heavy rain creates dangerous travel conditions and landslides in the Himalayas. Beth and I take a detour to a converted Maharaja palace in the Himalayan foothills of India, essentially an Ayurvedic spa. In our nightstand drawer, in place of a Bible, we find a copy of *Vedanta Treatise*, a book simplifying the ancient Hindu scripture, the Vedas. Another book! One in the bushes, one in the sand, and now one in a drawer.

That night a speaker lectures about the book and, of course, we are drawn in. We spend the evening and ensuing days discussing the Vedas, the Upanishads, and the Bhagavad Gita with our new friend. He speaks glowingly about his own teacher, the book's author Swami Parthasarathy, whom we feel inspired to meet. Within a few days, we leave the Himalayas and fly to Pune to meet Parthasarathy, where we spend the next several weeks studying at his academy, a term he prefers instead of "ashram."

Highly educated, a lawyer and university lecturer who teaches ethical leadership to many prominent international business students, Parthasarathy discourages the rituals and worshipful displays that most devotees express in the presence of their gurus. Instead, he directs his students to daily study, exercise, and a healthy, simple diet. There are no tridents, robes, or idols—which he regards as symbols. He doesn't worship symbols. He uses them to understand the psychology of religion. His practicality is its own lesson. One day I put my hands together in a sign of gratitude and respect, and he slaps them away. The message being it's not about me, it's about you. Become your own teacher.

* * *

I DO GRAPPLE WITH ANGER.

I must step back and listen. Usually, the best of me will come through.

"Anyone who perceives his shadow and his light simultaneously," wrote Jung, "sees himself from two sides and thus gets in the middle."

To note my "moods," to commune with them, it is like the "hearing of the Word." The moods speak. They have something to say. It's essential that I listen. I'm in "the middle" of it all.

 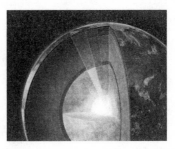

The transformation of anger "in the heated, sealed vessel," in "the middle" of myself as in the core-fire of the earth, the intensity of Consciousness comes out of the fire, out of the emotions that press in on me. I whirl from here. The feuding opposites, "shadow and light," come out of the fire, what heats me up, what drives me into confliction. Out of control, I burn everything down. But, contained, as in the earth, my thinking is stabilized—my voice of reason, it places me in the middle. It helps me to seek containment. I understand the turmoil. I am held within the "middle" in between right and wrong.

"Instead of arguing with the drives which carry us away, we prefer to cook them and…ask them what they want… That can be discovered by active imagination, or through a fantasy, or through

*experimenting with reality, but always with the introverted attitude
of observing objectively what the [anger] drive really wants."*

—Marie-Louise von Franz, *Alchemy*

* * *

BACK IN LA, OUR TRIP has inspired Beth to resume her studies,
and by midsummer she is admitted to Columbia University in
New York.

I am up for the change. Before we leave for New York, I get into
photography. I study with noted portraitist Greg Gorman and take
a couple of ten-day workshops in Oaxaca with photojournalist Mary
Ellen Mark. Both are encouraging of my work, and I see I'm pretty
good at it. It's pure interest, and I enjoy catching what I see. Pretty
much what analysis is about.

One night I attend a lecture at the C. G. Jung Institute. The
speaker is Rabbi Mordecai Finley. He lectures about Kabbalah, Jung,
and personal development. I like what he has to say. It's basically that
"the kingdom of God is *within* you."

He's easy to listen to, like Joseph Campbell. During the lecture, he
says something about "meeting God." Intrigued, I introduce myself
and ask if he has actually met God.

"Yes, I have," he says.

I smile and kiddingly ask, "What does he or she look like?"

"Light," he says.

Light can be seen in many ways. I can see it as Consciousness.
Yeah, I think Nature is ultimate Consciousness. It thinks in all kinds
of ways. It can be ultimate "Light" as an ongoing energy that is everywhere, and I can call this "God."

I attend some of Rabbi Finley's Saturday services. I like the story
of Moses leaving Egypt for the wilderness, or as I see it, leaving for
the depths of the Soul.

I'm up for the "Light."

* * *

Aʜ, ᴛʜɪs Sᴏᴜʟ ʙᴜsɪɴᴇss. How deep it can go. I suppose I'm embodied through Nature, through light, the sun, through everything that is, through all of Creation. I got the whole thing going on inside me. What is this stuff?

With the earth, I can call Her Mother, but this planet is an electromagnetic male (+) and female (−). Made in the image of this, embodying polarity, I must be androgynous. I've got the earth's polar field running through me! Pretty hard to shake it off. Not that I'm up to it. With the earth turning about the way it does, the sun appearing to rise and set, through polarity I can see in both directions, East and West. Well, yeah, I've got two eyes in my head! It makes some sense why I'm set up like this. In the East there's this thought about having a third eye in the middle of my forehead just above the two.

Well, it's not so much a real eye, but it stands for something. I can see it as the sun shining upon the face of my "two-eyed" earth. In the East, some people note this as the "third," mark the spot in red, and call it a bindi. It seems to balance things out. The earth seen through the light of the sun. Well yeah, absolutely.

What we do with light, well, it can get very creative. It can be for or against things. It's always in there with Imagination, all the ways to see what we're doing with ourselves, to light up the way. Then the question becomes, what are you going to do with what you see?

* * *

LATE THAT FALL I CLOSE UP the house, and Beth and I are in New York City. While she's in class, I'm outside in this great humanity that New York is. I spend a lot of time in Central Park, but I'm also just hanging out with people, always with my camera. I'm so steeped in photography. I look through photo books to see what great photographers are looking at. Overall, when I'm shooting, whatever resonates with me, catches my eye, I'm shooting it. That's it. It's all in the eye of the beholder. I hang out with Mary Ellen Mark at her studio. I meet Jay Maisel, one of the great street photographers, and we shoot together. I also connect with Duane Michals and his wonderful sense of humor. All of them tell me the same thing—just shoot, shoot, shoot!

And that's what I do. With my camera, I'm on the streets most of the day, all over the city. I'm not disguised or hiding behind sunglasses or underneath a hat. Just with my camera, I want to be around everybody. NYC is certainly the place for this. I'm looking at everything. I'm shooting everything. I'm into people, and, man, the city has them all! Unlike LA, where I'm in a car all the time, whizzing past it all, or hiking up into lonely places. In the city, I'm on the streets and in the subway with everybody. And everybody is happy to see Kramer—and the guy who played Kramer. I see there is so much friendliness and forgiveness. People come up to me, offer comfort, say how much they loved the show, and assure me everything's cool.

It has an effect on me. I walk out of my building onto the street, and I'm extroverted. This city really brings me out of myself. It's Kramer coming through the door! It's the Giddyup through and through!

* * *

BETH AND I ARE LIVING on the Upper West Side overlooking Central Park and the American Museum of Natural History. I meet the sun rising from our apartment, sitting out on our Juliet balcony, watching the light sweep over the city. Something else: our place is directly behind Jerry's building, an irony we were unaware of when we got the apartment. I can see his windows from our balcony! Once again, living in New York, I'm his next-door neighbor.

Jerry and I get together one day and as we're walking along Eighty-First, I retrieve an old framed corkboard from a pile of trash.

"What are you doing with that?" he asks.

"I'm keeping it," I say.

Jerry shakes his head. The idea of going through trash for something, that's not his thing.

"Jerry, it's perfectly good. Why throw it away? This would cost forty bucks at a stationery store." I mean it.

We both grin. It's Jerry and Kramer. There's no way out of it.

* * *

ONE DAY ON THE STREET, I run into one of Rabbi Finley's students.

"I heard you were here in the city," he says.

"Yes."

"What are you doing?" he asks.

"My fiancée is going to school here," I say.

"And you?" he wants to know.

"I'm finding the Light. Give Finley my love."

* * *

NOT TOO LONG AFTER THIS, I take the Eighty-First Street subway to Penn Station and I walk to a nearby photography store. I'm upgrading to a new camera. The man behind the counter helping me is a Hasidic Jew with a long, bushy beard. I imagine he's Walt Whitman. If only he were wearing a straw hat. If not for his suit and his expert knowledge of cameras, he could definitely pass as my man from the nineteenth century.

I like the feel and look of this new camera with lots of doodads that I don't know how to use yet.

"I'll probably have to get a teacher," I say.

He puts up a hand, like a crossing guard. STOP!

"No, no, don't get a teacher. *Figure it out on your own.* You'll be a better photographer."

It was excellent advice. For two and a half months, I work on learning how to shoot with this top-of-the-line camera. The more I play around with the f-stop and the ISO, like a tango to master, the more creative I get with this thing. All on my own, I'm getting pretty good with this camera. We're "talking to each other." What I think is just an inanimate object, a camera, isn't true. This camera is very much alive. We sync up. We're seeing through each other. And all of this comes about on my own.

My heart-work is very much like photography. I'm not just learning how to shoot, I'm learning how to see. It's about nuance and reflection, looking inward and outward through the appropriate lens, working on focus, and figuring out where and how to find the light, even in the dark. It doesn't happen in one shot. I have to make mistakes, miss, try again. It's an ongoing process. It doesn't end pain or suffering. The work actually shines a light on it. It reveals a picture of right and wrong, and always includes a chance to change, to seek improvement.

Starting out, I was more of an abstract shooter looking up to the likes of Minor White, Harry Callahan, and Aaron Siskind. I'm framing everything through the camera and shooting just what I see. I don't use Photoshop. "Not that there's anything wrong with that."

CHAPTER 31

The Light

I am reluctant to participate in the *Seinfeld* reunion that Larry David is cooking up on his HBO series *Curb Your Enthusiasm*. It's 2009, and I'm living in Manhattan when George Shapiro calls to tell me about the idea and asks if I will participate. Everyone else has said yes—Jerry, Jason, and Julia. It's exciting, he says.

The last thing I want to do is be in front of a TV camera, playing "myself" on Larry's show and stepping back into Kramer's shoes again. I'm literally and psychically thousands of miles away from both Kramer and Santa Monica's HBO.

So I tell George I'm not up for working anymore. Especially as Kramer. That's quite a character to start up again. It's been over a decade.

Poor George. He's trying to put a reunion show together and he needs all four of us to make it work.

"Give it some thought. This will be great for everybody."

After we hang up, the event at the Laugh Factory weighs on me. It's only been three years since then. It still hurts. What an almighty wrong that was! Still, it cut me loose. I think I'm better off for it. I've "crossed the line" into the other side of my Nature, and I'm contentedly retired. At sixty, I'm enjoying my days bebopping about Manhattan and Brooklyn and looking at everything through a camera.

As far out as I can get, New York City is a kind of ground wire to prevent my "spiritual life" from carrying me away.

George Shapiro and Howard West always grounded Jerry and kept the *Seinfeld* fold intact. They were always looking out for us when it came to the show. They had to. They were very much invested in *Seinfeld* as producers. How this included me, well, I really can't go against the grain. I'll always be a part of the show.

George has to draw me back into the fold. They really can't do a reunion show without me. I don't want to disappoint my old show mates who want this reunion. We went through years of tempering to get as good as we got. We did it together, contracts and all. And, above all, I still have Kramer's shoes...

"I don't want to hold up the train," I tell George. "Tell Larry that I'm on board. Sorry I put you through the hoops."

* * *

IN THE TEN YEARS SINCE *Seinfeld* has been off the air, Jerry has mentioned a few times that he's been approached to bring back the show. As far as I know, he's never taken it seriously, and I have always supported leaving it alone. "Why come back?" I once told him. "If it flops, it's just going to hurt the franchise." Another time, I suggested accepting a comeback offer, but only if we voice the show in Claymation. "They can't kill clay, Jerry."

Larry left *Seinfeld* after the seventh season to write for himself, to become his own show. He was on this path when we met on *Fridays*. He was always a performer first and foremost. Doing *Fridays*, he wrote to support himself as a comic actor. Many years later, writing a pilot with Jerry and creating the character George Costanza, Larry was delighted that he had Jason who could make his writing jump, but overall, Larry was always the comic actor that he is, indirectly performing through the character George.

I think he was as surprised as anyone at how good he got as a writer. He got so confident that he once said to me, "I gotcha two Emmys." That took me aback for a moment. I took it to mean that Larry didn't recognize my contribution as a performer, that it was all his writing that was winning the awards. I had to straighten that out in my head. I can't act without a script, but a script is lifeless without an actor. As an actor, the writing is behind you, and you're out there *in front* of the audience. You're the one who has to cook up the performance.

I was so out "in front," so full of the Kramer character and the pressure to come through, I realized only much later that I didn't thank Larry enough for all the writing he was putting into the show. I was serving the Kramer character as Larry was serving the show.

In retrospect, when Larry left, I don't think it was out of insecurity, or too much pressure, or that he didn't want to write anymore. It was Larry wanting to get out for himself, making it on his own, burning as a star through his own fire. With *Curb*, he's doing it. As much as I don't want to reunite, I feel an obligation to support him in this. The characters he wrote on *Seinfeld* for so many years, well, we can be there for him now.

* * *

I FLY TO LA AND REOPEN MY HOUSE for the first time in a couple of years. It feels good to be back at home sitting before the ocean, basking in the sun.

I wish I could say the same about the reunion. When I read the pages, it's clear that Larry is at the top of his game. The *Seinfeld* reunion is going to be spread over three episodes—first when Larry asks each of us to participate; then the table read; and finally, the actual show. In typical self-centeredness that defines Larry on *Curb* and nearly always backfires, it's all a gambit by him to get back with his ex-wife, Cheryl.

I'm concerned whether I can perform. It's been eleven years since I played Kramer! As for playing "myself," well, I'm even more uncomfortable about that for all the obvious reasons. I don't fit in. Our first big moment together is at the actual table read, as everybody comes in from their busy schedules, all working on projects, happy to see one another. I'm certainly not as accomplished. I don't work anymore. I feel more like an observer than a participant. I don't feel right here. I was much happier in Manhattan—out of the world of showbiz and into my own thing.

But I'm trying to be up and at 'em for the sake of the memories, yet I can see that everyone has moved on. Even Larry. He's hugging people! He's a hugger now. Did he just kiss Julia? All of them are on top of their game, beaming with success. I am not beaming. It might as well be the day we shot the pilot so many years ago, me sitting in the dark, alone with the alone, while the action is elsewhere.

The old *Seinfeld* soundstage has been re-created exactly the way it was for the seven seasons Larry was on the show. All of us take the same seats at the long table, and many of the same people are there. At the table with everyone, I feel dejected, as if the Laugh Factory night had just happened. Can they see it? Do they feel it? Stay cool, Michael.

* * *

I'm also self-conscious about my hair. It's unusually long and unkempt. It makes my face look gaunt. I think I've lost weight. Certainly, the weight of my confidence. At the table with everybody, I'm sort of in character, playing it as if *I have no look at all* for a co-star on a TV show, which is really the way I feel. I have no presence here. I feel like a ghost.

I'm mulling over my backstory. Well, I live in NYC. I don't work as an actor anymore. I take pictures for no one but me.

Maybe as "myself," I should have my camera, shoot pictures in my scenes. But I don't. I'm really not myself at all. And I don't want to give myself away.

In Larry's storyline, I'm to play myself in the show before I play Kramer. Playing Michael Richards as himself, well, again, I'm feeling out of it. Buck up! Let's get into it. I should include the Laugh Factory incident. That's myself, the person the viewing audience saw all over the news. Unfortunately, I'm not creative enough to talk to Larry about this, that maybe we should have a scene in the show where I'm really myself, talking to him about that night at the club, and some of what I've been through in the three years since then, basically that I'm not my old self. It's not a bad idea and could be quite powerful and affecting, raising real issues and breaking the fourth wall in the same way Larry has done on his show, but I ditch the idea. I fear not handling that incident well. More so, I don't want this reunion show to be all about my comedy club catastrophe.

Still, too bad. I should be playing my real self instead of fictionalizing it. This is what I've been working on these last few years. To finally get out of character altogether to be myself, play close to myself, to act from zero—to be the face behind the mask, a genuine human being not faking it. To get to myself behind anger, behind the insecurity that had me paralyzed at the Emmy Awards, or a failed TV show, or, more importantly, going crazy for being outwardly rejected by someone in the audience at a comedy club. Not being wanted. As "myself" on *Curb*, I can talk about inferiority! How such insecurity can lead to anger. A put-down to hold oneself up by, who wants to come out on top of me? Nobody wants to end up at the bottom. Be the loser. Give it all up. "You're not funny!" How am I myself now? You want myself on this show? Here's what's going on. *Stop! Let it go. Get the mask on. Get to hair and makeup!*

I decide to just play what's written. I'll do the best I can with the material that's given to me. I worked like that for years on *Seinfeld*. Give it to me and I'll get it done!

* * *

AFTER THE TABLE READ, Julia and Jason and Jerry mingle and feel pretty good about what's going on. I find myself standing off to the side, really out of it. I don't have the Giddyup. Larry senses this. He catches my attention and motions with his head for me to follow him. "I want to talk to you," he says. He leads me into a private room, where he shuts the door. In all the years I've known Larry, I've never had this type of intimacy with him, where it's just the two of us like this. "I'm going to make sure that you're okay here," he says. We should have shot this moment for the show!

This is the side of Larry that went out of the room and listened from behind a door when I first came in to read for Kessler/Kramer. Back then, he thought his presence would throw me. He didn't want to come across as a writer-producer in charge of me. Now, he doesn't want his show to throw me. I appreciate his care.

I do my best. Wardrobe does a great job finding some of Kramer's style of clothing, and I have the K-Man's shoes! They're like the "talented shoes" in the film *Tom Thumb*. I put them on, and the K-Man comes through. Giddyup! And then, back to myself.

* * *

BETH PICKS UP HER DEGREE at Columbia and we drive back to LA.

It's December 2010 and...this is it! After seven years together, Beth and I want to get married. Way back in the beginning of our relationship, she and I were so drawn to each other, yet we both tried to resist falling in love. We were trying to stay safe, knowing that there is shadow everywhere. After a painful divorce, I feared another commitment. After my first marriage, dramatic flings left me feeling empty. But after all the years of being together and smoothing our path through therapy, Beth and I are ready.

For Beth, giving birth at forty-two years old is not without its worries. A pregnancy at her "advanced maternal age" is considered medically risky. I'm in my early sixties, also at a riskier age. So as much as I would love to start a family and reexperience the joyous childhood years as I did with my daughter, maybe this time with a son, it's up to Beth. It's now or never.

She picks now. During the winter solstice and a total lunar eclipse, the first in 372 years, Beth and I exchange vows in a private ceremony in Big Sur. Framed by redwoods and jagged ocean cliffs, the setting couldn't be more beautiful. It even rains for good luck. And that night we create a family.

Beth has an easy pregnancy, while I finish all the jobs around the house that I have put off for years to get the place ready for what's to come. We just hope for a healthy baby no matter the gender.

On September 9, 2011, during a harvest moon, and following a long labor, Beth gives birth to our very healthy and very heavy baby boy. He's over ten pounds! We name him Antonio after his Italian grandfather, the only man in my family there for me as a kid. Beth and I are delighted to have this little big guy around.

* * *

IN 2013, I INTRODUCE ANTONIO to Kirstie Alley on the set of her short-lived TV Land series *Kirstie*. I have a supporting role on her show. It was Beth's idea. She heard about the show and the role of a chauffeur. Without me being in on it, she makes a few calls and an audition is set up. I go along with it and read for the network and get the part. TV Land's publicity was concerned that the press might go against me after my wipeout at the Laugh Factory, but the press never brought it up. They reviewed the show and treated me well. I will always be grateful to Kirstie and TV Land for all their support. They were up for sticking by me no matter what.

Kirstie and Rhea Perlman turn out to be two of the most talented women I have ever worked with, and I'm happy to be on board with these two pros. They are incredible to be around. Old hands on a TV set, we all get along well. Kirstie, like Jason Alexander, has a nearly photographic memory. Like him, she is off script as fast as the pages are put in her hands.

In fact, Jason guest-stars on an episode and has a few scenes with Kirstie. These two, off book, so fast together, are a delight to watch. I don't move so fast, but I get the job done. I miss you, Kirstie.

I consider some new offers to work, but nothing inspires interest. I just can't get at it anymore. I'm happy to be home with my family. I also make sure that my mother is comfortable in the twilight of her long life. I hang out with her, getting to know her more. She's getting dementia but still knows me and is happy to have me around. I'm all she's got. I'm looking out for her.

* * *

EVERY MORNING AT DAWN, I walk in the mountains with my devoted dog and gaze out at the eastern horizon. His unconditional love is a wonder to me.

The sun keeps the earth steady, the seasons in order. I'm all for order and light keeping it all going.

* * *

THIS IS MY FIRST TIME INSIDE a comedy club since that fateful night at the Laugh Factory. Most of the regulars at the Comedy Store are here attending a get-together honoring Mitzi Shore. She is ailing, her ability to communicate slipping away. She is seated in the large guest booth in the Main Room of the Store usually reserved for VIPs. She is certainly a VIP. Comics come up to her throughout the evening and pay their respects. When I step in for my moment, I sit by her side and hold her hands. She isn't present and can't respond. She is on the quay to the next world. I see it in her eyes.

"Thank you for all my times here at the Store, Mitzi," I say, then sit down at a small table in the back of the club. I used to kid that Mitzi was my mother in comedy and Budd Friedman was my father. In reality, I was born and raised at the Improv. Neither of my comedy "parents" ever abandoned me after the Laugh Factory show. You can always come home, they said. I just wasn't up for it.

A steady stream of comics and industry folks come to the stage one by one and say a few words about Mitzi and how much they love her. Some corporate guys who have taken over the Comedy Store approach me and kindly reiterate my place at the club. I can work there anytime. I appreciate that.

When I went down at the Laugh Factory, Budd Friedman called right away to tell me I had a place at the Improv if I wanted to work. He knew me and saw that comics were now entering a new world. We would all need to be aware that those freewheeling nights at the Improv were no longer the same with the advent of camera phones. The night when the two of us stood out on Melrose in our bathrobes watching most of his club burn down, well, we made it through that together. Watching me burn down, Budd was there to help me through it. I was grateful.

Back when I was performing in *Arsenic and Old Lace* at the Strand in London, Budd and his wife, Alix, came to see me in the play. In one scene, I did a little Kramer-ism that made the audience laugh, but afterward Budd lightly scolded me for it. I was in a different role now, and he wanted me to steer clear of that character. Be an actor! Bravo. It was the first time that Budd ever gave me a direct note. I took his direction. He was looking out for me. Yep, born and raised at the Improv.

We went out for dinner after my performance, and John Malkovich was at a nearby table with Kevin Kline. Budd noticed them. He loved those guys.

"Budd, go over and introduce yourself, tell 'em that you run the Improv. They'll love it!"

"No, no. I don't want to bother them," he said.

That surprised me. Budd had been around the biggest comedy stars in the business. But he was starstruck. I'm always starstruck, so who was I to talk? I continued to egg Budd to go over and say hello to John and Kevin. I was living vicariously through him. He went over to them and they talked for a minute or so. Budd knew how to get a conversation going. He returned to the table happy at having made contact.

"So, Budd, are you going to give them any times?" I asked.

He smiled.

After dinner, we strolled along the streets and came across a comedy club. Budd started to drift in that direction, but Alix called him back to her side.

"Budd!"

No clubs. They were on vacation.

But they came to see my play. I was delighted.

* * *

I'M LEAVING THE COMEDY STORE AGAIN. This time a different tribute. Robin has died.

When I heard the news, it was like the sun got dimmer. He must have been suffering a great deal. The illness was taking him down slowly. His magnificent talent waning.

I head for the door. From one room to another, from one lifetime to another...there I was, sitting in the Main Room at the Comedy Store, and now, it's in the past. Gone. A memory for a while. Gone. Adios.

In the Comedy Store parking lot, the valet guy takes my ticket to get my car. To my surprise, I'm standing next to Larry Brezner waiting for his car. Once my manager, along with Charlie, it's been a whole lot of years since we've seen each other. Larry has been managing Robin all this time.

"Larry. What was going on with Robin?"

"He was very unhappy," Larry says. "Depressed all the time."

I can only think of shift and change, the masks of my profession, the happy and sad, the comedy and tragedy in us all. I keep this to myself.

I see a softness in Larry's face. He is gentle. His eyes are kind and open-hearted. I always knew Larry as a hardball manager, but I can see that I didn't know him at all. This saddens me.

The death of Robin has brought us face to face. I wasn't that close to Larry when I was with Charlie. I had the feeling that Larry didn't think much of me. He once saw my act and was rather critical. "I really don't know what you're doing up there." I wasn't at my best that night. So what! Move on. Let it go. Robin died. All things pass!

Larry's car arrives.

I see that gentleness in Larry again. His eyes are from his heart. We hug and say, "Take care." It feels so final. Well, enjoy it while it lasts.

Soon he'll be diagnosed with leukemia. In less than a year, he will pass.

* * *

IN THE SUMMER OF 2018, I get my annual physical and find out my PSA level is too high. Soon I get the startling news: prostate cancer.

Well, it's my time to pass on, I think. My winter is upon me. Let my leaves fall softly to the ground, a return to source. But I have an eight-year-old son. My Antonio. He's only in second grade. I can hear my grandmother's broken English, "Live for the boy! Live for the boy!" Absolutely, yes! If I can.

My biopsy results are not great. My doctor suggests the treatment options and advises surgery to remove the prostate. I consult with three more specialists, one at the Mayo Clinic, another at Johns Hopkins, and my final stop at Cedars-Sinai in Los Angeles, where I see Dr. Matthew Bui.

I remember when Gore Vidal came back from Ravello to Los Angeles to address his medical needs and called those times his "Cedars-Sinai years." I guess these are mine.

Like the other doctors, Dr. Bui explains my options, including "watchful waiting," radiation therapy, or surgery. My cancer is stage one and localized within the prostate. In other words, we've detected it early and it hasn't spread. He feels that I am, at age seventy, still young and vigorous, "an excellent candidate" for a da Vinci robotic prostatectomy. Well, I'm not for "watchful waiting," sitting around for the cancer to make its move, most likely against me, and radiation therapy is not a guarantee to rid the cancer. To avoid any danger of spreading, I'm up for the prostatectomy.

"We don't make big incisions anymore," Dr. Bui tells me. "We make small, keyhole incisions, put a little telescope inside, and little robotic arms are inserted laparoscopically. It's more precise. It's very accurate. There's less trauma, quicker healing, and less pain. It's a game-changer when it comes to prostate surgery."

Human ingenuity at its best. I do want to live for this!

* * *

DR. BUI WAS BORN IN SAIGON, Vietnam, and came to the US with his family as refugees, escaping during the fall of Saigon in 1975. At that time, I was recently out of the army, an army that tore up his homeland, and now this brilliant man from Saigon is explaining how he was going to save my life. Even more ironically, Dr. Bui mentions the robotic technology he uses to perform the surgery was initially developed by the military!

So, what's it going to be? Annihilate each other or save ourselves?

I want to know more about Dr. Bui's remarkable story from refugee to world-renowned cancer specialist. "After we escaped, I received lots of help," he tells me. "I always felt this great sense of wanting to give back. I wanted to address some existential equation in the universe: How could I put my inquisitive mind to meaningful purpose?"

How the best of us comes about from challenging circumstances!

Dr. Bui says prostate cancer and breast cancer are the number one causes of cancer deaths in men and women. Yet women are much better at talking about breast cancer than men are about prostate cancer. "There's a kind of ego thing that gets in the way with men," he says. "There's a perception they won't be whole if they have the surgery."

I feel assured by Dr. Bui's calm manner and his extensive experience. Still, it feels like I'm about to have my kavorka cut out. Dr. Bui knows what's going through my mind. He's done thousands of these surgeries.

"When people get diagnosed with cancer, there's always a curtain of gloom that falls on them," he says. "It's normal. But Michael, if God came down from Heaven and told you that you had to pick a cancer, this is the one to pick. This one we can fix!"

Good to know I'm fixable—for now, anyway.

In January 2019, I undergo surgery. Recovery takes just a few weeks. I actually feel new and improved, in better shape than when I went in. My wife thinks so too!

Giddyup!

* * *

So now it's early 2022, and here I am doing something I never did before: I'm watching *Seinfeld*. Now that I'm writing this book, I'm watching the episodes, so many of them for the first time, remembering the hard work that went into creating such a great show. I see how funny Jason is. And Julia. And Jerry. And the guest talent. And the writing. And the way it's all shot. Wow, I'm in this too! I'm impressed. For weeks, Antonio and I sit together, watching the shows from start to finish, in sequence, all nine seasons. He's laughing, and I am aware of how quickly time passes. I'm looking at episodes made twenty-eight years ago! I'm reliving *Seinfeld* through my son, grateful to have put my interest in acting to a "meaningful purpose."

* * *

I have some regrets. How I think my life could have been better if only I knew what I know now. I'm reviewing my life, even making corrections for the next one. I do believe in the continuity of the Soul. Certainly, the continuity of Nature. Change is constant and universal. I change from here to there. It's so ongoing from wherever I am.

For the most part, I do know that the screwups in life are necessary; the irrational showing the way; sometimes funny, sometimes a horrible mess to attend to, to figure out the reason why. Always the reason why. Making my way through the rights and wrongs, like, what gets a laugh and what doesn't, today it's just good to see that all that hard work on *Seinfeld* is making my son laugh.

Mistakes are built into the course of a lifetime. Comedy is built upon the error. The pratfall usually gets a laugh, yet clowns are depicted with a tear. Suffering is upon all.

I'm keenly aware of the housekeeping still to be done. I'm grateful for this work, this home—the features of this world that I AM.

I forget how whole I am, how whole we are! We are of the earth. What we do to the earth, we do to ourselves. The earth is the soul of man. Return home, to the depths of soul. Nature or bust!

Light upon the Heart upon the Book of Nature

* * *

MY MOTHER IS A HUNDRED AND ONE YEARS OLD. She lives in a nursing home where she has round-the-clock care. Dementia has taken away most of her memories and her ability to clearly communicate, but she still recognizes me and knows my name and has a few moments of lucidity. On a recent visit, I help her into her wheelchair and push her outside to the rose garden, where we sit and enjoy the perfumed air and warmth of the afternoon sun.

We don't have to speak much. My hand on hers is enough. All that we have been through is enough to fill the silence—and we have been through it, on our own and together, starting with her decision to bring me into this world. All these years later we are still here.

"Mike, the sun feels so good," she says.

"Yes, it does, Mom."

She shuts her eyes and tilts her head up toward the sun. "Mmm, it feels so good to feel the light."

"The sun is in my heart, Mom."

"That's where the light comes from," she whispers.

*A*nd upon this quest, I stand before the light. East and west, from both directions, I rise and set, live and die. I am alpha and omega, a beginning and an end. Round and whole in this.

I am cosmic. I am "made in the image" of Creation. And this Nature is mindful of itself through me. I am death as much as life, a summer and a winter. How can I avoid my seasons?

How can I avoid time and the suffering that I am? The evil that I am? I am big bang. I am bomb and holocaust, war and its destruction. How do I avoid the magnitude of my soul?

I can't. I am the fullness of Nature, the whole of my humanity.

As Blake said, "God is divine imagination." As Einstein said, "A to B will get you somewhere but imagination will get you everywhere." As Muhammad Ali said, "The man who has no imagination has no wings." I am either limited in imagination or I use it to transcend my oblivion.

I am "everywhere" throughout space and time.

I am gathered together in the ark of my soul and shine as a star in the center of my night. I come and go as you do. I am humanity, fixed in this body-earth turning around a star.

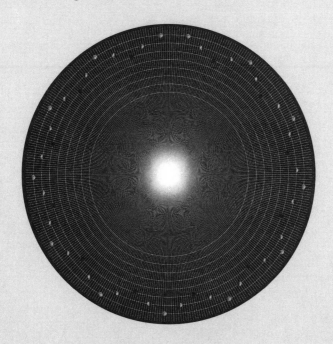

Acknowledgments

Here's something I've learned writing this book. You don't get to this point in a memoir, the last pages at the end, without a wellspring of appreciation and love for the people who helped you get this far. I certainly haven't. The list of people who helped me through this and so much more must begin with my wife Beth and my son Antonio, both of whom kept me sane and humored and ensured my heart was full. I remember beginning this adventure years ago with Beth. We sat in our living room with a legal pad and a computer and took a first stab at outlining the book. A view of the Pacific Ocean stretching endlessly was outside our bay window. I had no idea writing *Entrances and Exits* would be an adventure akin to crossing that great sea. It lasted three and a half years, and at times I wasn't sure if we were going to make it. Beth and Antonio were always optimistic. "Keep at it! It's going to be good!" And I did. They like the book. I hope you do, too.

I want to thank my friends and colleagues for inspiring the best in me and sticking close by. That list begins with Jerry Seinfeld—always a friend, and I thank you for your beautiful foreword—and my *Seinfeld* cast and crew for all the inspiring days working together that provided the stuff that I talk about in these pages. Thanks for nine incredible years of doing the show. What a family! As Jerry once told me, we didn't make the show for us, we made it for the audience, and he was right. The show keeps going and I'm delighted to still be bringing laughs to people more than thirty years after the first episode.

I must thank Elizabeth Much, my publicist, for connecting me to Todd Gold, my collaborator. Todd encouraged me to write so much of this book, and in the beginning, I cursed him when he left me to myself, to find my voice, to say what I mean, to get this book out of my system. Through it all, we became great friends. This was the icing on the cake.

The first draft of this manuscript was well over six hundred pages. It included a seventy-two-page appendix going much deeper into a spiritual ethos that I live by. It was so deeply personal that Todd and I thought that this work should be another book. I hope that happens one day. My editor Gretchen Young performed the essential job of trimming us down to four-hundred-plus pages. In a sense, she brought me down to earth. I also benefited from the help of an insightful copy editor, Jon Ford, and associate publisher, Madeline Sturgeon, for steadying us with encouragement as we got this book to publication. My best to Greg Johnson, our art director, who put the book together, combining text and images with great sensitivity and know-how. And to my publisher, Anthony Ziccardi, for providing me with such a sharp team! Thank you!

Writing was never a real strength of mine. I was a poor student in school. I misspell, mispronounce, and mix up words and idioms. The rules of grammar never landed. My wife, Beth, helped me with getting straight to what I mean. Again, there were times when I wasn't sure of myself as a writer but her encouragement kept me at it.

Joseph Mazzaferro delighted me with his concepts for the visual impact of my book—we kept his original idea for the book's cover. From here, thanks to my hair stylist, Craig Gangi, who connected me to the very talented photographer Tony Duran, who easily got the shot within minutes that became our cover. A big thanks to my book agent, Dan Strone, the CEO of Trident Media Group, for patiently directing me through all the intense stages of book making; a process that drove me a bit crazy at times, but thanks to Permuted Press for giving me everything I needed. And also, much gratitude to Trident Media's associate agent Claire Romine for her invaluable assistance in clearing so many images in this book.

I am grateful to my dear friend Janet Muff and her take on my manuscript, all of her great suggestions for clarifying the text. Also, to Janet's husband, Dr. Jim Boyce, who read my manuscript twice! And loved every page. His endorsement helped me through my final rewrites. And to my close friend John Langmore and his sense of humor, always on the lookout for anything I might say that people could slap me around with. To Dr. Stuart Lerner, our chats, and what's up with the world these days, a needed break to catch up with what's going on around me. For so many years, I thank the late Dr. John Dobbs for his counseling. Also, Dr. Mark Winborn, who told me right up front, before we began analysis, "You should write a book!" I had it in mind, but he certainly reminded me. Also to Dr. Stanton Marlan for his insight into dreams, depth psychology, and alchemical philosophy. And finally, to Donald Sloggy and his many years as a Jungian analyst, who endorsed my recovery, the way of the heart, and my return to public life.

Finally, thank you to my fans, for your support, the letters, and all your interest in my whereabouts and well-being. The feeling is mutual.

Photo and Illustration Credits

Kramer always leaning in on Jerry.

A rare look into Kramer's apartment. I made that red lamp.

Kramer eyeballing the librarian, Marion (Ashley Gardner). She might be looking up the word "kavorka."

Man, the powerful effects of that light from the Chicken Roaster!

Cement in the washer, mission accomplished!

It wasn't easy dealing with the power of the kavorka for nine seasons.

Pimp, prophet, or urban peacock? The man had an imagination.

One man's trash is another's treasure. "Enjoy it while it lasts."

This painting has been reproduced countless times but no one knows where the original is.

Kramer is sprung from another fine mess.

Kramer's sense of "reality"… it was always imagination.

The four of us in this together… forever.

Some of my early photography…

Los Angeles, 2009. © Michael Richards

Los Angeles, 2009. © Michael Richards

New York City, 2009. © Michael Richards

New York City, 2009. © Michael Richards

Santa Monica, 2009. © Michael Richards

New York City, 2010. © Michael Richards

Los Angeles, 2010. © Michael Richards

On my walk, a few thoughts…

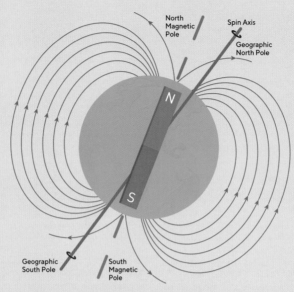

As Rumi had his pole, I *imagine* my pole in the magnetic Earth
both positive (+) and negative (−).

One early morning on the trail, I come upon a circle of flowers that someone created.
Not exactly an actual sun/moon wheel, but it's close and more than an adequate good
morning from a like-minded hiker. The next day on the trail, the circle is no longer.
Someone or something has wiped it away. It's gone. Outside, all is shift and change,
things come and go. It's all so temporal. But this circle of flowers is still around. I can
hold it together from *within* which is where it was before, from within someone who
placed it on the trail for others to see. We can see each other through the physical
world, and though it all passes away, I hold this circle within me, *spiritually*. It's eternal,
on-going, so present, so alive within me.

"In the heart of one who prays that one may meditate,
meditate as far as the infinite."

—GERSHOM SCHOLEM

Sunrise with my dog Leo…